ADULTS WITH INCAPACITY LEGISLATION

ADULTS WITH INCAPACITY LEGISLATION

Dr Carleton
Consultant Psychiatrist
IPCU Wishaw

Tele: 01698 366520
Fax: 01698 366020

Annotated by

Adrian D. Ward, MBE, LL.B.
Solicitor, Turnbull & Ward, Barrhead

W. GREEN

Published in 2008 by Thomson Reuters (Legal) Limited
(Registered in England and Wales,
Company No 1679046.
Registered office and address for service
100 Avenue Road, Swiss Cottage,
London, NW3 3PF) trading as W. Green

Typeset by LBJ Typesetting Ltd
of Kingsclere

Printed and bound in Great Britain by MPG Books Ltd, Bodmin, Cornwall.

No natural forests were destroyed to make this product;
only farmed timber was used and replanted.

A CIP catalogue record of this book is available from the British Library.

ISBN 978-0-414-01580-7

© 2008 Thomson Reuters (Legal) Limited

Thomson Reuters and the Thomson Reuters logo are trademarks of Thomson Reuters.

All rights reserved. UK statutory material in this publication is acknowledged as Crown copyright.

No part of this publication may be reproduced or transmitted in any form or by any means, or stored in any retrieval system of any nature without prior written permission, except for permitted fair dealing under the Copyright, Designs and Patents Act 1988, or in accordance with the terms of a licence issued by the Copyright Licensing Agency in respect of photocopying and/or reprographic reproduction. Applications for permission for other use of copyright material including permission to reproduce extracts in other published work shall be made to the publisher. Full acknowledgment of author, publisher and source must be given.

Preface

This book sets out, with annotations, the text of the Adults with Incapacity (Scotland) Act 2000 with all amendments up to and including those made by the Adult Support and Protection (Scotland) Act 2007, all of which have now been in force from April 1, 2008. Two small prospective amendments made by the Welfare Reform Act 2000, and due to come into force on October 27, 2008, are also included.

Appendix 1 contains, with commentary, the text of s.13ZA of the Social Work (Scotland) Act 1968, which has been in force since March 22, 2007, and which is important in relation to Pt. 6 of the Incapacity Act. Appendix 2 contains relevant regulations other than those which remain as set out in Appendix 2 to my book *Adult Incapacity* (W. Green, 2003).

My original annotations to the Incapacity Act appeared in Current Law Statutes. They were reprinted in Greens Annotated Acts along with Hilary Patrick's annotations to the Mental Health (Scotland) Act 1984 (W. Green, 2001). They were also reproduced in Mays' *Scottish Social Work Legislation* (W. Green, a looseleaf publication).

Since my original annotations were prepared we have had frequent amendments to the Incapacity Act, particularly by statutes in the years 2001, 2003, 2005 and 2007 (a sequence to be continued?), and developing case law. I have sought to cite the noteworthy cases of which I am aware at the points where they seem most relevant. There have also been developments in experience and practice, including as this work is being finalised the significant developments in the provision of caution described in the note to s.58 (6). The result of all of this has been substantially expanded and largely rewritten annotations, though I have retained with minimum alterations those passages which remain valid.

In a broader context, there has been the development of the whole subject of adult incapacity, of which matters covered by the Incapacity Act represent only part. Adult incapacity is now a recognised specialism for which accreditation by the Law Society of Scotland may be sought. It is a subject *sui generis*, potentially straddling all other areas of law and legal practice, and is recognised as such by Scottish Civil Law Reports—though categorisations less responsive to the essentially dynamic nature of law try to squeeze adult incapacity in as a sub-category of mental health (which it plainly is not) or of social welfare (social welfare presumably being a subdivision of personal welfare, one of the two topics—the other being property and financial matters—addressed by the Incapacity Act, which in turn covers only part of the subject of adult incapacity).

Nevertheless, reports and articles on the subject appear with increasing frequency, supplemented by decisions on the Scottish Courts Website (*www.scotcourts.gov.uk*, click on library, then court judgements, and search against "adults with incapacity") and much useful material on the Public Guardian's website (see General Note to s.6). The subject is also developing internationally, with reform in many jurisdictions and continued attention from the Council of Europe and the European Court of Human Rights. A surprising apparent exception is the United Nations. The unfortunate terms of Article 12.2 of the recent UN Convention on the Rights of Persons with Disabilities are considered in the Introduction and General Note. Read literally, it declares that all persons with disabilities

Preface

have full legal capacity. No, they do not, unless the dark legacies of the past are still allowed in some quarters to deny the very existence as human beings of people with serious intellectual disabilities. What requires to be emphasised is that they are entitled to full legal rights and status, and that the consequences of their incapacities must be recognised and adequately addressed. That must be stressed again and again and again, to counteract the forces otherwise constantly tugging back down the order of priorities, towards those dark shadows of the past, those people least able to advocate for themselves.

These annotations are written primarily for lawyers, but I hope that the updated text of the Incapacity Act and other material, including my annotations, in this volume will be helpful too for the wider readership to which *Adult Incapacity* was also addressed. Those to whom this work may seem at first too technical may care to start with the Public Guardian's website and the Codes of Practice, which include glossaries—explaining, for example, what lawyers mean by "caution" in this context, and how they pronounce it. Also to be recommended are Hilary Patrick's *Mental Health, Incapacity and the Law in Scotland* (Tottel, 2006) and her regular contributions to Scolag magazine.

As my own journey through the subject of adult incapacity has progressed, an accumulating cast of thousands deserves acknowledgement: lawyers in all branches of my profession; members of many other key professions; legislators, officials and administrators; members of voluntary organisations and those serving them; families and carers of people who may lack full capacity, and those people themselves; and all of the foregoing across many countries. Particular groups are all those who, over the years, have been colleagues on the Mental Health and Disability Sub-Committee of the Law Society of Scotland; and my fellow members of the Steering Group of the Alliance for the Promotion of the Incapable Adults Bill, of the Incapacity Act Implementation Steering Group, and the expert working party of which I am a member at the Council of Europe. Particular assistance reflected in the contents of this volume has been received from Sandra McDonald, Public Guardian, Donald Lyons, Director of the Mental Welfare Commission for Scotland, and Jill Hyslop of W. Green

And there is one more. Invisibly but indelibly present through every page of *Adult Incapacity*, all of these annotations and their predecessor, before that *A New View* and my input to *Mental Handicap and the Law*, and over the years countless articles, and conference and seminar papers, are the skilled hard work and commitment to meticulous standards of my secretary Evelyn Brookmire. It has been particularly challenging to strive for accuracy and consistency in the mass of detailed changes and cross-references which have formed much of her task on this occasion. If any blemishes, small or large, have survived undetected, the responsibility is mine.

Adrian D. Ward
August 26, 2008

Contents

	Page
Preface	v
Table of Cases	ix
Table of United Kingdom Statutes	xi
Table of Scottish Statutes	xiii
Table of Statutory Instruments	xix
Table of Scottish Statutory Instruments	xxi
Table of Abbreviations	xxiii
Contents of the Incapacity Act	xxv
Adults with Incapacity (Scotland) Act 2000	1

Appendix 1

s.13ZA of the Social Work (Scotland) Act 1968	183

Appendix 2

Note: List of SSI's reproduced in *Adult Incapacity* which remain unamended.	189
Act of Sederunt (Summary Applications, Statutory Applications and Appeals etc. Rules) (SI 1999/929)	190
Adults with Incapacity (Evidence in Relation to Dispensing with Intimation or Notification) (Scotland) Regulations (SSI 2001/79)	200
Adults with Incapacity (Supervision of Welfare Guardians etc. by Local Authorities) (Scotland) Regulations (SSI 2002/95)	201
Adults with Incapacity (Reports in Relation to Guardianship and Intervention Orders) (Scotland) Regulations (SSI 2002/96)	203
Adults with Incapacity (Recall of Guardians' Powers) (Scotland) Regulations (SSI 2002/97)	234
Adults with Incapacity (Ethics Committee) (Scotland) Regulations (2002/190)	273
Adults with Incapacity (Management of Residents' Finances) (No. 2) (Scotland) Regulations (2003/266)	276
Adults with Incapacity (Conditions and Circumstances Applicable to Three Year Medical Treatment Certificates) (Scotland) Regulations (2007/100)	280
Adults with Incapacity (Medical Treatment Certificates) (Scotland) Regulations (SSI 2007/104)	282
Adults with Incapacity (Requirements for Signing Medical Treatment Certificates) (Scotland) Regulations (2007/105)	284
Adults with Incapacity (Accounts and Funds) (Scotland) Regulations (SSI 2008/51)	285
Adults with Incapacity (Public Guardian's Fees) (Scotland) Regulations (SSI 2008/52)	287
Adults with Incapacity (Certificates in Relation to Powers of Attorney) (Scotland) Regulations (SSI 2008/56)	291

Contents

Adults with Incapacity (Public Guardian's Fees)(Scotland) Amendment Regulations 2008 (2008/238) 296

Index 307

Table of Cases

A's Guardian, Applicant, 2007 S.L.T. (Sh. Ct.) 69; 2006 G.W.D. 19–417 13
AD, Guardianship application in respect of, February 8, 2005, Glasgow Sh. Ct 134
Alexander v Metbro Ltd, 2004 S.L.T. 963; 2004 Rep. L.R. 119; 2004 G.W.D. 26–550,
    OH 18
Anderson, Petitioner, June 26, 2007, SC 33
Arthur v Arthur, 2005 S.C.L.R. 350, Sh. Ct. 114
B, Applicant, 2005 S.L.T. (Sh. Ct.) 95; 2005 G.W.D. 19–334 .... 18, 99
B's Curator Bonis, Noter, 1996 S.L.T. (Sh. Ct.) 27; 1995 S.C.L.R. 671 13
Brogan, Petitioner, 1986 S.L.T. 420, OH 127
Cooke v Telford, 2005 S.C.L.R. 367, Sh. Ct. 20, 107, 114, 120
D's Curator Bonis, Noter, 1998 S.L.T. 2; 1997 G.W.D. 13–538, OH 13
EB Applications in respect of, December 1, 2005, Glasgow Sh. Ct. 110
Edinburgh City Council v Z, 2005 S.L.T. (Sh. Ct.) 7; 2005 G.W.D. 5–68 .... 18, 125
Fraser v Paterson (No.1), 1987 S.L.T. 562; 1989 S.C.L.R. 577, OH 16
F.W., November 29, 2005, Glasgow Sh. Ct. 96, 106, 108
Galashan (Francis) and Lynn (John Scott) Applications in respect of, July 7, 2008,
    Edinburgh Sh. Ct.; 2008 G.W.D. 29–449 .... 26, 96
Glasgow City Council application for appointment of welfare guardian to AD, June 27,
    2005 .... 18, 107
H, May 6, 2008, Dunoon Sh. Ct. 112
H, Applicant, 2007 S.L.T. (Sh. Ct.) 5; 2006 G.W.D. 21–447 107
H.L. v U.K. (the "Bournewood case") (2004) 40 EHRR 761 184
H.M. v Switzerland (2002) ECHR 157 184
Kirkland, AW21/04, May 14, 2004, Sh. Ct. 95, 106
J, Renewal of guardianship of, June 30, 2008, Inverness Sh. Ct. 112, 117, 119
LC (Mrs), Application in respect of, May 18, 2005, Sh. Ct. 30
Law Hospital NHS Trust v Lord Advocate, 1996 S.C. 301; 1996 S.L.T. 848; [1996] 2
    F.L.R. 407; (1998) 39 B.M.L.R. 166; [1996] Fam. Law 670, IH 8, 93
M, Applicant, 2007 S.L.T. (Sh. Ct.) 24; 2006 G.W.D. 19–418 .... 33, 99
M v M, 2006 G.W.D. 17-331, Sh. Ct. 41, 43
McDowall's Executors v IRC [2004] STC (SCD) 22 33
McFarlane v Donaldson (1835) 13 S 725 127
Morris, Petitioner, 1986 117
Morris (No.2), Petitioner, 1991 117
Morris (No.3), Petitioner, 2002 117
Muldoon, Applicant, 2005 S.L.T. (Sh. Ct.) 52; 2005 S.C.L.R. 611; 2005 G.W.D. 5–57 9,
    184, 186
North Ayrshire Council v JM, 2004 S.C.L.R. 956, Sh. Ct. 9, 12, 111, 112, 114
O'B (J), Application by, AW55/2008, Glasgow 112
Pirie v Clydesdale Bank Plc, 2007 S.C.L.R. 18; 2006 G.W.D. 19–419, OH 9
RA, Application in respect of, January 17, 2008, Glasgow Sh. Ct. 20, 114
RL, Application in respect of, December 28, 2007, Glasgow Sh. Ct. 111
Riley v James Beaton & Co (Plumbers) Ltd, 2004 S.L.T. 1083; 2004 G.W.D. 31–635,
    OH 99, 111
Robertson (James), Summary Application, PF for the public interest, November 30,
    2007, Kirkcaldy Sh. Ct. 96
Rogers, Petitioner Unreported September 12, 2007, Sh. Ct. 111
Shtukaturov v Russia (App No.4409/05) (2008) 11 C.C.L. Rep. 440 4
Stork, Pursuer, 2004 S.C.L.R. 513, Sh. Ct. 20, 106, 107
T, Applicant, 2005 S.L.T. (Sh. Ct.) 97; 2005 G.W.D. 26–501 99
X and Y v The Netherlands, March 26, 1985 on application No. 16/1983/72/110 187

Table of United Kingdom Statutes

1849	Judicial Factors Act (12 & 13 Vict. c.51) 96, 147		1990	Law Reform (Miscellaneous Provisions) (Scotland) Act (c.40) 5
1921	Trusts (Scotland) Act (11 & 12 Geo.5 c.58) 95, 127			s.71 .... 5, 172
1968	Social Work (Scotland) Act (c.49) 153		1991	Age of Legal Capacity (Scotland) Act (c.50) ... 16, 126, 154
	s.3 .... 106, 153		1995	Children (Scotland) Act (c.36).. 126
	s.5 .... 109, 185			s.11(2)(b) 147
	s.13ZA .... v, 7, 13, 95, 109, 110, **183**, 184, 185, 186			Criminal Procedure (Scotland) Act (c.46) 106, 114, 127, 151
	s.94(1) 133, 153			s.84 8
1971	Powers of Attorney Act (c.27)		1999	Mental Health (Amendment) (Scotland) Act (c.32) 6
	s.3 39			
1984	Anatomy Act (c.14) 36		2000	Mental Capacity Act (c.9)
	Mental Health (Scotland) Act (c.36) .. 1, 7, 8, 16, 18, 20, 21, 27, 72, 94, 95, 105, 110, 127, 144, 151, 153, 171			s.5 185
			2007	Welfare Reform Act (c. 5) ..... v, 1
	s.3(2) 27			
	s.18 105			
	s.29(4) 26			
	s.37(2)(a) 127			
	s.41(2) 8			
	s.92(1) 100, 105			
	s.94 .... 6, 8, 80, 172			
	Sch.4 para.5 72			
	para.7(d) 72			
	para.8 72			

Table of Scottish Statutes

2000 Adults with Incapacity
  (Scotland) Act (asp 4) **1**
  Pt 1 .... 2, 5, **9**, 98, 105, 113, 172
  Pt 2 .. 2, 8, 18, 24, **32**, 37, 39, 172
  Pts 2–6 5
  Pt 3 .. 2, 5, 6, 7, 8, 13, 14, 18, 24,
      32, **47**, 48, 49, 50, 51, 60, 61,
      67, 69, 70, 71, 72, 79, 95, 99,
      109, 117, 125, 148, 172, 184
  Pt 4 ... 2, 6, 13, 14, 18, 24, 32, **72**,
      79, 81, 155, 172, 184
  Pt 5 .... 2, 6, 7, 12, 13, 14, 32, **82**,
      85, 86, 87, 90, 93, 184
  Pt 6 .... v, 1, 2, 6, 7, 17, 18, 24, 26,
      32, 47, 48, **94**, 95. 96, 105,
      109, 110, 127, 160, 172, 184,
      185, 186, 187
  Pt 7 .... 2, **146**
  s.1 .... 1, 5, 6, 8, **9**, 11, 12, 14, 15,
      18, 20, 30, 32, 37, 44, 47, 51,
      70, 72, 79, 82, 96, 98, 100,
      105, 106, 109, 110, 112, 113,
      114, 124, 130, 133, 146, 149,
      160, 172, 185
    (1) 12, 13, 37
    (1)–(4) 11
    (2) ... 13, 14, 37, 75, 77, 109,
      128
    (2)–(4) 5, 32, 48, 75, 85
    (2)–(5) 32, 72, 76
    (3) .. 13, 14, 15, 85, 107, 109,
      126, 136
    (4) 14, 15, 79, 101
      (a)   15, 20, 126, 129, 147
      (b) 15, 22
      (c) 15, 105
    (5) 5, 11, 16, 78, 126
    (6)   5, 11, 13, 16, 27, 32, 122,
      153, 186
    (7) 11, 17, 29, 36, 41, 46,
      130, 134, 136, 145, 149
  s.2 .... 9, **17**, 20, 41, 127, 129, 139,
      141
    (2) 18, 26, 105
    (3) 18, 32
    (4) 18, 30
  s.3 .. 9, **18**, 20, 22, 26, 56, 98, 102,
      105, 106, 107, 117, 132, 139,
      141
    (1) 20, 107
    (2) 105
      (a) 20, 29
      (b) 20, 106
      (c) 20, 106

    (d) 20, 99, 105, 107
  (3) .. 9, 15, 17, 29, 32, 39, 48,
      51, 72, 82
  (4) 20, 22, 100, 110
  (5) 20, 22, 100, 110
  (5A) 15, 20
  (5B) 15, 20
  (6) 20
s.4 .... 9, 17, **20**, 21, 153
  (1) 21
    (a) 21
    (b) 21
    (c) 21
  (3) 21
  (3B) 22
s.5 .... 9, **22**
s.6 .... v, 9, **22**, 24, 27, 31, 32
  (1) 23
    (b) 39
  (2) 39
    (a) 24, 139
    (b) 24, 39
    (c) .. 24, 32, 48, 148, 172
    (d) ... 24, 41, 48, 72, 77,
      148
    (da) 24, 31
    (e) 24, 48, 77, 161
    (f) 24, 27, 29
  (3) 24
s.7 .... 9, **24**
  (1) 25
    (d) 30
  (2) 25
  (3) 25
s.8 .... 9, 24, **25**, 41, 96, 132
  (1) 25
  (2) 26
s.9 ... 9, 16, **26**, 31, 32, 41, 42, 45
  (1) 29
    (c) 24, 27, 29
    (d) 27, 29, 32
    (g) 27, 29
  (2) 29
s.10 .... 9, **27**, 31, 32, 127
  (1)(a) 28, 29, 127, 139
    (b) 24, 27, 28, 29
    (c) 27, 29, 32
    (d) 29, 82
    (e) 27, 29
  (2) 29
  (3) 29
    (b) 41
  (4) 29
s.11 .. 9, 18, **29**, 30, 41, 45, 58, 62,
      75, 117

xiii

Table of Scottish Statutes

(1) .. 18, 29, 30, 45, 105, 127, 133
(2) .. 29, 30, 42, 45, 113, 118, 126, 136, 137, 139, 141, 143, 147
s.12 .. 9, 24, 27, **30**, 48, 72, 77, 82
   (1) 29, 30, 31
   (2) 24, 27, 29, 31
s.13 .... 9, **31**, 32, 41, 128
   (1) 31
     (e) 48
     (h) 82
s.14 ...... 9, 17, **31**, 36, 75, 82, 93
s.15 .... 5, 32, **33**, 36, 37, 172
   (1) 5
   (2) 5, 34
   (3) 34
   (3)(ba) 34, 36
   (4) 34
   (5) 5, 34, 153
s.16 .... 5, 32, **34**, 172
   (1) 5
   (1)–(4) 36, 172
   (2) 5
   (3)(ba) 36
     (c) 36
   (5) 5, 34
     (a) 36
     (b) 36
   (6) 36
   (7) 5, 34, 36, 153, 172
   (8) 36
s.16A 34, **36**
s.17 .... 5, **37**
s.18 .... 5, 34, **37**, 172
s.19 .... 5, 24, 34, **37**, 172
   (1) 38
   (2) 39
     (a) 39
     (c) 39
   (3) 34, 39
   (4) 39
   (5) 39
     (b) 34
   (6) 18, 39
s.20 .... 5, **39**, 45
   (1) 41
   (2) 41
     (b) 41
     (c) 29, 41
     (d) 41
     (e) 41
   (3) 41
     (a) 172
     (b) 27, 41
   (4) 18, 41
   (5) 41
s.21 .... 5, **41**, 100, 128, 172
s.22 .... 5, 27, **41**, 172
   (1)(d) 43
s.22A 3, 5, 33, **42**, 44

   (5) 44
s.23 .... 5, **44**, 172
   (1) 36, 45
   (2) 45
   (3) 27, 45
   (4) 36, 45
s.24 .... 5, **45**
   (1) 46
   (1A) 46
   (2) 32, 46
   (3) 46
   (4) 44, 46
s.24A **48**
   (1) 49
   (2) 49, 65
s.24B 3, 48, **49**, 71, 72, 98, 99, 105
   (1) 49, 72
   (2) 32, 67
     (a) 49
     (c) 49
s.24C **50**, 51, 61, 64, 69
s.24D **51**, 52, 53, 61, 64, 69
s.25 ..... 50, **51**, 52, 56, 61, 64, 70
   (1) 51
   (3) 51, 52
   (6) 52, 153
s.26 .... **53**, 54
   (1) 68
   (3)(a) 51
   (6)(b) 67
s.26A **53**, 59
   (1) 53
     (b) 53, 54
     (c) 54
   (4) 52, 54
s.26B 52, **54**, 56
s.26C **55**
   (1) 56
   (2) 56
   (3) 56
   (4) 56
   (5) 56
   (6)(b) 67
   (6)(c) 56
s.26D 52, **56**, 58, 61
s.26E 52, **56**, 58, 62
   (3)(c) 58
s.26F 54, **58**, 61
s.26G .. 50, 51, 53, 54, **58**, 59, 61, 65, 69
   (1) 59
   (3) 59
s.27 22, 51, 52, 55, 56, 58, **59**, 60, 64
s.27A **60**, 63, 64, 68, 70, 72
   (1) 61
     (d) 63
   (2) 61, 70
ss.27A–27G 60
s.27B **61**, 64, 68, 70

Table of Scottish Statutes

s.27C 22, **61**, 62, 63	(3) 14, 30, 75
(1)(a) 62	(4) 30, 75
(e) 62	(5) 14, 75
s.27D **62**	(6) 75
s.27E **63**	(7) 75
(4) 56	(8) 30, 45, 75
s.27F **63**	(9) 75
s.27G 60, 61, **63**	s.38 . . . . **75**, 172
(1) 60	s.39 . . . . 6, 73, 75, **76**, 172
(2) 60	(2) 76
s.28 . . . . 13, **64**, 65	(a) 77
(2) 13	(5) 76
s.28A **64**, 65	s.40 . . . . 6, 72, **77**
s.29 . . . . 64, **65**	(1) 77
s.30 . . . . **65**	(2) 24, 76, 77
(1) 49	(3) 24, 76, 77
(2) 49	(4) 77
s.30A **65**	s.41 . . . . 6, 76, **77**
s.30B **66**, 128	(f) 22
(1) 100	s.42 . . . . 6, **78**
(2) 148	s.43 . . . . 6, 76, **79**
s.31 . . . . **66**, 70, 72	s.44 . . . . 6, 76, **80**
(1) 67	(1) 80
(4) 67	(2) 80
s.31A 65, **67**	(3) 80
s.31B 58, 61, **67**	(4) 80
(4) 61	s.45 . . . . 6, 73, 77, **81**
(6) 68	(2) 74
s.31C **68**	(4) 81
s.31D 18, **69**	(6) 18
s.31E 6, 47, 48, **69**, 99	s.46 . . . . 6, 32, 72, **81**, 98, 105
(1) 49, 70	(1) 82
(2) 70	(2) 82
(3) 70	s.47 . . . . 6, 36, **82**, 89
(4) 70	(1) 24, 32, 82, 85
(5) 70	(a) 85
(6) 70	(1A) 6
(7) 49, 70	(b) 7
(8) 44, 70	(2) 85
s.32 3, 5, 6, 14, 32, 47, 48, 49, 59, **70**, 71	(2A) 7, 85, 87, 90
s.33 . . . . 48, **71**	(a) 86
(1) 72	(3) 85
(a) 49, 72	(4) 85
(2) 72	(5) 85
s.34 72	(6) 85
s.35 . . . . 6, **72**, 172	(7) 7, 85
(1) 73, 155	(8) 85
(a) 74	(9) 86
(b) 73	(10) 86
(c) 74	ss.47–48 6
(d) 73	s.48 . . . . 7, 85, **86**
(e) 73	(2) 36, 86
(2) 73	(3) 86
(3) 73, 74	s.49 . . . . 7, **86**, 98, 105
(4) 73	(1) 85
(5) 74	(2) 87
s.36 . . . . **74**	ss.49–50 6
s.37 . . . . 6, **74**, 76, 172	s.50 . . 8, 17, 36, **87**, 90, 93, 94, 98, 105
(1) 75	(1) 85, 89
(2) 13, 14, 75	(2) 89

Table of Scottish Statutes

(b) 85	(6B) 7, 105, 117
(c) 85	(6B)–(7) 105, 107
(3) 89	(7) 106
(4) 90	s.58 .... 14, **108**, 117
(5) 90	(1) 14, 95, 109, 136
(6) 90	(a) 14, 187
(7) 81, 89, 90	(b) 47, 105, 107, 109,
(8) 86, 89, 90	184
(9) 90	(2) 110
(10) 89	(3) 98, 99, 107, 110, 120,
s.51 .... 6, **90**	122, 136, 141
(1)(a) 93	(4) 105, 110, 117, 141
(2)(a) 93	(5) 105, 111, 120
(3) 22	(6) v, 100, 105, 111, 136, 141
(a) 93	(7) 127
(b) 93	(b) 112
(c) 93	(c) 112
(d) 93	(d) 112
(e) 93	s.59 ...... 105, **113**, 127, 131, 151
(f) 36, 93	(1)(a) 114
(3A)(a) 93	(b) 114
(b) 93	(2) 131
(c) 93	(3) 114
(4) 13, 93	(4) 114
(5) 93	(b) 114
(6) 93	(c) 114
(7) 93	(d) 114
s.52 .... 6, 17, 90, **93**	s.60 .. 18, 108, 111, **114**, 118, 119,
s.53 .... 95, **96**, 107, 127	171
(1) 187	(1) ... 116, 120, 122, 136, 141
(2) 100	(2) 117
(3) 24, 28, 98, 100, 105	(3) 106, 117
(4) 100, 105, 107	(3A) 106, 117
(5) 98	(4) 105
(b) 98	(b) 110
(6) 98, 100	(4A) 117
(7) 100	(5) 117
(a) 111	s.61 .... 7, **118**, 116, 145, 146, 172
(14) 98, 100	s.62 .... 95, 105, 111, **119**, 172
ss.53–56A 100	(1)(a) 105, 120
s.54 .... 41, 98, **100**, 128	(b) 105
s.55 .... 98, **100**	(2) 120
s.56 .... 7, 98, **101**, 118	(a) 120
(1) 98	(6) 56
(2) 102	(b) 120
(3)–(6) 102	(7) 56, 111
s.56A **102**	(b) 120
s.57 .. 95, 100, **102**, 105, 110, 141,	(9) 56
160	s.63 .... 56, 95, 105, **121**, 127
(1) 105	(1) 122
(1)–(4) 105	(8) 122
(2) 24, 28, 105, 114, 117, 125	s.64 .... 95, 100, 105, **122**
(3) 98, 100, 105, 106, 107	(1) ... 105, 110, 125, 126, 130
(b) 16	(a) 125
(3A) 98, 105, 106, 107	(a)–(d) 126
(3B) 98, 105, 106, 107	(b) 125
(3A)–(3B) 107	(d) 125
(4) 98, 100, 106, 107	(e) 16, 126, 130
(5) 107, 116, 127	(2) 36, 98, 110, 124, 126
(5)–(6A) 105, 107	(3) 126
(6) 105, 111, 116, 127	(4) 126, 144

Table of Scottish Statutes

(5) 96, 126	s.74 .... 95, 105, **140**
(6) 126	(2) 141
(7) 18, 29, 127, 139	(4) 105, 110, 141
(8) 107, 127	(5)(b) 141
(9) 30, 45,114, 127, 144, 151	s.75 .... 45, **141**
(10) 30, 45, 114, 118, 127	(1) 122
(11) 99, 124, 127	(2)(a) 122
(12) 127	(3) 45
s.65 .... 41, 100, **127**	(d) 143
s.66 .... 13, 127, **128**	(4) 45
(4) 129	(a) 143
(7) 18	(5) 136
(8) 18	s.75A **143**, 146
s.67 .... 100, **129**	(a)(i) 143
(1) 16, 126, 130	s.76 .... 45, 126, **143**
(2) 172	(3) 127, 144
(3) 98, 130	(4) 30
(4) 11, 98, 130	s.77 .... 98, **144**
(5) 130	(1) 145
(7) 130	(2) 145
s.68 .... **130**	(3) 145
(1) 131	(4) 102, 118, 145, 146
(2)–(4) 114	(5) 145
(3) 26, 114, 131	s.78 .... 3, 102, 118, 143, **145**, 146
(b) 132	(1)(a) 146
(4)(b) 131	(b) 145
(5) 131	s.79 .... 44, 102, 118, 145, **146**
(8) 18	s.79A 16, **146**, 147, 171
s.69 .... 131, **132**, 147	s.80 .... 8, **146**, 171
(2)–(4) 127	s.81 32, 48, 72, 98, 105, 132, **147**,
s.70 .... 95, **132**, 133, 134	149, 161
(1) 133	(1) 147
(2) 133	(2) 147
(4A) 134	s.81A **147**
(6) 134	s.82 ... 5, 8, 11, 14, 32, 37, 44, 48,
s.71 .... 45, 95, 105, **134**	51, 72, 78, 98, 105, 132, 147,
(1) 135	**148**, 161
(a) 114, 135, 142	(1) 149
(b) 122, 135	(2) 149
(c) 14, 109, 136, 142	s.83 .... 7, 32, 82, 98, 105, **149**
(2) 136	s.84 .... 114, 127, **149**
(3) 136	s.85 .... 8, 17, **151**
(4) 98, 99, 110, 136	s.86 ... 9, 25, 29, 31, 86, 127, 139,
(5) 136	**152**, 155
s.72 .... **136**	s.87 .... 21, 22, 72, **152**
(1) 95	(1) 48, 72, 90, 106, 153
(aa) 137	(2) 153
(2) 22, 137	(3) 153
(5) 18	(4) 153
(6) 18	s.88 .... 8, **154**
s.73 .... 29, 70, 135, **137**	(1) 95
(1) 139	s.89 .... **154**
(3) 95, 139	(1) 154
(a) 29	(2) 154
(b) 29	(3) 154
(3A) 139	Sched. 1 .... 72, 74, **154**
(5) 22	para.1 155
(8) 18, 139	(c) 155
(9) 18, 139	para.2 155
(10) 139	Sched. 2 .... 18, 24, 95, 100, 105,
s.73A **139**	127, **155**

Table of Scottish Statutes

para.1 160
   (1) 105, 126, 160
   (4) 105, 107, 160
   (5) 161
   (6) 160
   (7) 160
para.5 160
   (3) 160
para.6 .... 100, 102, 126, 127, 161
   (2) 22
para.7 128
   (4) 160
   (5) 160
para.8(6) 132, 147, 161
   (7) 132, 147, 161
Sched. 3 .... 2, 8, 17, 32, 98, 106, 151, **161**
para.1 (1)(b) 107
(1)(c) 99, 107
para.2 166
   (1)(c) 99, 107
   (3) 99, 107
para.4 32
Sched. 4 .... 8, 95, 105, 136, 147, 160, **166**
para.1 .... 95, 171
   (1) 171
   (2) 147, 171
   (3) 171
   (4) 171
   (5) 171
   (6) 171
   (7) 171
para.2 .... 95, 171
   (1) 171
   (2) 171
   (3) 171
para.3 .... 95, 171
para.4 .... 32, 41, 95, 172
   (1) 172
   (2) 172
   (3) 172
   (4) 172

para.5 172
   (1) 172
   (2) 172
   (3) 172
   (4) 172
para.6 .... 95, 171, 172
   (2) 172
   (3) 116, 172
   (3A) 125
   (3C) 172
   (6) 160
   (7) 18
para.7 .... 95, 172
   (a) 32
para.8 .... 32, 95
Sched. 5 .... 8, 147, **172**
para.1 .... 147, 154
para.14 102
para.17(1) 27
para.26 .... 114, 127, 151
Sched. 6 .... 8, 100, 105, 147, **179**

2001 Regulation of Care (Scotland) Act (asp 8) 2, 3, 6
2003 Mental Health (Care and Treatment) (Scotland) Act (asp 13) .. 3, 9, 16, 21, 27, 36, 85, 86, 99, 106, 108, 110, 153
   s.32(1) 106
      (2) 106
   s.328 16
2005 Smoking, Health and Social Care (Scotland) Act (asp 13) 3, 6
2006 Human Tissue (Scotland) Act (asp 4) 36
2007 Adult Support and Protection (Scotland) Act (asp 10) .. v, 1, 3, 5, 7, 8, 13, 27, 31, 33, 37, 43, 94, 95, 100, 107, 109, 111, 117, 133, 134, 140, 143, 170, 185
   Pt 1 .... 13, 95, 134
   s.57 (1)(d) 185
   s.64 .... 109, 184, 185, 186

Table of Statutory Instruments

1999 Act of Sederunt (Summary Applications, Statutory Applications and Appeals etc. Rules) (SI 1999/929) 18, 120, 122, 136, 141
- r. 3.16.1 .... **190**
- r. 3.16.2 .... **191**
- r. 3.16.3 .... **191**
- r. 3.16.4 .... **191**
  - (1) 117
  - (3) 117
  - (4) 117
- r. 3.16.5 .... 18, **192**
- r. 3.16.6 .... **192**
- r. 3.16.7 .... **192**
- r. 3.16.8 .... 116, **193**
  - (1) 116
  - (1A) 112, 116, 117
  - (2) 116
  - (3) 116
  - (4) 116
  - (5) 116
- r. 3.16.9 .... **193**
- r. 3.16.10 .... **193**
  - (6) 112
- r. 3.16.11 .... **194**
- r. 3.16.12 .... **194**
- r. 3.16.13 .... **194**
- Sched. **195**

2003 Health Professions Order 2001 (Consequential Amendments) Order 2003 (SI 2003/1590) 93

2007 Pharmacists and Pharmacy Technicians Order 2007 (SI 2007/289) 93

Table of Scottish Statutory Instruments

2001 Adults with Incapacity (Supervision of Welfare Attorneys by Local Authorities) (Scotland) Regulations (SSI 2001/77) .. **29, 41**

Adults with Incapacity (Evidence in Relation to Dispensing with Intimation or Notification) (Scotland) Regulations (SSI 2001/79) .. **30, 200**
reg.1 .... **200**
reg.2 .... **200**

Adults with Incapacity (Scotland) Act 2000 (Commencement No.1) Order (SSI 2001/81) **95**

2002 Adults with Incapacity (Supervision of Welfare Guardians etc by Local Authorities) (Scotland) Regulations (SSI 2002/95) .. **28, 201**
reg.1 .... **201**
reg.2 .... **201**
reg.3 .... **202**
reg.4 .... **202**

Adults with Incapacity (Reports in Relation to Guardianship and Intervention Orders) (Scotland) Regulations (SSI 2002/96) 105, **203**
reg.1 .... **203**
reg.2 .... **203**
reg.3 .... **203**
reg.4 .... **203**
reg.5 .... **204**
reg.6 .... **204**
Sched. 1 .... **205**
Sched. 8 .... **209**
Sched. 9 .... **221**
Sched. 10 .... **222**

Adults with Incapacity (Recall of Guardians' Powers) (Scotland) Regulations (SSI 2002/97) 139, **234**
reg.1 .... **234**
reg.2 .... **234**
reg.3 .... **234**
reg.4 .... **234**
reg.5 .... **235**
reg.6 .... **235**
reg.7 .... **235**

reg.8 .... **235**
reg.9 .... **235**
reg.10 .... **235**
reg.11 .... **235**
reg.12 .... **235**
Sched. 1 .... **237**
Sched. 2 .... **244**
Sched. 3 .... **251**
Sched. 4 .... **253**
Sched. 5 .... **257**
Sched. 6 .... **261**
Sched. 7 .... **263**
Sched. 8 .... **265**
Sched. 9 .... **269**

Adults with Incapacity (Non-compliance with Decisions of Welfare Guardians) (Scotland) Regulations (SSI 2002/98) .. 134

Adults with Incapacity (Ethics Committee) (Scotland) Regulations (SSI 2002/190) 93, **273**
reg.1 .... **273**
reg.2 .... **273**
reg.3 .... **273**
reg.4 .... **274**
reg.5 .... **274**
reg.6 .... **274**
reg.7 .... **274**

Adults with Incapacity (Specified Medical Treatments) (Scotland) Regulations (SSI 2002/275) 86

2003 Adults with Incapacity (Management of Residents' Finances) (Scotland) Revocation Regulations (SSI 2003/226) 76

Adults with Incapacity (Management of Residents Finances) (No.2) (Scotland) Regulations (SSI 2003/266) 72, **276**
reg.1 .... **276**
reg.2 .... **276**
reg.3 .... **276**
reg.4 .... **277**
reg.5 .... **277**
Sched. 1 .... **278**

Table of Scottish Statutory Instruments

2005 Adults with Incapacity
(Management of
Residents' Finances)
(Scotland) Regulations
(SSI 2005/610) 3, 72

2007 Adults with Incapacity
(Conditions and
Circumstances Applicable
to Three Year Medical
Treatment Certificates)
(Scotland) Regulations
(SSI 2007/100) 85, **280**
   reg.1 .... **280**
   reg.2 .... **280**
   reg.3 .... **280**

Adults with Incapacity
(Medical Treatment
Certificates (Scotland)
Regulations
(SSI 2007/104) 85, **282**
   reg.1 .... **282**
   reg.2 .... **282**
   reg.3 .... **282**
   Sched. **283**

Adults with Incapacity
(Requirements for Signing
Medical Treatment
Certificates) (Scotland)
Regulations
(SSI 2007/105) 85, **284**
   reg.1 .... **284**
   reg.2 .... **284**

2008 Adults with Incapacity
(Accounts and Funds)
(Scotland) Regulations
(SSI 2008/51) 48, **285**
   reg.1 .... **285**
   reg.2 .... **285**
   reg.3 .... **285**
   reg.4 .... **285**
   reg.5 .... **285**
   Sched. **286**

Adults with Incapacity (Public
Guardian's Fees)
(Scotland) Regulations
(SSI 2008/52) 25, **287**
   reg.1 .... **287**
   reg.2 .... **287**
   reg.3 .... **287**
   reg.4 .... **287**
   Sched. 1 .... **288**

Adults with Incapacity
(Certificates in Relation to
Powers of Attorney)
(Scotland) Regulations
(SSI 2008/56) 37, 44, **291**
   reg.1 .... **291**
   reg.2 .... **291**
   reg.3 .... **291**
   reg.4 .... **291**
   reg.5 .... **291**
   Sched. 1 .... **292**

Adults with Incapacity (Public
Guardian's Fees)
(Scotland) Amendment
Regulations
(SSI 2008/238) 25, **296**
   reg.1 .... **296**
   reg.2 .... **296**
   Sched. 1 .... **297**
   Sched. 2 .... **300**
   Sched. 3 .... **303**

Table of Abbreviations

"*Adult Incapacity*"	: "Adult Incapacity" by Adrian D. Ward, W. Green, 2003
"appointees"	: attorneys, persons authorised under intervention orders, guardians, withdrawers, managers of authorised establishments, or such of them as may be specified in the particular provision referred to
"CPA"	: continuing power of attorney
"CTO"	: community treatment order (under the 2003 Act)
"ECHR"	: European Convention on Human Rights
"MWC"	: Mental Welfare Commission for Scotland
"SLC Report"	: Scottish Law Commission *Report on Incapable Adults* (Report No. 151) published September, 1995
"SP OR"	: Scottish Parliament Official Report
"the Alliance"	: the Alliance for the Promotion of the Bill (now this Act): see "*Background*"; p.1
"this Act", "the Incapacity Act"	: Adults with Incapacity (Scotland) Act 2000 (asp 4)
"WPA"	: welfare power of attorney
"1968 Act"	: The Social Work (Scotland) Act 1968 (6 & 7 Eliz. 2, c.40)
"1984 Act"	: The Mental Health (Scotland) Act 1984 (c.36)
"2000 Act", "2000 text"	: The Incapacity Act as originally enacted
"2001 Act"	: The Regulation of Care (Scotland) Act 2001 (asp8)
"2003 Act"	: The Mental Health (Care and Treatment) (Scotland) Act 2003 (asp13)
"2005 Act"	: The Smoking, Health and Social Care (Scotland) Act 2005 (asp13)
"2007 Act"	: The Adult Support and Protection (Scotland) Act 2007 (asp10)

Contents of the Incapacity Act

Part 1
General

General

1. General principles and fundamental definitions

Judicial proceedings

2. Applications and other proceedings and appeals
3. Powers of sheriff
4. Power of Court of Session or sheriff with regard to nearest relative
5. Safeguarding of interests in Court of Session appeals or proceedings

The Public Guardian

6. The Public Guardian and his functions
7. The Public Guardian: further provision

Expenses in court proceedings

8. Expenses in court proceedings

The Mental Welfare Commission

9. Functions of the Mental Welfare Commission

Local authorities

10. Functions of local authorities

Intimation

11. Intimation not required in certain circumstances

Investigations

12. Investigations

Codes of practice

13. Codes of practice

Appeal against decision as to incapacity

14. Appeal against decision as to incapacity

Part 2
Continuing Powers of Attorney and Welfare Powers of Attorney

15. Creation of continuing power of attorney
16. Creation and exercise of welfare power of attorney
16A. Continuing and welfare power of attorney: accompanying certificate

Adults with Incapacity Legislation

17. Attorney not obliged to act in certain circumstances
18. Power of attorney not granted in accordance with this Act
19. Registration of continuing or welfare power of attorney
20. Powers of sheriff
21. Records: attorneys
22. Notification to Public Guardian
22A. Revocation of continuing or welfare power of attorney
23. Resignation of continuing or welfare attorney
24. Termination of continuing or welfare power of attorney

PART 3

ACCOUNTS AND FUNDS

24A. Intromission with funds
24B. Adults in respect of whom applications may be made

Authority to take preliminary steps

24C. Authority to provide information about funds
24D. Authority to open account in adult's name

Authority to intromit

25. Authority to intromit
26. Authority to intromit: application

Withdrawal certificates

26A. Withdrawal certificates

Joint and reserve withdrawers

26B. Addition of joint withdrawer
26C. Joint withdrawers: supplementary
26D. Reserve withdrawers: applications
26E. Reserve withdrawers: authority to act

Variation of withdrawer's authority

26F. Variation of withdrawal certificate

Authority to transfer specified sums

26G. Authority to transfer specified sums

Applications: general

27. Applications: general requirements
27A. Countersigning of applications
27B. Medical certificates
27C. Intimation of applications
27D. Determination of applications: applicant to be fit and proper
27E. Determination of applications: opportunity to make representations
27F. Referral of application to sheriff
27G. Multiple applications etc.

Fundholders

28. Fundholders of adult's current account and adult's second account

Contents of the Incapacity Act

28A. Fundholder of original account
29. Fundholder's liability

Withdrawers

30. Use of funds by withdrawer
30A. Notification of change of address
30B. Records and inquiries

Duration etc. of authority

31. Duration of withdrawal certificate
31A. Suspension and termination of authority
31B. Renewal of authority to intromit
31C. Duration of certificates issued under section 24C, 24D and 24G etc.

Appeals

31D. Appeals
31E. Transition from guardianship

Miscellaneous

32. Joint accounts

Interpretation

33. Interpretation of Part

PART 4

MANAGEMENT OF RESIDENTS' FINANCES

35. Application of Part 4
36. Registration for purposes of managing residents' finances
37. Residents whose affairs may be managed
38. Financial procedures and controls in registered establishments
39. Matters which may be managed
40. Supervisory bodies
41. Duties and functions of managers of authorised establishment
42. Authorisation of named manager to withdraw from resident's account
43. Statement of resident's affairs
44. Resident ceasing to be resident of authorised establishment
45. Appeal, revocation etc.
46. Disapplication of Part 4

PART 5

MEDICAL TREATMENT AND RESEARCH

47. Authority of persons responsible for medical treatment
48. Exceptions to authority to treat
49. Medical treatment where there is an application for intervention or guardianship order
50. Medical treatment where guardian etc. has been appointed
51. Authority for research
52. Appeal against decision as to medical treatment

PART 6
INTERVENTION ORDERS AND GUARDIANSHIP ORDERS

Intervention orders

53. Intervention orders
54. Records: intervention orders
55. Notification of change of address
56. Registration of intervention order relating to heritable property

Guardianship orders

57. Application for guardianship order
58. Disposal of application
59. Who may be appointed as guardian
60. Renewal of guardianship order by sheriff
61. Registration of guardianship order relating to heritable property

Joint and substitute guardians

62. Joint guardians
63. Substitute guardian

Functions etc. of guardian

64. Functions and duties of guardian
65. Records: guardians
66. Gifts
67. Effect of appointment and transactions of guardian
68. Reimbursement and remuneration of guardian
69. Forfeiture of guardian's remuneration
70. Non-compliance with decisions of guardian with welfare powers

Termination and variation of guardianship and replacement, removal or resignation of guardian

71. Replacement or removal of guardian or recall of guardianship by sheriff
72. Discharge of guardian with financial powers
73. Recall of powers of guardian
73A. Recall of chief social work officer's guardianship powers
74. Variation of guardianship order
75. Resignation of guardian
75A. Death of guardian
76. Change of habitual residence

Termination of authority to intervene and guardianship on death of adult

77. Termination of authority to intervene and guardianship on death of adult
78. Amendment of registration under section 61 on events affecting guardianship or death of adult
79. Protection of third parties: guardianship

Guardianship orders: children

79A. Guardianship orders: children

Contents of the Incapacity Act

Part 7

Miscellaneous

80. Future appointment of curator bonis etc. incompetent
81. Repayment of funds
81A. Public Guardian's power to obtain records
82. Limitation of liability
83. Offence of ill-treatment and wilful neglect
84. Application to guardians appointed under Criminal Procedure (Scotland) Act 1995
85. Jurisdiction and private international law
86. Regulations
87. Interpretation
88. Continuation of existing powers, minor and consequential amendments and repeals
89. Citation and commencement

Schedule 1—Managers of an establishment
Schedule 2—Management of estate of adult
Schedule 3—Jurisdiction and private international law
Schedule 4—Continuation of existing curators, tutors, guardians and attorneys under this Act
Schedule 5—Minor and consequential amendments
Schedule 6—Repeals

The Bill for this Act of the Scottish Parliament was passed by the Parliament on 29th March 2000 and received Royal Assent on 9th May 2000.

ADULTS WITH INCAPACITY (SCOTLAND) ACT 2000

2000 asp 4

An Act of the Scottish Parliament to make provision as to the property, financial affairs and personal welfare of adults who are incapable by reason of mental disorder or inability to communicate; and for connected purposes.

INTRODUCTION AND GENERAL NOTE
This book sets out, with annotations, the text of the Adults with Incapacity (Scotland) Act 2000 (asp4) ("this Act", "the Incapacity Act") with all amendments up to and including those made by the Adult Support and Protection (Scotland) Act 2007 (asp10) ("the 2007 Act"), which came fully into force on April 1, 2008, and with a few further amendments made by the Welfare Reform Act 2007 (c5) and due to come into force on October 27, 2008. It is intended to serve both as a volume which stands alone in its own right, and also as a companion volume to update and supplement my book *Adult Incapacity* (W. Green, 2003). The Incapacity Act, as originally enacted, was a radically reforming Act, which created in Scots Law a coherent modern code of provision as to decisions about the personal welfare of adults with incapacity, and the management of their property and financial affairs. It was "the first large Bill on a major policy area to be passed by the Scottish Parliament" (*per* Mr Iain Gray, Deputy Minister for Community Care, March 29, 2000—SP OR Vol. 5, No. 11, col. 1120). Previous fragmented, outdated and often harmful provision was in part substantially reformed, and in part superseded altogether. Thus from April 1, 2002, when Pt. 6 of the Incapacity Act came into force, no more curators bonis to adults, tutors or guardians under the Mental Health (Scotland) Act 1984 (c.36) ("the 1984 Act") could be appointed, and existing appointees became guardians under this Act. This Act introduced a new regime of intervention orders and guardianship orders; substantially reformed the law of powers of attorney; introduced a new procedure to obtain authority to intromit with funds, and reformed the law on joint accounts; introduced a new scheme of management of residents' finances which replaced previous 1984 Act hospital management and extended to a wider range of establishments; created a new authority to provide treatment, in addition to (but not replacing) the existing grounds in law on which medical treatment might be given; and contained provisions governing research, both research which is likely to produce real and direct benefit for the adult (so-called "therapeutic research") and, in strictly limited circumstances, research which is not ("non-therapeutic research"). Major new protections were created in the overriding principles in s.1; in new procedural, registration, supervisory and investigative provisions; and in the creation of a new offence of ill-treatment or wilful neglect. A new jurisdiction was vested in the sheriff court, and new powers were given to the Court of Session. The Accountant of Court became Public Guardian. Her responsibilities and powers were extended, as were those of the Mental Welfare Commission for Scotland ("MWC") and local authorities. The legislation is supplemented by regulations and codes of practice.

Background
In the period 1984-1990 attention was drawn to the deficiencies of existing law and suggestions were made for improvement: see, for example, *Dementia and the Law: The Challenge Ahead* (Scottish Action on Dementia, 1988) and Ward *Scots Law and the Mentally Handicapped* (1984) and *The Power to Act* (1990). In the same period tutors to adults were re-introduced in their modern form, the first such appointment being in 1986, initially to make good the lack of any true personal guardianship in Scots law (which role has now been taken over by welfare guardianship), and thereafter also on occasions to deal with single issues (now covered by intervention orders).

Internationally, the trend to reform accelerated during the same period. The Dependent Adults Acts of Alberta had already influenced the concept of revived tutors-dative. The process of reform in Scotland was particularly influenced by the Protection of Personal and Property Rights Act 1988 of New Zealand and the Betreuungsgesetz 1990 of Germany. Similar principles can be identified in all of these reforms, so that it is possible to generalise about "old law" and "new law": see *"Old law" and "new law"* below.

Adults with Incapacity Legislation

Formally, the process of reform commenced in Scotland with the Scottish Law Commission's Discussion Paper No. 94 "Mentally Disabled Adults: Legal Arrangements for Managing their Welfare and Finances" (September, 1991). Consultation was wide-ranging, with considerable input from relevant organisations and interested individuals, including representatives of the whole range of relevant disabilities. The Commission published its *Report on Incapable Adults* (Report No. 151, "SLC Report") in September, 1995. Government published its own Consultation Paper *Managing the Finances and Welfare of Incapable Adults* in February, 1997. There was increasing anxiety that the pace of deliberation did not match the urgency of the need for law reform. In December, 1997 a number of concerned organisations formed the "Alliance for the Promotion of the Incapable Adults Bill" ("the Alliance"). Membership rapidly grew to over 70 voluntary, professional and other organisations, including over 30 national organisations. Active campaigning publicised examples of both the inappropriate and harmful outcomes under existing law and the numbers of adults in Scotland at any one time affected by some form of incapacity, from causes including dementia (estimated in 1999 at some 61,000 in Scotland), moderate to severe learning disability (20,000), serious head injury (1,500 per annum in Scotland), and strokes and psychiatric hospital admissions (10,000 and 30,000 per annum respectively, not all of them entailing impairment of capacity). The Alliance estimated that approximately 100,000 adults in Scotland at any one time have impairment of capacity, and that estimate was subsequently quoted by the Scottish Executive. Put another way, the issues affect most families, sooner or later.

The Alliance was unsuccessful in its initial aim of achieving legislation by Westminster in 1998/1999. Lobbying of all of the main Scottish political parties resulted in commitments by all to support legislation in the first session of the Scottish Parliament. Those commitments were honoured. The Scottish Executive published its proposals in *Making the right moves: Rights and protection for adults with incapacity* in August, 1999. The Incapacity Act followed, providing vindication and commendation of the new legislative arrangements. First and foremost, where Westminster could not find time for such essential law reform, the Scottish Parliament delivered in its first session. Secondly, there was unprecedented openness, involvement of affected citizens, and responsiveness to their views, on the part of Scottish Executive Ministers and officials, the key Parliamentary Committees (principally the Justice and Home Affairs Committee, and also the Health and Community Care Committee), and the Parliament itself. Rapid publication of papers and proceedings on the Parliament's website encouraged this process. Considerable demands were placed upon MSPs both by this openness and by the stringencies of unicameral legislation (leaving some errors and blemishes, mostly now rectified, though some are mentioned in the annotations to sections and Schedules).

The Bill was introduced on October 8, 1999, accompanied by Explanatory Notes SP Bill 5—EN and Policy Memorandum SP Bill 5—PM. It was preceded by informal consideration by the Justice and Home Affairs Committee. That Committee then heard oral evidence on November 3, 9 and 17, 1999, also considered written evidence, and agreed its Stage 1 Report on December 1, 1999. The stage 1 debate took place on December 9, 1999. The Health and Community Care Committee also considered the Bill at stage 1, at meetings on November 16 and 17, 1999. Its Report appears as Appendix 1 to the Stage 1 Report. The Justice and Home Affairs Committee concluded stage 2 proceedings on March 1, 2000. Finally, the stage 3 debate took place on March 29, 2000, and after further amendment the Bill for this Act was passed on that date. A total of 327 amendments were tabled at stage 2, and 158 at stage 3.

Implementation, Review and Amendment
This Act received Royal Assent on May 9, 2000. Commencement was spread over a period of 43 months. The principal dates were April 2, 2001 (Pts. 1, 2, 3 and 7); April 1, 2002 (Pt. 6); July 1, 2002 (Pt. 5); and October 1, 2003 (Pt. 4, as by then amended by the Regulation of Care (Scotland) Act 2001 asp8). Final commencement was on November 4, 2004, in respect of those provisions of Sched. 3 which had awaited ratification in respect of Scotland of the Hague Convention of January 13, 2000 on the International Protection of Adults, Scotland being the first—and therefore initially only—country in the world in respect of which that Convention was ratified.

The implementation of this Act was overseen by an Implementation Steering Group. Regulations were made and Codes of Practice prepared. The Office of the Public Guardian was established, putting in place the systems to discharge the Public Guardian's functions under this Act, and recruiting and training staff. Major training programmes took place for social work and other local authority staff, medical professionals, lawyers and others. Needs

Introduction and General Note

for general public information were addressed. A project to monitor and assess progress and experience under the Act was established. The results were published in *The Adults with Incapacity (Scotland) Act 2000: Learning from Experience* (Scottish Executive, 2004). This was followed by a consultation exercise: see *Improving with Experience: Adults with Incapacity (Scotland) Act 2000 Consultation* (Scottish Executive, 2005), also *Summary of Responses to the Consultation Document "Improving with Experience"* (Scottish Executive, 2006). Resulting amendments to the Incapacity Act were proposed in the Adult Support and Protection (Scotland) Bill. Even during the passage of the Bill, there was significant further discussion. Indeed, Ministers and officials of Scottish Executive (now Scottish Government), and the Parliament itself, are to be commended for accepting that radically new legislation such as the Incapacity Act requires "aftercare" from both executive and legislature, and is almost bound to require subsequent improvement by amending legislation. As to discussion and amendment during the passage of the Bill itself, Lewis MacDonald, Deputy Minister for Health and Community Care, was clear as to the Executive's stance: "I welcome the support for the bill from all those who have spoken this afternoon. Euan Robson was right to emphasise that the ability to improve legislation as we learn from experience and practice is one of the dividends of devolution. The parliamentary process exists to enable legislation to be improved before it is enacted as well as after it has been in operation for some years. Rather than seeing the improvement of legislation by the parliamentary process as a failure of Government, we should see it as a success of Parliament and as a good example of how the Scottish Parliament was always intended to work". (Stage 3 debate, February 15, 2007, SPOR col. 32237). See also *Part 3* below. Whereas in 1999-2000 the Bill for the original Act was dealt with principally by the Justice and Home Affairs Committee (see above), the Bill for the 2007 Act was allocated to the Health Committee. Presumably by chance, rather than deliberately for continuity, Roseanna Cunningham MSP was Convenor of each committee at the relevant time.

There are some disappointing ineptitudes of draftsmanship in the amendments to the Incapacity Act inserted by the 2007 Act: see ss.22A, 24B, 32 and 78, and annotations thereto.

Prior to the 2007 Act, the Incapacity Act was amended by three statutes and four Statutory Instruments: see the Regulation of Care (Scotland) Act 2001 asp8; the Mental Health (Care and Treatment) (Scotland) Act 2003 asp13; the Smoking, Health and Social Care (Scotland) Act 2005 asp13; the Financial Services and Markets Act 2000 (Consequential Amendments and Appeals) Order SI 2001/3649; the Medicines for Human Use (Clinical Trials) Regulations SI 2004/1031; the Mental Health (Care and Treatment) (Scotland) Act 2003 (Modification of Enactments) Order SSI 2005/465; and the Adults with Incapacity (Management of Residents' Finances) (Scotland) Regulations SSI 2005/610.

"Old law" and "new law"
The descriptions of "old law" and "new law" referred to above, apply internationally and also in Scotland. "Old law" was typified by a "black and white" approach under which people were simplistically classed as sane or insane, fully capable and responsible or lacking all capability and responsibility, and so on. Procedures were equally simplistic: an assessment amounting to little more than a diagnosis resulted in a standardised outcome, often complete loss of legal capacity, and frequently of indefinite duration. "New law" recognises the great variety of intellectual disabilities and resulting impairments of capacity. In each case, such capacity as a person in fact has should be respected, safeguarded and if possible encouraged; and there requires to be a balance between providing special measures where they are needed, but on the other hand not restricting, discriminating or disqualifying any more than necessary.

Procedurally, the characteristics of "new law" are these. Firstly, a widely-drawn "gateway definition" ensures that procedures can be accessed by all who might benefit from them. Secondly, a coherent but flexible range of possible outcomes allows for appropriate measures to be taken in each individual case. Thirdly, there are governing principles to guide which special measures, if any, should be chosen and applied in each individual case. Fourthly, a process of assessment identifies the individual's circumstances, abilities, disabilities and needs, so that an appropriate individualised package of provision can be selected. Fifthly, similar principles to those governing the choice of provision are also applied to appointees (see definition of "appointees" in Definitions below) in the exercise of the powers conferred. Sixthly, adaptation of the package of provision to changes in needs and circumstances is ensured by time-limiting of appointments and requirements for ongoing review.

This Act takes account of *Principles Concerning the Legal Protection of Incapable Adults* (Council of Europe Recommendation No. R (99) 4 and explanatory memorandum). In its judgement of March 27, 2008 in *Shtukaturov v Russia* (Application No 4409/05) the European Court of Human Rights held that, in the circumstances of that case, non-compliance with the Recommendation resulted in a breach of Article 8 of the European Convention on Human Rights ("ECHR"). The court made the following significant general statement regarding the principles contained in the Recommendation: "Although these principles have no force of law for this Court, they may define a common European standard in this area." It may be helpful, and may on occasions be necessary, to have regard to the Recommendation in considering how our incapacity legislation should be interpreted.

Internationally, our Incapacity Act is itself looked to as an example of best practice in implementing Recommendation No R(99)4, and has received considerable attention from jurists. The Scottish experience of the Incapacity Act has influenced law reform processes in several countries, and continues to do so. Currently, the Scottish experience is assisting the Council of Europe in formulating a proposed *Recommendation on Principles concerning Powers of Attorney and Advance Directives for Incapacity*.

UN Convention
The UN Convention on the Rights of Persons with Disabilities of December 13, 2006 seeks to address from a global perspective all disabilities, including physical, sensory and intellectual disabilities. Article 12.1 re-affirms the right of all persons with disabilities to recognition everywhere as persons before the law. Article 12.2 provides that: "States Parties shall recognize that persons with disabilities enjoy legal capacity on an equal basis with others in all aspects of life." Subsequent references to "the exercise of legal capacity" point to an idiosyncratic use of "legal capacity" to mean an adult's rights and status themselves, rather than the ability to exercise and assert them. Under that usage "legal incapacity" refers to the diminution by law of an adult's rights and status, similar to that which might be imposed upon some criminals, or upon bankrupts. Persons with disabilities should never have such legal incapacity imposed upon them by reason of their disabilities.

Across the great range of intellectual disabilities, human rights and fundamental freedoms can be put at risk on the one hand by ascribing incapacity to those who have capacity but may require support in exercising their "legal capacity", but also on the other hand by suggesting that only support—rather than careful legal safeguards—is required by those lacking capacity, and whose apparent compliance is not a valid exercise of "legal capacity". The very essence of any adult incapacity regime is, in both creating and applying its provisions, to provide for both situations and to address in a balanced way the difficult task of drawing the delineation between them. The UN Declaration addresses the first situation in Article 12.3, which gives new authoritative force to existing best practice principles that where there is capacity but difficulty in exercising it, all necessary support should be given to facilitate, encourage and develop the exercise of capacity. Article 12.4 briefly re-states the main guiding principles applicable in the second situation where there is impairment of capacity and "measures that relate to the exercise of legal capacity" are required. However, Article 12.4 neither contains principles explicitly addressing such incapacities nor even acknowledges their existence. This lack of balance, coupled with the peculiar wording of Article 12.2, has unfortunately produced in much of the comment upon the Declaration a reinforcement of the "discrimination within anti-discrimination" which so often disadvantages people with impaired legal capacity (in the normal sense of that term). Specifically, it has become fashionable in some quarters to pretend that people in the second category above are in the first category, describing people who in fact have significant impairments of capacity as being "in need of support to make decisions". Failure to recognise the existence of a disability and its consequences is a form of discrimination, and often leads to further discrimination. "Supported decision-making" is for those who can, albeit with assistance, make their own valid decisions, though there is always a danger that the resulting decision may be more that of the supporter than of the adult. Where there is no relevant capacity, or only limited and partial capacity, what is required is a process of "constructing decisions" such as is described in Chapter 15 of *Adult Incapacity*. Because of these limitations and lack of balance in the UN Convention, the Council of Europe Recommendation No. R (99) 4, referred to in the preceding section, remains the principal starting-point for the continued development in Europe of laws to ensure the protection of the human rights and fundamental freedoms of those whose capacity to make valid decisions, and effectively to exercise and assert their rights, is impaired.

Introduction and General Note

Part 1
Part 1 of this Act defines "adults" as persons who have attained the age of 16 (s.1 (6)) and contains the "gateway" definition of incapacity (also s.1 (6)). The general principles which determine whether to intervene, and if so in what manner, are set out in s.1 (2)—(4). These, and the further principles in s.1 (5), apply to the actions of guardians, continuing and welfare attorneys, and managers of establishments. The importance of these general principles cannot be over-emphasised. They should be referred to in conjunction with almost every other provision of this Act. An example of their importance is that the limitation of liability in terms of s.82 is not available unless the principles have been complied with. Part 1 also contains general provisions regarding proceedings (including matters of intimation and expenses), appeals, and powers of the sheriff and of the Court of Session; general provisions regarding the Public Guardian, MWC and local authorities; and provisions regarding investigations, codes of practice and appeals against decisions as to incapacity. See General Note to Pt. 1 for an explanation of the layout of this Part, which appears somewhat haphazard on first reading.

Parts 2—6 contain the range of available provisions under this Act. The principles in s.1 apply to all of them.

Part 2
This Part provides the modern code of continuing powers of attorney (CPAs) and welfare powers of attorney (WPAs). Prior to the Law Reform (Miscellaneous Provisions) (Scotland) Act 1990 (c.40) it was thought that powers of attorney ceased to have effect upon the incapacity of the granter. Section 71 of that Act (repealed by this Act) provided that, unless containing a declaration to the contrary, a Power of Attorney executed after that Act came into force would remain effective following the incapacity of the granter. This was intended as an interim measure pending consideration by the Scottish Law Commission of the issues (*Hansard*, H.L. Vol. 522, col. 1649—October 25, 1990). In the following decade, serious concerns developed about the lack of safeguards against inappropriate purported grants of powers of attorney, and of protection for granters following loss of capacity. Those concerns increased with a developing trend towards including welfare as well as financial powers. CPAs are defined in this Act (s.15 (1) and (2)) as powers in relation to property and financial affairs which continue to have effect during incapacity. WPAs may be exercised in relation to welfare matters, but only during incapacity (s.16 (1), (2) and (5)). CPAs and WPAs granted after commencement of this Act are only valid if this Act's requirements are met (s.18). These include requirements for certification at time of granting of capacity and of no undue influence (ss.15, 16 and 16A), and requirements for registration with the Public Guardian before the power can be operated (s.19). There are requirements to notify various subsequent events to the Public Guardian (s.22). The formalities for revocation, introduced by the 2007 Act, mirror those for original grant, in that they require similar certification, and registration (s.22A). Anyone claiming an interest may apply to the sheriff to exercise various supervisory and other powers (s.20). Attorneys are not required to do anything which would be disproportionately burdensome or expensive (s.17), but must keep records (s.21), and must comply with the requirements of s.23 if they wish to resign. Powers in favour of a spouse end upon judicial separation, divorce or declaration of nullity, and in relation to any particular matters attorneys will be superseded by guardians with relevant powers, but there is protection for those continuing to act in good faith (s.24). CPAs end on the bankruptcy of granter or attorney, but WPAs do not (ss.15 (5) and 16 (7) respectively).

Part 3
Part 3 formerly contained two distinct provisions. Section 32 introduced an important reform by providing that where an account is held in joint names, then unless the contrary is specified one holder may continue to operate the account if the other loses relevant capacity. Previously, many couples had been advised to open joint accounts on the assumption that one could continue to operate if the other lost capacity, but banks and others took the view that incapacity of either joint holder terminated the mandate. The remainder of the original Pt. 3 contained relatively simple procedures to permit intromissions during incapacity with funds held by a "fundholder" (the definition covers banks, building societies "or other similar bodies").

Section 32 has been a success and has been retained unamended, except that it is no longer disapplied by appointment of an attorney or guardian, or grant of an intervention order (see General Note to s.32). The remainder of Pt. 3 was not a success, uptake being far less than anticipated. As the amendments to Pt. 3 multiplied during stage 2 of the Bill for the 2007 Act, the Executive superseded them with a single amendment (to that Bill) introduced by the Convenor of the Health Committee, Roseanna Cunningham MSP, as follows: "The prize for the longest-ever amendment in the history of the Scottish Parliament goes to the Executive for its amendment 107, which is a 15-page amendment to Pt. 2 of the bill. It proposes to replace totally Pt. 3 of the Adults with Incapacity (Scotland) Act 2000, which relates to the financial affairs of an adult with incapacity" (SPOR Health Committee December 19, 2006 col. 3302). Lewis Macdonald (Deputy Minister for Health and Community Care) explained: "When we considered the totality of those amendments, it seemed sensible to take the opportunity to replace the whole of Part 3 of the 2000 Act with a newly drafted Part 3, which we hope is more accessible and comprehensible." (*ibid*. col. 3305).

Part 3 (apart from s.32) has accordingly now been replaced in its entirety by the new scheme described in the General Note to Pt. 3 which, as there explained, is best viewed as a form of simplified and limited financial guardianship. A guardianship order under Pt. 6 may not be granted where any other means under this Act will suffice, therefore the new provisions of Pt. 3 will have a substantial impact on guardianship procedure, rendering Pt. 6 guardianship applications inappropriate in many situations where they were previously presented. It is also likely that many existing financial guardianships will be found to be no longer justified in relation to s.1 principles, so that in such cases advantage will be taken of the new s.31E which facilitates the transition from Pt. 6 guardianship to administration under Pt. 3. Withdrawals by authorised establishments are covered by Pt. 4 (s.42).

Part 4
Part 4 provides a scheme of management by "authorised establishments". Prior to this Act, the only such scheme was hospital management under the 1984 Act s.94. Many more adults with incapacity now live in a variety of establishments other than hospitals. The provisions of s.94 were in any event ripe for reform; indeed, the last pre-devolution Westminster legislation was the Mental Health (Amendment) (Scotland) Act 1999 (c.32) (introduced as a Private Member's Bill by Eric Clarke, MP) to permit unblocking of funds held for patients following discharge. Part 4 was the last Part of this Act to be brought into force, by which time it had already been amended by the Regulation of Care (Scotland) Act 2001 (asp8). It has since been further amended. The Pt. 4 scheme covers all categories of establishments defined in s.35, except for those "registered establishments" which opt out, subject to revocation under s.45. The principal supervisory body under Pt. 4 is the Scottish Commission for Regulation of Care or the Health Board, depending upon the category of establishment, rather than the Public Guardian as with other methods of management under this Act. For individual residents, the procedure includes medical certification, notification to the relevant supervisory body and intimation to the resident, nearest relative and named person (s.37). The matters which may be managed are limited to those specified in s.39. The relevant supervisory body has a duty to monitor authorised establishments and to investigate complaints (s.40). Duties are imposed on authorised establishments by s.41, and (as mentioned above) a procedure to authorise withdrawal of funds is contained in s.42. Sections 43 and 44 contain provisions, including a requirement to prepare a statement of affairs, in respect of residents who regain capacity or leave the establishment (or both). CPAs, guardianship and intervention orders, and other specific powers take precedence over Pt. 4 powers (s.46).

Part 5
Part 5 created a new authority to give medical treatment (ss.47—48); deals with medical treatment when guardianship or intervention orders have been sought or are in force, and where an attorney has relevant powers (ss.49—50); contains provisions about research (s.51); and contains general provisions for appeal on medical matters to the sheriff, and with leave of the sheriff to the Court of Session, by anyone having an interest (s.52). Part 5 was amended by the Smoking, Health and Social Care (Scotland) Act 2005 (asp13) ("the 2005 Act"). Under the 2000 text only doctors could issue certificates to authorise treatment under s.47 . The 2005 Act widened the range of certifiers (see s.47 (1A)). The 2000 text set a maximum of one year for authorisations. The 2005 Act permits authorisations for up to three years in certain circumstances. The 2005 Act also resolved some difficulties with the 2000 text, and made some other and consequential amendments.

During the passage of the original Bill controversy was focused, or rather mis-focused, upon Pt. 5, to an extent which occasionally distorted debate (see for example comments on "intervention" in the General Note to s.1). Prior to this Act, medical treatment which might

Introduction and General Note

otherwise be an assault could be rendered lawful in four ways: consent of the patient, valid consent on behalf of the patient, necessity, and statutory authority under the 1984 Act. Authority under Pt. 5 does not detract from these (s.47(2A)). It is used most often for treatment neither so acutely required as to be immediately justified by the principle of necessity, nor where it is otherwise necessary or appropriate to obtain a guardianship or intervention order. Doctors and other certifiers generally appear to prefer the certainty of this statutory authority to perceived uncertainty surrounding the principle of necessity, except where urgent circumstances do not immediately permit this. Certification by the medical practitioner primarily responsible for treatment, or other authorised certifier (see s.47 (1A) (b)) ("the certifier" in these annotations) will permit any procedure or treatment to promote or safeguard physical or mental health, given by the certifier or by others under the instructions, or with the approval or agreement, of the certifier. Some matters are excluded and regulations may exclude, or prescribe special requirements for, others (ss.47 (7) and 48). This authority does not apply where the certifier is aware of a pending application for a guardianship or intervention order with relevant medical powers: in that situation only emergency treatment may be given (s.49). Where there is a guardianship or intervention order, or a Power of Attorney, with relevant medical powers, treatment decisions will normally be taken, or consented to, by the relevant appointee. Section 50 provides that where there is agreement between certifier and appointee, any other person having an interest (including the doctor primarily responsible for the adult's treatment, where not the certifier) may appeal that decision to the Court of Session. Section 50 also deals with disagreements between certifier and appointee. The appointee's decision will stand unless the certifier asks MWC to nominate a "nominated practitioner", from a list maintained by the Commission, to consider the matter. The nominated practitioner must consult the appointee and (where reasonable and practicable) a person nominated by the appointee. Subject to further appeal to the Court of Session (which may also be made by anyone having an interest) the nominated practitioner decides the matter. Up to time of writing this procedure had never been used.

Part 6
Part 6 deals with intervention and guardianship orders, which may be granted by the sheriff. Orders may cover welfare matters, or financial and property matters, or both, and where guardianship is sought the court may grant an intervention order if that will suffice (but not vice versa). All applications require to be accompanied by two medical reports based upon examination and assessment within 30 days of the application, one of them by a "relevant medical practitioner" (see s.57 (6B)). A further report is required as to the general appropriateness of the order sought and the suitability of the proposed appointee. Where personal welfare powers are sought, this must be a social work report (from a mental health officer except where the only relevant disability is inability to communicate). Where only property or financial powers are sought, anyone with sufficient knowledge may make the report. Intervention orders take two forms. They may simply order specific action to be taken; or they may authorise an appointee to take specified action or make specified decisions.

In relation to guardians, Pt. 6 contains provisions as to who may be appointed; provisions regarding joint and substitute guardians; procedural matters including record-keeping; guardians' functions, responsibilities and powers; provisions in relation to termination and variation of guardianship and replacement, removal or resignation of the guardian; protections for third parties dealing with guardians; and other matters.

There are provisions regarding registration in the Sasine and Land Registers of intervention orders (s.56) and guardianship orders (s.61) affecting heritable property.

The 2007 Act introduced two important alternatives to Pt. 6 procedure. In relation to welfare matters, it did so by inserting a new s.13ZA in the Social Work (Scotland) Act 1968 ("the 1968 Act"). Because of the importance of this provision to practice under the Incapacity Act, the text of s.13ZA of the 1968 Act appears in Appendix 1, with an account of the background and commentary on the provisions and related guidance in the annotation. In relation to financial matters, it did so by replacing the previous Pt. 3 in the manner described above, and with the consequences for Pt. 6 discussed in the General Note for Pt. 3. The 2007 Act also introduced a simplified renewal procedure, a significant alteration to the provisions regarding caution, and other improvements summarised in the General Note for Pt. 6.

Part 7
Part 7 provides for an offence of ill-treatment and wilful neglect (s.83). Persons with powers under this Act who use funds improperly are liable to repay them with interest, but have

under s.82 a general exemption from liability for breach of duty of care or fiduciary duty where their actions or failure to act were reasonable and in good faith, and were in accordance with the general principles in s.1. Incapacity Act guardianship was substituted for 1984 Act guardianship in terms of the Criminal Procedure (Scotland) Act 1995 (c.46) (s.84).

Section 80 in conjunction with Sched. 4, which s.88 incorporates, contained important transitional (and some continuing) provisions. With some qualifications, appointments of curators or tutors to adults in force on April 1, 2002 became guardianships under the new Act, and are now subject to renewal provisions inserted by the 2007 Act. Appointments of curators bonis to children continue to be competent, but such appointees become guardians under this Act when the person reaches the age of 16, if the appointment does not then terminate. Existing 1984 Act guardians became guardians under the Incapacity Act, but with the fixed powers conferred in s.41 (2) of the 1984 Act. For all of the foregoing, proceedings pending on April 1, 2002 continued under previous law, but appointees became guardians under this Act. Various provisions of this Act were applied to existing attorneys when Pt. 2 came into force on April 02, 2001. Likewise, various provisions were applied to existing hospital managers acting under s.94 of the 1984 Act when Pt. 3 came into force, and their authority to manage continued for a maximum of three years.

Schedule 3, incorporated by s.85, and various provisions throughout this Act contain private international law provisions, which comply with the Hague Convention of January 13, 2000 on *The International Protection of Adults*. Sched. 3 also defines which sheriffdom has jurisdiction.

Part 7 also contains usual supplementary provisions including those covering interpretation and (by reference to Scheds. 5 and 6 respectively) statutory amendments and repeals.

Regulations
Regulations under (and some relevant to) the Incapacity Act were reproduced in Appendix 2 of *Adult Incapacity*. Amended and new regulations appear in Appendix 2 of this volume.

Codes of Practice
The following Codes of Practice, updated with effect from April 1, 2008, are available at *http://www.publicguardian-scotland.gov.uk/forms/codes.asp*:
 Code of Practice for Local Authorities exercising functions under the 2000 Act
 Code of Practice for Continuing and Welfare Attorneys
 Code of Practice for those authorised under the Access to Funds scheme
 Code of Practice for persons authorised under Intervention Orders and Guardians.

Updated with effect from January 31, 2008, and available at *http://www.scotland.gov.uk/Publications/2008/06/13114117/2*, is:
 Adults with Incapacity (Scotland) Act Part 5 Code of Practice.

Also relevant is the "Guidance for Local Authorities (March 2007) Provision of community care services to adults with incapacity".

Matters not covered by this Act
The SLC Report recommended legislation on the withholding and withdrawal of life-preserving treatment, and on advance directives. On the first topic, the Commission's Report was published prior to the decision in *Law Hospital NHS Trust v Lord Advocate*, 1996 SLT 848. The Scottish Executive decided to exclude both topics from this Act, on the basis that it is preferable that the courts should continue to develop the law, rather than that it should yet be fixed in statute. This did not prevent considerable debate of the first topic during the Parliamentary proceedings. The current law on withholding and withdrawal of treatment may be found in *Law Hospital*, above. There is no equivalent statement of current Scots law in relation to advance directives, but the position is reviewed in the SLC Report (paras. 5.41-5.46). In England, the Lord Chancellor provided a useful survey of the law in *Making Decisions*, October, 1999. With reference to s.50 (see under *Part 5* above) it is understood that MWC take the view (correctly, it is submitted) that patients, and therefore their appointees if so authorised, can refuse consent to proposed treatment but cannot demand that treatment be given or continued. It is understood that the cases where this point arose referred to in the General Note to s.50 were both cases of proposed withholding of life sustaining treatment, that in both cases MWC drew attention to relevant British Medical Association guidance, and that in consequence life sustaining treatment was initiated for a trial period.

Adults with Incapacity (Scotland) Act 2000 (Pt. 1)

PART 1
GENERAL

General

GENERAL NOTE
The content of Pt. 1 is summarised in the Introduction and General Note. After s.1, which sets out general principles and contains the key definitions of "adult", "incapable" and "incapacity", the layout of the remainder of Pt. 1, as enacted, is not as clear as in the original draft Bill appended to the SLC Report. Part 1 contains three substantive procedures: under s.3 (3), to apply to the sheriff to give directions to an appointee; under s.4, to apply to the Court of Session or the sheriff to make certain orders in respect of the nearest relative, and the nearest relative's functions; and under s.14, to appeal against a decision as to incapacity. General provisions regarding court procedures under this Act are contained in ss.2, 3, 5, 8 and 11 (s.11 deals with intimations and notifications generally). Sections 6 and 7 deal generally with the Public Guardian and her role; s.9 deals generally with the functions of MWC under this Act; s.10 deals generally with the functions of local authorities under this Act; and s.12 contains further provisions related to the functions of all three. Section 13 deals with codes of practice under this Act (whereas regulations are dealt with in s.86).

The draft Bill annexed to the SLC Report contained, in clause 2(5), a suggested provision that: "All applications and proceedings under this Act shall be disposed of by a sheriff nominated for the time being for that purpose by the sheriff principal, unless no such sheriff is available to do so." The Scottish Law Commission discussed choice of forum in paras. 2.18—2.31 of its Report. Although the option of using the courts had attracted most support, there was considerable support for the alternatives of tribunals or hearings, and considerable disquiet about the suitability of the courts, perceived disadvantages including that the courts would be "intimidating, legalistic, adversarial and only willing to look at the issues put in front of them, lacking in understanding of the needs of the mentally incapable, slow, expensive and associated with criminal proceedings". The Scottish Law Commission took the view that some (and therefore, by implication, not all) of the criticisms were unfounded; and also adopted, and described as "excellent", a suggestion by the Law Society of Scotland that proceedings under this Act should be conducted by specially selected "designated sheriffs". Not even the modest proposal in the draft Bill annexed to the SLC Report was adopted in this Act. Nevertheless, the shreival bench has addressed this new jurisdiction with care, and often enthusiasm. In the larger courts, notably Glasgow, some sheriffs have in practice specialised. Even where there has been no specialisation, there has been considerable investment of time and effort in developing competence, and in adapting the judicial role to meet the need to comply with the requirement of ECHR Art. 6 for a "fair" hearing in an area where most, if not all, other modern jurisdictions rest with specialised courts or tribunals because of the essential requirement for an informed and proactive, rather than traditionally reactive, judicial role. Moreover, that role requires both sensitivity in dealing with what are often distressing personal circumstances, and also robustness in defending fundamental rights of adults and their freedoms by reference to this Act's s.1 principles (e.g. see *North Ayrshire Council v J.M.* (Sh. Ct.) 2004 SCLR 956, and *Muldoon, Applicant* (Sh. Ct.) 2005 SCLR 611). In time there will no doubt be comparisons with the performance of Mental Health Tribunals operating under the 2003 Act. There was an expectation that in course of time there might be pressure to bring Incapacity Act and 2003 Act jurisdictions together in the same forum. However the requirements differ significantly. It appears to be the trend that contentious issues under the Incapacity Act demand primarily the competences and independence of judges, rather than the medical expertise possessed by Mental Health Tribunals. Moreover, the courts will continue to encounter issues of capacity and incapacity in areas other than the Incapacity Act jurisdiction itself (e.g. see *Pirie v Clydesdale Bank plc* (OH) 2007 SCLR 18). It is now much less easy to envisage a persuasive case for unifying the jurisdictions.

General principles and fundamental definitions
1.—(1) The principles set out in subsections (2) to (4) shall be given effect to in relation to any intervention in the affairs of an adult under or in pursuance of this Act, including any order made in or for the purpose of any proceedings under this Act for or in connection with an adult.

(2) There shall be no intervention in the affairs of an adult unless the person responsible for authorising or effecting the intervention is satisfied that the intervention will benefit the adult and that such benefit cannot reasonably be achieved without the intervention.

(3) Where it is determined that an intervention as mentioned in subsection (1) is to be made, such intervention shall be the least restrictive option in relation to the freedom of the adult, consistent with the purpose of the intervention.

(4) In determining if an intervention is to be made and, if so, what intervention is to be made, account shall be taken of—

- (a) the present and past wishes and feelings of the adult so far as they can be ascertained by any means of communication, whether human or by mechanical aid (whether of an interpretative nature or otherwise) appropriate to the adult;
- (b) the views of the nearest relative[, named person][1] and the primary carer of the adult, in so far as it is reasonable and practicable to do so;
- (c) the views of—
   - (i) any guardian, continuing attorney or welfare attorney of the adult who has powers relating to the proposed intervention; and
   - (ii) any person whom the sheriff has directed to be consulted,

  in so far as it is reasonable and practicable to do so; and
- (d) the views of any other person appearing to the person responsible for authorising or effecting the intervention to have an interest in the welfare of the adult or in the proposed intervention, where these views have been made known to the person responsible, in so far as it is reasonable and practicable to do so.

(5) Any guardian, continuing attorney, welfare attorney or manager of an establishment exercising functions under this Act or under any order of the sheriff in relation to an adult shall, in so far as it is reasonable and practicable to do so, encourage the adult to exercise whatever skills he has concerning his property, financial affairs or personal welfare, as the case may be, and to develop new such skills.

(6) For the purposes of this Act, and unless the context otherwise requires—

"adult" means a person who has attained the age of 16 years;
"incapable" means incapable of—

- (a) acting; or
- (b) making decisions; or
- (c) communicating decisions; or
- (d) understanding decisions; or
- (e) retaining the memory of decisions,

as mentioned in any provision of this Act, by reason of mental disorder or of inability to communicate because of physical disability; but a person shall not fall within this definition by reason only of a lack or

---

[1] Words inserted by Mental Health (Care and Treatment) (Scotland) Act 2003 (Modification of Enactments) Order 2005 (SSI 2005/465), Sch.1, para.28(2).

deficiency in a faculty of communication if that lack or deficiency can be made good by human or mechanical aid (whether of an interpretative nature or otherwise); and

"incapacity" shall be construed accordingly.

(7) In subsection (4)(c)(i) any reference to—

(a) a guardian shall include a reference to a guardian (however called) appointed under the law of any country to, or entitled under the law of any country to act for, an adult during his incapacity, if the guardianship is recognised by the law of Scotland;
(b) a continuing attorney shall include a reference to a person granted, under a contract, grant or appointment governed by the law of any country, powers (however expressed), relating to the granter's property or financial affairs and having continuing effect notwithstanding the granter's incapacity;
(c) a welfare attorney shall include a reference to a person granted, under a contract, grant or appointment governed by the law of any country, powers (however expressed) relating to the granter's personal welfare and having effect during the granter's incapacity.

DEFINITIONS
"adult" : s.1 (6)
"continuing attorney" : s.15 (2)
"incapable" : s.1 (6)
"incapacity" : s.1 (6)
"managers of an establishment" : s.35 (5) and Sched. 1
"mental disorder" : s.87 (1), referring to the definition in s.328 of the 2003 Act (and see Note to s.1 (6))
"named person" : s.87 (1), referring to the definition in s.329 of the 2003 Act
"nearest relative" : s.87 (1), referring to the definition in s.254 of the 2003 Act (but see s.4)
"primary carer" : s.87 (1)
"welfare attorney" : s.16 (2)

GENERAL NOTE
As emphasised in the Introduction and General Note, the provisions of this section should be referred to in conjunction with almost every other provision of this Act. This section contains the "gateway" definition of those to whom the provisions of this Act may be applied (subs. (6)), general principles applicable to all interventions under this Act (subs. (1)—(4)), duties upon stated appointees (subs. (5)) to encourage exercise and development of relevant skills, and provisions—replicated frequently throughout this Act—that references to relevant appointees include equivalent appointments under the law of any other country, if such appointment is recognised by Scots law (subs. (7)).

Appointees lose the protection of the limitation of liability provisions of s.82 in relation to any failure to act in accordance with the general principles in s.1. Guardians lose the benefit of the proviso to s.67 (4) if they have failed to comply *inter alia* with s.1.

In any intervention under this Act, it is important to recognise the distinction between child law and adult law. The test adopted in this Act is the application of general principles, as opposed to a "best interests" test. The latter term does not feature anywhere in this Act. This Act's approach is explained by this passage from the SLC Report:

> *"Our general principles do not rely on the concept of best interests of the incapable adult .... We consider that 'best interests' by itself is too vague and would require to be supplemented by further factors which have to be taken into account. We also consider that 'best interests' does not give due weight to the views of the adult, particularly to wishes and feelings which he or she had expressed while capable of doing so. The concept of best interests was developed in the context of child law where a child's level of understanding*

may not be high and will usually have been lower in the past. Incapable adults such as those who are mentally ill, head-injured, or suffering from dementia at the time when a decision has to be made in connection with them, will have possessed full mental powers before their present incapacity. We think it is wrong to equate such adults with children, and for that reason would avoid extending child law concepts to them. Accordingly, the general principles we set out below are framed without express reference to best interests".

The general principles referred to are those now set out in this section. The task is not to attempt paternalistically to decide what is in the adult's best interests, but to construct a decision for the adult with as much input as possible from the adult, or from what is known about the adult and the adult's background.

A methodology was proposed in Chapter 15 ("Constructing Decisions") of *Adult Incapacity* and adopted in the successful arguments for the respondent, Mrs M, in *North Ayrshire Council v J.M* (Sh. Ct.) 2004 SCLR 956. Mr M was seriously injured in an accident in 1987. After 15 years in hospital, authorities decided that it was appropriate to discharge him on the basis that he no longer needed full-time medical or nursing care. He and his wife, Mrs M, were happily married. They shared the same outlook and values. Mrs M was initially resistant to discharge because she feared that he would not receive the care which his difficult needs required. However a placement which appeared to be suitable was identified, the drawback being that it offered short-term rather than long-term care so that further decisions about suitable placement were likely to be required in 18 months to two years' time. The case before the sheriff was a contest between chief social work officer and Mrs M for appointment as welfare guardian. The central issue was whether the court should simply make its own objective decision as to what seemed to be in Mr M's best interests, or whether—having found that either would be suitable for appointment—the sheriff should arrive at a decision taking into account Mr M's known views which he had been able to express before his accident, the marriage which he and his wife had entered and sustained and the values which they shared. The sheriff appointed Mrs M as welfare guardian for a period of two years, so that the appointment would require to be reviewed when the next series of major decisions was likely to be required. In appointing Mrs M rather than the chief social work officer, the sheriff was guided by the general principles in s.1 of the Incapacity Act, rather than by any wider arguments (for example, based on the right to respect for private and family life under ECHR Article 8) which might have been resorted to if the Act's own principles had been less robust. The sheriff concluded that from all that was known of Mr M's past wishes and feelings, he would certainly have preferred his wife to be his guardian. The sheriff's decision appears to indicate that the conduct of Mrs M which caused the local authority to oppose her appointment in fact amounted to doing what one would expect a conscientious guardian to do. The sheriff correctly took his guidance from the general principles, and appears to have been correct in the way in which he interpreted them and applied them to the facts before him.

Incapacity jurisdiction entrusts to the court the rights and liberties of adults by definition unable to safeguard them for themselves, or to advocate for themselves. Others, including safeguarders when appointed, may assist; but responsibility rests with the court to ensure compliance with the general principles when authorising (or declining to authorise) any intervention, whether or not the proceedings are contested. As stated in the General Note to Pt. 1, this Act, and the circumstances which it addresses, demand an informed and proactive judicial role.

Subs. (1)
"Intervention" is not defined. In resisting attempts to introduce a definition, the Scottish Parliament appears to have concentrated almost exclusively on perceived difficulties in relation to the medical provisions of Pt. 5 (e.g. see SP OR Vol. 5, No. 11, cols. 1047–1058), and not to have weighed them against possible advantages of a definition for the broader provisions of this Act. It is clear from the debates that "intervention" means not only the various procedures under this Act, but also the acts and decisions of relevant appointees and others. Also, "an intervention can encompass a positive and a negative Act" (e.g. a decision to do something or a decision not to do it)—*per* Mr Angus MacKay, Deputy Minister for Justice, SP OR Vol. 5, No. 11, col. 1047. The multiplicity of circumstances and issues which can arise in relation to adults with incapacity may in time necessitate judicial interpretation, but in most situations difficulty will be avoided if it is remembered that a broad interpretation was clearly intended, encompassing (it is suggested) any decision, act or deliberate omission within the broad scope of this Act's provisions in any way affecting (or intended or having the potential to affect) the welfare, affairs, interests or status of an adult with incapacity.

Adults with Incapacity (Scotland) Act 2000 (Pt. 1)

Subs. (2)
This is now generally known as "the first principle".
"the person responsible for authorising or effecting the intervention". This will include the courts, the Public Guardian, managers of establishments both when deciding to seek certification under s.37 (2) and when acting thereafter, medical and other practitioners when certifying for purposes of Pts. 4 or 5, supervisory bodies when exercising powers in relation to individual adults, persons acting under any authority conferred by Pt. 3 or Pt. 5, and appointees of all kinds (see "Abbreviations"), p.xxiii.
"benefit". There should be no intervention merely because of incapacity (see subs. (6)), however severe. There must be both incapacity and need, and the intervention must meet that need. "benefit" is not defined in this Act, but the courts can be expected to adopt a broad definition. For example, there is nothing in the proceedings of the Scottish Parliament to suggest that it intended to curtail the previous trend of authorising curators bonis to make gifts or adopt Inheritance Tax saving measures where appropriate (see, for example, *B's Curator Bonis* (Sh. Ct.) 1995 SCLR 671 and *D's Curator Bonis* (Noter) 1997 GWD 13–538 and 1998 SLT 2). With due caution, "benefit" can reasonably be interpreted as encompassing overcoming the limitations created by incapacity, so as to permit something which the adult could reasonably be expected to have chosen to do if capable, even though of a gratuitous or unselfish nature. This interpretation is supported by the provisions of s.66 regarding gifts from the estate of an adult under guardianship (and is also supported by the commentary on s.28 (2) of the 2000 text in the official Explanatory Notes). For an example of benefit, broadly interpreted in this way, so great as to be described by the court as "inestimable", see *A's Guardian, Applicant* (a misnomer, because this was an application to appoint a guardian to A) 2007 SLT (Sh. Ct.) 69, where a guardian was appointed to a 45 year-old woman severely disabled, and rendered incapable, by multiple sclerosis, in terms which ensured that she would not be forcibly separated from her 16 year-old son. This Act itself contains provisions about making gifts (s.66) and participation in research from which the adult will not benefit directly (s.51(4)). The requirements of subs. (4) to ascertain the adult's own present or past wishes and feelings, and to consult, may assist in determining what could reasonably be regarded as "benefit" in difficult cases.
"such benefit cannot reasonably be achieved without the intervention". Even where there is both incapacity and need, and the intervention would meet that need, there must still be no intervention, in the legal sense, if the need can to a reasonable extent be met in some other way. Provision of treatment or care may allow the adult to regain sufficient capacity to make a decision. Patient explanation in relaxed and helpful surroundings, or re-writing legalese in plain English, or assistance with communication, may all enable the adult to act without formal intervention. It may be possible to remove the problem rather than impose intervention upon the adult, an approach which in some serious circumstances is now facilitated by Pt. 1 of the 2007 Act. Provision of appropriate facilities and services may suffice. The effect of this subsection is to create a positive obligation to take appropriate informal or other steps, where feasible and reasonable, when intervention would otherwise be necessary. However, neither this subsection nor any other provision of this Act sanctions the imposition *de facto* of intervention obtainable under this Act, without following this Act's procedures or other lawful procedure (e.g. see General Note in Appendix 1 to s.13ZA of the 1968 Act), upon an adult who appears to be compliant but cannot validly consent. To impose *de facto* provisions, such as guardianship powers, without the appropriate procedure to obtain those powers, and thus without the resulting monitoring and safeguards, would contravene ECHR Art. 6, and might amount to a deprivation of liberty contrary to Art. 5. Accordingly, in such situations not only is intervention under this Act not blocked by s.1 (2), but continuation of *de facto* arrangements without such intervention might be wrongful.
The requirements of subs. (2), and the above considerations, also apply to further intervention where other formal measures are already in place. Such measures may be within or outwith the scope of this Act. There should be no further intervention if the desired benefit can reasonably be achieved by more appropriate use of measures already in place in relation to the adult.
Finally and importantly, subs. (2) requires consideration to be given to the suitability of taking formal measures outwith the scope of this Act, subject to one apparent exception mentioned below. Even if, notwithstanding the view to the contrary expressed in the note to subs. (3) below, the requirement to review options under subs. (3) is limited to interventions within the scope of this Act, the references to intervention in subs. (2) certainly mean intervention under this Act (see subs. (1)), therefore one of the measures under this Act

Adults with Incapacity Legislation

should not be applied if the desired benefit could "reasonably be achieved" by initiating a formal measure outwith the scope of this Act. That does not give any primacy to measures outwith this Act, it is submitted, and merely includes them within the options to be considered, because consideration of what is reasonable in terms of subs. (2) should include *inter alia* what is "the least restrictive option in relation to the freedom of the adult", notwithstanding that that requirement appears expressly in subs. (3) rather than subs. (2). If the range of options under subs. (3) does include measures outwith this Act, then the practical result is precisely the same, and nowhere in this Act is one of these subss. (2) and (3) disapplied where the other applies. For discussion of the range of potentially relevant measures see *Adult Incapacity*, and for an older survey of measures under both Scots and English law see Ashton and Ward *Mental Handicap and the Law* (Sweet & Maxwell, 1992), where management techniques under Scots law are compared and evaluated in Chapter 10B. See also s.37 (2) and (5), and General Note thereto. There is one exception to the principle expounded in this paragraph, and it is an exception which "proves the rule". Section 58 (1) requires the sheriff to grant a guardianship application if the adult is incapable as defined in s.58 (1)(a) and if "no other means provided by or under this Act" would suffice. However, that limitation to measures under this Act does not apply to the recall and termination provisions of s.71 (1)(c), provision (ii) of which refers to the adult's interests being "satisfactorily safeguarded or promoted otherwise than by guardianship". Moreover, the s.1 principles apply fully to the disposal of guardianship applications, as they do to all other interventions. Again, the practical outcome will be the same.

Subs. (3)
This is the second principle.

Where there is incapacity and need, and need cannot be met without intervention, the principle of minimum necessary intervention applies, and the "least restrictive option in relation to the freedom of the adult" must be selected. This operates at three levels: the choice of procedure; where the chosen procedure offers such flexibility, the choice of powers conferred; and the decisions and actions, on an ongoing basis, of appointees and others authorised to act.

At the level of choice of procedure, the operation of a Power of Attorney will generally be the least restrictive of the options under this Act, because the Power will have been created by the adult, rather than imposed upon the adult. The provisions of s.58 mentioned at the end of the General Note to subs. (2) (above) effectively place guardianship as the most restrictive of the options under this Act. However, in balancing the other procedures, it is not possible to create a hierarchy unrelated to circumstances in individual cases, because subs. (3) refers to the degree of restriction of freedom, not (for example) the simplicity of the procedure, and there may be situations (again by way of example) where the protections afforded by a more formal procedure may represent a lesser restriction of the adult's freedom than a simpler alternative. This matter must be carefully addressed by anyone empowered to put in place any of the interventions provided for in those Parts. For example, if the managers of an establishment take Pt. 4 powers in circumstances where this does not in fact represent the option least restrictive of the adult's freedoms, then such contravention of s.1 disqualifies them from the limitation of liability under s.82.

While the interventions to which subs. (3) refers are interventions "under or in pursuance of this Act", the options to be considered are not explicitly so limited; and even if they were, the benefit principle in subs. (2) would require consideration of options. On those options, see the note to subs. (2) above.

At the level of powers granted, subs. (3) means, for example, that the powers granted to a guardian should be limited to those required or potentially required; the scope of intervention orders should be similarly limited; the rate of transfer of funds under Pt. 3 should be likewise limited; and so on.

At the ongoing level, subs. (3) must be observed by all appointees, by joint account holders operating under s.32, by anyone exercising in relation to the adult any of the powers under Pt. 5, and so on.

Subs. (4)
At the same three levels as are referred to in the foregoing General Note to subs. (3), in determining whether intervention is necessary and, if so, what is the least restrictive intervention, account must be taken of the present and past wishes and feelings of the adult (so far as they can be ascertained)—the third principle, and the views of those others specified

(so far as it is reasonable and practicable to do so)—the fourth principle. These requirements will clearly have been contravened if wishes and feelings of the adult could have been ascertained but were not, or views of others should have been ascertained but were not. Where they have been ascertained, issues may still arise as to whether account has been properly taken of them. While relative weight will always be a matter of balance in particular circumstances, and the elements of subs. (4) are not stated to be in order of priority, one would generally expect clear present wishes and feelings of the adult to take priority over those expressed in the past, and the adult's own wishes and feelings to take priority over the views of others.

Subs. (4)(a)
It is of major significance that the obligation to take account of the adult's wishes and feelings, if ascertainable, is absolute. This is merely emphasised by the inclusion of "by any means of communication . . ." and by the exclusion of the qualification, which appears in the ensuing paragraphs of this subsection, "insofar as it is reasonable and practicable to do so". If it is possible to ascertain wishes and feelings, that must be done.

As regards present wishes and feelings, research shows that advanced modern psychological techniques may allow the wishes and feelings of severely incapacitated people to be accessed, that their wishes and feelings when in such a situation may be very different from those expressed when viewing such circumstances hypothetically in the past, and that the incapacitating event may have caused a change of character rendering past wishes and feelings no longer relevant to the present adult—see, for example, *Neuropsychological assessment after extremely severe head injury in a case of life or death* (T.M. McMillan, "Brain Injury", 1997, Vol. 11, No. 7, 483–490) and *Neuropsychological assessment of a potential "euthanasia" case: a 5 year follow up* (T.M. McMillan and C.M. Herbert, "Brain Injury", 2000, Vol. 14, No. 2, 197–203), both of which articles relate to the same young woman who had been severely brain-damaged, following a road accident, and in respect of whom permission had been sought to terminate involuntary feeding. It is reasonable to suggest that where wishes and feelings have altered radically when confronted with the reality of an incapacitating condition, or have been altered by it, then the present adult should not be treated as irrevocably "owned" by the past adult, and (as suggested above) those present wishes and feelings should normally prevail.

As noted in the General Note to s.1 above, best interests, or words to similar effect, are not explicitly mentioned in s.1 or anywhere else in this Act. In the case of adults, however disabled, the adult's own wishes and feelings, present or past, should normally carry substantial weight, even when the views of other people as to what they consider to be in the adult's best interests may differ. Precedents from child law are unlikely to be relevant, appropriate or helpful. Of the freedoms referred to in subs. (3), the freedom of self-determination will be the most important in many cases.

Sometimes a delicate balance requires to be struck between clearly indicated wishes and feelings, and benefit. For example, as adults become older and more vulnerable, they may become more distressed by family conflict or its prospect than by the concessions which they believe could be made to avoid conflict; though that will rarely justify succumbing to unreasonable conflict which exploits such vulnerability.

See ss.3 (5A) and (5B) on the assistance which the court may receive from a person providing independent advocacy services in making the sheriff aware of the adult's wishes and feelings, in any application or proceedings under this Act.

Past wishes and feelings, which should be taken into account, should be distinguished from valid and unrevoked advance directives and the like, which may be legally binding (see "*Matters not covered by this Act*" in the Introduction and General Note).

Subss. 4(b) and (c)
The general requirement to take account of the views of those listed in these provisions does not detract from their specific roles under this Act. Thus, appointees will be the primary decision-makers within their powers, but should be consulted in other matters.

Subs. (4)(c)(i)
This requirement includes the obligations of those holding joint or dual appointments to consult the other appointees.

Subs. (4)(c)(ii)
Under s.3 (3) any person (including the adult) claiming an interest may apply to the sheriff to give directions.

Adults with Incapacity Legislation

Subs. (5)
A major criticism of previous law was that procedures such as curatory might deprive people of legal capacity for acts and transactions of which they would otherwise have been capable; or that the ethos of curatory often discouraged exercise and development of skills. The fifth principle, in this subsection, responds by creating a positive obligation, where it is reasonable and practicable to do so, to encourage the exercise and development of skills. In the case of guardians, see also s.64 (1)(e), under which guardians may be empowered to authorise the adult to carry out transactions, and s.67 (1) limiting the extent to which the guardianship order results in legal incapacity.

Subs. (6)
This subsection defines the two fundamental elements (which comprise the short title of this Act) of "adult" and "incapacity", thus defining the scope of this Act and those to whom its provisions may be applied. The commencement of the adult incapacity regime at age 16 co-ordinates appropriately with the Age of Legal Capacity (Scotland) Act 1991 (c.50). To avoid discontinuity for young people requiring guardians, s.79A permits guardianship applications under this Act to be commenced up to 3 months before age 16, though no order may take effect before that age.

The definition of "mental disorder" originally referred to the definition of that term in the 1984 Act. In relation to an amendment prompted by concerns as to whether the definition covered all of the causes of incapacity to which this Act was intended to apply, Mr Iain Gray, Deputy Minister for Community Care, said (SP OR Vol. 5, No. 11, col. 1043–1044): "If . . . . the amendment has been prompted by lingering concerns about whether the definition of mental disorder covers all the underlying conditions that should be included, specifically the effects of head injuries or a stroke, our medical and legal advice is that those conditions fall within the definition. That ties in with well-known international medical terminology. The definition already spells it out that mental disorder is "however caused or manifested". "However caused" is intended to cover whatever physical accident or illness led to the condition causing incapacity. The Executive acknowledges that the current definition of mental disorder in [the 1984 Act] needs to be reviewed and updated. That is why the Committee chaired by Bruce Millan was set up to undertake that work. When it reports, we will have the advantage of the Millan Committee's wide public consultation and expertise. We will then be able to maintain the advantages of consistency between incapacity law and mental health law. We will also avoid the likelihood of two changes to the existing definition in quick succession, which would be difficult for both professionals and the public to follow." The consistency anticipated by Mr Gray is now provided by s.328 of the 2003 Act in the following terms: "(1) Subject to subsection (2) below, in this Act 'mental disorder' means any—(a) mental illness; (b) personality disorder; or (c) learning disability, however caused or manifested; and cognate expressions shall be construed accordingly. (2) A person is not mentally disordered by reason only of any of the following—(a) sexual orientation; (b) sexual deviancy; (c) transsexualism; (d) transvestism; (e) dependence on, or use of, alcohol or drugs; (f) behaviour that causes, or is likely to cause, harassment, alarm or distress to any other person; (g) acting as no prudent person would act."

There is differentiation in some provisions of this Act between incapacity caused (wholly or partly) by mental disorder, and incapacity caused solely by inability to communicate due to physical disability. In relation to the latter, MWC generally does not have a role (see *inter alia* s.9) and the report under s.57 (3)(b) for guardianship and intervention order applications is provided by the chief social work officer rather than the mental health officer. The differentiation may present difficulties of interpretation in individual cases. In *Fraser v Paterson*, 1987 SLT 562, Lord Jauncey said of the victim of a stroke that while she "has very severe difficulties of communication she is very far from being of unsound mind in the sense in which that term is normally accepted by doctors and lawyers". Upon that description, one suspects that under this Act her incapacity might be classed as arising from an inability to communicate through physical disability, rather than from mental disorder, notwithstanding Mr Gray's apparent inclusion within the latter of all incapacity caused by strokes.

The definition of "incapable", as with other definitions in this Act, is "for the purposes of this Act". It will not necessarily be interpreted as coinciding with the tests of capacity for other purposes, such as determining whether a purported act or transaction is void. For example, the courts are unlikely to depart from their policy of reluctance to declare a person incapable of testamentary capacity, and might decline to apply—for that purpose—the element of "retaining the memory of decisions" in the case of someone who is incapable of retaining memory of the decision as to appropriate testamentary provision, yet who consistently and repeatedly reaches the same decision in a manner otherwise satisfying all relevant tests of capacity.

"retaining the memory of decisions" is in any event likely to be interpreted as referring to retention of memory to a degree, and for a duration, appropriate to the matter in question. No-one retains total and indefinite memory of all competent decisions. An element of proportionality is also likely to be applied to "understanding decisions".

"as mentioned in any provision of this Act" is significant. People are not to be classed as incapable in any general sense. They may be assessed as incapable for particular purposes. In any event, that would appear to be the appropriate understanding of this phrase in this Act in its final form, and a reasonable one. When the Bill was first introduced, the phrase served a somewhat different purpose, because some or all of the five elements (a)—(e) were quoted in relation to each relevant mention of "incapable" throughout this Act, but those references to individual elements were all removed by Scottish Executive amendments during stage 2.

Decisions as to the incapacity of an adult made by anyone other than the sheriff may be appealed to the sheriff under s.14, which also provides for appeal to the sheriff principal against decisions by the sheriff as to incapacity, with further appeal to the Court of Session.

Subs. (7)
This subsection contains provisions, replicated frequently throughout this Act, that references to specified appointees include reference to equivalent appointments under other jurisdictions, if recognised by Scots law. As mentioned in the Introduction and General Note, this Act complies with the Hague Convention of January 13, 2000 on *The International Protection of Adults*. Relevant private international law provisions are contained in Sched. 3, incorporated by s.85.

Judicial proceedings

Applications and other proceedings and appeals

2.—(1) This section shall apply for the purposes of any application which may be made to and any other proceedings before the sheriff under this Act.

(2) An application to the sheriff under this Act shall be made by summary application.

(3) Unless otherwise expressly provided for, any decision of the sheriff at first instance in any application to, or in any other proceedings before, him under this Act may be appealed to the sheriff principal, and the decision upon such appeal of the sheriff principal may be appealed, with the leave of the sheriff principal, to the Court of Session.

(4) Rules made under section 32 of the Sheriff Courts (Scotland) Act 1971 (c.58) may make provision as to the evidence which the sheriff shall take into account when deciding whether to give a direction under section 11(1).

GENERAL NOTE
This and the following section contain general provisions regarding sheriff court applications and other proceedings under this Act. Further general powers of both the sheriff and the Court of Session are contained in s.4. The Court of Session, and not the sheriff, has jurisdiction under s.50.

Jurisdiction in respect of intervention orders and guardianship orders under Pt. 6 is conferred on the sheriff. The sheriff's other powers include giving directions under s.3 (3) to anyone exercising functions conferred by this Act; making orders regarding the exercise of the functions of the nearest relative under s.4; hearing appeals as to incapacity under s.14; hearing appeals against decisions about medical treatment under s.52; and hearing various remits and appeals under the provisions listed in the next paragraph.

Appeal lies to the sheriff principal and thereafter (with leave of the sheriff principal) to the Court of Session, except where this Act provides otherwise. Appeals against a decision of a sheriff regarding medical treatment under s.52 lie (with the leave of the sheriff) direct to the

Court of Session. Matters in which the sheriff's decision is final include remits and appeals under the following provisions of this Act: in Pt. 2, ss.19 (6) and 20 (4); in Pt. 3, s.31D (which refers to several sections in Pt. 3); in Pt. 4, s.45 (6); in Pt. 6, ss.64 (7), 66 (7) and (8), 68 (8), 72 (5) and (6), and 73 (8) and (9); various matters in Sched. 2; and in Sched. 4, para. 6 (7).

Subs. (2)
This subsection provides that applications to the sheriff under this Act shall be made by summary application. See SI 1999/929 (as amended), reproduced in Appendix 2 (which inappropriately retains references to the 1984 Act in defining "nearest relative"). On "subsequent applications" see the General Note to s.60. There now seems to be a general recognition that terse traditional pleadings are inappropriate in Incapacity Act applications, and that full relevant information should be provided. It would appear to be good practice that the application should set out all of the information required by the sheriff to enable him to comply with the s.1 principles and with the specific procedural and other requirements incumbent upon him, so that he may if so minded properly grant the application. For example, in applications for appointments with financial powers, applicants should give as much information as is reasonably practicable, with values or estimated values, regarding assets. This will also assist in fixing caution, in cases where caution is still ordered. They should also provide such CV-type and other information as will assist the sheriff in deciding about suitability of any proposed appointee. Sheriff Baird referred in *B, Applicant*, 2005 SLT (Sh. Ct.) 95 (an application for an intervention order) to the importance of practitioners giving the court full information in the pleadings. One point about the form of application is that the prescribed form does not include pleas-in-law. Some traditionalist practitioners seem reluctant to produce an application without pleas-in-law, but it might be wise for them to consider the decision of Lady Paton in *Alexander v Metbro Limited*, 2004 SLT 963, a decision on whether pleas-in-law could still be added as optional extras under the new personal injuries rules in the Court of Session. She ruled that pleadings which included pleas-in-law should not be accepted. She quoted the observation of the Coulsfield Working Party that pleadings should "exclude mere stylistic standard phrases and ritual incantations". No similar deliberations seem to have preceded the promulgation of the prescribed form of applications under this Act, but standing Lady Paton's decision it may be safer for applicants to follow the prescribed form and omit pleas-in-law. Nevertheless, it is understood that in one sheriff court an application was returned for "correction" because it contained no plea-in-law.

Subs. (3)
See SI 1999/929, Form 24, in Appendix 2. In *City of Edinburgh Council v Z*, 2005 SLT (Sh. Ct.) 7, apparently the first appeal under this jurisdiction, it was noted that neither the Incapacity Act nor the relevant Rules specified the form of the note in an appeal to the Sheriff Principal. Sheriff Principal MacPhail recorded that: "I recommended that the appellant should follows the Rules prescribed for appeals in Ordinary Causes by Rule 31.4 of the Ordinary Cause Rules 1993". In *Application by Glasgow City Council for appointment of welfare guardian to AD*, June 27, 2005, Sheriff Principal Bowen considered the extent to which it was appropriate on appeal to consider questions of fact, and also considered the effect of the marking of an appeal upon any further procedure before the sheriff.

Subs. (4)
Section 11 (1), referred to in subs. (4), provides that the court may direct that intimation or notification should not be given to the adult where that would be likely to pose a serious risk to the adult's health. See General Note to s.11 and the case there cited, and SI 1999/929 rule 3.16.5.

Powers of sheriff
3.—(1) In an application or any other proceedings under this Act, the sheriff may make such consequential or ancillary order, provision or direction as he considers appropriate.

(2) Without prejudice to the generality of subsection (1) or to any other powers conferred by this Act, the sheriff may—

    (a) make any order granted by him subject to such conditions and restrictions as appear to him to be appropriate;

(b) order that any reports relating to the person who is the subject of the application or proceedings be lodged with the court or that the person be assessed or interviewed and that a report of such assessment or interview be lodged;
(c) make such further inquiry or call for such further information as appears to him to be appropriate;
(d) make such interim order as appears to him to be appropriate pending the disposal of the application or proceedings.

(3) On an application by any person (including the adult himself) claiming an interest in the property, financial affairs or personal welfare of an adult, the sheriff may give such directions to any person exercising—

(a) functions conferred by this Act; or
(b) functions of a like nature conferred by the law of any country,

as to the exercise of those functions and the taking of decisions or action in relation to the adult as appear to him to be appropriate.

(4) In an application or any other proceedings under this Act, the sheriff—

(a) shall consider whether it is necessary to appoint a person for the purpose of safeguarding the interests of the person who is the subject of the application or proceedings; and
(b) without prejudice to any existing power to appoint a person to represent the interests of the person who is the subject of the application or proceedings may, if he thinks fit, appoint a person to act for the purpose specified in paragraph (a).

(5) Safeguarding the interests of a person shall, for the purposes of subsection (4), include conveying his views so far as they are ascertainable to the sheriff; but if the sheriff considers that it is inappropriate that a person appointed to safeguard the interests of another under this section should also convey that other's views to the sheriff, the sheriff may appoint another person for that latter purpose only.

[(5A) In determining an application or any other proceedings under this Act, the sheriff shall, without prejudice to the generality of section 1(4)(a), take account of the wishes and feelings of the adult who is the subject of the application or proceedings so far as they are expressed by a person providing independent advocacy services.

(5B) In subsection (5A), "independent advocacy services" has the same meaning as it has in section 259(1) of the Mental Health (Care and Treatment) (Scotland) Act 2003 (asp 13).][2]

(6) The sheriff may, on an application by—

(a) the person authorised under the order;
(b) the adult; or
(c) any person entitled to apply for the order,

make an order varying the terms of an order granted under subsection (2)(a).

---

[2] Subsections (5A) and (5B) inserted by Adult Support and Protection (Scotland) Act 2007 (asp 10), s.55.

Adults with Incapacity Legislation

DEFINITIONS
"adult" : s.1 (6)
"independent advocacy services" : 2003 Act, s.259 (1)
"person claiming an interest" : s.87 (1)

GENERAL NOTE
This section, except for subs. (3) (described last in this General Note), contains general provisions regarding the powers of the sheriff in applications and other proceedings under this Act (which include those mentioned in the General Note to s.2). In developing this jurisdiction, and in responding to medical developments and social change, it will be helpful to the courts to have the broad discretionary powers conferred by this section. A major disadvantage of former 1984 Act guardianship procedure was that sheriffs were unable to make orders precisely directed to the particular needs of individual cases. Under this Act, the sheriff may make consequential or ancillary orders, provisions or directions (subs. (1)) and may attach conditions or restrictions to any order (subs. (2)(a)), which conditions and restrictions may be varied upon application under subs. (6). The procedural powers under subs. (2)(b) and (2)(c) enable the sheriff to order reports, assessments or interviews (and reports thereon), further inquiry and provision of further information. Interim orders may be made under subs. (2)(d).

Both Sheriff Vannet in *Frank Stork and others*, 2004 SCLR 513 and Sheriff Baird in *Cooke v Telford*, 2005 SCLR 367 held that subs. (1) does not confer any form of dispensing power. Sheriff Baird observed that he preferred to construe subs. (1) narrowly. The same sheriff used his discretionary powers in *Application in respect of R.A.* (Glasgow Sh. Ct., Scottish Courts Website January 17, 2008) to resolve a situation in which he had appointed a financial guardian who was refused caution, and had then received an unrelated application for appointment of another financial guardian to the same adult.

Subsections (4) and (5) deal with the appointment and functions of safeguarders. In all applications and other proceedings under this Act the sheriff is required to consider whether it is necessary to appoint a safeguarder. The power to appoint a safeguarder is in addition to, and does not replace, any existing powers to appoint someone to represent the interests of the adult, such as a curator *ad litem*. The safeguarder has a general function to safeguard the interests of the person who is the subject of the proceedings, including conveying that person's views to the sheriff "so far as they are ascertainable" (see General Note to s.1 (4)(a)). However, where the sheriff considers it inappropriate for the safeguarder to convey the person's views, the sheriff may appoint someone else to do so. To this rather large cast of potential players, subss. (5A) and (5B) now add the assistance of a person providing independent advocacy services in helping the wishes and feelings of the adult to be expressed. It is for the sheriff, guided by the s.1 principles, to manage this cast. On occasions, considerable professional and judicial experience may be required to assess the extent to which preferred wishes and feelings of the adult are demonstrably rather than speculatively such, and are indeed those of the adult rather than of one of these intermediaries. See note to subs. (4)(a) of s.1 on advanced modern psychological techniques.

Subsection (3) is oddly placed in this section, as it creates a separate procedure (to which, along with other procedures under this Act, the provisions of s.2 and the other provisions of s.3 apply) under which the adult, or anyone else claiming an interest in the property, financial affairs or personal welfare of the adult, may apply to the sheriff to make an order giving directions to appointees and others exercising functions under this Act.

Power of Court of Session or sheriff with regard to nearest relative
4.—(1) [. . .][3] the court may, having regard to section 1 and being satisfied that to do so will benefit [an adult with incapacity][4], make an order that—

> (a) certain information shall not be disclosed, or intimation of certain applications shall not be given, to the nearest relative of the adult;
> (b) the functions of the nearest relative of the adult shall, during the continuance in force of the order, be exercised by a person,

---

[3] Words repealed by Adult Support and Protection (Scotland) Act 2007 (asp 10), s.56(2)(a).
[4] Words substituted by Adult Support and Protection (Scotland) Act 2007 (asp 10), s.56(2)(b).

specified in the [order]⁵, who is not the nearest relative of the adult but who—

  (i) is a person who would otherwise be entitled to be the nearest relative in terms of this Act;
  (ii) in the opinion of the court is a proper person to act as the nearest relative; and
  (iii) is willing to so act; or

 (c) no person shall, during the continuance in force of the order, exercise the functions of the nearest relative.

(2) An order made under subsection (1) shall apply only to the exercise of the functions under this Act of the nearest relative.

(3) The court may [. . .]⁶ make an order varying the terms of an order granted under subsection (1).

[(3A) The court may make an order under subsection (1) or (3) only on the application of—

 (a) the adult to whom the application relates; or
 (b) any person claiming an interest in that adult's property, financial affairs or personal welfare.

(3B) The court may dispose of an application for an order under subsection (1) or (3) by making—

 (a) the order applied for; or
 (b) such other order under this section as it thinks fit.]⁷

(4) [. . .]⁸

DEFINITIONS
"adult" : s.1 (6)
"incapable" : s.1 (6)
"nearest relative" : s.87 (1), referring to the definition in s.254 of the 2003 Act (but see the provisions of this s.4)

GENERAL NOTE
This Act confers powers and functions on the nearest relative (see below). This s.4 and the related provisions of s.87 have been substantially amended and much improved since original enactment. The original 2000 text sought to cope with some unsatisfactory aspects of the definition in the 1984 Act, now superseded by the 2003 Act. The 2000 text also had the unsatisfactory features that applications under s.4 could not be made by the adult while capable, nor by anyone else.

The orders which may be made under s.4 remain the same. Under subs. (1)(a) the court may order that neither information nor intimation be given to the nearest relative. The court may order under subs. (1)(b) that someone else should exercise the functions of nearest relative, or under subs. (1)(c) that no-one should do so. Applications for such orders under subs. (1) and for variation of such orders under subs. (3) may now be made by, but only by, the adult (at any time, including in anticipation of subsequent incapacity) or any person claiming

---

⁵ Words substituted by Adult Support and Protection (Scotland) Act 2007 (asp 10), s.56(2)(c).
⁶ Words repealed by Adult Support and Protection (Scotland) Act 2007 (asp 10), s.56(3).
⁷ Subsections (3A) and (3B) inserted by Adult Support and Protection (Scotland) Act 2007 (asp 10), s.56(4).
⁸ Subsection repealed by Adult Support and Protection (Scotland) Act 2007 (asp 10), s.56(5).

an interest in the adult's affairs or welfare. Under subs. (3B) the court may now make the order sought, or any other order competent under this section.
See also General Note to s.87.
Provisions of this Act under which the nearest relative has functions or receives intimations include ss.1 (4)(b), 27, 27C, 37 (3), 41 (f), 51 (3), 72 (2), 73 (5) and Sched. 2, para. 6(2).

Safeguarding of interests in Court of Session appeals or proceedings
5.—(1) In determining any appeal or in any other proceedings under this Act the Court of Session—

(a) shall consider whether it is necessary to appoint a person for the purpose of safeguarding the interests of the person who is the subject of the appeal or other proceedings; and
(b) without prejudice to any existing power to appoint a person to represent the interests of the second mentioned person, may if it thinks fit appoint a person to act for the purpose specified in paragraph (a).

(2) Safeguarding the interests of a person shall, for the purposes of subsection (1), include conveying his views so far as they are ascertainable to the court; but if the court considers that it is inappropriate that a person appointed to safeguard the interests of another under this section should also convey that other's views to the court, the court may appoint another person for that latter purpose only.

General Note
This section contains provisions for appointment of safeguarders in Court of Session proceedings under this Act, similar to those for sheriff court proceedings contained in s.3 (4) and (5). See General Note to s.3.

The Public Guardian

The Public Guardian and his functions
6.—(1) The Accountant of Court shall be the Public Guardian.
(2) The Public Guardian shall have the following general functions under this Act—

(a) to supervise any guardian or any person who is authorised under an intervention order in the exercise of his functions relating to the property or financial affairs of the adult;
(b) to establish, maintain and make available during normal office hours for inspection by members of the public on payment of the prescribed fee, separate registers of—
   (i) all documents relating to continuing powers of attorney governed by the law of Scotland;
   (ii) all documents relating to welfare powers of attorney governed by the law of Scotland;
   (iii) all authorisations [relating to intromission][9] with funds under Part 3;
   (iv) all documents relating to guardianship orders under Part 6;
   (v) all documents relating to intervention orders under Part 6,

---

[9] Words substituted by Adult Support and Protection (Scotland) Act 2007 (asp 10), Sch.1, para.5(a).

Adults with Incapacity (Scotland) Act 2000 (Pt. 1)

in which he shall enter any matter which he is required to enter under this Act and any other matter of which he becomes aware relating to the existence or scope of the power, authorisation or order as the case may be;
(c) to receive and investigate any complaints regarding the exercise of functions relating to the property or financial affairs of an adult made—
   (i) in relation to continuing attorneys;
   (ii) concerning intromissions with funds under Part 3;
   (iii) in relation to guardians or persons authorised under intervention orders;
(d) to investigate any circumstances made known to him in which the property or financial affairs of an adult seem to him to be at risk;
[(da) to take part as a party in any proceedings before a court or to initiate such proceedings where he considers it necessary to do so to safeguard the property or financial affairs of an adult who is incapable for the purposes of this Act;][10]
(e) to provide, when requested to do so, a guardian, a continuing attorney, a withdrawer or a person authorised under an intervention order with information and advice about the performance of functions relating to property or financial affairs under this Act;
(f) to consult the Mental Welfare Commission and any local authority on cases or matters relating to the exercise of functions under this Act in which there is, or appears to be, a common interest.

(3) In subsection (2)(c) any reference to—

(a) a guardian shall include a reference to a guardian (however called) appointed under the law of any country to, or entitled under the law of any country to act for, an adult during his incapacity, if the guardianship is recognised by the law of Scotland;
(b) a continuing attorney shall include a reference to a person granted, under a contract, grant or appointment governed by the law of any country, powers (however expressed), relating to the granter's property or financial affairs and having continuing effect notwithstanding the granter's incapacity.

DEFINITIONS
"adult" : s.1 (6)
"continuing attorney" : s.15 (2)
"guardianship order" : s.58 (4)
"incapacity" : s.1 (6)
"intervention order" : s.53 (1)
"local authority" : s.87 (1) (referring to the Local Government etc. (Scotland) Act 1994 (c.39) s.2)
"Mental Welfare Commission" : s.87 (1) (referring to s.4 of the 2003 Act)
"power of attorney" : s.87 (1)
"prescribed" : s.87 (1) (and see s.86)
"Public Guardian" : s.6 (1)
"withdrawer" : s.26 (10)

GENERAL NOTE
This section helpfully brings together various general functions conferred upon the Public Guardian. Under subs. (1) the Accountant of Court became the Public Guardian. Both

---

[10] Inserted by Adult Support and Protection (Scotland) Act 2007 (asp 10), s.67.

holders of the position of Public Guardian have made massive, thoughtful and proactive contributions towards turning the intentions and ideals of this Act into reality for the benefit of people with impairments of capacity, and for the support and assistance of those with roles under this Act. The culture established among staff at the Office of the Public Guardian, and the service given by them, are likewise commendable, and worthy of study by other public offices. Almost inevitably, these annotations in places criticise some practices adopted by the Public Guardian. Such criticisms are exceptions which "prove the general rule".

Several of the provisions of s.6 must be read with the more detailed provisions of the Part referred to. The Public Guardian's functions, except for the functions of registration under subs. (2)(b) and consultation under subs. (2)(f), relate to property and financial affairs, and do not extend to personal welfare. The supervisory function in subs. (2)(a) should be read in conjunction with the provisions regarding intervention orders and guardians in Pt. 6, and Sched. 2. The record-keeping functions in subs. (2)(b) should be read in conjunction with Pt. 3 as regards CPAs and WPAs, and with the Parts quoted as regards the other matters specified. On the Public Guardian's practices in relation to CPAs and WPAs, see General Note to s.19. The function of dealing with complaints under subs. (2)(c) should be read in conjunction with Pt. 2 as regards CPAs, Pt. 3 as regards intromissions with funds and Pt. 6 as regards appointees under guardianship and intervention orders. Subsection (3) contains the usual inclusion of similar appointees under other jurisdictions.

Subsection (2)(d) contains an important provision that the Public Guardian should investigate where she becomes aware of circumstances in which the property or financial affairs of an adult seem to be at risk. In the context of this Act, this is likely to be interpreted as meaning risk containing an element of incapacity or apparent incapacity on the part of the adult. See s.12 for further powers following upon investigations under subss. (2)(c) and (d). See also the duties of local authorities to apply for intervention orders (s.53 (3)) and guardianship orders (s.57 (2)), though under subs. (2)(da) of this section the Public Guardian now has explicit powers to initiate or enter "any proceedings before a court" where she considers that necessary to safeguard the property or financial affairs of an adult who lacks relevant capacity. This wide-ranging power is not limited to proceedings under this Act. See s.8 regarding expenses. On investigatory duties under this Act, see also the duties under s.40 (2) and (3) of supervisory bodies in relation to management by authorised establishments under Pt. 4.

Under subs. (2)(e) the Public Guardian provides general information and advice by leaflets and on her website, as well as individual advice to appointees who seek it. Subsection (2)(f) contains provisions regarding consultation with MWC and local authorities which are replicated as regards the former in s.9 (1)(c) and as regards the latter in s.10 (1)(b). See also s.12 (2).

Relevant contact details are: The Office of the Public Guardian, Hadrian House, Callendar Business Park, Callendar Road, Falkirk FK1 1XR, Tel: 01324 678300; Fax: 01324 678301; Website: www.publicguardian-scotland.gov.uk.

The Public Guardian: further provision

7.—(1) The Scottish Ministers may prescribe—

(a) the form and content of the registers to be established and maintained under section 6(2)(b) and the manner and medium in which they are to be established and maintained;

(b) the form and content of any certificate which the Public Guardian is empowered to issue under this Act;

(c) the forms and procedure for the purposes of any application required or permitted to be made under this Act to the Public Guardian in relation to any matter;

(d) the evidence which the Public Guardian shall take into account when deciding under section 11(2) whether to dispense with intimation or notification to the adult.

(2) The Public Guardian may charge the prescribed fee for anything done by him in connection with any of his functions under this Act and he shall not be obliged to act until such fee is paid.

(3) Any certificate which the Public Guardian issues under this Act shall, for the purposes of any proceedings, be conclusive evidence of the matters contained in it.

DEFINITIONS
"adult" : s.1 (6)
"prescribe" : s.87 (1) (and see s.86)
"prescribed" : s.87 (1) (and see s.86)
"Public Guardian" : s.6 (1)

GENERAL NOTE
Powers to make regulations is conferred on the Scottish Ministers by s.86. Subsection (1) of this section lists the matters in relation to the Public Guardian's functions which may be governed by regulations, and subs. (2) provides that regulations may prescribe fees which the Public Guardian "may charge" (or may, on this wording, waive). Under subs. (3) certificates issued by the Public Guardian under the Act are conclusive for the purpose of any proceedings.

Subs. (2)
For fees chargeable by the Public Guardian see SSI 2008/52 as amended with effect from August 1, 2008 by SSI 2008/238.

Expenses in court proceedings

Expenses in court proceedings
8.—(1) Where in any court proceedings (other than, in the case of a local authority, an application under section 68(3)) the Public Guardian, Mental Welfare Commission or local authority is a party for the purpose of protecting the interests of an adult, the court may make an award of expenses against the adult or against any person whose actings have resulted in the proceedings.

(2) Where in any court proceedings (other than, in the case of a local authority, an application under section 68(3)) the Public Guardian, Mental Welfare Commission or local authority is a party for the purpose of representing the public interest, the court may make an award of expenses against any person whose actings have resulted in the proceedings or on whose part there has been unreasonable conduct in relation to the proceedings.

DEFINITIONS
"adult" : s.1 (6)
"local authority" : s.87 (1) (referring to the Local Government etc. (Scotland) Act 1994 (c.39) s.2)
"Mental Welfare Commission" : s.87 (1) (referring to s.4 of the 2003 Act)
"Public Guardian" : s.6 (1)

GENERAL NOTE
As introduced, this section would have empowered the court to award against the adult's estate expenses incurred by the Public Guardian, MWC or local authority both for protecting the adult's interests and also for representing the public interest. The Scottish Parliament unanimously supported the view that the adult's estate should not bear the cost of representing the public interest, except in (rare but possible) cases where the conduct of the incapable adult has resulted in the proceedings or has been unreasonable in relation to the proceedings. Accordingly, the expenses of the bodies referred to may in proceedings to protect the adult's interests be awarded against the adult or against anyone whose actings have caused the proceedings (subs. (1)), but the expenses of such bodies in representing the public interest

may be awarded only against a person (including the adult) whose actings have resulted in the proceedings or on whose part there has been unreasonable conduct in relation to the proceedings (subs. (2)).

Section 68 (3) contains specific provisions regarding the expenses of applications by a local authority to have the chief social work officer appointed guardian, and of subsequent applications by that officer as guardian.

There are no other express provisions in this Act regarding the expenses of court proceedings under it. Expenses would accordingly appear to be within the sheriff's discretion, either under the sheriff's general powers in s.3 or (as all applications under this Act are to be made by summary application, s.2 (2)) under the sheriff's inherent power to dispose of questions of expenses in summary applications (see Macphail *Sheriff Court Practice*, 3rd Ed. Para. 26.46). While expenses are not normally awarded in applications to the sheriff in his administrative, rather than judicial, capacity (ibid para. 26.47), the purposes of most, if not all, of the provisions of this Act for application, remit or appeal to the sheriff include ensuring compliance with ECHR Art. 6, therefore it seems unlikely that any procedure before the sheriff under this Act would be held to be administrative rather than judicial (but see ibid para. 26.38 for cases where, for purposes of right to appeal, decisions by the sheriff under the 1984 Act s.29 (4) were held to be administrative).

See the decision of Sheriff Mackie in *Applications by Francis Galashan and John Scott Lynn* (Edinburgh Sh. Ct. Scottish Courts Website July 7, 2008) for discussion of awards of expenses in Pt. 6 applications, and their interpretation. Sheriff Mackie held that unless an order for the expenses to be met from the adult's estate explicitly states otherwise, the expenses should be calculated according to the judicial table for party and party expenses.

The Mental Welfare Commission

Functions of the Mental Welfare Commission

9.—(1) [. . .][11] The Mental Welfare Commission shall have the following general functions under this Act in relation to any adult to whom this Act applies by reason of, or by reasons which include, mental disorder—

(a)–(b) [. . .][12]

(c) to consult the Public Guardian and any local authority on cases or matters relating to the exercise of functions under this Act in which there is, or appears to be, a common interest;

(d) where they are not satisfied with any investigation made by a local authority into a complaint made under section 10(1)(c), or where the local authority have failed to investigate the complaint, to receive and investigate any complaints relating to the exercise of functions relating to the personal welfare of the adult made—

(i) in relation to welfare attorneys;
(ii) in relation to guardians or persons authorised under intervention orders;

(e)–(f) [. . .][13];

(g) to provide a guardian, welfare attorney or person authorised under an intervention order, when requested to do so, with information and advice in connection with the performance of his functions in relation to personal welfare under this Act.

(2) A guardian or welfare attorney of such an adult or a person authorised under an intervention order in relation to such an adult or the

---

[11] Words repealed by Mental Health (Care and Treatment) (Scotland) Act 2003 (asp 13), Sch. 5.
[12] Repealed by Mental Health (Care and Treatment) (Scotland) Act 2003 (asp 13), Sch. 5.
[13] Repealed by Mental Health (Care and Treatment) (Scotland) Act 2003 (asp 13), Sch. 5.

local authority shall afford the Mental Welfare Commission all facilities necessary to enable them to carry out their functions in respect of the adult.
(3) In subsection (1)(d) any reference to—

(a) a guardian shall include a reference to a guardian (however called) appointed under the law of any country to, or entitled under the law of any country to act for, an adult during his incapacity, if the guardianship is recognised by the law of Scotland;
(b) a welfare attorney shall include a reference to a person granted, under a contract, grant or appointment governed by the law of any country, powers (however expressed) relating to the granter's personal welfare and having effect during the granter's incapacity.

DEFINITIONS
"adult" : s.1 (6)
"guardianship order" : s.58 (4)
"incapacity" : s.1 (6)
"intervention order" : s.53 (1)
"local authority" : s.87 (1) (referring to the Local Government etc. (Scotland) Act 1994 (c.39) s.2)
"mental disorder" : s.87 (1) (and see General Note to s.1 (6))
"Mental Welfare Commission" : s.87 (1) (referring to s.4 of the 2003 Act)
"Public Guardian" : s.6 (1)
"welfare attorney" : s.16 (2)

GENERAL NOTE
This section brings together the general functions of MWC under this Act, but requires to be read in conjunction with the 2003 Act. The general functions of the Public Guardian under s.6 are concerned with property and financial affairs, and the general functions of MWC under this section and of local authorities under s.10 are concerned with personal welfare, except for the duties of all to consult with each other. MWC functions under this Act are limited to adults to whom this Act applies by reason of mental disorder (or reasons which include mental disorder). Accordingly, MWC (unlike the Public Guardian and local authorities) has no role in relation to adults whose incapacity results solely from inability to communicate (see definition of "incapable" in s.1 (6)—for comment on possible difficulties see General Note to that subsection). However, for administrative simplicity the 2007 Act removed several references to the limitation to mental disorder cases: see, for example, the notification provisions regarding WPAs in ss.20 (3)(b)(iii), 22 and 23 (3).

Schedule 5, para. 17(1), still in force, limited the visiting and investigative functions of MWC under the 1984 Act s.3 (2) to detained patients, deleting the previous references to 1984 Act guardianship, but there are presumably no 1984 Act guardianships still in force.

Subsection (1)(c) replicates the provisions of s.6 (2)(f) and s.10 (1)(b) regarding consultation among the Public Guardian, MWC and local authorities. See also s.12 (2).

Subsection (1)(d) contains an additional function to receive and investigate complaints where MWC is not satisfied with a local authority investigation under s.10 (1)(c), or where the local authority has failed to investigate. See also s.12.

The function of providing information and advice under subs. (1)(g) duplicates the function of local authorities under s.10 (1)(e).

Local authorities

Functions of local authorities
10.—(1) A local authority shall have the following general functions under this Act—

(a) to supervise a guardian appointed with functions relating to the personal welfare of an adult in the exercise of those functions;

(b) to consult the Public Guardian and the Mental Welfare Commission on cases or matters relating to the exercise of functions under this Act in which there is, or appears to be, a common interest;
(c) to receive and investigate any complaints relating to the exercise of functions relating to the personal welfare of an adult made—
   (i) in relation to welfare attorneys;
   (ii) in relation to guardians or persons authorised under intervention orders;
(d) to investigate any circumstances made known to them in which the personal welfare of an adult seems to them to be at risk;
(e) to provide a guardian, welfare attorney or person authorised under an intervention order, when requested to do so, with information and advice in connection with the performance of his functions in relation to personal welfare under this Act.

(2) For the purposes of subsection (1)(d), "local authority" includes a local authority for an area in which the adult is present.

(3) The Scottish Ministers may make provision by regulations as regards the supervision by local authorities of the performance of their functions—

(a) by guardians, in relation to the personal welfare of adults under this Act;
(b) where the supervision has been ordered by the sheriff—
   (i) by persons authorised under intervention orders;
   (ii) by welfare attorneys.

(4) In subsection (1)(c) any reference to—

(a) a guardian shall include a reference to a guardian (however called) appointed under the law of any country to, or entitled under the law of any country to act for, an adult during his incapacity, if the guardianship is recognised by the law of Scotland;
(b) a welfare attorney shall include a reference to a person granted, under a contract, grant or appointment governed by the law of any country, powers (however expressed) relating to the granter's personal welfare and having effect during the granter's incapacity.

DEFINITIONS
"adult" : s. 1(6)
"incapacity" : s. 1(6)
"intervention order" : s. 53(1)
"local authority" : s.87(1) (referring to the Local Government etc. (Scotland) Act 1994 (c.39) s.2)
"Mental Welfare Commission" : s.87(1) (referring to s.4 of the 2003 Act)
"Public Guardian" : s.6 (1)
"welfare attorney" : s.16 (2)

GENERAL NOTE
This section brings together the general functions of local authorities under this Act. Except for the consultation provisions of subs. (1)(b), their functions under this section are limited to personal welfare matters. However, their duties to apply for intervention orders under s.53 (3) and guardianship orders under s.57 (2) relate to protection of the property or financial affairs of the adult, as well as personal welfare.
   On the local authority's supervision of guardians with welfare powers, under subs. (1)(a), see SSI 2002/95 as amended by SSI 2005/630. The draft Bill annexed to the SLC Report

Adults with Incapacity (Scotland) Act 2000 (Pt. 1)

contained, in clause 49(c), a requirement upon guardians to "comply with any order or demand made . . . by the local authority in relation to the personal welfare" of the adult. That provision was quite inappropriate, because guardians should not be the puppets of local authorities and on occasions may require, in the adult's best interests, to challenge local authorities. Accordingly, no equivalent provision was included in this Act, either as introduced or as enacted (cf. s.64 (7), which retains a requirement upon financial guardians to comply with orders or demands made by the Public Guardian). On the other hand, an amendment at stage 2 to alter "supervise" to "monitor" was unsuccessful (though the official Explanatory Notes use "monitor"). Moreover, under s.73 the local authority may (subject to right of appeal to the sheriff) recall the welfare powers of a guardian if the criteria in s.73 (3)(a) or (b) apply. Accordingly, it is probably reasonable to view the supervisory function under subs. (1)(a) as ensuring that guardians with welfare powers discharge their functions properly, but not inhibiting proper discharge of those functions even when that may entail conflict with the local authority. In any situation where there is a significant dispute between guardian and local authority as to whether the guardian is acting inappropriately, or on the other hand properly but in a manner inconvenient to the local authority, it would probably be better for the matter to be referred to MWC under s.9 (1), or to the sheriff for directions under s.3 (3).

As well as the duty to consult under subs. (1)(b) (see the related provisions of s.6 (2)(f) and s.9 (1)(c)) local authorities have a duty under s.9 (2) to afford MWC all facilities necessary to enable MWC to carry out its functions. See also s.12 (2).

The function of receiving and investigating complaints under subs. (1)(c) is subject to the similar function of MWC under s.9 (1)(d) where MWC is not satisfied with a local authority investigation, or the local authority has failed to investigate. In relation to subs. (1)(c), see also subs. (4) and the General Note to s.1 (7) and s.12 (1).

The local authority's function of providing information and advice under subs. (1)(e) replicate the MWC function under s.9 (1)(g). Subsection (2) empowers a local authority to investigate under subs. (1)(d) in relation to any adult present within that local authority's area, so that the local authority may "investigate, as a matter of urgency, circumstances in which the personal welfare of an adult may be at risk" (*per* Mr Iain Gray, Deputy Minister of Community Care, SP OR, Vol. 5, col. 1064). See also s.12 (1).

Subsection (3) provides for regulations by Scottish Ministers (see s.86) regarding the supervisory functions of local authorities both in relation to guardians under subs. (1)(a) (discussed above) and where supervision has been ordered by the sheriff of appointees under interim orders (see *inter alia* s.3 (2)(a)) and WPAs (see s.20 (2)(c) and SSI 2001/77, reproduced in *Adult Incapacity*).

Intimation

Intimation not required in certain circumstances

11.—(1) Where, apart from this subsection, intimation of any application or other proceedings under this Act, or notification of any interlocutor relating to such application or other proceedings, would be given to an adult and the court considers that the intimation or notification would be likely to pose a serious risk to the health of the adult the court may direct that such intimation or notification shall not be given.

(2) Where, apart from this subsection and subsection (1), any intimation or notification to him under this Act would be given by the Public Guardian to an adult and the Public Guardian considers that the intimation or notification would be likely to pose a serious risk to the health of the adult the Public Guardian shall not give the intimation or notification.

DEFINITIONS
"adult" : s.1 (6)
"Public Guardian" : s.6 (1)

GENERAL NOTE
This section addresses situations where intimation or notification to the adult would be likely to pose a serious risk to the adult's health. Under subs. (1), the court may dispense with

Adults with Incapacity Legislation

intimation or notification if it considers that there is such a risk. Under subs. (2), the Public Guardian must do so. There were criticisms that under former curatory procedure applications to dispense with service had been made lightly, and might on occasions have been related to convenience rather than to serious risk to health. The fact that the adult may be seriously upset by, and seek to oppose, an application is *prima facie* a reason to ensure that the adult hears about and fully understands the application, and is afforded an opportunity to oppose. Having regard to ECHR and s.1 principles, the courts require robust evidence before exercising discretion to dispense with intimation or notification.

In *Application in respect of Mrs L.C.* May 18, 2005, Sheriff Baird had before him reports which met the requirements of Rule 3.16.5 and s.11, but only to the extent of repeating the words of statute. Sheriff Baird pointed out that the court can only dispense with intimation if the court "considers" that intimation would be likely to pose a serious risk to the adult's health, therefore the court should not dispense with intimation unless the court has clear and specific information which will entitle the court to form the view that intimation would be likely to pose such a risk.

The chief social work officer must not notify under s.64 (9) when the sheriff has given a direction under subs. (1)—see s.64 (10), and see also s.76 (4). In case of similar risk to the adult's health, managers of establishments may under s.37 (8) seek a direction from their supervisory body that they need not notify the adult under s.37 (3) and (4).

See s.2 (4) as to rules regarding evidence to be taken into account under subs. (1), and s.7 (1)(d) as to regulations regarding evidence to be taken into account under subs. (2), and see SSI 2001/79 as amended by SSI 2005/445.

Investigations

Investigations

12.—(1) In consequence of any investigation carried out under—

(a) section 6(2)(c) or (d) by the Public Guardian;
(b) section 9(1)(d) [. . .][14] by the Mental Welfare Commission; or
(c) section 10(1)(c) or (d) by a local authority,

the Public Guardian, Mental Welfare Commission or local authority, as the case may be, may take such steps, including the making of an application to the sheriff, as seem to him or them to be necessary to safeguard the property, financial affairs or personal welfare, as the case may be, of the adult.

(2) For the purposes of any investigation mentioned in subsection (1), the Public Guardian, Mental Welfare Commission and local authority shall provide each other with such information and assistance as may be necessary to facilitate the investigation.

DEFINITIONS
"adult" : s.1 (6)
"local authority" : s.87 (1) (referring to the Local Government etc. (Scotland) Act 1994 (c.39) s.2)
"Mental Welfare Commission" : s.87 (1) (referring to s.4 of the 2003 Act)
"Public Guardian" : s.6 (1)

GENERAL NOTE
Following upon investigation under the powers referred to, the relevant authority is empowered by subs. (1) to make (any competent) application to the sheriff, or to take any other steps which that authority considers necessary to safeguard the adult's welfare, property

---

[14] Words repealed by Mental Health (Care and Treatment) (Scotland) Act 2003 (asp 13), Sch. 5.

or financial affairs. See General Notes to s.6, s.9 and s.10 regarding respective competencies in relation to personal welfare, and in relation to property and financial affairs, and see s.6 (2)(da) for the more extensive powers conferred on the Public Guardian by the 2007 Act.

Subsection (2), which chronologically would precede subs. (1) in relation to any particular investigation, requires provision of information and assistance in relation to such investigations among the relevant authorities.

Codes of practice

Codes of practice
13.—(1) The Scottish Ministers shall prepare, or cause to be prepared for their approval, and from time to time revise, or cause to be revised for their approval, codes of practice containing guidance as to the exercise by—

(a) local authorities and their chief social work officers and mental health officers;
(b) continuing and welfare attorneys;
(c) persons authorised under intervention orders;
(d) guardians;
(e) withdrawers;
(f) managers of authorised establishments;
(g) supervisory bodies;
(h) persons authorised to carry out medical treatment or research under Part 5,

of their functions under this Act and as to such other matters arising out of or connected with this Act as the Scottish Ministers consider appropriate.

(2) Before preparing or approving any code of practice under this Act or making or approving any alteration in it the Scottish Ministers shall consult such bodies as appear to them to be concerned.

(3) The Scottish Ministers shall lay copies of any such code and of any alteration in it before the Parliament.

(4) The Scottish Ministers shall publish every code of practice made under this Act as for the time being in force.

DEFINITIONS
"authorised establishments" : s.35 (2)
"chief social work officer" : Social Work (Scotland) Act 1968 (c.49) s.3 (presumed)
"continuing attorney" : s.15 (2)
"intervention order" : s.53 (1)
"local authority" : s.87 (1) (referring to the Local Government etc. (Scotland) Act 1994 (c.39) s.2)
"managers" : s.35 (5) and Sched. 1, para. 1
"medical treatment" : s.47 (4)
"mental health officer" : s.87 (1) (referring to 2003 Act s.329)
"Parliament, the" : Scotland Act 1998 s.126 (1)
"welfare attorney" : s.16 (2)
"withdrawer" : s.25 (6)

GENERAL NOTE
Subsection (1) lists the topics covered by the codes of practice, and the remaining subsections deal with consultation, laying before the Scottish Parliament, and publication. See Introduction and General Note for particulars of current codes of practice.

See s.86 regarding regulations.

Appeal against decision as to incapacity

Appeal against decision as to incapacity
14. A decision taken for the purposes of this Act, other than by the sheriff, as to the incapacity of an adult may be appealed by—

(a) the adult; or
(a) any person claiming an interest in the adult's property, financial affairs or personal welfare relating to the purpose for which the decision was taken,

to the sheriff or, where the decision was taken by the sheriff, to the sheriff principal and thence, with the leave of the sheriff principal, to the Court of Session.

DEFINITIONS
"adult" : s.1 (6)
"incapacity" : s.1 (6)
"person claiming an interest" : s.87 (1)

GENERAL NOTE
This section contains general rights to appeal against decisions under this Act as to incapacity of an adult. Appeals may be brought by that adult or by anyone claiming an interest. Where the decision was made by anyone other than the sheriff, appeal lies to the sheriff. Where the decision was made by the sheriff, appeal lies to the sheriff principal and thence, with leave of the sheriff principal, to the Court of Session. See also General Notes to ss.1 (6), 2 (3) and 47 (1).

PART 2

CONTINUING POWERS OF ATTORNEY AND WELFARE POWERS OF ATTORNEY

GENERAL NOTE
The content of Pt. 2 is summarised in the Introduction and General Note.

Part 2 applies only to continuing powers of attorney ("CPAs") and welfare powers of attorney ("WPAs"), as defined in s.15 and s.16 respectively, and references in the annotations to this Part to attorneys mean attorneys under such powers. In England and internationally, various terms are used for powers of attorney intended to enter into force, or to continue in force, in the event of the granter's incapacity. At time of writing it seems likely that the Scottish term "continuing power of attorney" will be adopted by the Council of Europe in its *Recommendation on Principles concerning powers of attorney and advance directives for incapacity*, but covering welfare powers as well as property and financial powers.

The principles in s.1 (2)—(4) apply generally to this Part, and the principles in s.1 (2)—(5) must be observed by attorneys.

To the extent that attorneys and others acting in accordance with the provisions of this Part exercise "functions conferred by this Act", the sheriff may give directions in accordance with s.3 (3).

Attorneys under CPAs are subject to investigation of complaints by the Public Guardian under s.6 (2)(c), and attorneys under WPAs to such investigation by MWC under s.9 (1)(d) and local authorities under s.10 (1)(c).

Attorneys may receive guidance and advice under ss.6, 9 and 10, and from codes of practice under s.13.

The provisions of Pt. 3 (other than s.32) and Pt. 4 are disapplied by ss.24B (2) and 46 respectively where there is an attorney with relevant powers. See General Note to s.16 regarding provisions concerning attorneys in Pt. 5. Guardians appointed with relevant powers under Pt. 6 supersede attorneys by virtue of s.24 (2).

Section 81 (repayment of funds), s.82 (limitation of liability) and s.83 (offence of ill-treatment and wilful neglect by persons "exercising powers under this Act relating to the personal welfare of an adult") apply to attorneys. The protection of s.82 is not available when the attorney has not acted in accordance with the s.1 principles.

On jurisdiction and related matters, see Sched. 3 and in particular para. 4 thereof.

For transitional provisions relevant to pre-2000 Act attorneys see Sched. 4, paras. 4, 7(a) and 8. The inclusion of WPAs in the transitional provisions would appear to have dispelled doubts which might have lingered as to the competency of welfare powers prior to this Act.

On changes introduced by the 2007 Act, see notes to relevant sections and also John Kerrigan *The Adult Support and Protection (Scotland) Act 2007—Problems?* 2008 SLT (News) 27, commented on in the General Note to s.22A.

See *Anderson, Petitioner* (Court of Session June 26, 2007, Scottish Courts Website) for a decision holding that it was not competent for the court to allow an attorney as such to appear on behalf of a party litigant.

See *McDowall's Executors v IRC*, [2004] STC (SCD) 22 and *M, Applicant*, 2007 SLT (Sh. Ct.) 24 on the interpretation of powers of attorney, which are strictly construed.

Creation of continuing power of attorney

15.—(1) Where an individual grants a power of attorney relating to his property or financial affairs in accordance with the following provisions of this section that power of attorney shall, notwithstanding any rule of law, continue to have effect in the event of the granter's becoming incapable in relation to decisions about the matter to which the power of attorney relates.

(2) In this Act a power of attorney granted under subsection (1) is referred to as a "continuing power of attorney" and a person on whom such power is conferred is referred to as a "continuing attorney".

(3) A continuing power of attorney shall be valid only if it is expressed in a written document which—

   (a) is subscribed by the granter;
   (b) incorporates a statement which clearly expresses the granter's intention that the power be a continuing power;
   [(ba) where the continuing power of attorney is exercisable only if the granter is determined to be incapable in relation to decisions about the matter to which the power relates, states that the granter has considered how such a determination may be made;][15]
   (c) incorporates a certificate in the prescribed form by [a practising solicitor][16] or by a member of another prescribed class that—

   (i) he has interviewed the granter immediately before the granter subscribed the document;
   (ii) he is satisfied, either because of his own knowledge of the granter or because he has consulted [another person][17] (whom he names in the certificate) who [has][18] knowledge of the granter, that at the time the continuing power of attorney is granted the granter understands its nature and extent;
   (iii) he has no reason to believe that the granter is acting under undue influence or that any other factor vitiates the granting of the power.

(4) [A practising solicitor][19] or member of another prescribed class may not grant a certificate under subsection (3)(c) if he is the person to whom the power of attorney has been granted.

[(5) It is declared that the rule of law which provides that an agent's authority ends in the event of the bankruptcy of the principal or the agent

---

[15] Inserted subject to savings specified in SSI 2007/334, art.4 by Adult Support and Protection (Scotland) Act 2007 (asp 10), s.57(1)(a).
[16] Substituted by Adult Support and Protection (Scotland) Act 2007 (asp 10), s.57(1)(b)(i).
[17] Substituted by Adult Support and Protection (Scotland) Act 2007 (asp 10), s.57(1)(b)(ii).
[18] Substituted by Adult Support and Protection (Scotland) Act 2007 (asp 10), s.57(1)(b)(iii).
[19] Substituted by Adult Support and Protection (Scotland) Act 2007 (asp 10), s.57(1)(c).

applies, and has applied since subsection (1) came into force, in relation to continuing powers of attorney.][20]

DEFINITIONS
"bankrupt" : s.87 (4)
"continuing attorney" : s.15 (2)
"continuing power of attorney" : s.15 (2)
"incapable" : s.1 (6)
"power of attorney" : s.87 (1)
"practising solicitor": s.87 (1)
"prescribed" : s.87 (1) (and see s.86)

GENERAL NOTE
Under subs. (1) a CPA granted in accordance with this section (and under s.18, only a CPA so granted) continues in force after the granter's incapacity. Subsection (2) defines "continuing power of attorney" and "continuing attorney" accordingly. Subsection (3) prescribes the four requisites for a CPA to be valid as such (and thus registrable under s.19, only registered CPAs being operable). The CPA must be subscribed by the granter; it must clearly state the granter's intention that it should be a CPA; it must incorporate a certificate in prescribed form by a solicitor or member of another prescribed class, who (subs. (4)) is not the grantee; and (after October 5, 2007) if it is to be exerciseable only if the granter lacks relevant capacity, it must state that the granter has considered how incapacity is to be determined.

"clearly" excludes potentially ambiguous powers, which can be encountered on occasion. It would be better practice to be unambiguous, one way or the other.

The certification provisions require certification of the granter's understanding of the nature and extent of the power of attorney, and also that the certifier has no reason to believe that the power is vitiated by undue influence or otherwise. Unless the certifier is confident as to the granter's capacity, he should consult someone (prior to April 1, 2008, more than one person) able to satisfy the certifier as to capacity, and should name in the certificate the person so consulted. These requirements address concerns that under previous law some granters may not have realised that powers of attorney continue in force following incapacity unless they state the contrary, and concerns about the circumstances in which powers have sometimes been granted, particularly by people vulnerable at time of granting. On certification, see also s.16A and SSI 2008/056.

At time of granting, consideration should be given as to whether the power is to be a "springing" power as provided for in s.19 (3), in which case subs. (3)(ba) will apply, and whether up to two additional copies should be issued upon registration under s.19 (5)(b).

Section 16 (5) and (7) contain provisions applicable only to WPAs, the converse of which provisions apply to CPAs. In particular, only WPAs have since April 2, 2001 been exempted from the general rule that powers of attorney fall upon the bankruptcy of granter or attorney, and that is now confirmed by subs. (5). There is no provision to revive a CPA upon discharge from bankruptcy.

Creation and exercise of welfare power of attorney
16.—(1) An individual may grant a power of attorney relating to his personal welfare in accordance with the following provisions of this section.

(2) In this Act a power of attorney granted under this section is referred to as a "welfare power of attorney" and an individual on whom such power is conferred is referred to as a "welfare attorney".

(3) A welfare power of attorney shall be valid only if it is expressed in a written document which—

    (a) is subscribed by the granter;
    (b) incorporates a statement which clearly expresses the granter's intention that the power be a welfare power to which this section applies;

---

[20] Inserted by Adult Support and Protection (Scotland) Act 2007 (asp 10), s.57(1)(d).

[(ba) states that the granter has considered how a determination as to whether he is incapable in relation to decisions about the matter to which the welfare power of attorney relates may be made for the purposes of subsection (5)(b);][21]

(c) incorporates a certificate in the prescribed form by [a practising solicitor][22] or by a member of another prescribed class that—

   (i) he has interviewed the granter immediately before the granter subscribed the document;

   (ii) he is satisfied, either because of his own knowledge of the granter or because he has consulted [another person][23] (whom he names in the certificate) who [has][24] knowledge of the granter, that at the time the welfare power of attorney is granted the granter understands its nature and extent;

   (iii) he has no reason to believe that the granter is acting under undue influence or that any other factor vitiates the granting of the power.

(4) [A practising solicitor][25] or member of another prescribed class may not grant a certificate under subsection (3)(c) if he is the person to whom the power of attorney has been granted.

(5) A welfare power of attorney—

(a) may be granted only to an individual (which does not include a person acting in his capacity as an officer of a local authority or other body established by or under an enactment); and

(b) shall not be exercisable unless—

   (i) the granter is incapable in relation to decisions about the matter to which the welfare power of attorney relates; or

   (ii) the welfare attorney reasonably believes that sub-paragraph (i) applies.

(6) A welfare attorney may not—

(a) place the granter in a hospital for the treatment of mental disorder against his will; [. . .][26]

(b) consent on behalf of the granter to any form of treatment [in relation to which the authority conferred by section 47(2) does not apply by virtue of regulations made under section 48(2)][27] [;

(c) make, on behalf of the granter, a request under section 4(1) of the Anatomy Act 1984 (c. 14);

(d) give, on behalf of the granter, an authorisation under, or by virtue of, section 6(1), 17, 29(1) or 42(1) of the Human Tissue (Scotland) Act 2006 (asp 4); or

(e) make, on behalf of the granter, a nomination under section 30(1) of that Act.][28]

---

[21] Inserted subject to savings specified in SSI 2007/334, art.4 by Adult Support and Protection (Scotland) Act 2007 (asp 10), s.57(2)(a).
[22] Substituted by Adult Support and Protection (Scotland) Act 2007 (asp 10), s.57(2)(b)(i).
[23] Substituted by Adult Support and Protection (Scotland) Act 2007 (asp 10), s.57(2)(b)(ii).
[24] Substituted by Adult Support and Protection (Scotland) Act 2007 (asp 10), s.57(2)(b)(iii).
[25] Substituted by Adult Support and Protection (Scotland) Act 2007 (asp 10), s.57(2)(c).
[26] Word repealed by Human Tissue (Scotland) Act 2006 (asp 4), s.57(2)(b).
[27] Substituted by Adult Support and Protection (Scotland) Act 2007 (asp 10), s.57(2)(d).
[28] Inserted by Human Tissue (Scotland) Act 2006 (asp 4), s.57(2)(b).

(7) A welfare power of attorney shall not come to an end in the event of the bankruptcy of the granter or the welfare attorney.

(8) Any reference to a welfare attorney—

(a) in relation to subsection (5)(b) in a case where the granter is habitually resident in Scotland; and
(b) in subsection (6),

shall include a reference to a person granted, under a contract, grant or appointment governed by the law of any country, powers (however expressed) relating to the granter's personal welfare and having effect during the granter's incapacity.

DEFINITIONS
"bankrupt" : s.87 (4)
"continuing power of attorney" : s.15 (2)
"incapable" : s.1 (6)
"incapacity" : s.1 (6)
"local authority" : s.87 (1) (referring to the Local Government etc. (Scotland) Act 1994 (c.39) s.2)
"mental disorder" : s.87 (1) (and see General Note to s.1 (6))
"power of attorney" : s.87 (1)
"practising solicitor" : s.87 (1)
"prescribed" : s.87 (1) (and see s.86)
"welfare attorney" : s.16 (2)
"welfare power of attorney" : s.16 (2)

GENERAL NOTE
Subsections (1)—(4) contain provisions in relation to WPAs substantially similar to those relating to CPAs in s.15 (see General Note to that section), though s.16 (3)(ba) differs from s.15 (3)(ba) because WPAs may be exercised only when the granter lacks relevant capacity (see s.16 (5)(b)). On subs. (3)(c), see also s.16A and SSI 2008/056. The remaining provisions of this section apply to WPAs only.

Under subs. (5)(a) only an individual may be attorney under a WPA. Section 23 (4), referring to s.23 (1) which in turn refers to WPAs as well as CPAs, appears to confirm that joint and substitute appointments remain competent under WPAs, and that the purpose of subs. (5)(a) is to exclude appointees who are not individuals. Appointees acting in their capacities as officers of local authorities and other statutory bodies are also excluded. Subsection (5)(b) provides that WPAs only take effect following loss of capacity. See also subs. (8) and General Note to s.1 (7). A general right of appeal against decisions by anyone as to incapacity is contained in s.14.

Under subs. (6) a welfare attorney may not place the granter in hospital for treatment of mental disorder against the granter's will (for which 2003 Act procedures remain necessary), or consent to any treatment excluded by regulations under s.48 (2) from the scope of the authority to treat under s.47, or make request that a body be used after death for anatomical examination under the Anatomy Act 1984, or give authorisation or make a nomination under the provisions referred to of the Human Tissue Act 2006 (cf. s.64 (2)), which refer to removal and use of body parts after death, live transplants, post-mortem examinations and use of tissue samples and organs. Provisions regarding medical treatment where a welfare attorney has been appointed are contained in s.50, and welfare attorneys may have a role under s.51 (3)(f) in relation to proposed research. With reference to subs. (6), see also subs. (8) and General Note to s.1 (7).

Under subs. (7) a WPA, unlike a CPA, continues in force notwithstanding the bankruptcy of granter or attorney.

Continuing and welfare power of attorney: accompanying certificate
16A. Where a document confers both—

(a) a continuing power of attorney; and

Adults with Incapacity (Scotland) Act 2000 (Pt. 2)

(b) a welfare power of attorney,

the validity requirements imposed by sections 15(3)(c) and 16(3)(c) may be satisfied by incorporating a single certificate which certifies the matters set out in those provisions.][29]

DEFINITIONS
"continuing power of attorney" : s.15 (2)
"welfare power of attorney" : s.16 (2)

GENERAL NOTE
Prior to the 2007 Act, a combined CPA and WPA required two certificates. This section now provides for a single certificate for both purposes. See SSI 2008/56.

Attorney not obliged to act in certain circumstances
17. A continuing or welfare attorney shall not be obliged to do anything which would otherwise be within the powers of the attorney if doing it would, in relation to its value or utility, be unduly burdensome or expensive.

DEFINITIONS
"continuing attorney" : s.15 (2)
"welfare attorney" : s.16 (2)

GENERAL NOTE
At common law attorneys have fiduciary duties and a duty of care, beyond which gratuitous attorneys do not have a specific duty to act. On the basis that a decision not to do something can be an "intervention" (see General Note to s.1 (1)), an attorney whose failure to act contravened the s.1 principles would be open to the various sanctions available under the Act against errant attorneys, and would lose the protection of s.82. However this s.17 specifically permits an attorney not to act in the circumstances to which it applies. Curiously, similar protection is not afforded to guardians, who would presumably require to justify inaction by reference to the s.1 principles (including the "benefit" principle in s.1 (2)).

Power of attorney not granted in accordance with this Act
18. A power of attorney granted after the commencement of this Act which is not granted in accordance with section 15 or 16 shall have no effect during any period when the granter is incapable in relation to decisions about the matter to which the power of attorney relates.

DEFINITIONS
"incapable" : s.1 (6)
"power of attorney" : s.87 (1)

GENERAL NOTE
See General Note for Pt. 2, and, as regards potentially ambiguous powers, General Note to s.15.

Registration of continuing or welfare power of attorney
19.—(1) A continuing or welfare attorney shall have no authority to act until the document conferring the power of attorney has been registered under this section.

---

[29] Section 16A inserted by Adult Support and Protection (Scotland) Act 2007 (asp 10), s.57(3).

Adults with Incapacity Legislation

(2) For the purposes of registration, the document conferring the power of attorney shall be sent to the Public Guardian who, if he is satisfied that a person appointed to act is prepared to act, shall—

(a) enter prescribed particulars of it in the register maintained by him under section 6(2)(b)(i) or (ii) as the case may be;
(b) send a copy of it with a certificate of registration to the sender;
(c) if it confers a welfare power of attorney, [give notice of the registration of the document to both the local authority and][30] the Mental Welfare Commission.

(3) The document conferring a continuing or welfare power of attorney may contain a condition that the Public Guardian shall not register it under this section until the occurrence of a specified event and in that case the Public Guardian shall not register it until he is satisfied that the specified event has occurred.

(4) A copy of a document conferring a continuing or welfare power of attorney authenticated by the Public Guardian shall be accepted for all purposes as sufficient evidence of the contents of the original and of any matter relating thereto appearing in the copy.

(5) The Public Guardian shall—

(a) on the registration of a document conferring a continuing or welfare power of attorney, send a copy of it to the granter; [. . .][31]
(b) where the document conferring the continuing or welfare power of attorney so requires, send a copy of it to not more than two specified individuals or holders of specified offices or positions.
[(c) where the document confers a welfare power of attorney and the local authority requests a copy of it, send such a copy to the local authority; and
(d) where the document confers a welfare power of attorney and the Mental Welfare Commission requests a copy of it, send such a copy to the Mental Welfare Commission.][32]

(6) A decision of the Public Guardian under subsection (2) as to whether or not a person is prepared to act or under subsection (3) as to whether or not the specified event has occurred may be appealed to the sheriff, whose decision shall be final.

DEFINITIONS
"continuing attorney" : s.15 (2)
"Mental Welfare Commission" : s.87 (1) (referring to s.4 of the 2003 Act)
"power of attorney" : s.87 (1)
"prescribed" : s.87 (1) (and see s.86)
"Public Guardian" : s.6 (1)
"welfare attorney" : s.16 (2)
"welfare power of attorney" : s.16 (2)

GENERAL NOTE
Subsection (1) requires registration before attorneys, under either CPAs or WPAs, may act. If an attorney under a CPA is empowered to act before any loss of capacity, and proposes to do so, the CPA should first be registered.

---

[30] Substituted by Adult Support and Protection (Scotland) Act 2007 (asp 10), s.57(4)(a).
[31] Repealed by Adult Support and Protection (Scotland) Act 2007 (asp 10), s.57(4)(b)(i).
[32] Inserted by Adult Support and Protection (Scotland) Act 2007 (asp 10), s.57(4)(b)(ii).

Before registering, the Public Guardian requires to receive under subs. (2) the power of attorney document and evidence of the attorney's willingness to act, normally provided by the attorney's signature to that effect on the registration application form. Under subs. (3), in the case of a "springing" power of attorney, evidence must be provided that the "springing" event has occurred. Upon receipt of the requisite information and payment of her fee (massively increased in July 2007 from £35 to £60 and further increased to £65 with effect from August 1, 2008), under subs. (2) the Public Guardian enters prescribed particulars in the relevant register; issues a copy of the power of attorney with certificate of registration to the person who sent in the relevant information; and under subs. (5) also issues a copy to the granter and up to two further copies in accordance with any requirements to that effect contained in the power of attorney (and in the relevant section of the registration application form). Some fundholders demand to see the original certificate of registration, sealed in accordance with the practice adopted by the original Public Guardian, with attached copy of the Power, in terms of his practice note of October 26, 2001. His successor has (at time of writing these notes) adopted the helpful practice of attaching to all copies issued by her a letter drawing attention to subs. (4). Copies of WPAs are now sent to MWC and the local authority on request only, though both are notified of all registrations of WPAs under subs. (2)(c).

The registration duties of the Public Guardian in relation to CPAs and WPAs are set out in both s.6 (2)(b) and s.19 (2). Unfortunately the current practice of the Public Guardian does not extend to the explicit requirements under s.6 (1)(b)(i) and (ii) to maintain public registers of CPA and WPA documents. Prior to the 2000 Act, most powers of attorney were registered in the Books of Council and Session, but not all were so registered, and it was not easy to trace those which were so registered. Not only was it very difficult to ascertain whether an adult had granted a power of attorney (though easy to ascertain the identity of the attorney and the powers granted once the relevant registration had been traced), but also very difficult to identify cases of—for example—several purported powers granted by the same adult without apparent reference to each other, or a suspiciously large number of powers granted for no obvious good reason in favour of the same grantee. One of the clear purposes of the reforms embodied in the 2000 Act was that all CPA and WPA documents should be publicly accessible, along with relevant other information recorded by the Public Guardian, from dedicated public registers. At time of writing the Public Guardian does not make these automatically available upon payment of the appropriate fee despite the clear terms of s.6 (2)(b). It would appear to be open to any aggrieved applicant to have her directed to do so under s.3 (3), but unfortunate if that should become necessary. However, she has refused to provide a copy of a Power of Attorney document to a child of a granter concerned to ascertain whether an attorney was acting within the powers conferred. She has in fact given much thought to the balance between publication, and issues of privacy, data protection and possible "targeting" of vulnerable people using publicly available information. While the Scottish Government and the Parliament have apparently been content to impose discriminatorily high fees upon such vulnerable people (see *Out of the wrong pocket*, 2008 JLSS 9), they have neglected—throughout the period of over seven years since Pt. 2 came into force—to ensure that the particulars to be registered be prescribed by regulations in terms of subs. (2)(a). However, on a proper reading of s.6 (2), and having regard to the SLC Report, that would appear to be relevant only to the additional particulars to be registered, and not the Power of Attorney documents themselves.

Subsection (4) provided another alternative in addition to the previously and still existing options of exhibiting the original power of attorney, or a registered extract from the Books of Council and Session, or a copy certified in accordance with the rather cumbersome requirements of Powers of Attorney Act 1971 (c.27), s.3. An advantage of authenticated copies under subs. (4) is that it is obvious that they are CPAs or WPAs, and they have become the versions most frequently used.

Subsection (6) provides for appeal to the sheriff as to the matters specified.

Powers of sheriff

20.—(1) An application for an order under subsection (2) may be made to the sheriff by any person claiming an interest in the property, financial affairs or personal welfare of the granter of a continuing or welfare power of attorney.

(2) Where, on an application being made under subsection (1), the sheriff is satisfied that the granter is incapable in relation to decisions

about, or of acting to safeguard or promote his interests in, his property, financial affairs or personal welfare insofar as the power of attorney relates to them, and that it is necessary to safeguard or promote these interests, he may make an order—

    (a) ordaining that the continuing attorney shall be subject to the supervision of the Public Guardian to such extent as may be specified in the order;

    (b) ordaining the continuing attorney to submit accounts in respect of any period specified in the order for audit to the Public Guardian;

    (c) ordaining that the welfare attorney shall be subject to the supervision of the local authority to such extent as may be specified in the order;

    (d) ordaining the welfare attorney to give a report to him as to the manner in which the welfare attorney has exercised his powers during any period specified in the order;

    (e) revoking—

        (i) any of the powers granted by the continuing or welfare power of attorney; or

        (ii) the appointment of an attorney.

(3) Where the sheriff makes an order under this section the sheriff clerk shall send a copy of the interlocutor containing the order to the Public Guardian who shall—

    (a) enter prescribed particulars in the register maintained by him under section 6(2)(b)(i) or (ii) as the case may be;

    (b) notify—

        (i) the granter;

        (ii) the continuing or welfare attorney;

        (iii) where it is the welfare attorney who is notified, the local authority and [. . .][33] the Mental Welfare Commission;

        (iv) where the sheriff makes an order under subsection (2)(c), the local autority.

(4) A decision of the sheriff under subsection (2)(a) to (d) shall be final.

(5) In this section any reference to—

    (a) a continuing power of attorney shall include a reference to a power (however expressed) under a contract, grant or appointment governed by the law of any country, relating to the granter's property or financial affairs and having continuing effect notwithstanding the granter's incapacity;

    (b) a welfare power of attorney shall include a reference to a power (however expressed) under a contract, grant or appointment governed by the law of any country, relating to the granter's personal welfare and having effect during the granter's incapacity,

and "continuing attorney" and "welfare attorney" shall be construed accordingly.

DEFINITIONS
"continuing attorney" : s.15 (2)

---

[33] Repealed by Adult Support and Protection (Scotland) Act 2007 (asp 10), s.57(5).

Adults with Incapacity (Scotland) Act 2000 (Pt. 2)

"continuing power of attorney" : s.15 (2)
"incapable" : s.1 (6)
"incapacity" : s.1 (6)
"local authority" : s.87 (1) (referring to the Local Government etc. (Scotland) Act 1994 (c.39) s.2)
"mental disorder" : s.87 (1) (and see General Note to s.1 (6))
"Mental Welfare Commission" : s.87 (1) (referring to s.4 of the 2003 Act)
"person claiming an interest" : s.87 (1)
"prescribed" : s.87 (1) (and see s.86)
"Public Guardian" : s.6 (1)
"welfare attorney" : s.16 (2)
"welfare power of attorney" : s.16 (2)

GENERAL NOTE
This section provides that application may be made to the sheriff by anyone within subs. (1) for any of the orders specified in subs. (2). Although this procedure is only available when the granter has lost capacity, "any period" in subs. (2)(b) could include a period prior to loss of capacity, if the attorney had acted then. Moreover, "any period" there and also in subs. (2)(d) could mean a period prior to this Part of this Act coming into force—see Sched. 4 para. 4.

Under subs. (3), any such order is notified to the Public Guardian, who registers it and notifies it as required by para. (b). Except for revocation under subs. (2)(e), decisions by the sheriff under subs. (2) are final (subs. (4)). On subs. (5), see General Note to s.1 (7).

M v M (Glasgow Sheriff Court November 2, 2006) was an application by one joint attorney under subs. (2)(e) for revocation of the appointment of the other joint attorney. The sheriff initially revoked the appointment *ad interim*, and his subsequent judgement explains the circumstances in which he considered it appropriate to do so. It later emerged that the granter had apparently revoked the pursuer's appointment, but there appears to have been doubt about the granter's capacity to do so. Thereafter the interim revocation was recalled but some of the attorney's powers revoked. The sheriff directed that a copy of his judgement be sent to the Public Guardian for investigation under s.6 (2)(d) of this Act. There was no further procedure. It is understood that the adult died before the case went to proof.

Regarding applications to the sheriff generally, see ss.2, 3 and 8. Regarding intimation and notification, both by the court and by the Public Guardian, see s.11. In relation to any order made under subs. (2)(c), see s.10 (3)(b).

On notification to MWC, see General Note to s.9.

Regulations
See SSI 2001/77, reproduced in *Adult Incapacity*.

Records: attorneys
21. A continuing or welfare attorney shall keep records of the exercise of his powers.

DEFINITIONS
"continuing attorney" : s.15 (2)
"welfare attorney" : s.16 (2)

GENERAL NOTE
Continuing attorneys may under s.20 (2)(b) be required by order of the sheriff to submit accounts in respect of "any period", so would require to keep sufficient financial records to be able to comply with such an order, if it were made. Moreover, they retain their duty (at common law and usually under the specific terms of the power of attorney) to account to the granter or the granter's executors upon the granter's recovery or death, respectively. In addition to such accounting obligations in the case of continuing attorneys, they and welfare attorneys under this section, like appointees under intervention and guardianship orders (ss.54 and 65 respectively), are required to keep records of the exercise of their powers. There is no provision for regulations, but the codes of practice issued under s.13 give guidance.

Notification to Public Guardian
22.—(1) After a document conferring a continuing or welfare power of attorney has been registered under section 19, the attorney shall notify the Public Guardian—

(a) of any change in his address;
(b) of any change in the address of the granter of the power of attorney;
(c) of the death of the granter of the power of attorney; or
(d) of any other event which results in the termination of the power of attorney,

and the Public Guardian shall enter prescribed particulars in the register maintained by him under section 6(2)(b)(i) or (ii) as the case may be and shall notify the granter (in the case of an event mentioned in paragraph (a) or (d)) and, where the power of attorney relates to the personal welfare of the adult, both the local authority and [. . .][34] the Mental Welfare Commission.

(2) If, after a document conferring a continuing or welfare power of attorney has been registered under section 19, the attorney dies, his personal representatives shall, if aware of the existence of the power of attorney, notify the Public Guardian who shall enter prescribed particulars in the register maintained by him under section 6(2)(b)(i) or (ii) as the case may be, and shall notify the granter and, where the power of attorney relates to the personal welfare of the adult, both the local authority and [. . .][35] the Mental Welfare Commission.

DEFINITIONS
"adult" : s.1 (6)
"continuing power of attorney" : s.15 (2)
"incapacity" : s.1 (6)
"local authority" : s.87 (1) (referring to the Local Government etc. (Scotland) Act 1994 (c.39) s.2)
"mental disorder" : s.87 (1) (and see General Note to s.1 (6))
"Mental Welfare Commission" : s.87 (1) (referring to s.4 of the 2003 Act)
"power of attorney" : s.87 (1)
"prescribed" : s.87 (1) (and see s.86)
"Public Guardian" : s.6 (1)
"welfare power of attorney" : s.16 (2)

GENERAL NOTE
This section provides for notification of various events to the Public Guardian; entry of them in the relevant register; and notification by the Public Guardian to various parties. On revocation, see s.22A. See s.11 (2) regarding circumstances in which notification must not be given.
On notification to MWC, see General Note to s.9.

Revocation of continuing or welfare power of attorney
22A.—(1) The granter of a continuing or welfare power of attorney may revoke the power of attorney (or any of the powers granted by it) after the document conferring the power of attorney has been registered under section 19 by giving a revocation notice to the Public Guardian.

(2) A revocation notice shall be valid only if it is expressed in a written document which—

(a) is subscribed by the granter; and
(b) incorporates a certificate in the prescribed form by a practising solicitor or by a member of another prescribed class that—

---

[34] Repealed by Adult Support and Protection (Scotland) Act 2007 (asp 10), s.57(6).
[35] Repealed by Adult Support and Protection (Scotland) Act 2007 (asp 10), s.57(6).

(i) he has interviewed the granter immediately before the granter subscribed the document;
(ii) he is satisfied, either because of his own knowledge of the granter or because he has consulted another person (whom he names in the certificate) who has knowledge of the granter, that at the time the revocation is made the granter understands its effect;
(iii) he has no reason to believe that the granter is acting under undue influence or that

any other factor vitiates the revocation of the power.

(3) The Public Guardian, on receiving a revocation notice, shall—

(a) enter the prescribed particulars of it in the register maintained by him under section 6(2)(b)(i) or (ii) as the case may be; and
(b) notify—
 (i) the continuing or welfare attorney; and
 (ii) where it is the welfare attorney who is notified, the local authority and the Mental Welfare Commission.

(4) A revocation has effect when the revocation notice is registered under this section.

(5) No liability shall be incurred by any person who acts in good faith in ignorance of the revocation of a power of attorney under this section. Nor shall any title to heritable property acquired by such a person be challengeable on that ground alone.][36]

DEFINITIONS
"continuing power of attorney" : s.15 (2)
"local authority" : s.87 (1) (referring to the Local Government etc. (Scotland) Act 1994 (c.39) s.2)
"Mental Welfare Commission" : s.87 (1) (referring to s.4 of the 2003 Act)
"power of attorney" : s.87 (1)
"practising solicitor : s.87 (1)
"prescribed" : s.87 (1) (and see s.86)
"Public Guardian" : s.6 (1)
"welfare power of attorney" : s.16 (2)

GENERAL NOTE
Under the 2000 text, the only provision regarding revocation was the requirement under s.22 (1)(d), which has been retained, to notify the Public Guardian of any event resulting in termination of the Power of Attorney. There was no express procedure for revocation by the granter. The 2007 Act introduces such a procedure. The Bill originally proposed simply notification in writing to the Public Guardian. The Law Society urged that the risks in relation to revocation could be similar to those in relation to granting, and required similar protections. This was accepted. The notice of revocation to the Public Guardian must now incorporate a similar certificate to the certificate required for original grant of the Power of Attorney. The revocation takes effect upon registration by the Public Guardian, but "any person" acting in good faith in ignorance of the revocation will not incur any liability, nor shall any title to heritage acquired by such a person be challengeable on that ground alone. See *M v M* (Glasgow Sheriff Court November 2, 2006) for the potential difficulties and uncertainties surrounding revocation prior to this amendment.

See also John Kerrigan's article *The Adult Support and Protection (Scotland) Act 2007— Problems?* 2008 SLT (News) 27 for a full discussion of this section and possible pitfalls, and for

---

[36] Section 22A inserted by Adult Support and Protection (Scotland) Act 2007 (asp 10), s.57(7).

recommendations as to prudent practice. Mr Kerrigan points out that it is regrettable that this section does not require the granter to intimate to the attorney the sending of the notice of revocation to the Public Guardian. It is clearly wise for the granter to do so, and to intimate also to any third party whose dealings with the attorney whose authority the granter wishes to terminate, so as to displace the "good faith" defence in subs. (5). Mr Kerrigan's greatest alarm, and much of his discussion, is predicated on his view that "any person" in subs. (5) does not include the attorney. He suggests that if the attorney were included, the requirement would include reference to the s.1 principles as in s.82. In the view of this annotator, that might well have been an appropriate proviso in the case of attorneys, but the sequence of events in s.22A clearly means that there will be an interval between registration and receipt of intimation, and if the legislature had intended to exclude the attorney from "any person" it would have required to say so expressly, and would have made other provisions to address the position of the attorney between registration and receipt of notification. Section 24 (4), part of the 2000 text, is in similar terms to s.22A (5), and it has never been suggested that "any person" in s.24 (4) excludes the attorney. In the scheme of this Act as a whole, "any person" would always appear to mean precisely what it says—see for example "any person who acts in good faith" in s.31E (8); and where a provision applies to third parties, that is the term which this Act uses—see for example s.79.

The elements of "grant" and "contract" are discussed in *Adult Incapacity* at 6–6 to 6–8, where it is suggested that in the provisions of this Act there referred to, "grant" refers to a unilateral act by the granter, followed by the contract established when the attorney accepts appointment. That is logical, and causes no problems, in relation to the sequence of grant followed by contract (which may be short or—for example when a substitute appointment is triggered—lengthy or even repeated). However, this poorly drafted section seems to ignore the contract element. Thus it fails to address termination of the appointment of an attorney, leaving the power in force, in circumstances which would leave a joint attorney still acting, or would trigger the appointment of a substitute attorney. In the converse situation of resignation by the attorney, s.23 requires intimation to both the granter and the Public Guardian. This requirement, in the very next section, renders even more disappointing the inept drafting of s.22A.

There must be doubt as to whether the Parliament really intended to create a strange new means of terminating a contract under which termination becomes effective upon intimation to a third party, the Public Guardian, leaving the other party in ignorance of such termination until subsequently told by the third party that it has already occurred. Prudent certifiers might opt for the view that, in the absence of clearer evidence to the contrary, the Parliament did not intend such a radical departure from the principles of common law which continue to apply to the contract of mandate, qualified only by the express provisions of this Act insofar as applicable. On that view, failure to intimate the revocation direct to the attorney(s) would be a factor vitiating the revocation, and evidence of such intimation would be required before the certificate could properly be issued.

For the prescribed form of certificate see SSI 2008/56.

Resignation of continuing or welfare attorney

23.—(1) A continuing or welfare attorney who wishes to resign after the document conferring the power of attorney has been registered under section 19 shall give notice in writing of his intention to do so to—

- (a) the granter of the power of attorney;
- (b) the Public Guardian;
- (c) any guardian or, where there is no guardian, the granter's primary carer;
- (d) the local authority, where they are supervising the welfare attorney.

(2) Subject to subsection (4), the resignation shall not have effect until the expiry of a period of 28 days commencing with the date of receipt by the Public Guardian of the notice given under subsection (1); and on its becoming effective the Public Guardian shall enter prescribed particulars in the register maintained by him under section 6(2)(b)(i) or (ii) as the case may be.

(3) Where the resignation is of a welfare attorney, the Public Guardian shall notify the local authority and [. . .][37] the Mental Welfare Commission.

(4) The resignation of a joint attorney, or an attorney in respect of whom the granter has appointed a substitute attorney, shall take effect on the receipt by the Public Guardian of notice under subsection (1)(b) if evidence that—

(a) the remaining joint attorney is willing to continue to act; or
(b) the substitute attorney is willing to act,

accompanies the notice.

DEFINITIONS
"adult" : s.1 (6)
"continuing attorney" : s.15 (2)
"incapacity" : s.1 (6)
"local authority" : s.87 (1) (referring to the Local Government etc. (Scotland) Act 1994 (c.39) s.2)
"mental disorder" : s.87 (1) (and see General Note to s.1 (6))
"Mental Welfare Commission" : s.87 (1) (referring to s.4 of the 2003 Act)
"power of attorney" : s.87 (1)
"prescribed" : s.87 (1) (and see s.86)
"primary carer" : s.87 (1)
"Public Guardian" : s.6 (1)
"welfare attorney" : s.16 (2)

GENERAL NOTE
Subsection (1) requires an attorney under a CPA or WPA who wishes to resign to give notice as there specified. Section 11 does not apply, so that notice must be given to the granter even if that would pose serious risk to the granter's health. This may be an unintentional omission, given the extent to which other provisions permit or require notice not to be given in such circumstances: s.11 permits the sheriff and requires the Public Guardian to dispense with any notice to the adult under this Act in such circumstances, so that (for example) the resignation of a guardian will not be notified in such circumstances (see s.75 (3) and (4), in conjunction with s.11 (2)); a direction by the sheriff under s.11 (1) is extended to subsequent notifications by the chief social work officer under s.64 (9) and (10) (or by him or the Public Guardian under s.76); and a similar direction may be given by supervisory bodies under s.37 (8) as to intimations by managers of establishments to residents. The solution for an attorney desiring for good reason to resign, and fearing such serious risk to the adult's health, would be to apply to the sheriff to revoke his own appointment under s.20 and to direct in terms of s.11(1) that intimation should not be given to the granter. There should be no doubts about the competence of this: s.75 envisages applications by guardians for their own removal (see General Notes to ss.71 and 75).

In the case of resignation of a welfare attorney, the Public Guardian in turn gives notification under subs. (3) (and is accordingly subject to s.11 (2)).

Subsection (2) provides for a 28–day delay, unless it is shown under subs. (4) that a joint or substitute attorney is available and willing to provide continuity.

On notification to MWC under subs. (3), see General Note to s.9.

Termination of continuing or welfare power of attorney

24.—(1) If the granter and the continuing or welfare attorney are married to each other the power of attorney shall, unless the document conferring it provides otherwise, come to an end upon the granting of—

(a) a decree of separation to either party;

---

[37] Repealed by Adult Support and Protection (Scotland) Act 2007 (asp 10), s.57(8).

Adults with Incapacity Legislation

(b) a decree of divorce to either party;
(c) declarator of nullity of the marriage.

[(1A) If the granter and the continuing or welfare attorney are in civil partnership with each other the power of attorney shall, unless the document conferring it provides otherwise, come to an end on the granting of—

(a) a decree of separation of the partners in the civil partnership;
(b) a decree of dissolution of the civil partnership;
(c) a declarator of nullity of the civil partnership.][38]

(2) The authority of a continuing or welfare attorney in relation to any matter shall come to an end on the appointment of a guardian with powers relating to that matter.

(3) In subsection (2) any reference to—

(a) a continuing attorney shall include a reference to a person granted, under a contract, grant or appointment governed by the law of any country, powers (however expressed), relating to the granter's property or financial affairs and having continuing effect notwithstanding the granter's incapacity;
(b) a welfare attorney shall include a reference to a person granted, under a contract, grant or appointment governed by the law of any country, powers (however expressed) relating to the granter's personal welfare and having effect during the granter's incapacity.

(4) No liability shall be incurred by any person who acts in good faith in ignorance of—

(a) the coming to an end of a power of attorney under subsection (1) [or subsection (1A)][39]; or
(b) the appointment of a guardian as mentioned in subsection (2),

nor shall any title to heritable property acquired by such a person be challengeable on those grounds alone.

DEFINITIONS
"continuing attorney" : s.15 (2)
"incapacity" : s.1 (6)
"power of attorney" : s.87 (1)
"welfare attorney" : s.16 (2)

GENERAL NOTE
When the granter and attorney are married or are civil partners, the power is terminated by judicial separation, divorce or dissolution, or declarator of nullity, unless the document specifies otherwise (subss. (1) and (1A)). In relation to particular matters, attorneys are superseded by guardians with relevant powers (sub. (2)). Subsection (4) provides protection for those continuing to act in good faith in ignorance of termination under subs. (1) or (2). On subs. (3), see General Note to s.1 (7).

---

[38] Inserted by Family Law (Scotland) Act 2006 (asp 2), s.36(a).
[39] Inserted by Family Law (Scotland) Act 2006 (asp 2), s.36(b).

PART 3[40]
ACCOUNTS AND FUNDS

Purposes and application of Part

GENERAL NOTE

For a general description of Pt. 3 see Introduction and General Note. The SLC Report identified "a need for a fairly simple method of withdrawing money from an incapable adult's bank account" (para. 4.6, see also paras. 4.1 and 4.4), and proposed the scheme which appeared in Pt. 3 of the 2000 text. However, that scheme was not a success. Uptake was disappointing. The scheme proved to be too rigid and limited. Difficulties were created by some procedural aspects, such as the requirement that the counter-signatory should know both applicant and adult.

Administration under this Act was, and still is, unnecessary when the adult's only significant finances are state benefits which can be administered by a DWP appointee. Procedure under this Act was, and still is, unnecessary to manage funds in a joint account which can be managed under s.32 (see below) without any procedure being necessary. The original scheme for management of funds under Pt. 3 was valuable in cases where funds which required to be used for the adult's benefit were held in an account in the adult's sole name which could not be accessed without procedure under this Act. However, that proved to be a relatively narrow stratum of cases, beyond which there were many more where the adult had further funds in different places. The theoretical solution in such cases was to obtain an intervention order to simplify the adult's affairs, followed by an application for authority to intromit. However, procedure to obtain an intervention order is substantially the same as for guardianship, so that the total procedure to obtain an intervention order followed by authority to intromit was greater than seeking financial guardianship.

Apart from s.32, the original Pt. 3 has been replaced in its entirety with effect from April 1, 2008. The new scheme is best understood if seen not so much as its predecessor with refinements, but rather as a new simplified form of financial guardianship. Procedurally, it is closer to the previous Pt. 3 in that the various forms of application are made to, and determined by, the Public Guardian (with right of appeal to the sheriff, whose decision is final). It is also similar to the previous Pt. 3 in that there are no provisions for caution or for annual accounting. Beyond those aspects, however, the nature and scope of the management arrangements which can be put in place under the new Pt. 3 have more in common with Pt. 6, and are better viewed as a new form of simplified and limited financial guardianship. The new Pt. 3 will accordingly have a major impact upon proceedings and administration under Pt. 6. The sheriff may not grant a guardianship application unless satisfied that: "no other means provided by or under this Act would be sufficient to enable the adult's interests in his property, financial affairs or personal welfare to be safeguarded or promoted" (s.58 (1)(b)). In every case where an application for financial guardianship powers is contemplated, advisers will require to consider carefully whether needs could be adequately met under Pt. 3. Likewise, the courts will require to test applications for financial guardianship powers with equal rigour against *inter alia* the full range of solutions now offered by Pt. 3. Furthermore, in accordance with s.1 principles, existing financial guardians require to be alert to circumstances in which guardianships can be ended and replaced with administration under Pt. 3. Such transitions of management are now facilitated by s.31E (q.v.).

It follows that advisers, the courts and existing financial guardians require to be fully conversant with the scope of the new scheme under Pt. 3. In brief summary, the new scheme permits individual or joint withdrawers, reserve withdrawers and organisations as withdrawers (the last not being an option under Pt. 6, except for local authorities as welfare guardians). The range of possible applications to the Public Guardian includes applications for authority to obtain information about the adult's assets; where the adult requires but does not have a suitable account to receive funds or income, to open such an account (termed "the adult's current account"); to open "the adult's second account" where, for example, a savings-type account is required to accumulate surplus funds at a better rate of interest; as under the

---

[40] Part 3 substituted by Adult Support and Protection (Scotland) Act 2007 (asp 10), s.58, subject to transitional provisions specified in SSI 2008/49, arts.3 and 4.

previous scheme, to obtain authority to intromit, under which the "withdrawer" will open a "designated account" which becomes the withdrawer's operating account; to transfer funds between different accounts in the adult's name (something for which a preliminary intervention order was often required in the past), to terminate existing standing orders and direct debits, and to close existing accounts; and to authorise payment of lump sums. Retained from the original scheme are the provisions under which the withdrawer sets out a "budget" of proposed expenditure, which is authorised by the Public Guardian. There is now improved flexibility when the "budget" requires to be amended.

In comparing the new form of limited financial guardianship under Pt. 3 with the existing provisions for financial management under Pt. 6, the question is no longer "when is Pt. 3 appropriate?" but rather "in what circumstances is Pt. 3 not appropriate?" The answer in the "Access to Funds Revised Code of Practice" is "where the adult has financial assets of a complex nature, for example, stocks and shares, investment bonds, etc to be managed". Further common examples will be cases where heritable property is to be sold, managed or acquired; where a tenancy is to be given up; where reparation or other remedies are to be pursued, or there is other litigation; where a business is to be managed, sold or wound up; and where tax-planning arrangements are contemplated. Even in such cases, Pt. 6 administration may be of limited duration, to be followed by Pt. 3 administration. In such cases it might be better to seek guardianship rather than an intervention order, because of the doubts discussed in the Note to s.24B, and because the transitional mechanism under s.31E is available only in relation to guardianship.

All of Pt. 3 is concerned with the scheme outlined above, except for s.32, which remains embedded in Pt. 3 (because there was no better place to put it) and which relates to joint rather than sole accounts. This brief provision has probably conferred more benefit in proportion to its length than any other in this Act, by permitting a holder of an account in joint names to continue to operate it when the other loses relevant capacity. Prior to this Act, many couples put assets in joint names, and indeed were often encouraged by voluntary organisations to do so, as a precaution *inter alia* against the risk of one losing capacity, only to discover that if one did lose capacity, then the bank or other fundholder would treat the mandate for the account as terminated. That only happens now if the account specifically so provides.

As indicated by its title, the relevant Code of Practice refers to "access to funds". Although that term does not appear in Pt. 3 or its heading, it is the best generic description of the range of measures available under Pt. 3. Also on terminology, note that of the definitions particular to Pt. 3 only "withdrawer" appears in s.87 (1) (the interpretation section for this Act), and only "fundholder" and "withdrawal certificate" appear in s.33 (the interpretation section for Pt. 3). The locations of the many other definitions particular to Pt. 3 are noted under "Definitions" in these annotations, where relevant.

The general principles in s.1 (2)–(4) apply to Pt. 3. Persons exercising functions under Pt. 3 may be given directions by the sheriff under s.3 (3), and intromissions under Pt. 3 are subject to the Public Guardian's investigative powers under s.6 (2)(c) and (d) and further powers under s.12. Withdrawers may seek information and advice from the Public Guardian under s.6 (2)(e), and guidance from Codes of Practice under s.13 (1)(e), in particular the Access to Funds Revised Code of Practice mentioned above.

Section 81 (repayment of funds) and s.82 (limitation of liability) apply to withdrawers. The protection of s.82 is not available where the withdrawer has not acted in accordance with the s.1 principles.

Regulations
See SSI 2008/51.

Intromissions with funds

24A.—(1) This Part makes provision for the authorisation of persons by the Public Guardian to intromit with the funds of an adult for the purposes mentioned in subsection (2).

(2) Those purposes are—

    (a) the payment of central and local government taxes for which the adult is responsible;

    (b) the provisions of sustenance, accommodation, fuel, clothing and related goods and services for the adult;

Adults with Incapacity (Scotland) Act 2000 (Pt. 3)

    (c) the provision of other services provided for the purposes of looking after or caring for the adult;
    (d) the settlement of debts owed by or incurred in respect of the adult, including any prescribed fees charged by the Public Guardian in connection with an application under this Part;
    (e) the payment for the provision of items other than those mentioned in paragraphs (a) to (d) such as the Public Guardian may, in any case, authorise.

DEFINITIONS
"adult" : s.1 (6)
"prescribed" : s.87 (1) (and see s.86)
"Public Guardian" : s.6 (1)

GENERAL NOTE
Subsection (1) is not a comprehensive statement of the scope of Pt. 3. The joint account provisions of s.32 do not involve authorisation by the Public Guardian, and are therefore not subject to subs. (2). Subsection (2) should be read subject to the limitation in s.30 (1) that funds used by a withdrawer must be applied only for the adult's benefit, and the extension in s.30 (2) allowing a withdrawer who lives with the adult to apply funds towards household expenses.

Adults in respect of whom applications may be made
24B.—(1) An application to the Public Guardian under this Part may be made only in relation to an adult who is incapable in relation to decisions about, or of safeguarding the adult's interests in, the funds to which the application relates.
    (2) But an application may not be made in the case of an adult in relation to whom—

    (a) there is a guardian of the type mentioned in section 33(1)(a) with powers relating to the funds in question;
    (b) there is a continuing attorney with powers relating to the funds in question; or
    (c) an intervention order relating to the funds in question has been granted.

DEFINITIONS
"adult" : s.1 (6)
"continuing attorney" : s.15 (2)
"incapable" : s.1 (6)
"intervention order" : s.53 (1)
"Public Guardian" : s.6 (1)

GENERAL NOTE

Subs. (1)
Applications to the Public Guardian under Pt. 3 are limited to adults with incapacity in relation to the relevant funds.

Subs. (2)(a)
The limitation to non-Scottish guardians described in s.33 (1)(a) presumably arises because s.31E (1), dealing with transition from guardianship to authority to intromit, explicitly envisages an application under Pt. 3 where there is a guardian, but non-Scottish guardians are explicitly excluded from s.31E (1) by s.31E (7).

Subs. (2)(c)
On the face of it, this provision—literally interpreted—would have the absurd effect of rendering Pt. 3 procedure unavailable where an intervention order (rather than a guardianship

order) had been granted expressly because the proceeds of transactions authorised by the intervention order, such as selling a house or realising investments, could thereafter be administered under Pt. 3. If it be assumed that the Parliament did not intend to create an absurdity, "and remains in force" must be implied at the end of this subsection. Also, it would appear to be wise for those drafting such intervention orders to exclude from the powers conferred any administration of the proceeds of such a realisation, beyond receiving them and putting them into an account, with explicit declaration that the intervention order does not relate to those funds once placed in such an account. It should however be noted that s.26G can now be used in circumstances previously requiring an intervention order.

Authority to take preliminary steps

Authority to provide information about funds
24C.—(1) This section applies where a person—

(a) believes than an adult holds funds in an account in the adult's sole name; but
(b) cannot make an application under section 25 or section 26G because the person does not know—

  (i) where the account is held;
  (ii) the account details;
  (iii) how much is held in the account; or
  (iv) any other information needed to complete the application.

(2) Where this section applies, the person may apply to the Public Guardian for a certificate authorising any fundholder to provide the person with such information as the person may reasonably require in order to make an application under section 25 or 26G.

(3) Where the Public Guardian grants an application under subsection (2), the Public Guardian must issue the certificate to the applicant.

(4) A fundholder presented with a certificate issued under subsection (3) is not prevented by—

(a) any obligation as to secrecy; or
(b) any other restriction on disclosure of information,

from providing the person who presents the certificate to it with such information as the person may reasonably require in order to make an application under section 25 or 26G about funds held by it on behalf of the adult.

DEFINITIONS
"adult" : s.1 (6)
"fundholder" : s.33 (2)
"Public Guardian" : s.6 (1)

GENERAL NOTE
This new provision arises from concerns of fundholders about whether and to whom they might properly release confidential information when an application for authority to intromit was proposed. They may now properly release confidential information to the person to whom the Public Guardian has issued a certificate under this section. The section requires that an application for authority to intromit under s.25, or an application for authority to transfer funds under s.26G, is contemplated, but the person to whom the certificate is issued is not bound to proceed with such an application once the information has been released. Some other procedure—or no procedure—may be shown to be appropriate. The confidentiality of the information provided, following release under this procedure, is not regulated by the Act.

The person who obtains the certificate is however bound by the s.1 principles, and it seems reasonable to suggest that common law fiduciary duties and duties of care referred to in s.82 apply to them. The Act does not expressly direct the fundholder to release information, but it would appear that upon submission of the certificate the fundholder becomes subject to the s.1 principles and could be subject to a direction under s.3 (3). For procedural requirements under this section see ss.27 *et seq.*

Authority to open account in adult's name
24D.—(1) This section applies where—

    (a) a person believes that—

        (i) an adult holds funds;
        (ii) an adult is entitled to income or other payments or is likely to become so entitled; or
        (iii) a fundholder holds funds on behalf of an adult; but

    (b) the adult does not have a suitable account in the adult's sole name in which the funds, income or other payments can be placed for the purposes of intromitting with the adult's funds under this Part.

(2) Where this section applies, the person may apply to the Public Guardian for a certificate authorising the opening of an account in the adult's name for the purpose of intromitting with the adult's funds.
(3) Where the Public Guardian grants an application under subsection (2), the Public Guardian must issue the certificate to the applicant.
(4) The certificate issued under subsection (3) may specify the kind of account which may be opened by a fundholder.
(5) A fundholder presented with a certificate issued under subsection (3) may open an account in the adult's name.
(6) But, if the certificate specifies a kind of account, the fundholder may open only an account of the type specified.
(7) On an account being opened in pursuance of subsection (5), the applicant must notify prescribed particulars of the account to the Public Guardian.

DEFINITIONS
"adult" : s.1 (6)
"fundholder" : s.33 (2)
"prescribed" : s.87 (1) (and see s.86)
"Public Guardian" : s.6 (1)

GENERAL NOTE
This section allows for a new account to be opened to receive and hold funds of the adult to be accessed for the purposes of subsequent administration under Pt. 3. Procedure under s.26G may be necessary to put funds into the new account. In some cases procedure under both s.24C and s.24D may be required prior to an application for authority to intromit. See s.25 (3) when applications under ss.24D and 25 (1) are submitted to the Public Guardian simultaneously. Where an account is opened under s.24D, that account is "the adult's current account" for the purposes of s.26 (3)(a). For procedural requirements under s.24D, see ss.27 *et seq.*

Authority to intromit

Authority to intromit
25.—(1) A person mentioned in subsection (2) may apply to the Public Guardian for a certificate authorising the person to intromit with an adult's funds.

(2) Those persons are—

(a) an individual (other than an individual acting in his capacity as an officer of a local authority or other body established by or under an enactment);
(b) two or more individuals who wish to act jointly; or
(c) a body (other than a manager of an authorised establishment within the meaning of section 35(2)).

(3) An application under subsection (1) which is accompanied by an application under section 24D may only be granted if—

(a) an account is opened in pursuance of section 24D(5); and
(b) prescribed particulars of that account are notified to the Public Guardian in pursuance of section 24D(7).

(4) Where the Public Guardian grants an application under subsection (1), the Public Guardian must—

(a) enter prescribed particulars in the register maintained by the Public Guardian under section 6(2)(b)(iii); and
(b) issue a certificate of authority (a "withdrawal certificate") to the applicant.

(5) No application may be made under subsection (1) if a person is already authorised to intromit with the funds of the adult to whom the application relates (unless the application is made by that person).

(6) In this Act, an individual or a body who holds a valid withdrawal certificate issued under this Part is referred to as a "withdrawer".

DEFINITIONS
"adult" : s.1 (6)
"prescribed" : s.87 (1) (and see s.86)
"Public Guardian" : s.6 (1)
"withdrawal certificate" : ss.25 (4)(b), 26E (3)(b) and 33 (2) (see also s.27G (3))
"withdrawer" : s.25 (6)

GENERAL NOTE
This section provides for applications for authority to intromit. If any such authority is already in force in respect of the same adult, only the existing withdrawer may make a subsequent application under this section. The range of permitted applicants has been extended to allow for joint withdrawers or a corporate withdrawer. As with guardianship, a joint withdrawer may be appointed at the outset or added subsequently under s.26B. A reserve withdrawer may be appointed under s.26D. For procedural requirements under s.25 see ss.27 *et seq.*

Subs. (3)
This subsection provides for simultaneous submission of an application under s.24D to open a new account and an application under this section for authority to intromit. The application under this section may only be granted once the new account has been opened and prescribed particulars notified to the Public Guardian.

Subs. (6)
The "withdrawer" becomes the "main withdrawer" in ss.26D and 26E, which provide for reserve withdrawers. Note that the account with which the withdrawer is authorised to intromit is termed the "specified account". That definition is contained neither in s.25 nor in s.26, but in s.26A (4).

Adults with Incapacity (Scotland) Act 2000 (Pt. 3)

Authority to intromit: application
26.—(1) An application under section 25(1) must—

(a) state the purposes of the proposed intromission with the adult's funds, setting out the specific sums relating to each purpose;
(b) specify an account held by a fundholder in the adult's sole name which the applicant wishes to use for the purpose of intromitting with the adult's funds (or be accompanied by an application under section 24D to open an account for that purpose);
(c) contain an undertaking that the applicant will open an account (the "designated account") solely for the purposes of—
   (i) receiving funds transferred under the authority of any certificate granted; and
   (ii) intromitting with those funds;

(2) The application may also specify another account held by a fundholder in the adult's sole name which the applicant also wishes to use for the purpose of intromitting with the adult's funds (or be accompanied by an application under section 24D to open an account for that purpose).
(3) In this Part—

(a) the account specified or, as the case may be, opened for the purposes of subsection (1)(b) is referred to as the adult's current account.
(b) the account specified or, as the case may be, opened for the purposes of subsection (2) is referred to as the adult's second account.

DEFINITIONS
"adult" : s.1 (6)
"the adult's current account" : s.26 (3)(a)
"the adult's second account" : s.26 (3)(b)
"designated account" : s.26 (1)(c)
"fundholder" : s.33 (2)

GENERAL NOTE
The application must contain a budget of proposed expenditure. Having regard to s.26A (1)(b), it will require to propose which payments within the budget shall be made by standing order, direct debit or otherwise from the adult's current account in accordance with that section. The application must either specify the account to be accessed, or must be accompanied by an application under s.24D to open a new account to be accessed. The account to be accessed was previously called the "specified account", and is now called "the adult's current account". The application must contain an undertaking to open the "designated account", which will be the operating account which will receive funds from the adult's current account, and from which the budgeted expenditure will be paid, except for payments made by standing order, direct debit or otherwise from the adult's current account under s.26A (1)(b). The application may also specify a "second account" in the adult's name, or be accompanied by an application under s.24D to open a "second account". Note that under s.26A (1) the certificate may authorise transfer of funds into the second account from the adult's current account and/or the designated account, but not out of the second account. It is envisaged that the second account will normally be a savings or deposit type of account in which surplus funds can be held at a higher rate of interest than in the designated account or the adult's current account. See the note to s.26G regarding the possibility of using procedure under that section to transfer funds out of the second account.

Withdrawal certificates

Withdrawal certificates
26A.—(1) A withdrawal certificate may—

(a) authorise the transfer of funds—
> (i) from the adult's current account to the designated account;
> (ii) from the adult's current account to the adult's second account;
> (iii) from the designated account to the adult's second account;

(b) authorise the continuance or making of arrangements for the regular or occasional payment of funds from the adult's current account for specified purposes (for example: by standing order or direct debit);

(c) authorise the withdrawal of funds from the designated account for specified purposes;

(d) place limits on the amount of funds that may be so transferred, paid or withdrawn.

(2) But such a certificate does not authorise a transfer of funds or payment that would cause—

(a) the adult's current account;
(b) the adult's second account; or
(c) the designated account,

to become overdrawn.

(3) If any of the accounts mentioned in paragraphs (a) to (c) of subsection (2) is overdrawn, the fundholder of that account has a right of relief against the withdrawer.

(4) In subsection (1)(b), "specified" means specified in the certificate of appointment.

DEFINITIONS
"the adult's current account" : s.26 (3)(a)
"the adult's second account" : s.26 (3)(b)
"the designated account" : s.26 (1)(c)
"fundholder" : s.33 (2)
"specified" : in s.26A (1)(b), the definition in s.26A (4) applies
"withdrawal certificate" : ss.25 (4)(b), 26E (3)(b) and 33 (2) (see also s.27G (3))

GENERAL NOTE
The withdrawal certificate may authorise transfer of funds among accounts as described in the General Note to s.26, but not otherwise. See s.26G and the note thereto for other transfers. The withdrawal certificate may authorise payments by standing order, direct debit or otherwise from the adult's current account and the withdrawal of funds from the designated account, in all cases for the purposes specified in the certificate. Previously the budget of authorised expenditure fixed in this way could only be altered by ending the previous authority and making a fresh application. Now variation is possible under s.26F.

The withdrawal certificate does not (and cannot) authorise overdrawing on the adult's current account, the adult's second account or the designated account, and if such overdrawing occurs the fundholder has a right of relief against the withdrawer.

The definition of "specified" in subs. (4) is applied only to subs. (1)(b), but it appears that it should be applied also to subs. (1)(c) to give meaning to that provision.

Joint and reserve withdrawers

Addition of joint withdrawer
26B.—(1) This section applies where an individual has or individuals have been appointed as a withdrawer in relation to an adult.

Adults with Incapacity (Scotland) Act 2000 (Pt. 3)

(2) Where this sections applies, another individual may apply to the Public Guardian for appointment as a joint withdrawer.

(3) An application under subsection (1) must be signed by the existing withdrawer.

(4) Where the Public Guardian grants an application under subsection (1), the Public Guardian must—

- (a) enter prescribed particulars in the register maintained by the Public Guardian under section 6(2)(b)(iii); and
- (b) issue a certificate of authority (a "withdrawal certificate") to the existing withdrawer and the applicant.

(5) Subject to sections 31(2) and 31A, a certificate issued under subsection (4)(b) is valid until the date on which the withdrawal certificate held by the existing withdrawer would cease to be valid under section 31(1) or 31E(6), as the case may be (regardless of any subsequent extension, reduction, termination or suspension of the existing withdrawer's authority).

(6) In this section, "the existing withdrawer" means the individual or individuals mentioned in subsection (1).

(7) In this Part, where two or more individuals are appointed as withdrawers, each individual is referred to as a "joint withdrawer".

DEFINITIONS
"adult" : s.1 (6)
"existing withdrawer" : s.26B (6)
"joint withdrawer" : s.26B (7)
"prescribed" : s.87 (1) (and see s.86)
"Public Guardian" : s.6 (1)
"withdrawal certificate" : ss.25 (4)(b), 26E (3)(b) and 33 (2) (see also s.27G (3))
"withdrawer" : s.25 (6)

GENERAL NOTE
Section 25 covers joint applications for authority to intromit. This s.26B applies when one or more withdrawers have already been authorised, and another person seeks to be added as a joint withdrawer. The joint appointment lasts for the duration of the existing appointment. For procedural requirements see ss.27 *et seq*.

Joint withdrawers: supplementary

26C.—(1) Joint withdrawers may, subject to subsection (2), exercise their functions individually, and each joint withdrawer is liable for any loss incurred by the adult arising out of—

- (a) the joint withdrawer's own acts or omissions; or
- (b) the joint withdrawer's failure to take reasonable steps to ensure that another joint withdrawer does not breach any duty of care or fiduciary duty owed to the adult.

(2) Where more than one joint withdrawer is liable under subsection (1), they are liable jointly and severally.

(3) A joint withdrawer must, before exercising any function conferred on the joint withdrawer, consult the other joint withdrawers, unless—

- (a) consultation would be impracticable in the circumstances; or
- (b) the joint withdrawers agree that consultation is not necessary.

(4) Where joint withdrawers disagree as to the exercise of their functions, one or more of them may apply to the Public Guardian for directions.

(5) Directions given by the Public Guardian in pursuance of subsection (4) may be appealed to the sheriff, whose decision is final.
(6) Where there are joint withdrawers—

(a) a third party in good faith is entitled to rely on the authority to act of any one or more of them; and
(b) section 31A(5) (interim authority) only applies where the Public Guardian terminates the authority of all of the joint withdrawers.

DEFINITIONS
"joint withdrawer" : s.26B (7)
"Public Guardian" : s.6 (1)

GENERAL NOTE
This section applies to all joint withdrawers, whether appointed under s.25 or s.26B. Subsections (1) and (2) mirror the provisions in relation to joint guardians of s.62 (6), and subss. (3) and (6)(c) mirror ss.62 (7) and (9) respectively. Under subss. (4) and (5) application may be made to the Public Guardian to resolve disputes between joint withdrawers, with appeal to the sheriff: but there is nothing to exclude application direct to the sheriff under s.3. The procedural provisions of s.27 *et seq* do not apply to an application to the Public Guardian under s.26C (4).

Reserve withdrawers: applications

26D.—(1) In any case where an individual is issued with a withdrawal certificate ("a main withdrawer"), the Public Guardian may, on an application by the main withdrawer, appoint another individual ("a reserve withdrawer") to act as a withdrawer in the event of the main withdrawer temporarily becoming unable to act.

(2) An application for appointment of a reserve withdrawer may be made at the time of the application under section 25 for a withdrawal certificate or at any later time.

(3) The application for appointment as a reserve withdrawer must be signed by the proposed reserve withdrawer.

(4) Where the Public Guardian grants the application, the Public Guardian must enter prescribed particulars in the register maintained by the Public Guardian under section 6(2)(b)(iii).

DEFINITIONS
"main withdrawer" : s.26D (1)
"prescribed" : s.87 (1) (and see s.86)
"Public Guardian" : s.6 (1)
"reserve withdrawer" : s.26D (1)
"withdrawal certificate" : ss.25 (4)(b), 26E (3)(b) and 33 (2) (see also s.27G (3))

GENERAL NOTE
This section and the next make provision for reserve withdrawers. Unlike joint withdrawers, reserve withdrawers cannot be equated to substitute guardians (under s.63). Differences include that under this section an application to appoint a reserve withdrawer may only be made by the main withdrawer; the reserve withdrawer is appointed to act only during temporary inability of the main withdrawer to act; and under s.27E (4) the authority of the reserve withdrawer terminates on termination of the main withdrawer's authority. For procedural requirements under s.26D see ss.27 *et seq.*

Reserve withdrawers: authority to act

26E.—(1) Where—

(a) a reserve withdrawer has been appointed under section 26D; and

(b) the main withdrawer considers that the main withdrawer is or will be unable to carry out some or all of the main withdrawer's functions under this Part,

the main withdrawer may notify the Public Guardian that the main withdrawer wishes the Public Guardian to authorise the reserve withdrawer to intromit with the adult's funds for a specified period.

(2) Where a reserve withdrawer becomes aware that the main withdrawer is unable—

(a) to carry out some or all of the main withdrawer's functions in relation to intromitting with the funds concerned; and
(b) to notify the Public Guardian under subsection (1),

the reserve withdrawer may apply to the Public Guardian for a certificate authorising the reserve withdrawer to intromit with the adult's funds for a specified period.

(3) The Public Guardian, on being notified under subsection (1), must or, on an application under subsection (2), may—

(a) enter prescribed particulars in the register maintained by him under section 6(2)(b)(iii);
(b) issue a certificate of authority (a "withdrawal certificate") to the reserve withdrawer; and
(c) notify the adult and the main withdrawer.

(4) The certificate issued under subsection (3)(b) is—

(a) valid for the specified period, or such shorter period as the Public Guardian thinks fit, but does not extend beyond the date on which the validity of the withdrawal certificate issued to the main withdrawer would cease under section 31(1) or 31E(6), as the case may be;
(b) suspended during any period when the authority of the main withdrawer is suspended;
(c) terminated if the authority of the main withdrawer is terminated.

(5) The main withdrawer and the reserve withdrawer are liable (jointly and severally) for any loss incurred by the adult arising out of the reserve withdrawer's acts or omissions.

(6) In this section, "specified" means specified in the notice or, as the case may be, application.

DEFINITIONS
"adult" : s.1 (6)
"main withdrawer" : s.26D (1)
"prescribed" : s.87 (1) (and see s.86)
"Public Guardian" : s.6 (1)
"specified" : s.26E (6)
"reserve withdrawer" : s.26D (1)
"withdrawal certificate" : ss.25 (4)(b), 26E (3)(b) and 33 (2) (see also s.27G (3))

GENERAL NOTE
Normally the reserve withdrawer's authority to start acting will be triggered by the main withdrawer, but the Public Guardian has discretion to authorise the reserve withdrawer upon

Adults with Incapacity Legislation

application by the reserve withdrawer if the main withdrawer is unable to act and also unable to notify the Public Guardian. The authority of the reserve withdrawer may last for the remainder of the duration of the main withdrawer's appointment, or for a specified shorter period. See also note to s.26D. The procedural provisions of ss.27 *et seq* do not apply to procedure under this s.26E. Regarding notification to the adult under s.26E (3)(c), see s.11 regarding circumstances in which intimation must not be given to the adult.

Variation of withdrawer's authority

Variation of withdrawal certificate
26F.—(1) The Public Guardian may—

(a) on the application of a withdrawer, or
(b) if notified under section 30A,

vary the withdrawal certificate (the "existing certificate") issued to the withdrawer.
(2) But a withdrawal certificate may not be varied under this section so as to alter the period of validity of the certificate.
(3) Where the Public Guardian decides to vary the withdrawal certificate under subsection (1), the Public Guardian must—

(a) enter prescribed particulars in the register maintained by the Public Guardian under section 6(2)(b)(iii); and
(b) issue a varied withdrawal certificate to the withdrawer.

(4) The existing certificate ceases to be valid on the date the varied certificate is issued under subsection (3)(b).

DEFINITIONS
"prescribed" : s.87 (1) (and see s.86)
"Public Guardian" : s.6 (1)
"withdrawal certificate" : ss.25 (4)(b), 26E (3)(b) and 33 (2) (see also s.27G (3))
"withdrawer" : s.25 (6)

GENERAL NOTE
The former provisions for authority to intromit did not permit variation of the withdrawal certificate: variation could only be achieved by a fresh application. This section now provides a procedure for variation. It is likely to be used most commonly to alter the items in the approved budget, or to vary the amounts. This section may not be used to alter the duration of the authority: see s.31B for circumstances in which the validity of a withdrawal certificate may be extended. For procedural requirements under s.26F see ss.27 *et seq*.

Authority to transfer funds

Authority to transfer specified sums
26G.—(1) A person mentioned in subsection (2) may apply to the Public Guardian for a certificate authorising the transfer of a specified sum from a specified account ("the original account") in an adult's sole name to—

(a) the designated account;
(b) the adult's current account;
(c) the adult's second account; or
(d) such other account as may be specified.

(2) Those persons are—

Adults with Incapacity (Scotland) Act 2000 (Pt. 3)

(a) a withdrawer;
(b) a person who has applied for a withdrawal certificate under section 25;

(3) An application under subsection (1) may also seek authority—

(a) to close the original account;
(b) to terminate an arrangement for the payment of funds from the original account to another account (for example: a standing order or direct debit).

(4) Where the Public Guardian grants an application under subsection (1), the Public Guardian must—

(a) enter prescribed particulars in the register maintained by the Public Guardian under section 6(2)(b)(iii); and
(b) issue the certificate to the applicant.

(5) In this section, "specified" means specified in the application under subsection (1) or, as the case may be, in the certificate granted under subsection (4).

DEFINITIONS
"the adult's current account" : s.26 (3)(a)
"the adult's second account" : s.26 (3)(b)
"designated account" : s.26 (1)(c)
"the original account" : s.26G (1)
"prescribed" : s.87 (1) (and see s.86)
"Public Guardian" : s.6 (1)
"specified" : s.26G (5)
"withdrawal certificate" : ss.25 (4)(b), 26E (3)(b) and 33 (2) (see also s.27G (3))
"withdrawer" : s.25 (6)

GENERAL NOTE
This section provides a procedure to authorise a withdrawer, or a person who has applied for a withdrawal certificate, to transfer a specified sum from an account in the adult's sole name ("the original account") into the designated account, the adult's current account, the adult's second account or such other account as may be specified in the application. Under subs. (3) the application may also seek authority to close the original account and/or to terminate standing orders, direct debits or other payment arrangements from it.

Subs. (1)
A question arises whether the explicit mention of the designated account, the adult's current account and the adult's second account as transferee account signals an intention that the normal use of the procedure will be to consolidate funds in those accounts, but with discretion to the Public Guardian to authorise any other account as the transferee account; or whether the express mention of the designated account, the adult's current account and the adult's second account as transferee accounts must be interpreted as excluding them from coming within the definition of the "original account" because they are not similarly mentioned expressly in that definition. This commentator favours the former interpretation, so that this provision would provide a means to transfer funds out of the adult's second account (see note to s.26A). It must be regarded as significant that although the original account must be an account in the adult's sole name, "such other account as may be specified" apparently need not be in the adult's sole name. It would appear that the transferee account could perhaps be, for example, a joint account operated under s.32. For procedural requirements under s.26G, see ss.27 *et seq.*

Applications: general

Applications: general requirements
27.—(1) An application under section 24C, 24D, 25, 26B, 26D, 26F or 26G must—

(a) be signed by the applicant;
(b) contain the name and addresses of the nearest relative, named person and primary carer of the adult, if known;
(c) be submitted to the Public Guardian no later than 14 days after—
  (i) where it is required to be countersigned under section 27A, the day the application is so countersigned, or
  (ii) in any other case, the day the application is signed by the applicant as mentioned in paragraph (a).

DEFINITIONS
"adult" : s.1 (6)
"named person" : s.87 (1) (referring to the definition in s.329 of the 2003 Act)
"nearest relative" : s.87 (1), subject to s.87 (2) and (3) (but see s.4)
"primary carer": s.87 (1)
"Public Guardian" : s.6 (1)

GENERAL NOTE
This section and the following ss.27A—27G contain procedural provisions common to various applications under Pt. 3. Note that there are variations at the beginning of each of those sections as to the procedures to which they apply. Note also that provisions regarding registration and issue of certificates by the Public Guardian are covered in the specific sections relating to each procedure, but s.27G (2) permits combined certificates. Under this s.27 all applications must be signed by the applicant and must give details (if known) of the nearest relative, named person and primary carer. Where applications require to be countersigned under s.27A, they must be submitted to the Public Guardian within 14 days of countersignature. Where they do not require to be countersigned, they must be submitted to the Public Guardian within 14 days of signature by the applicant.

Section 27G (1) permits the Public Guardian to disapply this s.27 in relation to multiple applications to which s.27G applies. See the composite application form ATF2.

Countersigning of applications

27A.—(1) An application under section 24C, 24D, 25, or 26B must be countersigned by a person who must declare in the application that—

(a) the person knows the applicant and has known the applicant for at least one year prior to the date of the application;
(b) the person is not any of the following—
  (i) a relative of or person residing with the applicant or the adult;
  (ii) a director or employee of the fundholder;
  (iii) a solicitor acting on behalf of the adult or any other person mentioned in this paragraph in relation to any matter under this Act;
  (iv) the medical practitioner who has issued the certificate under section 27B in connection with the application;
  (v) a guardian of the adult;
  (vi) a welfare or continuing attorney of the adult;
  (vii) a person who is authorised under an intervention order in relation to the adult;
(c) the person believes the information contained in the application to be true; and
(d) the person believes the applicant to be a fit and proper person to intromit with the adult's funds.

(2) An application under section 26D (reserve withdrawers) must be countersigned by a person who must declare in the application the matters

Adults with Incapacity (Scotland) Act 2000 (Pt. 3)

set out in paragraphs (a) to (d) of subsection (1) but with references in those paragraphs to "applicant" read as references to the proposed reserve withdrawer.

(3) This section does not apply to an application made by a body.

DEFINITIONS
"adult" : s.1 (6)
"continuing attorney" : s.15 (2)
"fundholder" : s.33 (2)
"guardian" : s.33 (1)(a)
"intervention order" : s.53 (1)
"reserve withdrawer" : s.26D (1)
"welfare attorney" : s.16 (2)

GENERAL NOTE
Previously, the countersignatory under Pt. 3 required to be a person within a prescribed category, and required to have known the applicant for at least two years and also to know the adult. Not uncommonly it was difficult, and sometimes it was impossible, to find a qualified signatory who knew the adult as well as having known the applicant for two years. The requirements for the countersignatory to be a person in a prescribed class, and to know the adult as well as the applicant, have been dropped. The countersignatory now requires to have known the applicant for one year. To the previous lists of persons disqualified to be countersignatories there have been added guardians, welfare and continuing attorneys and a person authorised under an intervention order. It would seem that former holders of these positions are not excluded. As before, the countersignatory is required to declare that he or she believes the information contained in the application to be true and believes the applicant to be a fit and proper person to intromit with the adult's funds. Subsection (2) adapts the provisions of subs. (1) to an application under s.26D to appoint a reserve withdrawer. The provisions of this section do not apply to applications under s.26F to vary the withdrawal certificate, or under s.26G to transfer funds, or to any application by a body rather than an individual. The provisions of this section may under s.31B (4) be disapplied by the Public Guardian in relation to a renewal application under s.31B, and under s.27G in relation to multiple applications under s.27G.

Medical certificates

27B. An application under section 24C, 24D, or 25 must be accompanied by a certificate in prescribed form from a medical practitioner that the adult is—

(a) incapable in relation to decisions about; or
(b) incapable of acting to safeguard or promote the adult's interests in,

the adult's funds.

DEFINITIONS
"adult" : s.1 (6)
"incapable" : s.1 (6)
"prescribed" : s.87 (1) (and see s.86)

GENERAL NOTE
Medical certificates under this section are required only for applications for authority to provide information under s.24C, applications to open an account in the adult's name under s.24D, and applications for authority to intromit under s.25. The provisions of this section may under s.31B (4) be disapplied by the Public Guardian in relation to a renewal application under s.31B, and under s.27G in relation to multiple applications under s.27G.

Intimation of applications

27C.—(1) On receipt of a competent application under section 24C, 24D, 25, 26B, 26D, 26F or 26G, the Public Guardian must intimate the application to—

Adults with Incapacity Legislation

(a) the adult;
(b) the adult's nearest relative;
(c) the adult's primary carer;
(d) the adult's named person;
(e) where the applicant is—

(i) the individual mentioned in both paragraph (b) and (c); or
(ii) a body other than a local authority,

the chief social work officer of the local authority; and
(f) any other person who the Public Guardian considers has an interest in the application.

(2) A competent application is an application which complies with section 27 and, where appropriate, sections 27A and 27B.

DEFINITIONS
"adult" : s.1 (6)
"competent application" : s.27C (2)
"local authority" : s.87 (1) (referring to the Local Government etc. (Scotland) Act 1994 (c.39) s.2)
"named person" : s.87 (1) (referring to the definition in s.329 of the 2003 Act)
"nearest relative" : s.87 (1), subject to s.87 (2) and (3) (but see s.4)
"primary carer" : s.87 (1)
"Public Guardian" : s.6 (1)

GENERAL NOTE
This section sets out the intimation requirements for all applications other than applications to authorise reserve withdrawers to act under s.26E.

Subs. (1)(a)
See s.11 for provisions disapplying the requirement to intimate to the adult.

Subs. (1)(e)
For most purposes under this Act the role of the chief social work officer of the local authority is in relation to personal welfare matters rather than financial matters. Applications to which s.27C applies must however be notified to the chief social work officer of the local authority in two circumstances, firstly where the applicant is both nearest relative and primary carer, and secondly where the applicant is a body rather than an individual (and is not the local authority).

Determination of applications: applicant to be fit and proper
27D.—(1) The Public Guardian may grant an application made under section 24C, 24D, 25, 26B or 26D only if satisfied that—

(a) the applicant in an application under section 24C, 24D, 25 or 26B, or
(b) the proposed reserve withdrawer in an application under section 26D,

is a fit and proper person to intromit with the funds of the adult.

(2) In deciding whether a person is fit and proper, the Public Guardian must have regard to any guidance issued in relation to that matter by the Scottish Ministers.

DEFINITIONS
"Public Guardian" : s.6 (1)
"reserve withdrawer" : s.26D (1)

General Note
For all of the categories of application requiring countersignature under s.27A, the Public Guardian may grant the application only if satisfied that the applicant is a fit and proper person to intromit with the adult's funds. The evidence to this effect will normally be provided by the countersignatory in accordance with s.27A (1)(d). A countersignatory's certificate is not required in respect of a proposed reserve withdrawer, but the Public Guardian nevertheless requires to be satisfied that a proposed reserve withdrawer is a fit and proper person to intromit with the adult's funds.

Determination of applications: opportunity to make representations
27E.—(1) The Public Guardian must not grant an application under section 24C, 24D, 25, 26B, 26D, 26F or 26G without affording to any person who receives intimation of the application under section 27C or any other person who wishes to object an opportunity to make representations.

(2) Where the Public Guardian proposes to refuse the application the Public Guardian must intimate the proposed decision to the applicant and advise the applicant of the prescribed period within which the applicant may object to the proposed refusal.

(3) The Public Guardian must not refuse an application without affording to the applicant, if the applicant objects, an opportunity to make representations.

Definitions
"prescribed" : s.87 (1) (and see s.86)
"Public Guardian" : s.6 (1)

General Note
Any person who receives intimation under the intimation provisions of s.27C, or any other person who wishes to object, must have an opportunity to make representations. A proposal to refuse an application must be intimated by the Public Guardian to the applicant. The applicant may object to the proposed refusal, in which case the Public Guardian must give the applicant an opportunity to make representations, before actually refusing the application.

Referral of application to sheriff
27F.—(1) The Public Guardian may remit an application under section 24C, 24D, 25,26B, 26D, 26F or 26G for determination by the sheriff at the instance of—

(a) the Public Guardian;
(b) the applicant; or
(c) any person who objects to the granting of the application.

(2) The sheriff's decision on an application remitted under subsection (1) is final.

Definitions
"Public Guardian" : s.6 (1)

General Note
This section provides a procedure for determination of applications by the sheriff, whose decision is final.

Multiple applications etc.
27G.—(1) Where a person who has made an application under section 24C, 24D or 25 in respect of an adult makes another application under any of those sections in respect of the same adult, the Public Guardian may disapply any of the provisions in sections 27 to 27B to that application.

(2) Where the Public Guardian is to issue more than one certificate under this Part to the same person, the Public Guardian may instead issue a combined certificate to the person.

(3) References in this Part to a withdrawal certificate or other certificate issued under this Part include references to any combined certificate issued by the Public Guardian instead of the withdrawal or other certificate.

DEFINITIONS
"withdrawal certificate" : ss.25 (4)(b), 26E (3)(b) and 33 (2) (see also s.27G (3))
"Public Guardian" : s.6 (1)
"adult" : s.1 (6)

GENERAL NOTE
This section applies where the same person makes in respect of the same adult more than one application under any of the provisions of ss.24C (applications for authority to provide information), 24D (authority to open an account) and 25 (authority to intromit). The Public Guardian may disapply any of the provisions of ss.27, 27A and 27B, and may issue a combined certificate instead of separate certificates. See the composite application form ATF2.

Fundholders

Fundholders of adult's current account and adult's second account

28.—(1) The fundholder of an adult's current account may act on the instructions of a withdrawer to the extent authorised by the withdrawal certificate issued to the withdrawer.

(2) The fundholder of an adult's current account presented with a withdrawal certificate must not allow any operations to be carried out on that account other than those carried out in accordance with the certificate by the withdrawer.

(3) The fundholder of an adult's current account or an adult's second account presented with a withdrawal certificate may provide the withdrawer with a copy of any statement or other correspondence issued by the fundholder to the adult during the period when the withdrawal certificate is valid.

DEFINITIONS
"adult's current account" : s.26 (3)(a)
"adult's second account" : s.26 (3)(b)
"fundholder" : s.33 (2)
"withdrawal certificate" : ss.25 (4)(b), 26E (3)(b) and 33 (2) (see also s.27G (3))
"withdrawer" : s.25 (6)

GENERAL NOTE
This section authorises fundholders to operate the adult's current account in accordance with, but only in accordance with, the authority contained in the withdrawal certificate. This section also authorises the fundholder to provide the withdrawer with copies of statements and other correspondence issued to the adult during the period covered by the withdrawal certificate. On disclosure of information by fundholders, see also s.24C. On the fundholder's liability, see s.29.

Fundholder of original account

28A.—The fundholder of an original account may act on the instructions of a withdrawer to the extent authorised by the certificate issued to the withdrawer under section 26G(4).

DEFINITIONS
"fundholder" : s.33 (2)

"original account" : s.26G (1)
"withdrawer" : s.25 (6)

GENERAL NOTE
This section authorises fundholders to act in accordance with authority under s.26G to transfer funds from "the original account" as defined in s.26G, to close the original account, and to terminate standing order, direct debit and other payment arrangements. See also the provisions of s.29 regarding the fundholder's liability.

Fundholder's liability

29.—The fundholder of an account mentioned in section 28 or 28A is liable to the adult for any funds removed from the account under that section at any time when it was aware that the withdrawer's authority had been terminated or suspended by the Public Guardian under section 31A but, on meeting such liability, the fundholder of the account has a right of relief against the withdrawer.

DEFINITIONS
"Public Guardian" : s.6 (1)
"withdrawer" : s.25 (6)
"adult" : s.1 (6)
"fundholder" : s.33 (2)

GENERAL NOTE
This section applies where funds are removed from an account in accordance with ss.28 or 28A when the fundholder was aware that the withdrawer's authority had been terminated or suspended by the Public Guardian under s.31A. The fundholder is liable to the adult for funds so removed, with a right of relief against the withdrawer.

Withdrawers

Use of funds by withdrawer

30.—(1) Any funds used by the withdrawer must be applied only for the benefit of the adult.

(2) Despite subsection (1), where the withdrawer lives with the adult, the withdrawer may, to the extent authorised by the certificate, apply any funds withdrawn towards household expenses.

DEFINITIONS
"adult" : s.1 (6)
"withdrawer" : s.25 (6)

GENERAL NOTE
This section applies in addition to the terms of s.24A (2).

Notification of change of address

30A.—(1) A withdrawer must notify the Public Guardian—

(a) of any change in the withdrawer's address; and
(b) of any change in the address of the adult.

(2) A notice under subsection (1) must be given within 7 days of the date of the change to which it relates.

DEFINITIONS
"adult" : s.1 (6)

"Public Guardian" : s.6 (1)
"withdrawer" : s.25 (6)

GENERAL NOTE
This section requires withdrawers to notify the Public Guardian within seven days of any change in the address of the withdrawer or the adult.

Records and inquiries
30B.—(1) A withdrawer must keep records of the exercise of the withdrawer's powers.

(2) The Public Guardian may make inquiries from time to time as to the manner in which a withdrawer has exercised the withdrawer's functions under this Part.

DEFINITIONS
"Public Guardian" : s.6 (1)
"withdrawer" : s.25 (6)

GENERAL NOTE
The withdrawer must keep records and the Public Guardian must from time to time make enquiries, but neither the nature of the records nor the nature or frequency of the enquiries are specified.

Duration etc. of authority

Duration of withdrawal certificate
31.—(1) Unless this Part provides otherwise, a withdrawal certificate issued under section 25 is valid for a period of 3 years commencing with the date of issue of the certificate.

(2) The Public Guardian may reduce or extend the period of validity of a withdrawal certificate; and an extension may be without limit of time.

(3) Subsections (1) and (2) are without prejudice to the right of the withdrawer to make subsequent applications under section 25 after the withdrawal certificate ceases to be valid or, as the case may be, a suspension or termination of the withdrawer's authority.

(4) The validity of a withdrawal certificate ceases—

(a) on the appointment of a guardian with powers relating to the funds or account in question;
(b) on the granting of an intervention order relating to the funds or account in question; or
(c) on a continuing attorney's acquiring authority to act in relation to the funds or account in question,

but no liability is incurred by any person who acts in good faith under this Part in ignorance of the withdrawal certificate ceasing to be valid under this subsection.

DEFINITIONS
"continuing attorney" : s.15 (2)
"intervention order" : s.53 (1)
"Public Guardian" : s.6 (1)
"withdrawal certificate" : ss.25 (4)(b), 26E (3)(b) and 33 (2) (see also s.27G (3))
"withdrawer" : s.25 (6)

Adults with Incapacity (Scotland) Act 2000 (Pt. 3)

GENERAL NOTE
As with initial guardianship appointments, the normal duration of a withdrawal certificate is three years (subs. (1)) but the period may be varied by the Public Guardian. In cases of elderly adults whose capacity will not improve, guardianships are frequently granted without limit of time: the Public Guardian may do likewise with withdrawal certificates. Section 24B (2) sets out circumstances in which Pt. 3 applications may not be made: s.31 (4) provides that a withdrawal certificate will cease if any of those circumstances subsequently arise, but with protection for anyone acting in good faith and unaware of the cessation. There are no mandatory notification provisions under s.31 (4), but it would obviously be sensible for the new appointee to ensure that notice is given as may be appropriate.

Suspension and termination of authority
31A.—(1) The Public Guardian may suspend or terminate the authority of a withdrawer under a withdrawal certificate.

(2) The Public Guardian must without delay intimate the suspension or termination to—

  (a) the withdrawer whose authority is suspended or terminated;
  (b) any other joint withdrawer;
  (c) any reserve withdrawer; and
  (d) the fundholder of the designated account; and
  (e) such other persons as the Public Guardian thinks fit.

(3) A suspension or termination under subsection (1) suspends or, as the case may be, terminates all operations on the designated account by the withdrawer whose authority is suspended or terminated.

(4) The Public Guardian must on suspending or terminating the authority of the withdrawer enter prescribed particulars in the register maintained by the Public Guardian under section 6(2)(b)(iii).

(5) The Public Guardian may on terminating the authority of the withdrawer issue to the withdrawer an interim withdrawal certificate to continue to intromit with the adult's funds for a period not exceeding 4 weeks from the date of the termination.

DEFINITIONS
"designated account" : s.26 (1)(c)
"fundholder" : s.33 (2)
"joint withdrawer" : s.26B (7)
"prescribed" : s.87 (1) (and see s.86)
"Public Guardian" : s.6 (1)
"reserve withdrawer" : s.26D (1)
"withdrawal certificate" : ss.25 (4)(b), 26E (3)(b) and 33 (2) (see also s.27G (3))

GENERAL NOTE
This section permits the Public Guardian to suspend or terminate the withdrawer's authority to act. The Public Guardian may in effect give up to four weeks' notice of termination by issuing an interim withdrawal certificate: otherwise the termination takes immediate effect, as do all suspensions. Under s.26C (6)(b), where there are joint withdrawers an interim certificate may only be issued if the authority of all of them is terminated. Otherwise, the remaining withdrawer(s) continue(s) to act. The mandatory notification provisions of this section do not include the adult, but one would expect the Public Guardian to notify the adult if (for example) authority to withdraw was terminated because the adult had regained relevant capacity.

Renewal of authority to intromit
31B.—(1) This section applies to an application under section 25 if condition A or B is satisfied.

(2) Condition A is that the application is made by a person holding an existing withdrawal certificate.

(3) Condition B is that—

> (a) the main withdrawer has died or become incapable or the main withdrawer's authority under this Part has been terminated; and
> (b) the application is made, without undue delay, by an individual who was the reserve withdrawer at the time of the death, incapacity, or termination, as the case may be.

(4) Where this section applies, the Public Guardian may disapply any of the provisions in sections 26(1), 27A and 27B to an application to which this section applies (but may require the applicant to provide such other information as the Public Guardian requires to determine the application).

(5) Where condition A is satisfied in relation to an application under section 25, the existing withdrawal certificate will continue to be valid until the application is determined.

(6) Where an application to which this section applies is granted, the existing withdrawal certificate ceases to be valid.

DEFINITIONS
"incapable" : s.1 (6)
"Public Guardian" : s.6 (1)
"reserve withdrawer" : s.26D (1)
"withdrawal certificate": ss.25 (4)(b), 26E (3)(b) and 33 (2) (see also s.27G (3))
"withdrawer" : s.25 (6)

GENERAL NOTE
Where the holder of an existing withdrawal certificate makes a fresh application for a withdrawal certificate, the Public Guardian may disapply any of the provisions of s.26 (1) (which contains the requirements for a statement of purposes and amounts of proposed intromissions, a statement of the account to be accessed and an undertaking to open the designated account), s.27A (requiring applications to be countersigned) and s.27B (requiring a medical certificate), and (as with guardianship) the existing withdrawal certificate will if necessary continue to be valid until the fresh application is determined, in order to avoid a gap. The Public Guardian may also disapply any of the provisions in ss.26 (1), 27A and 27B in the case of an application by a reserve withdrawer made without undue delay following the death, incapacity or termination of authority of the main withdrawer.

Subsection (6) makes it clear that two withdrawal certificates may not exist in parallel. The fresh withdrawal certificate will supersede the previous one.

Duration of certificates issued under section 24C, 24D, and 26G etc.

31C.—(1) A certificate issued under section 24C, 24D or 26G is valid for such period as it may specify.

(2) But the Public Guardian may cancel the certificate at any time before the end of any period so specified.

(3) The Public Guardian must without delay intimate such a cancellation to—

> (a) the person to whom the certificate was issued,
> (b) where the certificate was issued under section 26G, the fundholder of the original account, and
> (c) such other persons as the Public Guardian thinks fit.

DEFINITIONS
"fundholder" : s.33 (2)
"Public Guardian" : s.6 (1)

GENERAL NOTE
Certificates of authority to provide information about funds (under s.24C), certificates of authority to open an account in the adult's name (under s.24D) and certificates authorising transfer of specified sums (under s.26G) are all valid for the period specified in the relevant certificate, but may be cancelled by the Public Guardian in accordance with the provisions of this section. Note that, as with suspension or termination of a withdrawal certificate, there is no requirement to intimate cancellation to the adult.

Appeals

Appeals
31D.—(1) A decision of the Public Guardian—

(a) to grant or refuse an application under section 24C, 24D, 25, 26B, 26D, 26E, 26F or 26G;
(b) to refuse to remit an application to the sheriff under section 27F;
(c) to reduce or extend the period of validity of a withdrawal certificate under section 31(2); or
(d) to suspend or terminate the authority of a withdrawer under section 31A,

may be appealed to the sheriff.
(2) The sheriff's decision on an appeal under subsection (1) is final.

DEFINITIONS
"Public Guardian" : s.6 (1)
"withdrawal certificate" : ss.25 (4)(b), 26E (3)(b) and 33 (2) (see also s.27G (3))
"withdrawer" : s.25 (6)

GENERAL NOTE
The range of decisions which may be made by the Public Guardian under Pt. 3 may be appealed to the sheriff, whose decision is final.

Transition from guardianship
31E.—(1) This section applies where—

(a) there is a guardian with powers relating to the property or financial affairs of an adult; and
(b) an application is made under section 25 in relation to the adult's funds.

(2) Section 27A does not apply to the application if it is made by the adult's guardian.
(3) The Public Guardian may disapply section 27B to the application.
(4) Where—

(a) it appears to the Public Guardian that, if the application were granted, the adult's interests in the adult's property and affairs can be satisfactorily safeguarded or promoted otherwise than by the existing guardianship; and
(b) the Public Guardian proposes to grant the application,

the Public Guardian must initiate the recall of the guardianship under section 73.

(5) The Public Guardian may not grant the application unless the guardianship is recalled.

(6) Where the Public Guardian grants the application, the withdrawal certificate issued to the withdrawer is valid for such period as the Public Guardian specifies at the time the Public Guardian grants the application.

(7) This section does not apply, and no application under this Part may be made, in the case of an adult if there is a person who is—

(a) appointed or otherwise entitled under the law of any country other than Scotland to act as a guardian (however called) in relation to the adult's property and financial affairs during the adult's incapacity, and

(b) recognised by the law of Scotland as the adult's guardian.

(8) Despite subsection (7), no liability is incurred by any person who acts in good faith under this Part in ignorance of any guardian of the type mentioned in that subsection.

DEFINITIONS
"adult" : s.1 (6)
"Public Guardian" : s.6 (1)
"withdrawer" : s.25 (6)

GENERAL NOTE
Under the previous Pt. 3, the Public Guardian helpfully assisted financial guardians to make the transition from guardianship to Pt. 3 administration, so far as her powers and judicious exercise of discretion enabled her to do so. Under the s.1 principles, guardians have a duty to convert financial guardianship to Pt. 3 administration when Pt. 3 administration will suffice and there is no significant prospect of guardianship powers being required in future. With the enhanced provisions of the new Pt. 3, such transitions are likely to become more frequent. This section facilitates the process of transition by disapplying the requirement for counter-signature under s.27A (per subs. (2)) and giving the Public Guardian discretion to disapply the requirement for a medical certificate under s.27B (per subs. (3)): which is likely to be appropriate in cases where the certificate for the guardianship application (or most recent renewal) confirms that incapacity is permanent, and the Public Guardian has no reason to think otherwise.

Subsections (4), (5) and (6) set out the mechanism for implementing the transition in the circumstances described in subs. (1), namely where there is an existing financial guardianship and an application for authority to intromit under s.25 is made. The Public Guardian will consider whether the proposed transition from guardianship to authority to intromit is appropriate and whether she proposes to grant the application. If so, she will initiate recall of the guardianship under the recall procedure provided for under s.73. Authority to intromit may only actually be granted if and when the guardianship has been recalled. The Public Guardian then will grant a withdrawal certificate for such period as she may specify: which appears to displace the presumption in favour of a three-year duration in s.31. In the case of an elderly adult with permanent impairment of capacity, where the guardianship order was without limit of time, the Public Guardian may well be disposed to issue a withdrawal certificate also without limit of time.

Under subs. (7), non-Scottish guardianships cannot be superseded by authority to intromit in this way. Subsection (8) protects anyone acting in good faith under this section, in ignorance of the existence of a non-Scottish guardianship.

Miscellaneous

Joint accounts
32.—Where an individual who along with one or more others is the holder of a joint account with a fundholder becomes incapable in relation to

decisions about, or of safeguarding the individual's interests in, the funds in the account, any other joint account holder may continue to operate the account unless—

(a) the terms of the account provide otherwise; or
(b) the joint account holder is barred by an order of any court from so doing.

DEFINITIONS
"fundholder" : s.33 (2)
"incapable" : s.1 (6)

GENERAL NOTE
This section stands alone. It permits one holder of an account in joint names, operable by either, to continue to intromit during incapacity of the other (or, where they are several and each may operate alone, remaining holders to intromit during the incapacity of one), unless the terms of the account or a court order provide otherwise. Those holding and opening joint accounts operable by each require to be alert to this provision, as in some cases (including many joint accounts operated for commercial purposes) they may wish to opt out of this provision.

Since April 1, 2008 this section is no longer disapplied where there is a guardian or continuing attorney with powers relating to such an account, or an intervention order is granted in relation thereto. That is because s.34 of the 2000 text disapplied the whole of Pt. 3 in such circumstances, whereas s.24B now provides that no application may be made to the Public Guardian in such circumstances: and s.32, unlike the remainder of Pt 3, does not require an application to the Public Guardian.

Interpretation

Interpretation of Part
33.—(1) In section 24B, 27A and 31 any reference to—

(a) a guardian includes a reference to a guardian (however called) appointed under the law of any country to, or entitled under the law of any country to act for, an adult during his incapacity, if the guardianship is recognised by the law of Scotland;
(b) a continuing attorney includes a reference to a person granted, under a contract, grant or appointment governed by the law of any country, powers (however expressed) relating to the granter's property or financial affairs and having continuing effect notwithstanding the granter's incapacity.
(c) a welfare attorney includes a reference to a person granted, under a contract, grant or appointment governed by the law of any country, powers (however expressed) relating to the granter's personal welfare and having effect during the granter's incapacity.

(2) In this Part—

"fundholder" means a bank, building society or other similar body which holds funds on behalf of another person,
"withdrawal certificate" means a certificate issued under section 25, 26B, 26E, 26F or 31A.

DEFINITIONS
"adult" : s.1 (6)

"continuing attorney" : s.15 (2)
"incapacity" : s.1 (6)
"welfare attorney" : s.16 (2)

GENERAL NOTE
Under subs. (1) there is only limited application of Pt. 3 to foreign guardians and attorneys. They are excluded from relevant provisions of Pt. 3 except that a foreign guardian or attorney, like Scottish equivalents, may not be counter-signatory under s.27A, and the appointment of a foreign guardian with relevant powers terminates authority to intromit under s.31 in the same way as appointment of a Scottish guardian. The reference in subs. (1) to s.24B is strangely circular, as s.24B explicitly excludes any guardian or attorney such as is referred to in s.33 (1)(a).

Subsection (2) for some reason only contains two of the definitions applicable to Pt. 3. Other definitions are spread through Pt. 3, their locations being noted under "Definitions" in these annotations, as relevant. The general interpretation section of this Act is s.87, but of the Definitions particular to Pt. 3 only "withdrawer" is referred to in s.87 (1).

34. [*See fn.40 at the beginning of Pt. 3*]

PART 4

MANAGEMENT OF RESIDENTS' FINANCES

GENERAL NOTE
The scheme of management of residents' finances under this Part is described in the Introduction and General Note. Part 4 is disapplied where appointees specified in s.46 have relevant powers.

The general principles in s.1 (2)—(5) apply to Pt. 4. "The managers" of different categories of establishment are as defined in Sched. 1, and the principal supervisory role is vested in the relevant "supervisory body" as defined in s.40. However, persons exercising functions under Pt. 4 may be given directions by the sheriff under s.3 (3), and management under Pt. 4 does not exclude the investigative powers of the Public Guardian under s.6 (2)(d) (see also s.12). Section 81 (repayment of funds) and s.82 (limitation of liability) apply to managers of establishments, but they lose protection under s.82 if they fail to comply with the general principles in s.1.

For transitional provisions relevant to pre-2000 Act management of funds under the 1984 Act, see Sched. 4, paras. 5, 7(d) and 8.

Regulations
See SSI 2003/266 and SSI 2005/610.

Application of Part 4
35.—(1)[41] Subject to subsection (3), this Part applies to the management of the matters set out in section 39 relating to any resident of any of the following establishments—

(a) a health service hospital;
(b) an independent hospital [. . .][42] [or private psychiatric hospital][43];
(c) a State hospital;
(d) a care home service; and
(e) a limited registration service.

(2) In this Part establishments mentioned in paragraph (b), [(d) or (e)][44] of subsection (1) are referred to as "registered establishments", all other

---

[41] Substituted by Regulation of Care (Scotland) Act 2001 (asp 8), Sch.3, para.23(2)(a).
[42] Words repealed by Mental Health (Care and Treatment) (Scotland) Act 2003 (asp 13) Sch.5.
[43] Words inserted by Adults with Incapacity (Management of Residents' Finances) (Scotland) Regulations 2005 (SSI 2005/610), reg.2.
[44] Words substituted by Regulation of Care (Scotland) Act 2001 (asp 8), Sch.3, para.23(2)(b).

Adults with Incapacity (Scotland) Act 2000 (Pt. 4)

establishments mentioned in subsection (1) are referred to as "unregistered establishments", and registered and unregistered establishments together are referred to as "authorised establishments".

(3) This Part shall not apply to a registered establishment where notice in writing is given to the supervisory body by—

(a) the managers of the registered establishment; or
(b) an applicant, [under section 7(1) of the Regulation of Care (Scotland) Act 2001 (asp 8), for registration of the service which comprises that][45] establishment,

that it shall not apply.

(4) The Scottish Ministers may by regulations amend the list of authorised establishments set out in subsection (1).

(5) In this Part, "the managers" has the meaning set out in schedule 1; and "resident" in relation to an authorised establishment means an adult whose main residence for the time being is the authorised establishment or [whose detention is authorised by virtue of the Criminal Procedure (Scotland) Act 1995 (c.46) or the 2003 Act][46].

(6)[47] Expressions used in subsection (1) and in the Regulation of Care (Scotland) Act 2001 have the same meanings in that subsection as in that Act.

DEFINITIONS
"2003 Act, the": The Mental Health (Care and Treatment) (Scotland) Act 2003 (asp13) (per s.87 (1))
"adult" : s.1 (6)
"authorised establishments" : s.35 (2)
"care home service" : Regulation of Care (Scotland) Act 2001 (asp8) ("the 2001 Act") ss.2 (3) and 77 (1) (per s.35 (6))
"establishments" : s.35 (1)
"health service hospital": 2001 Act s.77 (1) (per s.35 (6))
"independent hospital" : 2001 Act s.77 (1) and (2) (per s.35 (6))
"limited registration service" : 2001 Act ss.8 (4) and 77 (1) (per s.35 (6))
"managers" : s.35 (5) and Sched. 1, para. 1
"nursing home" : The Nursing Homes Registration (Scotland) Act 1938 (c.73) s.10 (2) and (3)
"private psychiatric hospital" : 2001 Act s.77 (1) (per s.35 (6))
"registered establishments" : s.35 (2)
"resident" : s.35 (5)
"State hospital" : s.87 (1) (referring to the National Health Service (Scotland) Act 1978 (c.29) s.102)
"supervisory body" : s.40 (1)
"unregistered establishments" : s.35 (2)

GENERAL NOTE
Part 4 relates to the management of the affairs specified in s.39 of residents in "authorised establishments", being all establishments within the categories listed in subs. (1), except for those "registered establishments" which opt out under subs. (3), subject to any amendments to the list of authorised establishments by regulations under subs. (4), and subject (in the case of individual establishments) to revocation by the relevant supervisory body under s.45. Under subs. (2), authorised establishments are divided into those in categories (b), (d) and (e) of

---

[45] Words substituted by Regulation of Care (Scotland) Act 2001 (asp 8), Sch.3, para.23(2)(c).
[46] Words substituted by Mental Health (Care and Treatment) (Scotland) Act 2003 (asp 13), Sch.4, para.9(2).
[47] Inserted by Regulation of Care (Scotland) Act 2001 (asp 8), Sch.3, para.23(2)(d).

subs. (1), termed "registered establishments", and those within categories (a) and (c), which are termed "unregistered establishments". Subsection (5) incorporates the definition, in respect of different categories of authorised establishments, of "managers" set out in Sched. 1, and defines "resident".

Subs. (3)
Note that opting out is competent in relation to registered establishments only, not unregistered establishments (as to which see General Note above).
See also s.45 (2).

Registration for purposes of managing residents' finances
36. [. . .][48]

Residents whose affairs may be managed
37.—(1) The managers of an authorised establishment shall be entitled to manage on behalf of any resident in the establishment in relation to whom a certificate has been issued under subsection (2) any of the matters set out in section 39.

(2) Where the managers of an authorised establishment, having considered all other appropriate courses of action, have decided that management on behalf of the resident of the matters set out in section 39 by them is the most appropriate course of action, they shall cause to be examined by a medical practitioner any resident in the establishment who they believe may be incapable in relation to decisions as to, or of safeguarding his interest in, any of the resident's affairs referred to in section 39; and if the medical practitioner finds that the resident is so incapable he shall issue a certificate in prescribed form to that effect.

(3) Subject to subsection (8), the managers of the authorised establishment shall intimate their intention of requiring an examination under subsection (2) to the resident and to the resident's nearest relative [and named person][49].

(4) Subject to subsection (8), the managers of the authorised establishment shall—

  (a) send a copy of the certificate to the resident and to the supervisory body, who shall notify the resident's nearest relative [and named person][50];
  (b) notify the resident and the supervisory body that they intend to manage the resident's affairs.

(5) Notification under subsection (4)(b) shall include a statement as to what other courses of action had been considered and why they were not considered appropriate.

(6) The medical practitioner who certifies under this section shall not—

  (a) be related to the resident or to any of the managers of the authorised establishment;
  (b) have any direct or indirect financial interest in the authorised establishment.

---

[48] Repealed by Regulation of Care (Scotland) Act 2001 (asp 8), Sch.4.
[49] Words inserted by Mental Health (Care and Treatment) (Scotland) Act 2003 (Modification of Enactments) Order 2005 (SSI 2005/465), Sch.1, para.28(4)(a).
[50] Words inserted by Mental Health (Care and Treatment) (Scotland) Act 2003 (Modification of Enactments) Order 2005 (SSI 2005/465), Sch.1, para.28(4)(b).

(7) A certificate—
  (a) shall be reviewed where it appears to the managers of the authorised establishment, the medical practitioner who certifies under this section or any person having an interest in any of the resident's affairs mentioned in section 39 that there has been any change in the condition or circumstances of the resident bearing on the resident's incapacity; and
  (b) shall expire 3 years after it was issued.

(8) If the managers of the authorised establishment consider that intimation to the resident under subsection (3) or any action under subsection (4) would be likely to pose a serious risk to the health of the resident they may apply to the supervisory body for a direction that they need not make the intimation or take the action.

(9) The Scottish Ministers may prescribe the evidence which the supervisory body shall take into account in reaching a decision under subsection (8).

DEFINITIONS
"authorised establishments" : s.35 (2)
"establishments" : s.35 (1)
"incapable" : s.1 (6)
"incapacity" : s.1 (6)
"managers" : s.35 (5) and Sched. 1, para. 1
"named person" : s.87 (1) (referring to the definition in s.329 of the 2003 Act)
"nearest relative" : s.87 (1), subject to s.87 (2) and (3) (but see s.4)
"prescribe" : s.87 (1) (and see s.86)
"prescribed" : s.87 (1) (and see s.86)
"resident" : s.35 (5)
"supervisory body" : s.40 (1)

GENERAL NOTE
This section sets out the procedure under which the managers of an authorised establishment become entitled to manage the affairs, as defined in s.39, of an individual resident. If the managers decide that such management is the most appropriate course of action (see General Note on subs. (2) below), they give intimation under subs. (3) (subject to subs. (8)) and have the resident examined by a medical practitioner (who is not disqualified by subs. (6)) under subs. (2). If the requirements of subs. (2) are met, the medical practitioner issues a certificate, which under subs. (1) entitles the managers of the establishment to manage that resident's affairs. Upon issue of the certificate, the managers and the supervisory body give notification in terms of subs. (4) (subject to subs. (8)) and subs. (5).

Subsection (7) prescribes circumstances in which the certificate must be reviewed, and provides that it shall expire three months after issue. Subsections (8) and (9) deal with situations where intimation and notification to the resident would be likely to pose a serious risk to the resident's health (cf. s.11).

Subs. (2)
The managers must comply with the general principles in s.1 (2)—(4), and in so doing must meet the particular requirements of subs. (2) of this section. Under subs. (5) they must give notification, upon issue of the certificate, of the other courses of action considered and why they were considered inappropriate. Having regard to s.1 (2) the option of no intervention must always be considered.

For appeals to the sheriff against decisions as to incapacity, see s.14.

Financial procedures and controls in registered establishments
38. [. . .][51]

---

[51] Repealed by Regulation of Care (Scotland) Act 2001 (asp 8), Sch.4.

Matters which may be managed

39.—(1) The matters which may be managed under this Part by the managers of an authorised establishment are—

(a) claiming, receiving, holding and spending any pension, benefit, allowance or other payment other than under the Social Security Contributions and Benefits Act 1992 (c.4)[, the State Pensions Credit Act 2002 (c.16)][52] [or Part 1 of the Welfare Reform Act 2007][53];

(b) claiming, receiving, holding and spending any money to which a resident is entitled;

(c) holding any other moveable property to which the resident is entitled;

(d) disposing of such moveable property,

and in this Part these matters, or any of them, are referred to as residents' affairs; and cognate expressions shall be construed accordingly.

(2) In managing these matters, the managers of an authorised establishment shall—

(a) act only for the benefit of the resident; and

(b) have regard to the sentimental value that any item might have for the resident, or would have but for the resident's incapacity.

(3) The managers of an authorised establishment shall not, without the consent of the supervisory body, manage any matter if that matter has a value greater than that which is prescribed for the purposes of this subsection.

(4) The supervisory body may in relation to an individual resident permit the managers of the authorised establishment to manage any matter which has a value greater than that which is prescribed in relation to it under subsection (3).

(5) For the purpose of this section, "manage" denotes no greater responsibility than complying with the duties set out in this section.

DEFINITIONS
"authorised establishments" : s.35 (2)
"incapacity" : s.1 (6)
"managers" : s.35 (5) and Sched. 1, para. 1
"prescribed" : s.87 (1) (and see s.86)
"resident" : s.35 (5)
"residents' affairs" : s.39 (1)
"supervisory body" : s.40 (1)

GENERAL NOTE
This section defines the "resident's affairs" which managers of authorised establishments may manage, following certification under s.37. SSI 2003/226 sets maximum limits for such management, beyond which the permission of the relevant supervisory body is required.

The managers must comply with subs. (2) and their responsibility to manage is limited as provided in subs. (5), but they must also comply with the general principles in s.1 (2)–(5), and with ss.41, 43 and 44. They are subject to the supervisory body's powers under s.40 (2) and (3).

---

[52] Inserted by Adult Support and Protection (Scotland) Act 2007 (asp 10), Sch.1, para.5(b).
[53] Prospectively amended by Welfare Reform Act 2007 (c.5), s.22(2). Amendment being brought into force on 27 October 2008 by SI 2008/787.

Subs. (2)(a)
On "benefit", see General Note on subs. (2) of s.1.

Supervisory bodies
40.—[(1) The supervisory body for the purposes of this Part is, in relation to—

(a) a registered establishment, the Scottish Commission for the Regulation of Care; and
(b) an unregistered establishment, the Health Board for the area in which the establishment is situated;][54]

and any reference in this Part to an authorised establishment in relation to a supervisory body is a reference to an authorised establishment for which the supervisory body is responsible.

(2) [The][55] supervisory body shall from time to time make inquiry as to the manner in which the managers of an authorised establishment are carrying out the management of residents' affairs and in particular the manner in which they are carrying out their functions under section 41.

(3) [The][56] supervisory body shall investigate any complaint received as to the manner in which the managers of an authorised establishment are managing residents' affairs.

(4) The Scottish Ministers may[, as respects any authorised establishment, amend subsection (1) by substituting for the supervisory body allotted to that establishment a different supervisory body.][57]

DEFINITIONS
"authorised establishments" : s.35 (2)
"local authority" : s.87 (1) (referring to the Local Government etc. (Scotland) Act 1994 (c.39) s.2)
"managers" : s.35 (5) and Sched. 1, para. 1
"registered establishments" : s.35 (2)
"residents' affairs" : s.39 (1)
"supervisory body" : s.40 (1)

GENERAL NOTE
Subsection (1) defines supervisory bodies and subs. (4) provides for amendment by regulation. The supervisory body for a national health service hospital is the Health Board for the area where it is situated. For other authorised establishments, the Scottish Commission for the Regulation of Care is the supervisory body.

The powers of the supervisory body under subss. (2) and (3) are similar to those of the Public Guardian, in relation respectively to other methods of management and adults generally, in s.6 (2)(d) and (e). The sanctions available to the supervisory body include those contained in s.45. Supervisory bodies do not have powers equivalent to those of the Public Guardian (and others) under s.12.

Duties and functions of managers of authorised establishment
41. The managers of an authorised establishment shall, in relation to residents whose affairs they are managing under section 39—

(a) claim, receive and hold any pension, benefit, allowance or other payment to which the resident is entitled other than under the

---

[54] Words substituted by Regulation of Care (Scotland) Act 2001 (asp 8), Sch.3, para.23(3)(a).
[55] Words substituted by Regulation of Care (Scotland) Act 2001 (asp 8), Sch.3, para.23(3)(b).
[56] Words substituted by Regulation of Care (Scotland) Act 2001 (asp 8), Sch.3, para.23(3)(b).
[57] Words substituted by Regulation of Care (Scotland) Act 2001 (asp 8), Sch.3, para.23(3)(c).

Social Security Contributions and Benefits Act 1992 (c.4)[, the State Pensions Credit Act 2002 (c.16)][58] [or Part 1 of the Welfare Reform Act 2007][59];
(b) keep the funds of residents separate from the funds of the establishment;
(c) comply with any requirements of the supervisory body as respects keeping the funds of residents separate or distinguishable from each other;
(d) ensure that where, at any time, the total amount of funds held on behalf of any resident exceeds such sum as may from time to time be prescribed they shall be placed so as to earn interest;
(e) keep records of all transactions made in relation to the funds held by them in respect of each resident for whose benefit the funds are held and managed and, in particular, ensure that details of the balance and any interest due to each resident can be ascertained at any time;
(f) produce such records when requested to do so by the resident, his nearest relative[, his named person][60] or the supervisory body;
(g) spend money only on items or services which are of benefit to the resident on whose behalf the funds are held;
(h) not spend money on items or services which are provided by the establishment to or for such resident as part of its normal service;
(i) make proper provision for indemnifying residents against any loss attributable to—
   (i) any act or omission on the part of the managers of the establishment in exercising the powers conferred by this Part or of others for whom the managers are responsible or attributable to any expenditure in breach of paragraph (g);
   (ii) any breach of duty, misuse of funds or failure to act reasonably and in good faith on the part of the managers.

DEFINITIONS
"authorised establishments" : s.35 (2)
"establishments" : s.35 (1)
"managers" : s.35 (5) and Sched. 1, para. 1
"named person" : s.87 (1) (referring to the definition in s.329 of the 2003 Act)
"nearest relative" : s.87 (1), subject to s.87 (2) and (3) (but see s.4)
"prescribed" : s.87 (1) (and see s.86)
"resident" : s.35 (5)
"supervisory body" : s.40 (1)

GENERAL NOTE
In addition to the duties and functions listed, managers must by s.1 (5), insofar as it is reasonable and practicable to do so, encourage the adult to exercise existing skills and develop new skills, and they lose the protection of s.82 if they fail to do so.

Authorisation of named manager to withdraw from resident's account
42.—(1) On an application in writing by the managers of an authorised establishment the supervisory body may issue a certificate of authority under this section in relation to any resident named in the application.

---

[58] Inserted by Adult Support and Protection (Scotland) Act 2007 (asp 10), Sch.1, para.5(c).
[59] Prospectively amended by Welfare Reform Act 2007 (c. 5), s.22(3). Amendment being brought into force on 27 October 2008 by SI 2008/787.
[60] Words inserted by Mental Health (Care and Treatment) (Scotland) Act 2003 (Modification of Enactments) Order 2005 (SSI 2005/465), Sch.1, para.28(5).

(2) An application under subsection (1) shall specify one or more persons (being managers, officers or members of staff of the establishment) who shall exercise the authority conferred by this section.

(3) A certificate of authority shall be signed by the officer of the supervisory body authorised by the body to do so and shall—

    (a) specify accounts or other funds of the resident;
    (b) name the persons specified in the application (the "authorised persons");
    (c) specify the period of validity of the certificate of authority, being a period not exceeding the period of validity of the certificate issued under section 37(2).

(4) The authorised persons may make withdrawals from such account or source of funds of the named resident as is specified in the certificate of authority and the fundholder may make payments accordingly.

(5) The supervisory body may at any time after it has issued a certificate of authority, revoke it and if it does so it shall notify the fundholder of the revocation.

DEFINITIONS
"authorised establishments" : s.35 (2)
"authorised persons" : s.42 (2) and (3)(b)
"fundholder" : s.33 (2) (and see General Note to Pt. 3)
"managers" : s.35 (5) and Sched. 1, para. 1
"resident" : s.35 (5)
"supervisory body" : s.40 (1)

GENERAL NOTE
Under this section, managers of an authorised establishment may apply to their supervisory body for a certificate permitting one or more "authorised persons" to make specified withdrawals from specified accounts or other funds of the resident. This provision lacks several of the safeguards and controls under the equivalent procedure in Pt. 3, including intimation provisions equivalent to those in Pt. 3 or in the preceding provisions of Pt. 4, but as with any intervention the s.1 principles apply, including the requirement to take account of the present and past wishes of the resident, if ascertainable, and the views of others, under s.1 (4).

Statement of resident's affairs

43.—(1) In this section, "resident" means a resident of an authorised establishment whose affairs are being managed in accordance with the provisions of this Part and "statement" means a statement of the affairs of the resident.

(2) Where a resident ceases to be incapable of managing his affairs, the managers of the establishment shall prepare a statement as at the date on which he ceases to be incapable and shall give a copy to him.

(3) Where a resident moves from an authorised establishment to another authorised establishment, the managers of the establishment from which he moves shall, except where he has ceased to be incapable, prepare a statement as at the date on which he moves and shall send a copy of the statement to the managers of the other establishment.

(4) Where a resident leaves an authorised establishment, other than to move to another authorised establishment and except where he has ceased to be incapable, the managers of the establishment shall prepare a statement as at the date on which he leaves and shall give a copy of the statement to any person who appears to them to be the person who will manage his affairs.

DEFINITIONS
"authorised establishments" : s.35 (2)
"incapable" : s.1 (6)
"managers" : s.35 (5) and Sched. 1, para. 1
"resident" : s.43 (1)

GENERAL NOTE
This section provides for the preparation and issue of a statement of affairs where the resident regains capacity or leaves the establishment.

Resident ceasing to be resident of authorised establishment

44.—(1) Where a resident ceases to be a resident of an authorised establishment, or ceases to be incapable, the managers of the establishment shall continue, for a period not exceeding 3 months from the date on which he ceases to be a resident or, as the case may be, to be incapable, to manage his affairs while such other arrangements as are necessary for managing his affairs are being made.

(2) At the end of the period referred to in subsection (1) during which the managers of the establishment have continued to manage the resident's affairs, they shall prepare a statement and shall give a copy of it to—

(a) the resident, if he has ceased to be incapable; or
(b) any person who appears to them to be the person who will manage his affairs.

(3) Where a resident ceases to be a resident of an authorised establishment and his affairs are to be managed by another establishment, authority or person (including himself) the managers of the establishment shall take such steps as are necessary to transfer his affairs to that establishment, authority or person, as the case may be.

(4) Where a resident ceases to be a resident of an authorised establishment the managers of the establishment shall within 14 days of that event inform—

(a) the supervisory body; and
(b) where the resident has not ceased to be incapable and has moved neither—

(i) to another authorised establishment; nor
(ii) into the care of a local authority,

the local authority of the area in which they expect him to reside.

DEFINITIONS
"authorised establishments" : s.35 (2)
"incapable" : s.1 (6)
"local authority" : s.87 (1) (referring to the Local Government etc. (Scotland) Act 1994 (c.39) s.2)
"managers of an establishment" : s.35 (5) and Sched. 1
"resident" : s.35 (5)
"supervisory body" : s.40 (1)

GENERAL NOTE
Until s.94 of the 1984 Act was amended by the Mental Health (Amendment) (Scotland) Act 1999 there were significant problems with blocked funds held by hospital managers who failed to take appropriate steps prior to discharge, because their authority to manage ceased

abruptly upon discharge. This section allows management under Pt. 4 to continue for up to three months after discharge (subs. (1)); provides for preparation and issue of statements upon conclusion of such extended management (subs. (2)); provides for transfer of management to managers of another establishment (subs. (3)); and provides for notification within 14 days when a resident has ceased to reside in the establishment (subs. (4)).

Appeal, revocation etc.
45.—(1) Where it appears to [the][61] supervisory body that the managers of an authorised establishment are no longer operating as such or have failed to comply with any requirement of this Part or that, for any other reason, it is no longer appropriate that they should continue to manage residents' affairs it may revoke [that power to manage][62].
(2) [. . .][63]
(3) Where a [. . .][64] a power to manage has been revoked under this section, the supervisory body shall within a period of 14 days from such revocation take over management of the residents' affairs and, where they do so, comply with the requirements imposed by and under this Part upon the managers of an authorised establishment.
(4) The supervisory body shall, within the period of 3 months after taking over management of residents' affairs under subsection (3), cause that management to be transferred to such other establishment, authority or person (who may be the resident) as they consider appropriate.
(5) Where the supervisory body is satisfied that the circumstances mentioned in subsection (1) no longer apply in relation to an establishment whose power to manage it has revoked, it may annul the revocation of the power and, where necessary, of the registration.
(6) Any decision of [the][65] supervisory body may be appealed to the sheriff, whose decision shall be final.

DEFINITIONS
"authorised establishments" : s.35 (2)
"managers" : s.35 (5) and Sched. 1, para. 1
"registered establishments" : s.35 (2)
"resident" : s.35 (5)
"residents' affairs" : s.39 (1)
"supervisory body" : s.40 (1)

GENERAL NOTE
This section provides for revocation of the power to manage. The supervisory body must within 14 days take over management themselves, and within three months thereafter transfer management to some other establishment, authority or person, or to the resident himself (under subs. (4), which clearly envisages any appropriate method of management, not limited to management under Pt. 4). Revocation may subsequently be cancelled. Decisions under this section may be appealed to the sheriff, whose decision is final.

Disapplication of Part 4
46.—(1) This Part shall not apply to any of the matters which may be managed under section 39 if—

>   (a) there is a guardian, continuing attorney, or other person with powers relating to that matter; or

---

[61] Words substituted by Regulation of Care (Scotland) Act 2001 (asp 8), Sch.3, para.23(4)(a).
[62] Words substituted by Regulation of Care (Scotland) Act 2001 (asp 8), Sch.3, para.23(4)(b).
[63] Repealed by Regulation of Care (Scotland) Act 2001 (asp 8), Sch.3, para.23(4)(c).
[64] Words repealed by Regulation of Care (Scotland) Act 2001 (asp 8), Sch.3, para.23(4)(d).
[65] Words substituted by Regulation of Care (Scotland) Act 2001 (asp 8), Sch.3, para.23(4)(e).

(b) an intervention order has been granted relating to that matter,

but no liability shall be incurred by any person who acts in good faith under this Part in ignorance of any guardian, continuing attorney, other person or intervention order.

(2) In this section any reference to—

(a) a guardian shall include a reference to a guardian (however called) appointed under the law of any country to, or entitled under the law of any country to act for, an adult during his incapacity, if the guardianship is recognised by the law of Scotland;
(b) a continuing attorney shall include a reference to a person granted, under a contract, grant or appointment governed by the law of any country, powers (however expressed), relating to the granter's property or financial affairs and having continuing effect notwithstanding the granter's incapacity.

DEFINITIONS
"adult" : s.1 (6)
"continuing attorney" : s.15 (2)
"incapacity" : s.1 (6)
"intervention order" : s.53 (1)

GENERAL NOTE
Part 4 is disapplied where an appointee listed in subs. (1), or an equivalent under subs. (2), has relevant powers, but there is protection for those acting in good faith and in ignorance of the relevant appointment.

PART 5

MEDICAL TREATMENT AND RESEARCH

GENERAL NOTE
See description of Pt. 5 in the Introduction and General Note. While this is in some respects the most self-contained Part of this Act, provisions of other Parts which apply to the subject-matter of Pt. 5, and to those exercising functions under this Part, include the following:

- the general principles in s.1;
- the powers of the sheriff to give directions under s.3 (3);
- the investigative powers of the local authority under s.10 (1)(d), with related provisions in s.12;
- the provisions regarding codes of practice in s.13 (1)(h);
- appeals against decisions about incapacity under s.14;
- the offence of ill-treatment and wilful neglect under s.83.

In these annotations to Pt. 5, the person who issues a certificate under s.47 (1) is called the "certifier", though the text of this Act does not adopt that or any other definition.

Authority of persons responsible for medical treatment
47.—(1) This section applies where [any of the persons mentioned in subsection (1A)][66]—

(a) is of the opinion that [an adult][67] is incapable in relation to a decision about the medical treatment in question; and

---

[66] Words substituted by Smoking, Health and Social Care (Scotland) Act 2005 (asp 13), s.35(2)(a)(i).
[67] Words substituted by Smoking, Health and Social Care (Scotland) Act 2005 (asp 13), s.35(2)(a)(ii).

Adults with Incapacity (Scotland) Act 2000 (Pt. 5)

    (b) has certified in accordance with subsection (5) that he is of this opinion.

(1A) [68] The persons are—

    (a) the medical practitioner primarily responsible for the medical treatment of the adult;
    (b) a person who is—
        (i) a dental practitioner;
        (ii) an ophthalmic optician;
        (iii) a registered nurse; or
        (iv) an individual who falls within such description of persons as may be prescribed by the Scottish Ministers,

who satisfies such requirements as may be so prescribed and who is primarily responsible for medical treatment of the kind in question.

(2) [. . .][69] the [person who by virtue of subsection (1) has issued a certificate for the purposes of that subsection][70] shall have, during the period specified in the certificate, authority to do what is reasonable in the circumstances, in relation to [. . .][71] [the medical treatment in question][72], to safeguard or promote the physical or mental health of the adult.

[(2A) Subsection (2)—

    (a) does not affect any authority conferred by any other enactment or rule of law; and
    (b) is subject to—
        (i) the following provisions of this section;
        (ii) sections 49 and 50; and
        (iii) sections 234, 237, 240, 242, 243 and 244 of the 2003 Act.][73]

(3) The authority conferred by subsection (2) shall be exercisable also by any other person who is authorised by the [person on whom that authority is conferred][74] to carry out [the medical treatment in question][75] and who is acting—

    (a) on his behalf under his instructions; or
    (b) with his approval or agreement.

(4) In this Part "medical treatment" includes any procedure or treatment designed to safeguard or promote physical or mental health.

(5) A certificate for the purposes of subsection (1) shall be in the prescribed form and shall specify the period during which the authority conferred by subsection (2) shall subsist, being a period which—

---

[68] Inserted by Smoking, Health and Social Care (Scotland) Act 2005 (asp 13), s.35(2)(b).
[69] Words repealed by Adult Support and Protection (Scotland) Act 2007 (asp 10), Sch.2.
[70] Words substituted by Smoking, Health and Social Care (Scotland) Act 2005 (asp 13), s.35(2)(c)(i).
[71] Words repealed by Adult Support and Protection (Scotland) Act 2007 (asp 10), Sch.2.
[72] Words substituted by Smoking, Health and Social Care (Scotland) Act 2005 (asp 13), s.35(2)(c)(ii).
[73] Inserted by Adult Support and Protection (Scotland) Act 2007 (asp 10), Sch.1, para.5(d).
[74] Words substituted by Smoking, Health and Social Care (Scotland) Act 2005 (asp 13), s.35(2)(d)(i).
[75] Words substituted by Smoking, Health and Social Care (Scotland) Act 2005 (asp 13), s.35(2)(d)(ii).

(a) the [person who issues the certificate][76] considers appropriate to the condition or circumstances of the adult; but
(b) [does not exceed—
  (i) one year; or
  (ii) if, in the opinion of the person issuing the certificate any of the conditions or circumstances prescribed by the Scottish Ministers applies as respects the adult, 3 years,

from][77] the date of the examination on which the certificate is based.

(6) If after issuing a certificate, the [person who issued it][78] is of the opinion that the condition or circumstances of the adult have changed he may—

(a) revoke the certificate;
(b) issue a new certificate specifying such period [not exceeding—
  (i) one year; or
  (ii) if, in the opinion of that person any of the conditions or circumstances prescribed by the Scottish Ministers apply as respects the adult, 3 years,

from][79] the date of revocation of the old certificate as he considers appropriate to the new condition or circumstances of the adult.

(7) The authority conferred by subsection (2) shall not authorise—

(a) the use of force or detention, unless it is immediately necessary and only for so long as is necessary in the circumstances;
(b) action which would be inconsistent with any decision by a competent court;
(c) placing an adult in a hospital for the treatment of mental disorder against his will.

(8) [. . .][80]

(9) Subject to subsection (10), where any question as to the authority of any person to provide medical treatment in pursuance of subsection (2)—

(a) is the subject of proceedings in any court (other than for the purposes of any application to the court made under regulations made under section 48); and
(b) has not been determined,

medical treatment authorised by subsection (2) shall not be given unless it is authorised by any other enactment or rule of law for the preservation of the life of the adult or the prevention of serious deterioration in his medical condition.

---

[76] Words substituted by Smoking, Health and Social Care (Scotland) Act 2005 (asp 13), s.35(2)(e)(i).
[77] Words substituted by Smoking, Health and Social Care (Scotland) Act 2005 (asp 13), s.35(2)(e)(ii).
[78] Words substituted by Smoking, Health and Social Care (Scotland) Act 2005 (asp 13), s.35(2)(f)(i).
[79] Words substituted by Smoking, Health and Social Care (Scotland) Act 2005 (asp 13), s.35(2)(f)(ii).
[80] Repealed by Adult Support and Protection (Scotland) Act 2007 (asp 10), Sch.2.

(10) Nothing in subsection (9) shall authorise the provision of any medical treatment where an interdict has been granted and continues to have effect prohibiting the provision of such medical treatment.

(11)[81] In subsection (1A)—

"dental practitioner" has the same meaning as in section 108(1) of the National Health Service (Scotland) Act 1978 (c.29);
"ophthalmic optician" means a person registered in either of the registers kept under section 7 of the Opticians Act 1989 (c.44) of ophthalmic opticians.

DEFINITIONS
"ophthalmic optician" : see subs. (11)
"dental practitioner" : see subs. (11)
"adult" : s.1 (6)
"certifier" (in annotations only) : see General Note for Pt. 5
"incapable" : s.1 (6)
"medical treatment" : s.47 (4)
"mental disorder" : s.87 (1) (and see General Note to s.1 (6))
"prescribed" : s.87 (1) (and see s.86)

GENERAL NOTE
See section on Pt. 5 in the Introduction and General Note. If the certifier considers that the adult is incapable as described in subs. (1)(a), he may proceed to certify in accordance with subss. (1) and (5), but must comply with s.1 (2)–(4) in so doing. Certification authorises treatment under subss. (2) and (3) except where the certifier is aware of a pending application for a relevant intervention or guardianship order (s.49 (1)); or where there is an appointee with relevant powers in terms of s.50 (1) and paras. (b) and (c) of s.50 (2) both apply. There are no provisions for notification or registration of certification. The certificate will be for an appropriate period up to the maximum periods provided for in subs. (5), and may be revoked or replaced if the adult's condition or circumstances change (subs. (6)). Renewal is not prohibited. Medical treatment which may be authorised is as defined in subs. (4), subject to the exceptions in subss. (2A), (7), (9) and (10) and in s.48.

The deletion of previous s.47 (8) by the 2003 Act resolved the inconsistency identified in para. 14–45 of *Adult Incapacity*.

Relevant regulations are SSI 2007/100, SSI 2007/104 and SSI 2007/105.

Subs. (2A)
This subsection effectively repeats the proviso in s.47 (2) of the 2000 text, which was to the effect that authority under this section was: "Without prejudice to any authority conferred by any other enactment or rule of law".

Subs. (3)
This could apply to the clinical team, family and carers, and others.

Subs. (4)
The Bill as introduced offered a more detailed definition (s.44 (2) of the Bill as introduced). The definition in this Act was substituted by Executive amendment at stage 2. If issues of interpretation arise, reference to the extensive parliamentary proceedings on this topic may assist. See also regulations under s.48.

Subs. (7)
Use of force or detention under the exception to (a) would clearly be an intervention, so that as well as being immediately necessary and of minimum duration, the nature and degree of force would require to comply *inter alia* with the requirements of s.1 (3) that it should represent "the least restrictive option in relation to the freedom of the adult, consistent with the purpose of the intervention".

---

[81] Inserted by Smoking, Health and Social Care (Scotland) Act 2005 (asp 13), s.35(2)(g).

2003 Act procedures, if necessary, would normally be preferred under para. (a), and remain the only competent procedure in respect of para. (c).

Subs. (9)
See also subs. (2A)(a) and discussion of Pt. 5 in Introduction and General Note.

Subs. (10)
Interdicts could be sought by people endeavouring to ensure the effectiveness of advance directives. See also s.50 (8).

Exceptions to authority to treat
48.—(1) [. . .][82]
(2) The Scottish Ministers may by regulations specify medical treatment, or a class or classes of medical treatment, in relation to which the authority conferred by section 47(2) shall not apply and make provision about the medical treatment, or a class or classes of medical treatment, in relation to which that authority does apply.
(3) Regulations made under subsection (2) may provide for the circumstances in which the specified medical treatment or specified class or classes of medical treatment may be carried out.

DEFINITIONS
"1984 Act, the" : The Mental Health (Scotland) Act 1984 (c.36) (per s.87 (1))
"medical treatment" : s.47 (4)
"mental disorder" : s.87 (1) (and see General Note to s.1 (6))

GENERAL NOTE

Subss. (2) and (3)
The draft Bill annexed to the SLC Report proposed two categories of matters, the contents of both to be partly specified in the legislation and partly prescribed by regulations. One category would be of matters requiring approval of the sheriff, and the other would require a second opinion from an independent doctor appointed for the purpose by MWC. This Act as introduced and enacted widened the regulatory powers of Scottish ministers (see s.86) to prescribe treatments to which the new authority specifically does apply; treatments to which it does not apply; treatments to which special requirements may apply; and what those special requirements should be. See SSI 2002/275 as amended by SSI 2002/302, reproduced in *Adult Incapacity*.

Medical treatment where there is an application for intervention or guardianship order
49.—(1) [Subsection (2) of section 47][83] shall not apply if, to the knowledge of the [person on whom authority is conferred by that subsection][84], an application for an intervention order or a guardianship order with power in relation to any medical treatment referred to in that subsection has been made to the sheriff and has not been determined.
(2) Until the application has been finally determined, medical treatment authorised by section 47(2) shall not be given unless it is authorised by any other enactment or rule of law for the preservation of the life of the adult or the prevention of serious deterioration in his medical condition.

---

[82] Repealed by Mental Health (Care and Treatment) (Scotland) Act 2003 (asp 13), Sch.5, para.1.
[83] Words substituted by Smoking, Health and Social Care (Scotland) Act 2005 (asp 13), s.35(3)(a).
[84] Words substituted by Smoking, Health and Social Care (Scotland) Act 2005 (asp 13), s.35(3)(b).

Adults with Incapacity (Scotland) Act 2000 (Pt. 5)

(3) Nothing in subsection (2) shall authorise the provision of any medical treatment where an interdict has been granted and continues to have effect prohibiting the provision of such medical treatment.

DEFINITIONS
"adult" : s.1 (6)
"guardianship order" : s.58 (4)
"intervention order" : s.53 (1)
"medical treatment" : s.47 (4)

GENERAL NOTE

Subs. (2)
See also s.47 (2A) and discussion of Pt. 5 in Introduction and General Note.

Medical treatment where guardian etc. has been appointed
50.—(1) This section applies where a guardian or a welfare attorney has been appointed or a person has been authorised under an intervention order with power in relation to any medical treatment referred to in section 47.
(2) The authority conferred by section 47(2) shall not apply where—

  (a) subsection (1) applies;
  (b) the [person who issued the certificate for the purposes of section 47(1)][85] is aware of the appointment or, as the case may be, authorisation; and
  (c) it would be reasonable and practicable for that [person][86] to obtain the consent of the guardian, welfare attorney or person authorised under the intervention order, as the case may be, to any proposed medical treatment but he has failed to do so.

(3) Where the [person who issued the certificate for the purposes of section 47(1)][87] has consulted the guardian, welfare attorney or person authorised under the intervention order and there is no disagreement as to the medical treatment of the adult, [the medical practitioner primarily responsible for the medical treatment of the adult (in a case where the person who so issued the certificate was someone other than that practitioner) or any person having an interest][88] in the personal welfare of the adult may appeal the decision as to the medical treatment to the Court of Session.
(4) Where the [person who issued the certificate for the purposes of section 47(1)][89] has consulted the guardian, welfare attorney or person authorised under the intervention order and there is a disagreement as to the medical treatment of the adult, the [person who issued the certificate][90]

---

[85] Words substituted by Smoking, Health and Social Care (Scotland) Act 2005 (asp 13), s.35(4)(a)(i).
[86] Words substituted by Smoking, Health and Social Care (Scotland) Act 2005 (asp 13), s.35(4)(a)(ii).
[87] Words substituted by Smoking, Health and Social Care (Scotland) Act 2005 (asp 13), s.35(4)(b)(i).
[88] Words substituted by Smoking, Health and Social Care (Scotland) Act 2005 (asp 13), s.35(4)(b)(ii).
[89] Words substituted by Smoking, Health and Social Care (Scotland) Act 2005 (asp 13), s.35(4)(c)(i).
[90] Words substituted by Smoking, Health and Social Care (Scotland) Act 2005 (asp 13), s.35(4)(c)(ii).

shall request the Mental Welfare Commission to nominate [a practitioner who the Commission consider has professional knowledge or expertise relevant to medical treatment of the kind in question (the "nominated practitioner")][91] from the list established and maintained by them under subsection (9) to give an opinion as to the medical treatment proposed.

(5) Where the [nominated practitioner][92] certifies that, in his opinion, having regard to all the circumstances and having consulted the guardian, welfare attorney or person authorised under the intervention order as the case may be and, if it is reasonable and practicable to do so, a person nominated by such guardian, welfare attorney or person authorised under the intervention order as the case may be, the proposed medical treatment should be given, the [person who issued the certificate for the purposes of section 47(1)][93] may give the treatment or may authorise any other person to give the treatment notwithstanding the disagreement with the guardian, welfare attorney, or person authorised under the intervention order, as the case may be.

(6) Where the [nominated practitioner][94] certifies that, in his opinion, having regard to all the circumstances and having consulted the guardian, welfare attorney or person authorised under the intervention order as the case may be and, if it is reasonable and practicable to do so, a person nominated by such guardian, welfare attorney or person authorised under the intervention order as the case may be, the proposed medical treatment should or, as the case may be, should not be given, the medical practitioner primarily responsible for the medical treatment of the adult, or any person having an interest in the personal welfare of the adult [(including, where the certificate issued for the purposes of section 47(1) was issued by another person, that person)][95], may apply to the Court of Session for a determination as to whether the proposed treatment should be given or not.

(7) Subject to subsection (8), where an appeal has been made to the Court of Session under subsection (3) or an application has been made under subsection (6), and has not been determined, medical treatment authorised by section 47(2) shall not be given unless it is authorised by any other enactment or rule of law for the preservation of the life of the adult or the prevention of serious deterioration in his medical condition.

(8) Nothing in subsection (7) shall authorise the provision of any medical treatment where an interdict has been granted and continues to have effect prohibiting the giving of such medical treatment.

(9) The Mental Welfare Commission shall establish and maintain a list of [practitioners][96] from whom they shall nominate the [practitioner][97] who is to give the opinion under subsection (4).

---

[91] Words substituted by Smoking, Health and Social Care (Scotland) Act 2005 (asp 13), s.35(4)(c)(iii)
[92] Words substituted by Smoking, Health and Social Care (Scotland) Act 2005 (asp 13), s.35(4)(d)(i).
[93] Words substituted by Smoking, Health and Social Care (Scotland) Act 2005 (asp 13), s.35(4)(d)(ii).
[94] Words substituted by Smoking, Health and Social Care (Scotland) Act 2005 (asp 13), s.35(4)(e)(i).
[95] Inserted by Smoking, Health and Social Care (Scotland) Act 2005 (asp 13), s.35(4)(e)(ii).
[96] Words substituted by Smoking, Health and Social Care (Scotland) Act 2005 (asp 13), s.35(4)(f)(i).
[97] Words substituted by Smoking, Health and Social Care (Scotland) Act 2005 (asp 13), s.35(4)(f)(ii).

(10) In this section any reference to—

(a) a guardian shall include a reference to a guardian (however called) appointed under the law of any country to, or entitled under the law of any country to act for, an adult during his incapacity, if the guardianship is recognised by the law of Scotland;
(b) a welfare attorney shall include a reference to a person granted, under a contract, grant or appointment governed by the law of any country, powers (however expressed) relating to the granter's personal welfare and having effect during the granter's incapacity.

Definitions
"adult" : s.1 (6)
"certifier" (in annotations only) : see General Note for Pt. 5
"incapacity" : s.1 (6)
"intervention order" : s.53 (1)
"medical treatment" : s.47 (4)
"Mental Welfare Commission" : s.87 (1) (referring to s.4 of the 2003 Act), "MWC" in these annotations
"welfare attorney" : s.16 (2)

General Note
References in this General Note to appointees mean appointees listed in subs. (1) and their equivalents in terms of subs. (10).

The relationship between appointees and medical practitioners regarding medical decisions, and the resolution of disagreements between them, attracted lively debate throughout the law reform process preceding this Act and the ensuing parliamentary proceedings. In these matters this Act as enacted differed radically from the Bill as introduced, which in turn differed substantially from the draft Bill annexed to the SLC Report. The SLC draft Bill proposed that the medical practitioner, upon obtaining a second opinion, could override the appointee. The SLC proposal "evolved from discussion with representatives of some of the Royal Colleges in Scotland" (para. 5.38), without any of the wider consultation which had characterised the SLC's work generally, and ran into wide-ranging and strong opposition on the grounds that doctors should not be able to override either an attorney expressly empowered by the patient to decide such matters, or a guardian expressly empowered by the court to do so, at least without the involvement of the court. It was also asserted that people likely to be appointed attorneys and guardians are more likely to know well the patient and the patient's medical history, and many examples were given of imposition by consultants, without discussion, of treatments already known to have failed or to have had undesirable consequences. Accordingly, the Act as introduced equated refusal by the appointee with refusal by the patient, subject to application to the Court of Session by the doctor. This prompted fears that inappropriate refusals by appointees might go unchallenged, to the detriment of the patient, because doctors lacked the will or resources to apply to the Court of Session. Suggestions that the Executive might revert substantially to the SLC proposal appeared to suit no-one. The Alliance adhered to the original objection to the SLC proposal, but also took the view that if appointees were to be overruled by anyone other than a court, that should only be done by someone who was—and was clearly seen to be—competent, independent and independently appointed, and there should be right of further recourse to the courts. Another element which emerged was the need to allow input from other parties with a clear interest, such as close relatives other than the appointee. The final form of this section was adopted by amendment at stage 3, and sought reasonably to accommodate all of these concerns.

Where there is an appointee with relevant powers, the authority under s.47 only applies if one of the criteria in subs. (2) of this section does not apply.

Where there is no disagreement between the appointee and the certifier, anyone "having an interest" (see below) may appeal to the Court of Session (subs. (3)), pending which appeal subss. (7) and (8) apply. Where the certifier is not the medical practitioner primarily responsible for the medical treatment of the adult, that practitioner may now likewise appeal to the Court of Session.

Adults with Incapacity Legislation

For situations where there is disagreement between the appointee and the certifier, MWC maintains a list of practitioners (subs. (9)) from which, in individual cases, it nominates a "nominated practitioner" upon request by the certifier (subs. (4)—MWC maintains a 24–hour answering service). Pending a decision by the nominated practitioner, subss. (7) and (8) apply.

The nominated practitioner must have regard to all the circumstances, must consult the appointee, and (where it is reasonable and practicable to do so) must consult someone nominated for the purpose by the appointee (subss. (5) and (6)). If the nominated practitioner then certifies that the proposed treatment should be given, it may be given (subs. (5)). The decision of the nominated practitioner, either way, may be challenged in the Court of Session by the certifier or by anyone having an interest. It may likewise be challenged in the Court of Session by the medical practitioner primarily responsible for the adult's treatment even when that practitioner was not the certifier. Pending determination of the appeal, subss. (7) and (8) apply.

The existence of mechanisms to resolve issues can be conducive to resolution by agreement without formally triggering those mechanisms. It is essential that the mechanisms in this section should have received careful consideration, and should be available if required, but it is notable—and indeed commendable—that up to time of writing these annotations the procedures in this section have never been used. It is understood that on three occasions MWC has been approached with regard to possible use, but on one occasion an attorney was unable to demonstrate that relevant powers had been conferred on the attorney, and on the other occasions MWC took the view (correctly, it is submitted) that appointees had no greater powers than the patient and could not demand that treatment be given, as opposed to refusing consent to proposed treatment, so that procedure under this section was not appropriate (see *Matters not covered by this Act* in Introduction and General Note).

On subs. (7) see also s.47 (2A) and discussion of Pt. 5 in Introduction and General Note.

Note that while a "person claiming an interest" is used frequently in this Act (and defined non-exclusively in s.87 (1)), the appeal provisions of ss.50 and 52 refer uniquely to "any person having an interest", which is not defined in this Act. See *Adult Incapacity* para. 14–59.

Authority for research

51.—(1) No surgical, medical, nursing, dental or psychological research shall be carried out on any adult who is incapable in relation to a decision about participation in the research unless—

    (a) research of a similar nature cannot be carried out on an adult who is capable in relation to such a decision; and

    (a) the circumstances mentioned in subsection (2) are satisfied.

(2) The circumstances referred to in subsection (1) are that—

    (a) the purpose of the research is to obtain knowledge of—

        (i) the causes, diagnosis, treatment or care of the adult's incapacity; or

        (ii) the effect of any treatment or care given during his incapacity to the adult which relates to that incapacity; and

    (b) [Subject to subsection (3A)][98], the conditions mentioned in subsection (3) are fulfilled.

(3) The conditions are—

    (a) the research is likely to produce real and direct benefit to the adult;

    (b) the adult does not indicate unwillingness to participate in the research;

---

[98] Inserted by Medicines for Human Use (Clinical Trials) Regulations 2004 (SI 2004/1031), Sch.10(1), para.21(a), subject to transitional provisions specified in Sch.12.

Adults with Incapacity (Scotland) Act 2000 (Pt. 5)

    (c) the research has been approved by the Ethics Committee;
    (d) the research entails no foreseeable risk, or only a minimal foreseeable risk, to the adult;
    (e) the research imposes no discomfort, or only minimal discomfort, on the adult; and
    (f) consent has been obtained from any guardian or welfare attorney who has power to consent to the adult's participation in research or, where there is no such guardian or welfare attorney, from the adult's nearest relative.

[(3A) Where the research consists of a clinical trial of a medicinal product, the research may be carried out—

    (a) without being approved by the Ethics Committee, if a favourable opinion on the trial has been given by an ethics committee, other than the Ethics Committee, in accordance with regulation 15 of the Medicines for Human Use (Clinical Trials) Regulations 2004; [. . .][99]
    (b) without the consent of any guardian or welfare attorney, or the adult's nearest relative, if—
        (i) it has not been practicable to contact any such person before the decision to enter the adult as a subject of the clinical trial is made, and
        (ii) consent has been obtained from a person, other than a person connected with the conduct of the clinical trial, who is—
            (A) the doctor primarily responsible for the medical treatment provided to that adult, or
            (B) a person nominated by the relevant health care provider.][100]

[(c) without the consent of any guardian or welfare attorney, or the adult's nearest relative, if—
    (i) treatment is being, or is about to be, provided for an adult who is incapable in relation to a decision about participation in the research as a matter of urgency;
    (ii) having regard to the nature of the clinical trial and of the particular circumstances of the case it is necessary to take action for the purposes of the clinical trial as a matter of urgency;
    (iii) it has not been reasonably practicable to obtain the consent of any such person;
    (iv) it has not been reasonably practicable to obtain the consent of any of the persons mentioned in paragraph (b)(ii)(A) or (B); and
    (v) the action to be taken is carried out in accordance with a procedure approved by the Ethics Committee or any other ethics committee or by an appeal panel appointed under

---

[99] Words repealed by Medicines for Human Use (Clinical Trials) Amendment (No.2) Regulations 2006 (SI 2006/2984), reg.3(a).
[100] Inserted by Medicines for Human Use (Clinical Trials) Regulations 2004 (SI 2004/1031), Sch.10(1), para.21(b), subject to transitional provisions specified in Sch.12.

Schedule 4 of the Medicines for Human Use (Clinical Trials) Regulations 2004 (S.I. 2004/1031) at the time it gave its favourable opinion in relation to the clinical trial.][101]

(4) Where the research is not likely to produce real and direct benefit to the adult, it may nevertheless be carried out if it will contribute through significant improvement in the scientific understanding of the adult's incapacity to the attainment of real and direct benefit to the adult or to other persons having the same incapacity, provided the other circumstances or conditions mentioned in subsections (1) to (3) are fulfilled.

(5) In granting approval under subsection (3)(c), the Ethics Committee may impose such conditions as it sees fit.

(6) The Ethics Committee shall be constituted by regulations made by the Scottish Ministers and such regulations may make provision as to the composition of, appointments to and procedures of the Ethics Committee and may make such provision for the payment of such remuneration, expenses and superannuation as the Scottish Ministers may determine.

(7) Regulations made by the Scottish Ministers under subsection (6) may prescribe particular matters which the Ethics Committee shall take into account when deciding whether to approve any research under this Part.

(8) In this section any reference to—

(a) a guardian shall include a reference to a guardian (however called) appointed under the law of any country to, or entitled under the law of any country to act for, an adult during his incapacity, if the guardianship is recognised by the law of Scotland;
(b) a welfare attorney shall include a reference to a person granted, under a contract, grant or appointment governed by the law of any country, powers (however expressed) relating to the granter's personal welfare and having effect during the granter's incapacity.

[(9) In this section—

"clinical trial on a medicinal product" means a clinical trial as defined by regulation 2(1) of the Medicines for Human Use (Clinical Trials) Regulations 2004;
"an ethics committee" has the meaning given by that regulation;
"person connected with the conduct of the trial" and "relevant health care provider" have the meanings given by Schedule 1 to those regulations.][102]

DEFINITIONS
"adult" : s.1 (6)
"an ethics committee" : s.51 (9)
"clinical trial on a medicinal product" : s.51 (9)
"incapable" : s.1 (6)
"incapacity" : s.1 (6)
"nearest relative" : s.87 (1), subject to s.87 (2) and (3) (but see s.4)
"person connected with the conduct of the trial" : s.51 (9)

---

[101] Inserted by Medicines for Human Use (Clinical Trials) Amendment (No.2) Regulations 2006 (SI 2006/2984), reg.3(b).
[102] Inserted by Medicines for Human Use (Clinical Trials) Regulations 2004 (SI 2004/1031), Sch.10(1), para.21(c), subject to transitional provisions specified in Sch.12.

Adults with Incapacity (Scotland) Act 2000 (Pt. 5)

"prescribe" : s.87 (1) (and see s.86)
"relevant health care provider" : s.51 (9)
"the Ethics Committee" : s.51 (6)
"welfare attorney" : s.16 (2)

GENERAL NOTE
"There is virtually no authority in Scotland as to the legality of research on people incapable of consenting to their participation" .... "We consider that there should be legislative authority and regulation of research on mentally incapable people in place of the present legal near-vacuum" (SLC Report, para. 5.65).

This section prohibits research on adults with incapacity in that regard unless research of a similar nature cannot be carried out on a capable adult (subs. (1)(a)); the purpose of the research complies with subs. (2)(a); conditions (b), (d) and (e) in subs. (3) apply; either condition (a) of subs. (3) or the provisions of subs. (4) apply; and either condition (c) of subs. (3) or subs (3A)(a) applies; and either condition (f) of subs. (3), or subs. (3A)(b), or subs. (3A)(c) applies. Condition (c) requires approval by the Ethics Committee, constituted in accordance with subs. (6), which may be required under subs. (7) to take prescribed matters into account, and may attach conditions to approval under subs. (5).

Subsection (4) governs research which is not likely to produce real and direct benefit to the adult who is the subject of that research. Examples given in the course of discussion of this provision included research into Alzheimer's disease which can only be carried out upon people in an advanced state of the disease, and likely to benefit people in an early stage or not yet suffering from the disease; and research which can only be carried out upon people following serious head injuries, likely to benefit others as to precautions or best initial treatment.

Relevant regulations are SSI 2002/190 as amended by SI 2003/1590, SSI 2004/212, SSI 2007/22, and SI 2007/289.

Appeal against decision as to medical treatment

52.—Any decision taken for the purposes of this Part, other than a decision by a medical practitioner under section 50, as to the medical treatment of the adult may be appealed by any person having an interest in the personal welfare of the adult to the sheriff and thence, with the leave of the sheriff, to the Court of Session.

DEFINITIONS
"adult" : s.1 (6)
"medical treatment" : s.47 (4)

GENERAL NOTE
This section differs from appeal provisions in other Parts of this Act, where (generally) either the sheriff's decision is final, or appeal lies from the sheriff to the sheriff principal, and thence (with leave of the sheriff principal) to the Court of Session. Section 50 contains its own unique appeal provisions, under which appeal lies direct to the Court of Session. The role accorded to the Court of Session by ss.50 and 52 allows that court, with authority and consistency, to develop the law in relation to matters which may arise from Pt. 5 of this Act, in like manner as it was considered appropriate that the Court of Session should continue to be able to deal with further issues which might arise in relation to withholding and withdrawal of life-preserving treatment following upon *Law Hospital NHS Trust v Lord Advocate*, 1996 SLT 848 (see comments under *"Matters not covered by this Act"* in Introduction and General Note). The *parens patriae* jurisdiction, exercised in that case, is unaffected by this Act, although it would appear to be competent for such matters to be dealt with alternatively by an intervention order.

While decisions concerning medical treatment under Pt. 5 may be appealed by the route provided in s.52, appeals to the sheriff against decisions as to incapacity under s.14 do not appear to be excluded in relation to Pt. 5. In some cases there would appear to be a choice as to whether an appeal to the sheriff should be taken as an appeal against a decision as to incapacity in terms of s.14 or as an appeal as to medical treatment in terms of s.52. In the former case, the appeal may be brought by the adult or "any person claiming an interest"; in the latter, by "any person having an interest" (on which see last paragraph of General Note to s.50). In the former case, further appeal lies next to the sheriff principal; in the latter, to the Court of Session.

See last paragraph of General Note to s.50 regarding "any person having an interest".

Part 6

Intervention Orders and Guardianship Orders

Intervention orders

GENERAL NOTE

As suggested in the description of Pt. 6 in the Introduction and General Note, which outlines the provisions of this Part, the scheme of intervention and guardianship orders is best approached as an entirely new scheme which came into force on April 1, 2002, rather than by comparison with the previous law relating to curators bonis, tutors and 1984 Act guardians. The ethos and many fundamental aspects of the current regime differ fundamentally from "old law"—see sections on *"Old law"* and *"new law"* and *Part 1* in Introduction and General Note. Those familiar with the previous law will have noted features of it, usually in amended form, reflected in this Act, but these should be approached in the context of this Act as a whole rather than as representing continuity of former provision.

The 2007 Act made several improvements to Pt. 6, all of which are now in force from April 1, 2008. The 2007 Act introduced a simplified renewal procedure. For renewals, only one medical report is now required. It must be provided by an approved medical practitioner (or other "relevant medical practitioner"—see below). For financial guardianship, the only other report required is a report from the Public Guardian, concerning the applicant's conduct as financial guardian and the applicant's suitability to continue. For welfare guardianship, a report from the mental health officer will still be required. The sheriff may dispense with a hearing. This procedure should make renewal less burdensome, and perhaps reduce the number of unduly lengthy initial appointments.

All transitional appointments will expire on October 5, 2009, if not renewed before that. The new simplified renewal procedure will be applicable. In response to concerns by the Law Society that some adults may lose their guardianships because their guardians are unaware of this change, a successful amendment requires the Public Guardian to notify financial guardians of the new provisions, and local authorities to notify welfare guardians; and in response to concerns by the Law Society about the status of joint guardians appointed under this Act to transitional guardians, it has been clarified by amendment that the relevant new provisions will apply also to such joint guardians.

Caution is no longer mandatory. In relation to both intervention orders and guardianship orders relating to property or financial affairs, this Act provides that the sheriff "may" order caution, rather than that he "shall" do so. It is also now possible to give "other security".

On managing the timetable of Pt. 6 applications, medical reports will now be valid even where the medical examination of the adult was carried out more than 30 days before the application was lodged, provided that the sheriff is satisfied that, since the examination was carried out, there has been no change in circumstances which might be relevant to matters set out in the report. The Bill for the 2007 Act as introduced referred to a requirement that the adult's condition is unlikely to have improved, but the Law Society pointed out successfully that this was not the appropriate test: the adult's condition could have improved, but capacity could remain equally impaired in relation to circumstances and needs.

It is now possible to commence guardianship applications three months before a young person attains the age of 16, though guardianship will only commence from that age. This provision is designed to avoid a gap between child guardianship and adult guardianship where capacity is significantly impaired.

There are two alternatives to the approved medical practitioner's report. Firstly, where the adult is not present in Scotland the relevant report may be provided by a person holding qualifications equivalent to those of an approved medical practitioner who has consulted the Mental Welfare Commission for Scotland ("MWC" in these annotations) about the report. Secondly, a report may be provided by "a person of such other description as the Scottish Ministers may prescribe". The "approved medical practitioner" and these alternatives are encompassed within the new definition of "relevant medical practitioner", who must now provide one of the medical reports (and also the only medical report under the new renewal procedure).

Section 70 of this Act contains a procedure under which the court can make an order ordaining the adult, or any person named in the order, to implement a decision of a welfare guardian. The sheriff may now, on cause shown, disapply the intimation requirement and the corresponding right to object within a prescribed period. In some such situations the new adult protection powers under Pt. 1 of the 2007 Act might be the better option.

Previously interim guardianship was limited to three months. Sheriffs are now able to grant interim guardianships for three months or for a longer period up to a maximum of six months.

The discharge powers of the Public Guardian in relation to financial guardianships under s.72 (1) of this Act are now extended to include cases where the guardianship order has expired. The recall powers of MWC under s.73 (3) of this Act are now limited to mental disorder cases. A new procedure has been created for recall of guardianship by the local authority where the chief social work officer is guardian. Where a guardian dies, the guardian's personal representative—if aware of the guardianship—is now required to notify the Public Guardian, who in turn notifies the adult, the local authority and (in mental disorder cases) MWC; registers particulars; and issues a fresh certificate to any surviving joint guardian, and/or to any substitute guardian.

As mentioned in the Introduction and General Note, the 2007 Act also introduced two important alternatives to Pt. 6 procedure, namely the new procedure under the new s.13ZA of the 1968 Act (see the text thereof and General Note thereto in Appendix 1) and the new access to funds provisions of Pt. 3 (see in particular the General Note for Pt. 3).

The scope of intervention orders, and some general aspects of the law relating to them, are discussed in the General Note to s.53. General aspects of the law relating to guardianship are mentioned in the General Note to s.57, and the potential scope of guardianship orders is discussed in the General Note to s.64.

Provisions of other Parts of this Act of particular relevance are mentioned in the General Note to Pt. 3 (access to funds under that Part as an alternative to Pt. 6 procedures), the General Note to s.53 (intervention orders), the General Note to s.57 (guardianship) and the General Note to subs. (1) of s.58 (alternatives to guardianship).

Appointees under intervention and guardianship orders with property and financial powers, unlike curators bonis prior to this Act, are not trustees in terms of the Trusts (Scotland) Act 1921 (11 & 12 Geo.5 c.58) and other legislation.

For transitional provisions relevant to pre–2000 Act curators, tutors and 1984 Act guardians, see Sched. 4, paras. 1, 2, 3, 6, 7 and 8.

Jurisdiction
Under the transitional provisions of this Act, all existing curators bonis and tutors to adults became guardians under this Act on April 1, 2002 (see s.88 (1), Sched. 4 and SSI 2001/81). The only exceptions were the very limited ones contained in para. 6 of Sched. 4. All of the rest of this Act's regime has applied to such transitional guardians from April 1, 2002. Thus, provisions which apply to transitional guardians just as they apply to guardians appointed after commencement include the various provisions in Pt. 6 and Sched. 2 under which the sheriff has jurisdiction in relation to intervention and guardianship orders, and jurisdiction will normally follow the habitual residence of the adult. Also applicable to transitional guardians are the various procedures subsequent to initial appointment such as replacement, removal or recall under s.71; variation of powers under s.74; appointment of a joint guardian under s.62; and appointment of a substitute guardian under s.63. There were nevertheless suggestions in more than one case that where it was desired to replace a transitional guardian originally appointed by the Court of Session, it would be necessary to apply to that court for discharge. Such application would have been not only unnecessary but in this commentator's view also incompetent. The appropriate procedure is an application to the sheriff under s.71, equally applicable to guardians appointed under this Act and to transitional guardians, whatever their source of original appointment. The point of necessity (though not competence) was dealt with by Sheriff Baird at Glasgow Sheriff Court in *Kirkland* (AW21/04 Glasgow Sh. Ct., May 14, 2004). After going through the relevant statutory provisions in his judgement, the sheriff concluded the note to his interlocutor by referring also to the benefit principle. "It seemed to me" he wrote "that the Sheriff Court does have the power to grant the order which is sought, and that it is not necessary to incur the extra expense involved in bringing petitions before two separate courts in order to achieve something which is desirable and necessary, and which is

always, in any event, overseen by the Office of the Public Guardian, and where the expense has to be met from the resources of the adult himself'. See also *F.W.* (Glasgow Sh. Ct., November 29, 2005).

There were likewise suggestions that application under the "old régime" for authority to encroach on capital was still required by transitional guardians even after commencement. Not only was the old régime swept away with the repeal inter alia of the Judicial Factors Act 1849 as it applied to tutors and curators, but in terms of s.64 (5) of this Act financial guardians are entitled (subject to certain provisos) to use the capital and income of the adult's estate to purchase assets, services or accommodation so as to enhance the adult's quality of life, and it would be wrongful for them to fail to encroach on capital where doing so would accord with this Act's s.1 principles. That also has applied to transitional guardians from April 1, 2002.

Curator ad litem or Part 6 appointment?
In *Summary Application by James Robertson, PF for the public interest* (Kirkcaldy Sh. Ct. November 30, 2007, Scottish Courts Website) the sheriff considered and approved the views expressed in *Adult Incapacity* para. 10–43 that in order to conduct proceedings a guardianship order should normally be preferred over a curator *ad litem* where other guardianship powers are required or likely to be required, and that an intervention order should normally be preferred if no other powers are likely to be required.

Expenses
See the decision of Sheriff Mackie in *Applications by Francis Galashan and John Scott Lynn* (Edinburgh Sh. Ct. July 7, 2008, Scottish Courts Website) for discussion of awards of expenses in Pt. 6 applications, and their interpretation. Unless an order for the expenses to be met from the adult's estate explicitly states otherwise, the expenses should be calculated according to the judicial table for party and party expenses. See also General Note to s.8.

Intervention orders

53.—(1) The sheriff may, on an application by any person (including the adult himself) claiming an interest in the property, financial affairs or personal welfare of an adult, if he is satisfied that the adult is incapable of taking the action, or is incapable in relation to the decision about his property, financial affairs or personal welfare to which the application relates, make an order (in this Act referred to as an "intervention order").

(2) In considering an application under subsection (1), the sheriff shall have regard to any intervention order or guardianship order which may have been previously made in relation to the adult, and to any order varying, or ancillary to, such an order.

(3) Where it appears to the local authority that—

(a) the adult is incapable as mentioned in subsection (1); and
(b) no application has been made or is likely to be made for an order under this section in relation to the decision to which the application under this subsection relates; and
(c) an intervention order is necessary for the protection of the property, financial affairs or personal welfare of the adult,

they shall apply under this section for an order.

(4) [Subsections (3), (3A), (3B) and (4) of section 57][103] shall apply to an application under this section and, for this purpose, for the reference to the individual or office holder nominated for appointment as guardian there shall be substituted a reference to a person nominated in such application.

(5) An intervention order may—

(a) direct the taking of any action specified in the order;

---

[103] Substituted by Adult Support and Protection (Scotland) Act 2007 (asp 10), s.59(1)(a).

(b) authorise the person nominated in the application to take such action or make such decision in relation to the property, financial affairs or personal welfare of the adult as is specified in the order;

(6) Where an intervention order directs the acquisition of accommodation for, or the disposal of any accommodation used for the time being as a dwelling house by, the adult, the consent of the Public Guardian as respects the consideration shall be required before the accommodation is acquired or, as the case may be, disposed of.

(7) In making or varying an intervention order the sheriff may, [. . .][104] in the case of an intervention order relating to property or financial affairs [. . .][105] require the person authorised under the order to find caution [or to give such other security as the sheriff thinks fit][106].

(8) The sheriff may, on an application by—

(a) the person authorised under the intervention order; or
(b) the adult; or
(c) any person claiming an interest in the property, financial affairs or personal welfare of the adult,

make an order varying the terms of, or recalling, the intervention order or any other order made for the purposes of the intervention order.

(9) Anything done under an intervention order shall have the same effect as if done by the adult if he had the capacity to do so.

(10) Where an intervention order is made, the sheriff clerk shall forthwith send a copy of the interlocutor containing the order to the Public Guardian who shall—

(a) enter in the register maintained by him under section 6(2)(b)(v) such particulars of the order as may be prescribed; [. . .][107]
[(aa) when satisfied that the person authorised under the order has found caution or given other security if so required, issue a certificate of appointment to the person; and][108]
(b) notify the adult, the local authority and (in a case where the adult's incapacity is by reason of, or reasons which include, mental disorder and the intervention order relates to the adult's personal welfare or factors which include it) the Mental Welfare Commission [of the terms of the interlocutor][109].

(11) A transaction for value between a person authorised under an intervention order, purporting to act as such, and a third party acting in good faith shall not be invalid on the ground only that—

(a) the person acted outwith the scope of his authority;
(b) the person failed to observe any requirement, whether substantive or procedural, imposed by or under this Act or by the sheriff or by the Public Guardian; or
(c) there was any irregularity whether substantive or procedural in the authorisation of the person.

---

[104] Repealed by Adult Support and Protection (Scotland) Act 2007 (asp 10), s.59(1)(b)(i).
[105] Repealed by Adult Support and Protection (Scotland) Act 2007 (asp 10), s.59(1)(b)(i).
[106] Inserted by Adult Support and Protection (Scotland) Act 2007 (asp 10), s.59(1)(b)(ii).
[107] Repealed by Adult Support and Protection (Scotland) Act 2007 (asp 10), s.59(1)(c)(i).
[108] Inserted by Adult Support and Protection (Scotland) Act 2007 (asp 10), s.59(1)(c)(ii).
[109] Inserted by Adult Support and Protection (Scotland) Act 2007 (asp 10), s.59(1)(c)(iii).

(12) A person authorised under an intervention order may recover from the estate of the adult the amount of such reasonable outlays as he incurs in doing anything directed or authorised under the order.

(13) Where a third party has acquired, in good faith and for value, title to any interest in heritable property from a person authorised under an intervention order that title shall not be challengeable on the ground only—

(a) of any irregularity of procedure in the making of the intervention order; or
(b) that the person authorised under the intervention order has acted outwith the scope of the authority.

(14) Sections 64(2) and 67(3) and (4) shall apply to an intervention order as they apply to a guardianship order and, for this purpose, for any reference to a guardian there shall be substituted a reference to the person authorised under the order.

DEFINITIONS
"adult" : s.1 (6)
"guardianship order" : s.58 (4)
"incapable" : s.1 (6)
"incapacity" : s.1 (6)
"intervention order" : s.53 (1)
"local authority" : s.87 (1) (referring to the Local Government etc. (Scotland) Act 1994 (c.39) s.2)
"mental disorder" : s.87 (1) (and see General Note to s.1 (6))
"Mental Welfare Commission" : s.87 (1) (referring to s.4 of the 2003 Act)
"office holder" : s.87 (1)
"person claiming an interest" : s.87 (1)
"prescribed" : s.87 (1) (and see s.86)
"Public Guardian" : s.6 (1)

GENERAL NOTE
Intervention orders are dealt with in this section, in the next following ss.54, 55 and 56, in the provisions of s.57 (3), (3A), (3B) and (4) as applied and adapted by subs. (4) of this section, the provisions of s.64 (2) and s.67 (3) and (4) as applied and adapted by subs. (14) of this section, and ss.71 (4) and 77. Provisions of other Parts of this Act of particular relevance are in Pt. 1 generally (and especially the general principles in s.1 and the sheriff's powers in s.3), in ss.24B, 46, 49, 50, 58 (3), 81, 82 and 83, and in Sched. 3.

Intervention orders may take two forms. They may direct the taking of specified action; or they may authorise the appointee to take specified action or make a specified decision (subs. (5)). There appears to be no reason why an intervention order should not do both, where appropriate. The order may be directed to personal welfare, or property and financial affairs, or both (see, e.g., subs. (5)(b)). Examples of particular matters which might be addressed are given in this Act itself. Subsection (6) (matters requiring the Public Guardian's consent) refers to the acquisition or disposal of residential accommodation: the language would appear to include interests as owner, tenant or lessee—s.56 (1) refers to orders vesting in the appointee right to deal with, convey or manage any interest in heritable property which is recorded or registered (or capable of being recorded or registered). Short-term powers previously conferred upon tutors-dative are likely to be available: examples include dealing with an interest in testate or intestate succession, including a legal rights entitlement, and dealing with a proposed deed of family arrangement or the proposed establishment of a trust in lieu of outright payment of an interest in succession; or making particular decisions about medical treatment. Also likely to be available are orders to take steps hitherto authorised by grants of special powers to curators bonis, where guardianship is not needed. More than one intervention order may be granted or in force at the same time, and an intervention order may be granted or in force concurrently with a guardianship order.

Within the whole field or property, financial affairs and personal welfare, the possible scope of intervention orders is only definitively circumscribed by the exclusions specified in s.64 (2), which include matters where 2003 Act procedures will prevail. While s.64 (11) provides for the scope of guardianship powers to be defined, and thus *inter alia* limited, by regulations, there is no equivalent provision in relation to the scope of intervention orders. There is no limitation to matters which were competent to curators, tutors or others under pre–2000 Act law.

It would appear that an intervention order could be sought in a matter in which the *parens patriae* jurisdiction also remains competent, such as authorising the discontinuance of treatment for a patient in a persistent vegetative state. It would probably be better practice for applicants to continue to take such matters to the Court of Session under the *parens patriae* jurisdiction, but it would not seem that a sheriff could refuse to deal with such an application on grounds of competency.

For jurisdiction in emergencies, see Sched. 3 paras. 1(1)(c), and 2(1)(c) and (3). The sheriff's general power to make interim orders under s.3 (2)(d) may be helpful where there is urgency.

The sheriff may grant an intervention order where guardianship has been sought (s.58 (3)) or is recalled (s.71 (4)), but not vice versa, therefore if there is room for doubt as to which might be considered appropriate by the court, it is safer to present a guardianship application. Likewise, to avoid duplication of procedure it is generally better to submit a guardianship application where it is envisaged that an intervention order in property and financial matters, and welfare guardianship (or the converse), will probably be shown to be the appropriate outcome. Guardianship may also now be preferable to an intervention order where a future transition to Pt. 3 management is envisaged, because of the doubts discussed in the General Note to s.24B, and because the transitional mechanism under s.31E is available in relation to guardianship but not intervention orders. Decisions relevant to the use of intervention orders since their introduction in 2002 include the following:

Hugh Riley v James Beaton & Company (Plumbers) Limited and others, opinion dated June 14, 2004 of Lord MacKay of Drumadoon (Court of Session, Outer House). The Pursuer sought damages because of alleged exposure to asbestos. On April 1, 2004 the sheriff at Edinburgh granted an intervention order authorising the Pursuer's wife to conduct the action on his behalf. She was given "the fullest powers in relation to the conduct of the Action as if she were herself the Pursuer", various powers being explicitly stated. Lord MacKay held that, a copy of the intervention order having been presented to the court, it was not necessary for the court to make any further order. In particular it was unnecessary to require Mrs Riley to sist herself as a party to the action. The intervention order gave Mrs Riley sufficient authority to give the Pursuer's solicitors any instructions that they might require in order to bring the action to a conclusion. Any award of expenses in favour of the Defenders would require to be borne by the Pursuer. Mrs Riley was entitled to recover from his estate such reasonable outlays as she might incur in connection with the action.

F.B. Applicant, decision by Sheriff John Baird dated May 13, 2005 (reported as *B, Applicant*, 2005 SLT (Sh. Ct.) 95). Sheriff Baird pointed out the wide potential scope of intervention orders. It was claimed that the adult's late husband had developed lung disease due to exposure to dust in the course of his employment as a coal miner. An intervention order was granted authorising the adult's son to have himself confirmed as executor in his father's estate and to negotiate settlement of the claims of both of his parents.

Application in respect of Mrs H.T., decision by Sheriff John Baird dated July 12, 2005 (reported as *T, Applicant*, 2005 SLT (Sh. Ct.) 97). An intervention order was granted authorising the adult's solicitor to execute a codicil. One of the adult's two sons was deceased. She specifically instructed her solicitor that she wished her surviving son to be her principal beneficiary, and left her house to him. She retained affection for her other son's widow, did not wish to exclude the widow from benefit, and left the residue of her estate—which was expected to be modest—to the widow. The adult had also granted a Power of Attorney in favour of her surviving son and his wife. The Power of Attorney included power to sell the house, and such sale had become necessary. It was feared that this would defeat the intention of her Will. The sheriff authorised execution of a codicil making it clear that not just the house, but also the net free proceeds of sale thereof, were to be left to the son.

Application in respect of Mr D.M. (Glasgow Sheriff Court AW36/06, decision dated April 28, 2006) (reported as *M, Applicant*, 2007 SLT (Sh. Ct.) 24). This was an application by the three children of the adult, who were executors of his late wife. He had granted a Power of Attorney in favour of two of them, but it did not authorise them to discharge or renounce any claim for legal rights. Her Will left her entire estate to the children, and it appears from the sheriff's note that he was satisfied that both she and the adult intended that her estate should pass directly to them. The court granted an intervention order authorising the children, as applicants, to execute on the adult's behalf a discharge or renunciation of his *ius relicti* in the estate of his late wife. The sheriff was satisfied that in the circumstances the s.1 principles, including the benefit test, were met.

The specific provisions of ss.53–56A are clearly expressed and require little further comment.

Subs. (2)
The sheriff requires to have regard to the history of any previous intervention and guardianship orders in relation to the adult, and also to any currently in force.

The sheriff must also have regard to the general principles in s.1, and must consider whether he should appoint a safeguarder (or someone in addition to the safeguarder to ascertain and convey the adult's views) (s.3 (4) and (5)).

Subs. (3)
This subsection substantially replicated, in relation to intervention orders, the provisions of the 1984 Act s.92 (1) (repealed by Sched. 6) in relation to curatory petitions.

Subs. (4)
The requirements of s.57 (3) for reports and the provisions in s.57 (4) for intimation are incorporated by this subsection. See General Note to s.57.

Subs. (6)
Cf. Sched. 2 para. 6 in relation to guardianship orders. This subsection assumes that the transaction will have been authorised in principle in the intervention order, so that the Public Guardian's consent will be required as regards consideration only. As under guardianship, terms other than the consideration do not require such consent: see Note to Sched. 2 para. 6.

Subs. (7)
Prior to amendment by the 2007 Act, caution was mandatory—as for guardianship—except only where the appointee was unable to find caution, yet was considered by the court to be suitable for appointment. There is now no presumption for or against caution. There is also the alternative of offering some other security where caution might otherwise be required. See General Note to subs. (6) of s.58.

Subs. (14)
See General Notes to ss.64 and 67.

Records: intervention orders
54. A person authorised under an intervention order shall keep records of the exercise of his powers.

DEFINITIONS
"intervention order" : s.53 (1)

GENERAL NOTE
The accounting and other requirements of Sched. 2 apply only to guardians and not (unless the sheriff were so to direct) to appointees under intervention orders. However, such appointees, like attorneys (s.21), withdrawers (s.30B (1)) and guardians (s.65), are required to keep records of the exercise of their powers.

Notification of change of address
55. After particulars relating to an intervention order are entered in the register under section 53 the person authorised under the intervention order shall [, not later than 7 days after any change of the person's or the adult's address, notify the Public Guardian of the change who][110] shall enter

---

[110] Substituted by Adult Support and Protection (Scotland) Act 2007 (asp 10), s.59(2).

prescribed particulars in the register maintained by him under section 6(2)(b)(v) and notify the local authority and (in a case where the adult's incapacity is by reason of, or reasons which include, mental disorder and the intervention order relates to the adult's personal welfare or factors which include it) the Mental Welfare Commission.

DEFINITIONS
"adult" : s.1 (6)
"incapacity" : s.1 (6)
"intervention order" : s.53 (1)
"local authority" : s.87 (1) (referring to the Local Government etc. (Scotland) Act 1994 (c.39) s.2)
"mental disorder" : s.87 (1) (and see General Note to s.1 (6))
"Mental Welfare Commission" : s.87 (1) (referring to 2003 Act s.4)
"prescribed" : s.87 (1) (and see s.86)
"Public Guardian" : s.6 (1)

Registration of intervention order relating to heritable property
56.—(1) This section applies where the sheriff makes an intervention order which vests in the person authorised under the order any right to deal with, convey or manage any interest in heritable property which is recorded or is capable of being recorded in the General Register of Sasines or is registered or is capable of being registered in the Land Register of Scotland.

(2) In making such an order the sheriff shall specify each property affected by the order, in such terms as enable it to be identified in the Register of Sasines or, as the case may be, the Land Register of Scotland.

(3) The person authorised under the order shall forthwith apply to the Keeper of the Registers of Scotland for recording of the interlocutor containing the order in the General Register of Sasines or, as the case may be, for registering of it in the Land Register of Scotland.

(4) An application under subsection (3) shall contain—

(a) the name and address of the person authorised under the order;
(b) a statement that the person authorised under the order has powers relating to each property specified in the order;
(c) a copy of the interlocutor.

(5) Where the interlocutor is to be recorded in the General Register of Sasines, the Keeper shall—

(a) record the interlocutor in the Register; and
(b) endorse the interlocutor to the effect that it has been so recorded.

(6) Where the interlocutor is to be registered in the Land Register of Scotland, the Keeper shall update the title sheet of the property to show it.

(7) The person authorised under the order shall send the endorsed interlocutor or, as the case may be, the updated Land Certificate or an office copy thereof to the Public Guardian who shall enter prescribed particulars of it in the register maintained by him under section 6(2)(b)(v).

DEFINITIONS
"intervention order" : s.53 (1)
"prescribed" : s.87 (1) (and see s.86)
"Public Guardian" : s.6 (1)

Adults with Incapacity Legislation

GENERAL NOTE
Where an intervention order vests in the appointee right to deal with, convey or manage any interest in heritable property which is recorded or registered (or capable of being recorded or registered), then a conveyancing description must be included in the order (subs. (2)), and the order must be recorded or registered in accordance with subss. (3)–(6) and thereafter submitted to the Public Guardian for her to make an appropriate entry in her register. Section 61 contains similar provisions in relation to guardianship orders. Section 77 (4) provides protection for third parties acting in good faith. Sections 78 and 79 apply only to guardianship, and not to intervention orders. Paragraph 6 of Sched. 2 applies to the purchase or disposal of accommodation by guardians only, and not under intervention orders, but it would be open to the sheriff to exercise his powers under s.3 to apply similar requirements to an intervention order. Paragraph 14 of Sched. 5 amended the indemnity provisions of the Land Registration (Scotland) Act 1979 (c.33) to take account of this Act.

Death of person authorised to intervene
56A.—[111] Where a person authorised under an intervention order dies, the person's personal representatives shall, if aware of the existence of the authority, notify the Public Guardian who shall—

> (a) notify—
>> (i) the adult;
>> (ii) the local authority; and
>> (iii) in a case where the adult's incapacity is by reason of, or reasons which include, mental disorder and the intervention order relates to the adult's personal welfare or factors including it, the Mental Welfare Commission; and
>
> (b) enter prescribed particulars in the register maintained under section 6(2)(b)(v).

DEFINITIONS
"adult" : s.1 (6)
"intervention order" : s.53 (1)
"local authority" : s.87 (1) (referring to the Local Government etc. (Scotland) Act 1994 (c.39) s.2)
"Mental Welfare Commission" : s.87 (1) (referring to 2003 Act s.4)
"prescribed" : s.87 (1) (and see s.86)
"Public Guardian" : s.6 (1)

Guardianship orders

Application for guardianship order
57.—(1) An application may be made under this section by any person (including the adult himself) claiming an interest in the property, financial affairs or personal welfare of an adult to the sheriff for an order appointing an individual or office holder as guardian in relation to the adult's property, financial affairs or personal welfare.
  (2) Where it appears to the local authority that—

> (a) the conditions mentioned in section 58(1)(a) and (b) apply to the adult; and
> (b) no application has been made or is likely to be made for an order under this section; and

---
[111] Inserted by Adult Support and Protection (Scotland) Act 2007 (asp 10), s.59(3).

(c) a guardianship order is necessary for the protection of the property, financial affairs or personal welfare of the adult,

they shall apply under this section for an order.

(3) There shall be lodged in court along with an application under this section—

(a) reports, in prescribed form, of an examination and assessment of the adult carried out not more than 30 days before the lodging of the application by at least two medical practitioners one of whom, in a case where the incapacity is by reason of mental disorder, must be [a relevant][112] medical practitioner [. . .][113];
(b) where the application relates to the personal welfare of the adult, a report, in prescribed form, from the mental health officer, (but where it is in jeopardy only because of the inability of the adult to communicate, from the chief social work officer), containing his opinion as to—
   (i) the general appropriateness of the order sought, based on an interview and assessment of the adult carried out not more than 30 days before the lodging of the application; and
   (ii) the suitability of the individual nominated in the application to be appointed guardian; and
(c) where the application relates only to the property or financial affairs of the adult, a report, in prescribed form, based on an interview and assessment of the adult carried out not more than 30 days before the lodging of the application, by a person who has sufficient knowledge to make such a report as to the matters referred to in paragraph (b)(i) and (ii).

[(3A) Subsection (3B) applies where a report lodged under subsection (3)(a) relates to an examination and assessment carried out more than 30 days before the lodging of the application.

(3B) Where this subsection applies, the sheriff may, despite subsection (3)(a), continue to consider the application if satisfied that there has been no change in circumstances since the examination and assessment was carried out which may be relevant to matters set out in the report.][114]

(4) Where an applicant claims an interest in the personal welfare of the adult and is not the local authority, he shall give notice to the chief social work officer of his intention to make an application under this section and the report referred to in subsection (3)(b) shall be prepared by the chief social work officer or, as the case may be, the mental health officer, within 21 days of the date of the notice.

(5) The sheriff may, on an application being made to him, at any time before the disposal of the application made under this section, make an order for the appointment of an interim guardian.

(6) The appointment of an interim guardian in pursuance of this section shall, unless recalled earlier, cease to have effect—

(a) on the appointment of a guardian under section 58; or

---

[112] Substituted by Adult Support and Protection (Scotland) Act 2007 (asp 10), s.60(1)(a).
[113] Words repealed by Mental Health (Care and Treatment) (Scotland) Act 2003 (asp 13), Sch.5.
[114] Inserted by Adult Support and Protection (Scotland) Act 2007 (asp 10), s.60(1)(b).

(b) at the end of the [effective period][115],

whichever is the earlier.

[(6A) The "effective period", for the purposes of subsection (6), means—

(a) the period of 3 months beginning with the date of appointment; or
(b) such longer period (not exceeding 6 months) beginning with that date as the sheriff may specify in the order.

(6B) In subsection (3)(a), "relevant medical practitioner" means—

(a) an approved medical practitioner;
(b) where the adult concerned is not present in Scotland, a person who—
  (i) holds qualifications recognised in the place where the adult is present and has special experience in relation to the diagnosis and treatment of mental disorder which correspond to the qualifications and experience needed to be an approved medical practitioner; and
  (ii) has consulted the Mental Welfare Commission for Scotland about the report concerned; or
(c) any other type of individual described (by reference to skills, qualifications, experience or otherwise) by regulations made by the Scottish Ministers.

(6C) The Scottish Ministers shall consult the Mental Welfare Commission before making regulations under subsection (6B)(c).][116]

[(7) In subsection [(6B)][117], "approved medical practitioner" has the meaning given by section 22 of the 2003 Act.][118]

DEFINITIONS
"adult" : s.1 (6)
"application" : s.2 (2)
"approved medical practitioner" : s.57 (7) (referring to s.22 of the 2003 Act)
"chief social work officer" : Social Work (Scotland) Act 1968 (c.49) s.3 (presumed)
"effective period" : s.57 (6A)
"guardianship order" : s.58 (4)
"incapacity" : s.1 (6)
"local authority" : s.87 (1) (referring to the Local Government etc. (Scotland) Act 1994 (c.39) s.2)
"mental disorder" : s.87 (1) (and see General Note to s.1 (6))
"mental health officer" : s.87 (1) (referring to s.329 of the 2003 Act)
"Mental Welfare Commission" : s.87 (1) (referring to 2003 Act s.4)
"office holder" : s.87 (1)
"person claiming an interest" : s.87 (1)
"prescribed" : s.87 (1) (and see s.86)
"relevant medical practitioner" : s.57 (6B)

---

[115] Substituted by Adult Support and Protection (Scotland) Act 2007 (asp 10), s.60(1)(c).
[116] Inserted by Adult Support and Protection (Scotland) Act 2007 (asp 10), s.60(1)(d).
[117] Substituted by Adult Support and Protection (Scotland) Act 2007 (asp 10), s.60(1)(e).
[118] Inserted by Mental Health (Care and Treatment) (Scotland) Act 2003 (asp 13), Sch.4, para.9(4)(b).

Adults with Incapacity (Scotland) Act 2000 (Pt. 6)

GENERAL NOTE
Guardianship is dealt with in this and the remaining sections of Pt. 6, and in Sched. 2. Provisions of other Parts of this Act of particular relevance are in Pt. 1 generally (and especially the general principles in s.1 and the sheriff's powers in s.3), in ss.24B, 46, 49, 50, 81, 82 and 83, and in Scheds. 3 and 4.

Like appointments of tutors-dative as revived in the last two decades of last century, and unlike appointments of former curators bonis, guardianship orders are limited as to duration (ss.58 (4) and 60 (4)) and flexible as to powers granted (s.64 (1)). Former 1984 Act guardianship had the former quality but lacked the latter. The potential scope of guardianship orders is discussed in the General Note to s.64.

Subsections (1)–(4) and (6B)–(7) of this section deal with the initiation of guardianship applications, and subss. (5)–(6A) deal with the appointment of interim guardians, for a period of from three to six months. In dealing with the application, the sheriff must comply with the general principles in s.1, and also has the powers and duties in s.3. Under s.59 the sheriff requires to be satisfied that the proposed guardian is suitable and has consented, and as to the other requirements of that section. Dual (or multiple), joint and substitute appointments may be sought in terms of ss.58 (5), 62 and 63 respectively. Other matters which applicants may wish to consider at time of application are whether the sheriff should be requested to make any interim order under s.3 (2)(d) (as well as or instead of any interim appointment under subss. (5) and (6) of this section), or to exercise any of his other discretionary powers under s.3; to direct in terms of s.11 (1) that intimation should not be given to the adult; to dispense with caution in terms of s.58 (6); to dispense with a management plan in terms of Sched. 2 para. 1(1); to confer in terms of Sched. 2 para. 1(4) powers which may be exercised prior to approval of the management plan; or to specify in terms of s.1 (4)(c)(ii) anyone whom the guardian should consult.

Subs. (1)
On the form of application and procedure, see note to s.2 (2).

Subs. (2)
This subsection substantially replicated, in relation to guardianship applications, the provisions of the 1984 Act s.92 (1) (repealed by Sched. 6) in relation to curatory petitions, but see also the similar provisions in relation to intervention orders in s.53 (3) and the requirement of s.58 (1)(b) not to grant a guardianship order where another option under this Act would suffice.

Subs. (3)
This subsection also applies, suitably adapted, to applications for intervention orders (s.53 (4)). Three reports in prescribed form (see SSI 2002/96 as amended by SSI 2008/55) are required, all based on assessments, subject to subss. (3A) and (3B), carried out within 30 days before lodging of the application. Two of them are medical reports. Where incapacity results from mental disorder, then (as with applications under the 1984 Act s.18) one must be from "a relevant medical practitioner" (see subs. (6B)). The third is a report as to general appropriateness of the order sought and suitability of the proposed guardian. Where personal welfare powers are sought (whether or not combined with property and financial powers) this third report must be provided by the mental health officer, or by the chief social work officer if incapacity arises from inability to communicate only. Where only property and financial powers are sought, anyone with sufficient knowledge may provide the third report. The sheriff can order additional reports or information, further assessments or interviews, and make further inquiries, under s.3 (2).

There seems to be some confusion about which applications under this Act require the three reports specified in this subs. (3), and which do not. Some sheriff clerks initially looked for the full range of reports for all types of application, and some staff in the Office of the Public Guardian also did so. To demand reports where they are not required by this Act, and where the circumstances demonstrate no benefit to the adult or necessity in doing so, would contravene the s.1 principles. This Act is explicit about where the three reports are required. They are required for: initial appointment (s.57); appointment of a joint guardian at time of initial application (under s.62 (1)(a)); and a variation under s.74 which adds welfare powers to what was previously a financial guardianship, or vice versa (per s.74 (4)). The three reports are not required for subsequent appointment of a joint guardian under s.62 (1)(b); appointment of a substitute guardian under s.63; replacement, removal or recall under s.71; or for variation under s.74, except where the variation would confer for the first time welfare powers upon a guardian who previously had property and financial powers only, or vice versa. The three reports under s.57 (3) are not required for all of the other applications, remits and appeals to the sheriff under the Incapacity Act. The sheriff has discretion under s.3 (2)(b) and (c) to order reports or make further enquiry, but such discretionary powers should only be exercised where there are *prima facie* reasons for doing so, and where it would be in accordance with the s.1 principles to do so. On the other hand, in applications such as for appointment of additional or replacement guardians (where the formal reports are not a statutory requirement) it will generally be helpful to obtain and produce a simple letter from a doctor—often the general practitioner—confirming, if such be the case, that there have been no significant changes in the adult's condition and capabilities since the original appointment. This can be helpful to the applicant's agent, and to the court, in cases where the original appointment was several years ago under former procedures, and the existing guardian is thus a transitional guardian. In *Kirkland*, (AW21/04 Glasgow Sh. Ct., May 14, 2004), Sheriff Baird stated that in such cases he would be satisfied with a "short, recent, medical report confirming that there has been no change in the adult's condition", and in *F.W.* (Glasgow Sh. Ct., November 29, 2005), he confirmed that such a medical report need not be provided by an "approved medical practitioner" (as defined in s.57 (7)).

Renewal applications now have their own particular requirements: see s.60 (3) and (3A).

There have been cases where applicants have been passed from one local authority to another when seeking a mental health officer's report for an application. It would appear that the position is this. This Act is concerned with the factual, objective test of "the area in which the adult resides" (or, in the case of the jurisdiction provisions in Sched. 3, the place where "the adult is habitually resident"). It is reasonable to assume that these tests are predicated upon the situation of an adult with impaired capacity who is not able to make valid choices and decisions which would be relevant to tests based on intention. This Act does not require applicants to approach any particular mental health officer with a request for a report. Section 57 (4) requires the applicant, in welfare cases, to give notice to the chief social work officer of the applicant's intention to make an application. That notice triggers the requirement for the mental health officer's report to be prepared within 21 days of the date of the notice. This Act refers sometimes to "the chief social work officer of the local authority" and sometimes simply to "the chief social work officer", but there is no reason to think that the phrases are not used synonymously. "The chief social work officer" is not defined in this Act, but is defined in s.3 of the 1968 Act as the person appointed to that position by the local authority. There appears to be no reason to consider that this Act, in any of its provisions, when referring to the chief social work officer refers to any person other than the chief social work officer appointed in terms of s.3 of the 1968 Act by the local authority which is the relevant authority in terms of this Act. Section 87(1) of this Act specifies that "references to a local authority shall be construed as references to the local authority for the area in which the adult resides". Once notice under s.57 (4) has been given to that chief social work officer, it is for the chief social work officer, not the applicant, to determine which mental health officer should prepare the report. Under s.32 (1) of the 2003 Act local authorities appoint persons satisfying the requirements of s.32 (2) of the 2003 Act to discharge "in relation to their [i.e. the local authority's] area" the functions of mental health officers under the Criminal Procedure (Scotland) Act 1995 (c46), the Incapacity Act and the 2003 Act itself. It is understood that there are arrangements between some local authorities under which the report may be prepared by a mental health officer employed by the local authority funding a placement outside that authority's area, where notice has been properly given to the chief social work officer for the placement area. There also appear to be some peripatetic mental health officers who divide their time among different authorities. The practical concerns of applicants are to ascertain which sheriff court has jurisdiction, to give notice to the correct chief social work officer, and to receive timeously a report prepared by a mental health officer given that task by or with the authority of the chief social work officer.

Subss. (3A) and (3B)
These subsections introduce a degree of flexibility absent from the 2000 text, which did not qualify "carried out not more than 30 days before the lodging of the application" each time those words appear in s.57 (3). Difficulties in "managing the timetable" were inevitable.

In *Frank Stork and others*, 2004 SCLR 513, the mental health officer's report had not been prepared within the 21–day period required by s.57 (4), and in consequence the medical reports were—by the time that the application was lodged in court—older than the 30 days required in terms of s.57 (3). Sheriff Vannet rejected a submission that he had discretion under s.3 (1) to allow the application to be received notwithstanding these deficiencies (see also *Cooke v Telford* 2005 SCLR (Sh. Ct.) 367 and note to s.3 (1)). Instead he interpreted "shall" in s.57 (3) as being "directory rather than mandatory". He concluded that: "Such an interpretation appears to me to be in harmony with the purpose and principles of the Act". He referred to the benefit principle in commenting that: "If the provisions of s.57 (3) and (4) are to be strictly enforced, then the Pursuers will have to go to the trouble and expense of instructing examinations and assessments of [the adult] of new, and will have to raise a new application and obtain another report from the mental health officer. Lest the subject of the application be forgotten, such a course would mean that [the adult] would have to undergo examination and assessment again by two medical practitioners. I do not believe that the legislature intended such a result. It goes against the whole spirit behind the Act." Sheriff Principal Bowen gave further consideration to this issue, and addressed the status of out-of-date reports, in *Application by Glasgow City Council for appointment of welfare guardian to AD*, June 27, 2005. Subsections (3A) and (3B) now give effect to the common-sense approach of these learned sheriffs. Where a medical report is lodged it is now valid even where the medical examination of the adult was carried out more than 30 days previously, provided that the sheriff is satisfied that, since the examination was carried out, there has been no change in circumstances which might be relevant to matters set out in the report. The Bill for the 2007 Act as introduced referred to a requirement that the adult's condition is unlikely to have improved, but the Law Society pointed out successfully that this was not the appropriate test: the adult's condition could have improved, but capacity could remain equally impaired in relation to circumstances and needs. It is to be recommended that applicants should still use all reasonable endeavours to comply with the 30–day requirement. If they stray beyond it, they will have to persuade the sheriff that it is appropriate to apply the new provision. In some cases since April 1, 2008, where mental health officers have been aware of likely delay, they have helpfully—on request—confirmed in their reports that there has been no change in circumstances since the medical examinations were carried out. The courts appear to be willing to accept an explanation and request to exercise discretion under these subsections by covering letter submitting the application.

Subs. (4)
This subsection, which like subss. (3)—(3B) also applies (suitably adapted) to applications for intervention orders (s.53 (4)), meets concerns that under the draft Bill annexed to the SLC Report applicants other than local authorities could encounter delays in obtaining reports. There may be workload and resource implications for mental health officers and their employing authorities, but it is clearly essential that there should either be such a time limit or an alternative source of reports for applicants, and the Parliament opted for the former. Even so, local authorities sometimes fail to comply—e.g. see *Stork*, above.

Subss. (5)–(6A)
The availability of interim appointments may be valuable in urgent situations, but the wording indicates that the application requires first to have been competently initiated, so that the reports needed in terms of subs. (3) would require to have been obtained, unless the sheriff were to be persuaded that his powers under s.3 enabled him to respond to an emergency before all the requirements of subs. (3) had been met.

Care should be taken to ensure that the sheriff is asked to confer upon the interim guardian such powers as will be required to address the matters necessitating the appointment, including any in terms of Sched. 2 para. 1(4). See Sched. 3 paras. 1(1)(c), and 2(1)(c) and (3), regarding jurisdiction in emergencies. See s.64 (8) as to the duty of interim guardians to make monthly reports.

Having regard to s.58 (1)(b), and also s.1 (3), interim guardianship should not be sought where an interim order under s.3 (2)(d), or an intervention order under ss.53 or 58 (3), would suffice.

The 2000 text limited interim appointments to a maximum of three months, giving rise to expressions of judicial concern in some cases. Sheriffs may now grant interim guardianships for three months or for a longer period up to a maximum of six months.

Subss. (6B)–(7)
H, Applicant, 2007 SLT (Sh. Ct.) 5 was an application to appoint a financial guardian who had property in Scotland, thus founding jurisdiction under Sched. 3, para. 1(1)(b), but who, after living in Scotland for over 60 years, had returned to her native Northern Ireland and was

resident in a care home there. Both medical reports were submitted by medical practitioners practising in Northern Ireland, and certified by an appropriate health authority there. It was held that neither satisfied the requirement for a report from an "approved medical practitioner" in terms of the 2000 text as amended by the 2003 Act, though either would suffice for the second medical report. In *F.W.*, (Glasgow Sh. Ct., November 29, 2005), the sheriff mentioned *obiter* that he had encountered a similar issue in a previous case. There are now two alternatives to the "approved medical practitioner". Firstly, where the adult is not present in Scotland the relevant report may be provided by a person who holds qualifications equivalent to those of an approved medical practitioner and who has consulted MWC about the report. Secondly, such a report may simply be provided by "a person of such other description as the Scottish Ministers may prescribe". The "approved medical practitioner" and these alternatives are encompassed within the new definition of "relevant medical practitioner", who must now provide one of the medical reports (and also the only medical report under the new renewal procedure—see s.60).

Disposal of application
58.—(1) Where the sheriff is satisfied in considering an application under section 57 that—

- (a) the adult is incapable in relation to decisions about, or of acting to safeguard or promote his interests in, his property, financial affairs or personal welfare, and is likely to continue to be so incapable; and
- (b) no other means provided by or under this Act would be sufficient to enable the adult's interests in his property, financial affairs or personal welfare to be safeguarded or promoted,

he may grant the application.

(2) In considering an application under section 57, the sheriff shall have regard to any intervention order or guardianship order which may have been previously made in relation to the adult, and to any order varying, or ancillary to, such an order.

(3) Where the sheriff is satisfied that an intervention order would be sufficient as mentioned in subsection (1), he may treat the application under this section as an application for an intervention order under section 53 and may make such order as appears to him to be appropriate.

(4) Where the sheriff grants the application under section 57 he shall make an order (in this Act referred to as a "guardianship order") appointing the individual or office holder nominated in the application to be the guardian of the adult for a period of 3 years or such other period (including an indefinite period) as, on cause shown, he may determine.

(5) Where more than one individual or office holder is nominated in the application, a guardianship order may, without prejudice to the power under section 62(1) to appoint joint guardians, appoint two or more guardians to exercise different powers in relation to the adult.

(6) In making a guardianship order relating to the property or financial affairs of the adult the sheriff [may][119] require an individual appointed as guardian to find caution [or to give such other security as the sheriff thinks fit][120].

(7) Where the sheriff makes a guardianship order the sheriff clerk shall forthwith send a copy of the interlocutor containing the order to the Public Guardian who shall—

---

[119] Substituted by Adult Support and Protection (Scotland) Act 2007 (asp 10), s.60(2)(a)(i).
[120] Inserted by Adult Support and Protection (Scotland) Act 2007 (asp 10), s.60(2)(a)(ii).

Adults with Incapacity (Scotland) Act 2000 (Pt. 6)

(a) enter prescribed particulars of the appointment in the register maintained by him under section 6(2)(b)(iv);
(b) when satisfied that the guardian has found caution [or given other security][121] if so required, issue a certificate of appointment to the guardian;
(c) notify the adult of the appointment of the guardian; and
(d) notify the local authority and (in a case where the incapacity of the adult is by reason of, or reasons which include, mental disorder and the guardianship order relates to the adult's personal welfare or factors which include it) the Mental Welfare Commission of the terms of the interlocutor.

DEFINITIONS
"adult" : s.1 (6)
"guardianship order" : s.58 (4)
"incapable" : s.1 (6)
"incapacity" : s.1 (6)
"intervention order" : s.53 (1)
"local authority" : s.87 (1) (referring to the Local Government etc. (Scotland) Act 1994 (c.39) s.2)
"mental disorder" : s.87 (1) (and see General Note to s.1 (6))
"Mental Welfare Commission" : s.87 (1) (referring to s.4 of the 2003 Act)
"office holder" : s.87 (1)
"prescribed" : s.87 (1) (and see s.86)
"Public Guardian" : s.6 (1)

GENERAL NOTE

Subs. (1)
Paragraph (b) effectively declares guardianship to be the most restrictive of the options available under this Act in terms of s.1 (3)—see General Note to that subsection. As there noted, the recall and termination provisions of this Act refer to any alternatives, not limited to those under this Act (see s.71 (1)(c)(ii)). At time of application, an alternative outwith this Act might well be preferable by reference to the principle of benefit (s.1 (2)) and the least restrictive option (s.1 (3)). The difference is that the precedence of alternatives under this Act is in terms of s.58 (1)(b) explicit and mandatory, whereas consideration of alternatives outwith this Act implies a wider discretion by reference to the s.1 principles; and in some cases it may be relevant for the court to note that the Parliament has chosen not to give to any alternative outwith this Act the same status in this regard as alternatives under this Act.

The General Note to Pt. 3 emphasises the importance of the new provisions of that Part, introduced by the 2007 Act, as potential alternatives to financial and property orders under Pt. 6.

There has been much debate about when to invoke Pt. 6 at all. That debate focused upon issues leading up to the insertion, by s.64 of the 2007 Act, of the new s.13ZA of the 1968 Act, and the publication of related "Guidance for Local Authorities (March 2007) Provision of community care services to adults with incapacity", which in terms of s.5 of the 1968 Act is binding upon local authorities. Those issues, s.13ZA and the guidance, and their relationship to this Act, are described and discussed in the General Note to s.13ZA (Appendix 1 *infra*). Put briefly, it is suggested that the following conclusions would be reasonable: (a) the s.1 principles of this Act require an element of proportionality, so that a Pt. 6 application is unlikely to be justified for only interventions which satisfy the three requirements of being minor, non-controversial and fully in accordance with the s.1 principles; (b) there is a clear distinction between public law duties to make services available, and private law questions of accepting those services and consenting to any interventions which may occur in consequence of such acceptance, a distinction that can only be bridged by explicit provision such as that now

---
[121] Inserted by Adult Support and Protection (Scotland) Act 2007 (asp 10), s.60(2)(b).

contained in s.13ZA of the 1968 Act; and (c) it is difficult to envisage any circumstances in which it would be appropriate for a court to refuse a Pt. 6 application by reference to the availability of procedure under s.13ZA of the 1968 Act.

In *Applications in respect of E.B.* (Glasgow Sh. Ct., December 1, 2005), it was submitted that the powers sought in an application to renew welfare guardianship could be authorised under a community treatment order (CTO) and that the mental health officer could apply to the mental health tribunal to vary those powers. Even place of residence could be varied under a CTO. It was submitted that guardianship was unnecessary. The sheriff renewed the welfare guardianship. He said that he did not find the decision an easy one to take. He concluded that it was not right to concentrate on whether a welfare guardianship under this Act or a CTO under the 2003 Act would be the less restrictive option. He believed that the question should be whether the proposed intervention under this Act would benefit the adult and, if so, whether such benefit could reasonably be achieved without such intervention. The sheriff was swayed by concern as to what would happen when the CTO was discharged. The adult would leave hospital with nowhere to go. She could well become homeless. Without appropriate support, she would be unable to cope or to look after herself.

Subs. (2)
The sheriff requires to have regard to the history of relevant orders concerning the adult, and to any currently in force.

The sheriff is also obliged to apply the principles contained in s.1, and must consider whether he should appoint a safeguarder (or someone in addition to the safeguarder to ascertain and convey the adult's views) (s.3 (4) and (5)).

Subs. (3)
One of the many disadvantages of the law as it stood prior to this Act was that if one procedure had been initiated and found to be inappropriate, it was generally necessary to re-commence *ab initio* with another. Thus, for example, an unreported 1984 Act guardianship application in Glasgow Sheriff Court in 2000 was continued to allow the Court of Session to be petitioned for appointment of tutors-dative, on the basis that such powers were more appropriate to meet the needs of the case, allowing an elderly lady to return home with suitable powers in place to facilitate a prompt response if her physical health deteriorated. This Act seeks to achieve a "one-door" approach, under which personal and/or property powers, and anything from an intervention order through guardianship with limited powers to guardianship with extensive powers, may be granted following upon the same application. Experience indicates that sheriffs will not infrequently find it appropriate to grant an order differing from that sought at the outset. Under this subsection they are empowered to grant an intervention order where guardianship has been sought in the application, but note that the combined effect of this subsection and subs. (1)(b) is that they are obliged to do so where an intervention order is appropriate and will suffice. Section 71 (4) empowers them to grant an intervention order when recalling a guardianship order. They cannot grant a guardianship order where an intervention order has been sought. In cases of doubt, an applicant may apply for guardianship but seek to persuade the sheriff to grant an intervention order under s.58 (3), or to grant one type of order in welfare matters and the other in financial and property matters. As the procedural requirements for both types of order are the same, alternative craves might technically be possible, but could raise difficulties over what accompanying reports should be submitted and whether two sets of reports could properly be issued.

Subs. (4)
The initial duration of the order is dealt with in this subsection. See s.64 (1) and (2) as regards the powers conferred. Unless cause be shown for longer duration, the maximum for initial appointment is three years and the maximum for renewals (s.60 (4)(b)) is five years. It would appear that where property and financial powers are conferred under variation procedure on a guardian hitherto having welfare powers only, or vice versa, the normal initial maximum for those new powers will be three years, because s.74 (4) requires such variation to proceed as a fresh application under s.57.

A flaw of curatory procedure was that appointments were generally indefinite, so that the suitability of the appointment was not reviewed. Following re-introduction of tutors-dative in 1986, a small number of unlimited appointments were granted, but the Court of Session thereafter addressed the question of suitable duration with care, requiring good reason to appoint for more than five years and not exceeding ten years (see Ashton and Ward *Mental*

Adults with Incapacity (Scotland) Act 2000 (Pt. 6)

Handicap and the Law, pp 138-139), though welfare tutory lacked the monitoring and supervision of guardianship. In the case of adults with learning disabilities, capabilities may continue to develop during their 20's, but remain relatively static for long periods thereafter, so that requiring guardians to re-apply after three years, and every five years thereafter, could in some cases be unduly burdensome, and longer appointments likely, on cause shown, to be appropriate and acceptable. In the case of an adult who is elderly or has a terminal condition, where capacity is irreversible, an indefinite appointment may be reasonable, rather than risking putting all concerned through renewal procedure should the adult happen to survive rather longer than anticipated. Indeed, anything other than an appointment explicitly for the lifetime of the adult—a formulation now adopted by some sheriffs—may contravene the benefit principle. On the other hand, where there are significant issues or significant concerns, less than three years may be appropriate. In *North Ayrshire Council v J.M.* (Sh. Ct.) 2004 SCLR 956 a welfare guardian was appointed for two years. It should be remembered that under statutory guardianship the fixed duration on first appointment was in 1984 halved from one year to six months. In applying this Act's principles to this issue, as one must, the relevant question may be: is there likely to be benefit to the adult in requiring everyone to go through the renewal procedure? In some cases the considerable trouble and cost of renewal procedure has been a consideration in granting orders for longer than might otherwise have been the case. That concern is reduced, though not eliminated, by the simplified renewal procedure introduced by the 2007 Act (see s.60 and note thereto). It remains the case that the effect of this subsection is to place a clear onus on an applicant seeking initial appointment for more than three years (and s.60 (4)(b) creates a similar onus for renewals exceeding five years).

By inference from the wording of s.57 (6), where there has been an initial interim appointment, the three years will run from the commencement of the full appointment.

Subs. (5)
For joint guardians generally, including those sharing the same powers, see s.62. This subsection refers to dual (or multiple) appointments of guardians each exercising different powers. Section 62 (7) envisages agreed allocation of functions among joint guardians.

Subs. (6)
Under the 2000 text, the sheriff had discretion to dispense with caution only where the proposed appointee was unable to obtain caution. Otherwise, caution had to be found. Until recently the only cautioners were Royal & Sun Alliance and Zurich GSG. Annual premiums could be up to 0.75% of the estate, a very significant cost on a substantial estate. It was difficult not to see it as an advantage when both companies declined to provide caution for an eminently reputable and suitable guardian, so that the court could be asked to dispense with caution altogether in terms of the original s.58 (6). That happened in one unreported case where the total value of the estate was around £750,000, saving the estate an annual charge for caution of at least £4,500, and possibly up to £5,625. It also happened in relation to a slightly smaller estate (see *Application in respect of R.L.*, below). In some recent cases where caution was available, but the sheriff took the view that the cost would have been unduly burdensome in relation to the benefit derived for the adult, the court fixed caution at nil. In *Hugh Riley v James Beaton & Company (Plumbers) Limited and others*, opinion dated June 14, 2004 of Lord MacKay of Drumadoon (Court of Session, Outer House), it was noted that the sheriff had not made any order for caution, yet had not held that s.53 (7)(a) applied. Lord MacKay simply observed that: "no party insisted on caution being found in the circumstances of the present action". In *Rogers, Petr.*, Glasgow Sh. Ct., September 12, 2007 (unreported but commented on in 2007 SLT (News) 280) the sheriff appears to have taken the extreme view of requiring a guardian to fund caution from his personal resources. That appears to have been in conflict with the fundamental separation (as in trust law) of the patrimonies of guardian and adult, and the prohibition on intermingling them. Where—as in *Rogers*, according to the commentary referred to—the adult's financial circumstances were such that the cost of caution would fall upon the guardian personally, and could not otherwise be met, it is difficult to understand how the sheriff concluded that the court had no discretion under the 2000 text to dispense with caution. In some circumstances a cautionary company has sought to require that all intromissions by a lay guardian should be under the joint control of the lay guardian and a solicitor (see *Application in respect of R.L.*, Glasgow Sh. Ct., December 28, 2007, Scottish Courts Website). In one case the guardian was prepared to lodge a sum in security, in lieu of caution, but the Incapacity Act as it stood would not permit this. These issues have been addressed by the 2007 Act. Caution is no longer mandatory. In relation to both intervention

orders and guardianship orders relating to property or financial affairs, whether to impose caution is now a matter in the discretion of the sheriff. This subsection now provides that the sheriff "may" order caution, rather than that he "shall" do so. It is also now possible for the guardian to give "other security". The new wording on caution appears to create no presumption for or against caution. It will be interesting to see whether sheriffs are able to develop a consistent policy on this. As always under this Act, the test is to be found in the s.1 principles.

Under this new provision, in *H* (Dunoon Sh. Ct., May 6, 2008) the sheriff initially ordered caution because the guardian was resident overseas but subsequently dispensed with caution when advised that the potential cautioner was not prepared to offer caution to a non-resident guardian. The sheriff referred to another such case in *Application in respect of R.L.* (see above). In *Renewal of guardianship of J* (Inverness Sh. Ct., June 30, 2008) the previous lay financial guardian had run into difficulties with accounting requirements and successfully sought his own replacement as financial guardian, upon renewal of the guardianship, with a professional guardian. Caution had previously cost the adult £5,000 per annum. Upon becoming aware of the difficulties, the cautioner withdrew caution, so that for the last several months of that guardian's tenure there was no caution. The sheriff dispensed with caution in respect of the new financial guardian. Increasingly caution has become an umbrella only available when there is no prospect of rain. Under the new provision, circumstances which may cause a sheriff to order caution may also cause the only companies hitherto offering caution to decline to provide it. The Public Guardian has however recently achieved success in her efforts to improve the situation by negotiating arrangements under which Norwich Union, through HSBC Insurance Brokers Limited, offers caution without individual assessment of each case, relying instead upon court scrutiny of appointments and the supervision thereafter by the Office of the Public Guardian. Application procedure is simple and quick for bonds up to £500,000, and reasonably straightforward and quick above that level. The first premium covers an 18-month period, to allow the Public Guardian to review the case before the due date for the next premium, which next and all subsequent premiums are for 12-month periods. In all cases premiums are charged on a fixed, published scale. The lowest band has a maximum cover of £5,000 with an initial premium of £45 and subsequent annual premiums of £30 each. For cover of £100,000, the premiums are £300 and £200 respectively, increasing pro rata above that level up to cover of £500,000 (premiums of £1,500 and £1,000 respectively). Bonds are cancellable only with the permission of the sheriff, even if a premium is unpaid. This service is available in addition to those offered by other cautioners, or the option of "other security". It is for the prospective guardian to choose. The new arrangements are described and welcomed in *Application by J. O'B.* (Glasgow, AW55/2008, Scottish Courts Website August 14, 2008).

It remains the case that the only certainty is that where caution is ordered and provided, it will represent a depredation—often a significant one—upon the adult's annual income. It is understood that there have been no cautionary claims under this Act. Caution, or its equivalent, is not a requirement of the *Principles Concerning the Legal Protection of Incapable Adults* (see *"Old law" and "new law"*, Introduction and General Note, *supra*). Theoretically and historically, caution is a commendable concept in Scots law. It is nevertheless necessary in each case to justify the cost of caution by reference to the benefit principle of s.1.

Where the proposed guardian is a solicitor, some sheriffs have taken the view that where the cover afforded by the Master Policy of the Law Society of Scotland is sufficient, it is not necessary for the purpose of protecting the finances and assets of the adult to order that caution be found (see, for example *North Ayrshire Council v J.M.* 2004 SCLR 956). The view of the Law Society is that the Master Policy does not provide appropriate cover.

The Public Guardian (unlike the Accountant of Court under former law) has no power to vary caution. In appropriate cases, caution should be defined by reference to the value of the adult's estate from time to time, rather than as a permanently fixed sum, and under SI 1999/929 rule 3.16.8(1A) may now be calculated and expressed as a percentage of the value of the adult's estate. On "other security" see SI 1999/929 rule 3.16.10(6).

On caution, see also Alan Eccles, *A Cautionary Tale*, 2008 SLT (News) 59 and James Inglis and Arlene McDaid, *Rogers, Petitioner*, 2007 SLT (News) 280.

Subs. (7)(b)
Under curatory, purely administrative delays in producing caution sometimes caused appointments to fall. There is no time limit in this section, but for some reason the relevant rules of court introduced such a requirement. Because of the difficulties hitherto over caution, the

time limit set by the sheriff is sometimes exceeded. Some courts are content to deal with that situation by correspondence: the applicant's agent writes to the court with an explanation and, if satisfied that it is appropriate to do so, the sheriff instructs the sheriff clerk to write to the Public Guardian advising that the sheriff requires no action to be taken and has no objection to the certificate of appointment being issued. That would appear to be appropriate practice and in accordance with the s.1 principles, except of course where consideration of the circumstances and those principles would indicate that more formal procedure should be followed.

Subs. (7)(c)
The Public Guardian is obliged by s.11 (2) not to intimate to the adult when doing so would be likely to pose serious risk to the adult's health.

Subs. (7)(d)
The authorities to be notified are those with supervisory and investigative powers under Pt. 1.

Who may be appointed as guardian
59.—(1) The sheriff may appoint as guardian—

(a) any individual whom he considers to be suitable for appointment and who has consented to being appointed;
(b) where the guardianship order is to relate only to the personal welfare of the adult, the chief social work officer of the local authority.

(2) Where the guardianship order is to relate to the property and financial affairs and to the personal welfare of the adult and joint guardians are to be appointed, the chief social work officer of the local authority may be appointed guardian in relation only to the personal welfare of the adult.
(3) The sheriff shall not appoint an individual as guardian to an adult unless he is satisfied that the individual is aware of—

(a) the adult's circumstances and condition and of the needs arising from such circumstances and condition; and
(a) the functions of a guardian.

(4) In determining if an individual is suitable for appointment as guardian, the sheriff shall have regard to—

(a) the accessibility of the individual to the adult and to his primary carer;
(b) the ability of the individual to carry out the functions of guardian;
(c) any likely conflict of interest between the adult and the individual;
(d) any undue concentration of power which is likely to arise in the individual over the adult;
(e) any adverse effects which the appointment of the individual would have on the interests of the adult;
(d) such other matters as appear to him to be appropriate.

(5) Paragraphs (c) and (d) of subsection (4) shall not be regarded as applying to an individual by reason only of his being a close relative of, or person residing with, the adult.

DEFINITIONS
"adult" : s.1 (6)
"chief social work officer" : Social Work (Scotland) Act 1968 (c.49) s.3 (presumed)

"guardianship order" : s.58 (4)
"local authority" : s.87 (1) (referring to the Local Government etc. (Scotland) Act 1994 (c.39) s.2)
"primary carer": s.87 (1)

GENERAL NOTE
See s.64 (9) and (10) when the chief social work officer is guardian, and see also s.68 (2)–(4). This section distinguishes between an "individual" (subs. (1)(a)) and the chief social work officer (subs. (1)(b)), so that the requirements of subss. (3) and (4) do not apply to the latter. That this is the Parliament's intention is confirmed by the terms of s.71 (1)(a), and should be seen in the context of the local authority's duty under s.57 (2) to apply for appointment when a guardian is needed and no-one else is doing so, and the provisions of s.68 (3) that the appointment of the chief social work officer as guardian will not cost the adult anything. These are "safety-net" provisions to ensure that the protection of welfare guardianship will be available without cost to those who need it. However the sheriff may require to consider competing applications, one proposing an individual as welfare guardian and the other proposing the chief social work officer. If the sheriff is satisfied that a welfare guardian is needed and that the individual meets the requirements of subs. (3), then assessment of the suitability of the individual in relation to the criteria in subs. (4) is likely to include comparative assessment of those criteria in relation to the alternative of the chief social work officer. If the adult is substantially dependent on local authority services, an individual who—considered alone—is suitable to be the guardian may frequently be more suitable than the chief social work officer as regards the criteria in paras. (c) and (d) of subs. (4), and also para. (b) thereof (in that ability to carry out the function will reasonably include sufficient independence to represent the adult's interests effectively when dealing with authorities). Article V of the Declaration on General and Special Rights of the Mentally Retarded of the International League of Societies for Persons with Mental Handicap (not incorporated into any international obligations, but persuasive) includes a provision that: "No person rendering direct services to the mentally retarded should also serve as his guardian". An example of competition for appointment between the local authority and a close relative was *North Ayrshire Council v J.M.* (Sh. Ct.) 2004 SCLR 956—see General Notre to s.1. In that case the respondent entered the process by minute, proposed herself as guardian, and was appointed. The competency of such procedure was challenged in *Arthur v Arthur* (Sh. Ct.) 2005 SCLR 350. The sheriff held the procedure to be competent, and that in any event under this section the sheriff may appoint "any individual" whom he considers suitable and who consents, and who need not be the applicant, nor a person nominated by minute. There have in fact been a number of cases where a contest has been resolved by a "neutral" appointment—often, as financial guardian, of a "neutral" solicitor. In *Cooke v Telford* (Sh. Ct.) 2005 SCLR 367 it was held that a respondent seeking appointment required to lodge a minute to that effect, and that it was incompetent to do so only in answers and not by minute. In *Application in respect of R.A.* (Glasgow Sh. Ct., January 17, 2008, Scottish Courts Website) an applicant was held to suitable as a welfare guardian, but unsuitable as a financial guardian because of a conviction for embezzlement several years earlier. The situation only came to light when the applicant was refused caution and another person applied for appointment as financial guardian. See the decision for the manner in which the sheriff resolved the procedural issues.

The requirements of subs. (1)(a) are substantially the same as were those for appointment of tutors-dative by the Court of Session under previous law.

For appointments under Criminal Procedure (Scotland) Act 1995 (c.46) as amended by s.84 and Sched. 5 para. 26 of this Act, the guardian is the local authority or a person approved by the local authority.

Renewal of guardianship order by sheriff
60.—(1) At any time before the end of a period in respect of which a guardianship order has been made or renewed, an application may be made to the sheriff under this section by the guardian for the renewal of such order, and where such an application is so made, the order shall continue to have effect until the application is determined.

(2) Where it appears to the local authority that an application for renewal of a guardianship order under subsection (1) is necessary but that

no such application has been made or is likely to be made, they shall apply under subsection (1) for the renewal of such an order and, where such an application is so made, the order shall continue to have effect until the application is determined.

[(3) There must be lodged in court along with an application under this section—

- (a) at least one report, in the prescribed form, of an examination and assessment of the adult carried out by a medical practitioner not more than 30 days before the lodging of the application,
- (b) where the application relates to the adult's personal welfare, a report, in the prescribed form, from the mental health officer (but where it is in jeopardy only because of the adult's inability to communicate, from the chief social work officer), containing the officer's opinion as to—
    - (i) the general appropriateness of continuing the guardianship, based on an interview and assessment of the adult carried out not more than 30 days before the lodging of the application; and
    - (ii) the suitability of the applicant to continue to be the adult's guardian; and
- (c) where the application relates to the adult's property or financial affairs, a report from the Public Guardian, in the prescribed form, containing the Public Guardian's opinion as to—
    - (i) the applicant's conduct as the adult's guardian; and
    - (ii) the suitability of the applicant to continue to be the adult's guardian.

(3A) In a case where the incapacity is by reason of mental disorder—

- (a) where a single report is lodged under subsection (3)(a), the related examination and assessment must be carried out by a relevant medical practitioner;
- (b) where 2 or more reports are so lodged, at least one of the related examinations and assessments must be carried out by a relevant medical practitioner.

"Relevant medical practitioner" has the same meaning in this subsection as it has in section 57(3)(a) (see definition in section 57(6B)).][122]

(4) Section 58 shall apply to an application under this section as it applies to an application under section 57; and for the purposes of so applying that section—

- (a) references to the making of a guardianship order and the appointment of a guardian (however expressed) shall be construed as references to, respectively, the renewal of the order and the continuation of appointment;
- (b) for subsection (4) there shall be substituted—

    "(4) Where the sheriff grants an application under section 60, he may continue the guardianship order for a period of 5 years

---

[122] Substituted by Adult Support and Protection (Scotland) Act 2007 (asp 10), s.60(3)(a).

or for such other period (including an indefinite period) as, on cause shown, he may determine.".

[(4A) A sheriff may determine an application made under this section without hearing the parties.][123]

(5) Where the sheriff refuses an application under this section, the sheriff clerk shall forthwith send a copy of the interlocutor containing the refusal to the Public Guardian who shall—

(a) enter prescribed particulars in the register maintained by him under section 6(2)(b)(iv); and
(b) notify the adult and the local authority and (in a case where the adult's incapacity is by reason of, or reasons which include, mental disorder and the guardianship order relates to the adult's personal welfare or factors which include it) the Mental Welfare Commission.

DEFINITIONS
"adult" : s.1 (6)
"guardianship order" : s.58 (4)
"incapacity" : s.1 (6)
"local authority" : s.87 (1) (referring to the Local Government etc. (Scotland) Act 1994 (c.39) s.2)
"mental disorder" : s.87 (1) (and see General Note to s.1 (6))
"Mental Welfare Commission" : s.87 (1) (referring to s.4 of the 2003 Act)
"prescribed" : s.87 (1) (and see s.86)
"Public Guardian" : s.6 (1)
"relevant medical practitioner" : s.57 (6B)

GENERAL NOTE

Subs. (1)
Applications for renewal may be made in good time before expiry, but where renewal has been sought at any time before expiry the previous appointment will automatically continue beyond its original expiry date pending determination of the renewal application. However, applicants who miss the expiry date should note that the interim guardianship provisions of s.57 (5) and (6) require that the application, with relevant reports, must first be lodged (see General Note to those subsections). See Sched. 4, para. 6 (3) for expiry of transitional guardianships, and see General Note to s.61 where a transitional guardianship includes powers over heritable property.

Rule 3.16.8 of SI 1999/929 applies to some but not all subsequent applications and proceedings, including renewal applications. It provides that application should be by minute in the process (rule 3.16.8(1), see also rule 3.16.8(1A)), and for prompt transmission of a relevant process held in a different sheriff court (rules 3.16.8(2) and (3)). Rule 3.16.8 applies only to applications and proceedings "subsequent to an initial application or proceeding considered by the sheriff", therefore it appears that in the case of transitional guardianships deriving from Court of Session appointments the first "subsequent application" under this Act should be by a fresh application under the preceding rules. In the case of old pre-Act Sheriff Court appointments, it may be wise to check whether the original process is still available, and if there is difficulty in that regard to enquire whether the court would prefer a fresh application rather than a minute.

Rule 3.16.8(1A) provides that the minute in "subsequent applications" should be governed by Chapter 14 of the Ordinary Cause Rules. Rules 3.16.8(4) and (5) apply specifically to renewals. The insertion and terms of rule 3.16.8(5) appear to be unfortunate. It provides that renewal applications should be served on the local authority and (for welfare guardianships

---

[123] Inserted by Adult Support and Protection (Scotland) Act 2007 (asp 10), s.60(3)(b).

Adults with Incapacity (Scotland) Act 2000 (Pt. 6)

arising from mental disorder) MWC, but those requirements appear also in rule 3.16.4(1), the only difference being the qualification "where appropriate" in the latter. It is inconceivable that there should be intimation only to the local authority and MWC. To fail to intimate to the adult, except in accordance with s.11, would contravene ECHR and the whole tenor of this Act, including the mandatory duty in s.1(4)(a). It is difficult to see how there could be compliance with s.1(4)(b) and (c) without intimating upon all of the parties there specified. In financial cases, it would be difficult to ensure compliance with s.1(2) and (3) without intimation to the Public Guardian, so as to ascertain—for example—whether Pt. 3 administration rather than renewal of guardianship would be appropriate (the Public Guardian's report under s.60(3)(c) addresses only the conduct and suitability of the guardian, not the suitability of continuing the guardianship). Rule 3.16.8(1A) adds the further potential difficulty that unless the sheriff directs otherwise intimation will be in accordance with the forms referred to in Chapter 14 of the Ordinary Cause Rules, which are ill-adapted to Incapacity Act procedure, for example in containing no equivalent of rules 3.16.4(3) and (4). It will clearly be helpful for the courts to take care in framing the first orders upon submission of all subsequent applications, and sensible for applicants to specify in some detail the terms of the first order sought.

Subs (2)
The local authority has a similar duty under this subsection to its duty under s.57 (2) in relation to initial applications.

Subs. (3), (3A) and (4A)
A fundamental characteristic of modern guardianship procedures is that they should be time-limited to ensure that they are fully reviewed. Experience of the modern, revived use of tutors-dative largely shaped the fundamentals of guardianship under this Act. Modern use of tutory-dative was introduced by *Morris, Petitioner* (1986), in which the petitioners sought (and were granted) limited specified powers and an appointment of limited duration so that their appointment was renewed in *Morris (No 2)* 1991 and again in *Morris (No 3)* 2002. Under this Act, a situation developed in which the important principle of time-limited appointments, on basic human rights grounds, often came into conflict with the "benefit" principle because the cumbersomeness, potential trouble to the adult and costs of renewal procedure were the same as for original applications, and probably greater than was contemplated when this Act was originally enacted. It became increasingly clear that a simplified renewal procedure was needed. This has now been provided by the 2007 Act. Renewal procedure now differs from initial applications in three ways:

(a) Only one medical report is required. It must be provided by a "relevant medical practitioner" (see s.57 (6B) and note thereto).
(b) In relation to financial guardianship, the only other report required is from the Public Guardian, concerning the applicant's conduct as financial guardian, and the applicant's suitability to continue (a report from the mental health officer remains necessary where there are welfare powers).
(c) The sheriff may dispense with a hearing.

Accordingly, for renewal the reports required will be as follows: welfare guardianship—a report from an approved practitioner and a report from the mental health officer; financial guardianship—a report from an approved practitioner and a report from the Public Guardian; combined guardianship—reports from an approved practitioner, the mental health officer and the Public Guardian.

As with all applications, if the sheriff considers that more information or reports are required, he may order these under s.3 of this Act. It would appear that the option to dispense with a hearing is only available if renewal is not combined with alterations such as a change of guardian or appointment of a joint or substitute guardian (all of which elements were combined in *Renewal of guardianship of J* (Inverness Sh. Ct., June 30, 2008)).

Subs. (4)
Section 58 applies as adapted in terms of this subsection, the most significant difference being the increase in maximum duration (subject to cause being shown for longer) from three years to five years: on duration of initial appointment and renewal, see General Note to subs. (4) of s.58.

Subs. (5)
Refusal of an application for renewal requires to be notified and registered in accordance with this subsection. The Public Guardian is however obliged by s.11 (2) not to intimate to the adult where doing so would be likely to pose serious risk to the adult's health.

Registration of guardianship order relating to heritable property

61.—(1) This section applies where the sheriff makes a guardianship order which vests in the guardian any right of the adult to deal with, convey or manage any interest in heritable property which is recorded or is capable of being recorded in the General Register of Sasines or is registered or is capable of being registered in the Land Register of Scotland.

(2) In making such an order the sheriff shall specify each property affected by the order, in such terms as enable it to be identified in the Register of Sasines or, as the case may be, the Land Register of Scotland.

(3) The guardian shall, after finding caution [or giving other security][124] if so required, forthwith apply to the Keeper of the Registers of Scotland for recording of the interlocutor containing the order in the General Register of Sasines or, as the case may be, registering of it in the Land Register of Scotland.

(4) An application under subsection (3) shall contain—

(a) the name and address of the guardian;
(b) a statement that the guardian has powers relating to each property specified in the order;
(c) a copy of the interlocutor.

(5) Where the interlocutor is to be recorded in the General Register of Sasines, the Keeper shall—

(a) record the interlocutor in the Register; and
(b) endorse the interlocutor to the effect that it has been so recorded.

(6) Where the interlocutor is to be registered in the Land Register of Scotland, the Keeper shall update the title sheet of the property to show the interlocutor.

(7) The guardian shall send the endorsed interlocutor or, as the case may be, the updated Land Certificate or an office copy thereof to the Public Guardian who shall enter prescribed particulars of it in the register maintained by him under section 6(2)(b)(iv).

DEFINITIONS
"adult" : s.1 (6)
"guardianship order" : s.58 (4)
"prescribed" : s.87 (1) (and see s.86)
"Public Guardian" : s.6 (1)

GENERAL NOTE
See General Note to s.56, which contains similar provisions in relation to intervention orders. In the case of guardianship, s.78 requires various events to be recorded or registered, and s.79 provides protection (in addition to the protection under s.77 (4)) to third parties.

There is no requirement for transitional guardians to record or register in similar manner. In such cases it may be considered appropriate upon renewal of the guardianship (see s.60 and

---

[124] Inserted by Adult Support and Protection (Scotland) Act 2007 (asp 10), s.60(4).

Adults with Incapacity (Scotland) Act 2000 (Pt. 6)

General Note thereto) to include a conveyancing description in the interlocutor, and to record or register the interlocutor as with a new appointment. This was done in *Renewal of guardianship of J* (see General Note to s.60).

Joint and substitute guardians

Joint guardians
62.—(1) An application may be made to the sheriff—
- (a) by two or more individuals seeking appointment, for their appointment as joint guardians to an adult; or
- (b) by an individual seeking appointment, for his appointment as an additional guardian to an adult jointly with one or more existing guardians.

(2) Joint guardians shall not be appointed to an adult unless—
- (a) the individuals so appointed are parents, siblings or children of the adult; or
- (b) the sheriff is satisfied that, in the circumstances, it is appropriate to appoint as joint guardians individuals who are not related to the adult as mentioned in paragraph (a).

(3) Where an application is made under subsection (1)(a), sections 58 and 59 shall apply for the purposes of the disposal of that application as they apply for the disposal of an application under section 57.

(4) In deciding if an individual is suitable for appointment as additional guardian under subsection (1)(b), the sheriff shall have regard to the matters set out in section 59(3) to (5).

(5) Where the sheriff appoints an additional guardian under this section, the sheriff clerk shall send a copy of the order appointing him to the Public Guardian who shall—
- (a) enter prescribed particulars in the register maintained by him under section 6(2)(b)(iv) of this Act;
- (b) when satisfied that the additional guardian has found caution [or given other security][125] if so required, issue a certificate of appointment to the additional guardian and a new certificate of appointment to the existing guardian;
- (c) notify the adult and the local authority and (in a case where the adult's incapacity is by reason of, or reasons which include, mental disorder and the guardianship order relates to the adult's personal welfare or factors which include it) the Mental Welfare Commission.

(6) Joint guardians may, subject to subsection (7), exercise their functions individually, and each guardian shall be liable for any loss or injury caused to the adult arising out of—
- (a) his own acts or omissions; or
- (b) his failure to take reasonable steps to ensure that a joint guardian does not breach any duty of care or fiduciary duty owed to the adult,

---

[125] Inserted by Adult Support and Protection (Scotland) Act 2007 (asp 10), s.60(5).

and where more than one such guardian is so liable they shall be liable jointly and severally.

(7) A joint guardian shall, before exercising any functions conferred on him, consult the other joint guardians, unless—

(a) consultation would be impracticable in the circumstances; or
(b) the joint guardians agree that consultation is not necessary.

(8) Where joint guardians disagree as to the exercise of their functions, either or both of them may apply to the sheriff for directions under section 3.

(9) Where there are joint guardians, a third party in good faith is entitled to rely on the authority to act of any one or more of them.

DEFINITIONS
"adult" : s.1 (6)
"guardianship order" : s.58 (4)
"incapacity" : s.1 (6)
"local authority" : s.87 (1) (referring to the Local Government etc. (Scotland) Act 1994 (c.39) s.2)
"mental disorder" : s.87 (1) (and see General Note to s.1 (6))
"Mental Welfare Commission" : s.87 (1) (referring to s.4 of the 2003 Act)
"prescribed" : s.87 (1) (and see s.86)
"Public Guardian" : s.6 (1)

GENERAL NOTE
The majority of appointments of tutors-dative, since revived in 1986, were joint appointments, and up to three joint tutors were not uncommon. In the case of appointments to young adults, these often comprised both parents and one other person to ensure the availability of decision-making if both parents were abroad or became unable for any reason to act. There were also applications to add another tutor to existing appointments. Several individuals so appointed were more distant relatives than specified in s.62 (2)(a), or unrelated. See the variety of appointments described in *Adult Incapacity*, 10–19, and previously in Ashton and Ward *Mental Handicap and the Law*, p138. At least one appointment of unrelated carers, there suggested to be competent, was since made. It is suggested that s.62 (2) does not create any presumption against joint appointees who are not relatives, merely a requirement to satisfy the court as to appropriateness. For sole appointments, which are more critical to the extent that all powers granted are concentrated in one individual, there is nothing in the Act to suggest that close relatives are to be preferred for appointment, and it would be naive to assume that close relationship to the adult would by itself ensure harmonious discharge of joint responsibilities.

See s.58 (5) for joint appointees each with different powers (better termed dual appointees).

The procedural provisions for an additional appointment cross-refer to appropriate provisions for original appointment. In *Cooke v Telford* (Sh. Ct.) 2005 SCLR 367 it was held that a joint appointment required a single joint application, in terms of s.62 (1)(a). A respondent could not competently seek appointment jointly with the applicant. This accords with common sense: it is difficult to see how it could be in the adult's interests to be served by guardians forced into a joint appointment resisted by at least one of them. Although this case was disposed of on points of competency, the sheriff nevertheless addressed the merits "recognising that I may be wrong to have come to the view on competency which I did, and in any event in deference to the submissions made on the merits of the case". The sheriff's approach to the assessment of the merits is likely to be instructive for practitioners preparing pleadings and submissions in contested cases; and indeed for practitioners preparing applications, whether contested or not.

For procedure in "subsequent applications" under subs. (1)(b) see second paragraph of General Note to subs. (3) of s.58, SI 1999/929, and General Note to subs. (1) of s.60.

Subs. (7)(b) implies that agreed allocation of functions would be competent for the purposes of this subsection (but subs. (6)(b) would still apply).

The remaining provisions of this section are clear and succinct, do not require further comment, but are important.

Adults with Incapacity (Scotland) Act 2000 (Pt. 6)

Substitute guardian
63.—(1) In any case where an individual is appointed as guardian under section 58 the sheriff may, on an application, appoint to act as guardian in the event of the guardian so appointed becoming unable to act any individual or office holder who could competently be appointed by virtue of section 59.

(2) In this Act an individual appointed under section 58 and an individual or office holder appointed under this section are referred to respectively as an "original guardian" and a "substitute guardian".

(3) The appointment of a substitute guardian shall be for the same period as the appointment of the original guardian under section 58(4).

(4) An application for appointment as a substitute guardian may be made at the time of the application for the appointment of the original guardian or at any time thereafter.

(5) In making an order appointing an individual as substitute guardian with powers relating to the property or financial affairs of the adult the sheriff [may][126] require an individual appointed as substitute guardian to find caution [or to give such other security as the sheriff thinks fit][127].

(6) Subsection (1) shall apply to an individual who, having been appointed as a substitute guardian subsequently, by virtue of this section, becomes the guardian as it applies to an individual appointed under section 58 and, for this purpose, any reference in this section to the "original guardian" shall be construed accordingly.

(7) Where the sheriff appoints a substitute guardian (other than a substitute guardian appointed in the same order as an original guardian) under subsection (1), the sheriff clerk shall send a copy of the interlocutor containing the order appointing the substitute guardian to the Public Guardian who shall—

  (a) enter prescribed particulars in the register maintained by him under section 6(2)(b)(iv); and
  (b) notify the adult, the original guardian and the local authority and (in a case where the adult's incapacity is by reason of, or by reasons which include, mental disorder and the guardianship order relates to the adult's personal welfare or factors which include it) the Mental Welfare Commission.

(8) On the death or incapacity of the original guardian, the substitute guardian shall, without undue delay, notify the Public Guardian—

  (a) of the death or incapacity (and where the original guardian has died, provide the Public Guardian with documentary evidence of the death); and
  (b) whether or not he is prepared to act as guardian.

(9) The Public Guardian on being notified under subsection (8) shall, if the substitute guardian is prepared to act—

  (a) enter prescribed particulars in the register maintained by him under section 6(2)(b)(iv);
  (b) when satisfied that the substitute guardian has found caution [or given other security][128] if so required, issue the substitute guardian with a certificate of appointment;

---

[126] Substituted by Adult Support and Protection (Scotland) Act 2007 (asp 10), s.60(6)(a)(i).
[127] Inserted by Adult Support and Protection (Scotland) Act 2007 (asp 10), s.60(6)(a)(ii).
[128] Inserted by Adult Support and Protection (Scotland) Act 2007 (asp 10), s.60(6)(b).

(c) notify the adult, the original guardian, the local authority and (in a case where the adult's incapacity is by reason of, or by reasons which include, mental disorder and the guardianship order relates to the adult's personal welfare or factors which include it) the Mental Welfare Commission that the substitute guardian is acting.

(10) Unless otherwise specified in the order appointing him, the substitute guardian shall have the same functions and powers as those exercisable by the original guardian immediately before the event mentioned in subsection (1).

DEFINITIONS
"adult" : s.1 (6)
"guardianship order" : s.58 (4)
"incapacity" : s.1 (6)
"local authority" : s.87 (1) (referring to the Local Government etc. (Scotland) Act 1994 (c.39) s.2)
"mental disorder" : s.87 (1) (and see General Note to s.1 (6))
"Mental Welfare Commission" : s.87 (1) (referring to s.4 of the 2003 Act)
"office holder" : s.87 (1)
"original guardian" : s.63 (2)
"prescribed" : s.87 (1) (and see s.86)
"Public Guardian" : s.6 (1)
"substitute guardian" : s.63 (2)

GENERAL NOTE
Substitute appointments were an innovation under this Act. Typically, where both parents are appointed joint guardians with welfare powers to a relatively young adult with permanent incapacities, a sibling may be appointed as substitute. An alternative is a joint appointment, imposing immediate responsibility (which may not be desired) but allowing such appointee to act without any delay or further formalities during temporary absence, illness or other unavailability of the other appointees. In this section, although subs. (1) refers to the original guardian being "unable to act", subs. (8) limits substitution to the death or incapacity of the original guardian, and as the definition of incapacity in s.1 (6) is not disapplied, substitution will not be competent in the event of disabling physical incapacity. However, substitution may take effect upon removal or resignation of a guardian (s.71 (1)(b)(ii), and s.75 (1) and (2)(a)(ii), respectively). To the extent that appointments of substitute guardians, rather than joint guardians, are sought, the provisions of this section apply, and are self-explanatory. For procedure in "subsequent applications" under subs. (4) see second paragraph of General Note to subs. (3) of s.58, SI 1999/929, and General Note to subs. (1) of s.60.

Functions etc. of guardian

Functions and duties of guardian
64.—(1) Subject to the provisions of this section, an order appointing a guardian may confer on him—

(a) power to deal with such particular matters in relation to the property, financial affairs or personal welfare of the adult as may be specified in the order;
(b) power to deal with all aspects of the personal welfare of the adult, or with such aspects as may be specified in the order;
(c) power to pursue or defend an action of declarator of nullity of marriage, or of divorce or separation in the name of the adult;
(d) power to manage the property or financial affairs of the adult, or such parts of them as may be specified in the order;
(e) power to authorise the adult to carry out such transactions or categories of transactions as the guardian may specify.

(2) A guardian may not—

Adults with Incapacity (Scotland) Act 2000 (Pt. 6)

    (a) place the adult in a hospital for the treatment of mental disorder against his will; [. . .]¹²⁹
    (b) consent on behalf of the adult to any form of treatment [in relation to which the authority conferred by section 47(2) does not apply by virtue of regulations made under section 48(2)]¹³⁰ [;
    (c) make, on behalf of the adult, a request under section 4(1) of the Anatomy Act 1984 (c. 14);
    (d) give, on behalf of the adult, an authorisation under, or by virtue of, section 6(1), 17, 29(1) or 42(1) of the Human Tissue (Scotland) Act 2006 (asp 4); or
    (e) make, on behalf of the adult, a nomination under section 30(1) of that Act.]¹³¹

(3) A guardian shall (unless prohibited by an order of the sheriff and subject to any conditions or restrictions specified in such an order) have power by virtue of his appointment to act as the adult's legal representative in relation to any matter within the scope of the power conferred by the guardianship order.

(4) The guardian shall not later than 7 days after any change of his own or the adult's address notify the Public Guardian who shall—

    (a) notify the adult (in a case where it is the guardian's address which has changed), the local authority and (in a case where the adult's incapacity is by reason of, or reasons which include, mental disorder and the guardianship order relates to the adult's personal welfare or factors which include it) the Mental Welfare Commission of the change; and
    (b) enter prescribed particulars in the register maintained by him under section 6(2)(b)(iv).

(5) A guardian having powers relating to the property or financial affairs of the adult shall, subject to-

    (a) such restrictions as may be imposed by the court;
    (b) any management plan prepared under paragraph 1 of schedule 2; or
    (c) paragraph 6 of that schedule,

be entitled to use the capital and income of the adult's estate for the purpose of purchasing assets, services or accommodation so as to enhance the adult's quality of life.

(6) The guardian may arrange for some or all of his functions to be exercised by one or more persons acting on his behalf but shall not be entitled to surrender or transfer any part of them to another person.

(7) The guardian shall comply with any order or demand made by the Public Guardian in relation to the property or financial affairs of the adult in so far as so complying would be within the scope of his authority; and where the guardian fails to do so the sheriff may, on the application of the Public Guardian, make an order to the like effect as the order or demand made by the Public Guardian, and the sheriff's decision shall be final.

---

[129] Words repealed by Human Tissue (Scotland) Act 2006 (asp 4), s.57(3)(a).
[130] Substituted by Adult Support and Protection (Scotland) Act 2007 (asp 10), s.60(7).
[131] Inserted by Human Tissue (Scotland) Act 2006 (asp 4), s.57(3)(b).

(8) An interim guardian appointed under section 57(5) having powers relating to—

(a) the property or financial affairs of an adult shall report to the Public Guardian;
(b) the personal welfare of an adult shall report to the chief social work officer of the local authority,

every month as to his exercise of those powers.

(9) Where the chief social work officer of the local authority has been appointed guardian he shall, not later than 7 working days after his appointment, notify any person who received notification under section 58(7) of the appointment of the name of the officer responsible at any time for carrying out the functions and duties of guardian.

(10) If, in relation to the appointment of the chief social work officer as guardian, the sheriff has directed that that intimation or notification of any application or other proceedings should not be given to the adult, the chief social work officer shall not notify the adult under subsection (9).

(11) The Scottish Ministers may by regulations define the scope of the powers which may be conferred on a guardian under subsection (1) and the conditions under which they shall be exercised.

(12) Schedule 2 (which makes provision as to the guardian's management of the estate of an adult) has effect.

DEFINITIONS
"adult" : s.1 (6)
"chief social work officer" : Social Work (Scotland) Act 1968 (c.49) s.3 (presumed)
"guardianship order" : s.58 (4)
"incapacity" : s.1 (6)
"local authority" : s.87 (1) (referring to the Local Government etc. (Scotland) Act 1994 (c.39) s.2)
"mental disorder" : s.87 (1) (and see General Note to s.1 (6))
"Mental Welfare Commission" : s.87 (1) (referring to s.4 of the 2003 Act)
"prescribed" : s.87 (1) (and see s.86)
"Public Guardian" : s.6 (1)

GENERAL NOTE
The Scottish Ministers may by regulations under subs. (11) define the scope of the powers which may be conferred on a guardian but so far have not done so. In the absence of such regulations, within the wide field of property, financial affairs and personal welfare, the possible scope of guardianship is only definitively circumscribed by the exclusions in subs. (2). Beyond that, it would appear that the outer boundaries will only be set by any judicial interpretation of "deal with" and "manage", and of "all aspects of . . . . personal welfare" and "property or financial affairs", and by the legislative competence of the Parliament. It is to be anticipated that issues will more frequently arise as to whether powers sought are appropriate and necessary, rather than competent, and as to whether a guardian's acts or proposed acts are within the powers which have been conferred upon him. In specifying personal welfare powers, former practice in petitions to appoint tutors-dative proved to be of assistance. As to property and financial powers, styles for powers of attorney (or for trustees' powers) may assist as starting-points, but only as such, because such documents are often widely drawn, whereas powers conferred upon guardians require to be the minimum shown to be necessary in order to comply with s.1. A lengthy list of possible property and financial powers is set out in some 50 paragraphs and sub-paragraphs in a schedule to New Zealand's Protection of Property and Personal Rights Act 1988 (see chapter XII of Ward *The Power to Act*).

The general principles do not require the powers conferred to be limited to those immediately necessary. Powers reasonably likely to be required during the period of the order should be included. There will usually be disadvantage rather than benefit to the adult and the adult's interests, and thus contravention of the benefit principle, in requiring a succession of applications to meet needs which have already been identified.

Some applicants have adopted a practice of seeking long lists of financial powers in cases where the adult lacks any significant management capability, and what are appropriate are plenary powers under s.64 (1)(d). If plenary powers are appropriate, then all that is necessary is to seek (in the words of s.64 (1)(d)) "power to manage the property and financial affairs of the adult". If within the scope of those plenary powers it is anticipated that the guardian will require to deal with a particular matter, such as selling a house or pursuing an action of reparation, then the applicant may crave both plenary powers in terms of s.64 (1)(d) and also, expressly without prejudice to the scope of the plenary powers sought, power under s.64 (1)(a) to deal with specified particular matters. One might have reservations about seeking simply "power to deal with all aspects of the personal welfare of the adult" in terms of s.64 (1)(b). Particularly in the case of welfare powers, it might be more helpful for the guardian and for those dealing with the guardian for "aspects" to be specified in the order, albeit in quite broad terms; and from the adult's point of view, this would better ensure compliance with the first and second general principles. However, the fine-tuning of what powers are actually exercised, and in what way, can only be achieved by proper observance of the general principles by the guardian. That applies to plenary powers as well as to broadly expressed but more specific powers. Where incapacity is partial only, it is essential that powers be limited. However, there are some cases where plenary welfare powers are likely to be appropriate to avoid the risk of a need arising which is not covered by the specific powers granted, thus imposing on all concerned the trouble and expense of an application for additional powers. In such cases, it will generally be preferable still to seek in explicit terms (and without prejudice to the scope of the plenary powers) the welfare powers which can be predicted to be required. In these matters it may be appropriate to make a distinction between financial and welfare matters, because of the very personal nature of welfare powers, and also because it is usually not too difficult to express succinctly all of the types of particular welfare powers likely to be required in any one case.

The foregoing is not a justification for granting excessive powers or retaining powers which have become excessive. In particular, financial guardians under the transitional provisions, who were formerly curators bonis, are of course obliged to follow the general principles. The plenary powers which they automatically inherited may be inappropriate. If so, they should make application to replace their plenary powers with limited powers, or at least to do so upon renewal (see Sched. 4 para. 6 (3A)), or even to replace financial guardianship with management under Pt. 3 (see General Note to Pt. 3).

There have been cases where local authorities proceeding under s.57 (2) have sought only welfare guardianship when there has been a clear requirement also for financial guardianship. By determining that they ought to proceed under s.57 (2), and then failing to seek financial powers as well as welfare powers if these are required, the local authority would appear to be automatically putting themselves in breach of their obligation under s.57 (2). It is good practice for an application for financial powers only briefly to demonstrate why welfare powers are not sought, and vice versa, and instructed solicitors should always enquire, even though initial instructions focus upon one of those aspects only.

In at least one unreported case a guardianship order authorised the guardian to sell the adult's house, but contained no other powers whatsoever. Thus the guardian had no power to bank, invest or otherwise manage the proceeds of sale. That would appear to have been a quite inept order, and it is surprising that it got as far as being granted in such terms. It is obvious, but needs to be stressed, that guardians only have the powers granted, either specifically or generically by the grant of plenary powers in terms of the first alternatives in ss.64 (1)(b) and (d). This point arose incidentally in the decision of Sheriff Principal (as he then was) MacPhail in *City of Edinburgh Council v Z*, 2005 SLT (Sh. Ct.) 7, the first appeal under this jurisdiction. Three specific welfare powers were granted, but they were described as "additional powers". The Sheriff Principal pointed out that they could not be described as additional powers "because if they were to be deleted from the Interlocutor, the guardian would not have any other powers. A guardianship order does not of itself confer any powers on the guardian .... The capacity of the adult remains unaffected in relation to any matter which is not within the scope of the authority of the guardian".

Such difficulties should be avoided if applicants follow what, it is suggested, is the proper practice of relating the powers sought to specific provisions of s.64 (1).

Questions have arisen as to the extent to which the sheriff should review the guardian's powers in applications where such review is not mandatory, such as applications for appointment of a joint, substitute or replacement guardian. The point may arise in particular where the existing guardian has plenary powers under this Act's transitional provisions. From the adult's point of view, what is important in terms of the second general principle (s.1 (3)) is that there is no unnecessary or excessive exercise of powers. That can be achieved in two ways. The first is for the powers themselves to be limited, but the second is for the guardian to be reasonably conscientious in implementing the guardian's obligation to comply with the second principle. Of these two, the guardian's conduct is the more important, because only a relatively "broad-brush" approach can be applied to conferring powers, and any fine-tuning must come from the guardian. It seems reasonable to suggest caution in narrowing the powers of a guardian acting properly and responsibly in this and other respects: it would be unfortunate to remove powers which seem to be unnecessary, only to find that due to changed circumstances or unexpected developments the guardian requires subsequently to seek reinstatement of some of those powers. The first principle is relevant here: if powers are to be narrowed, that must achieve a benefit for the adult, and should not be a merely "paper" exercise which makes no difference to the adult.

Subs. (1)
Paragraphs (a)—(d) provide the sheriff with the necessary flexibility to achieve the least restrictive option in terms of s.1 (3), and para. (e) facilitates compliance with the obligations of guardians to encourage the exercise and development of skills under s.1 (5) (see General Notes on subss. (3) and (5) of s.1, and see also s.67 (1) and (5)).

Subs. (2)
This subsection applies also to appointees under intervention orders.

Subs. (3)
Schedule 5 inserts references to "legal representative" in the Heritable Securities (Scotland) Act 1894 (c.44) by para. 7 and the Offices, Shops and Railway Premises Act 1963 (c.41) by para. 9. There are many more insertions of express references to guardians. It is intended that "legal representative" (which is not defined) should extend more widely than statutory references to the phrase. The Explanatory Notes to this Act included the example of instructing a solicitor on the adult's behalf. The concept of "legal representative" is well developed in child law (see, for example, Children (Scotland) Act 1995 (c.36) and Age of Legal Capacity (Scotland) Act 1991 (c.50) as amended thereby). Great caution should be exercised in applying principles or precedents of child law to adults with incapacity, as they may often be inappropriate (see, for example, third paragraph of General Note to subs. (4)(a) of s.1). However, as demonstrated in Wilkinson & Norrie *Parent and Child*, 2nd Ed. paras. 15.28 et seq., the concept of legal representation has its origins in tutory. Tutory in turn was in its origins a concept common both to children and to adults with incapacity, therefore child law may (with appropriate caution) be a source of guidance in any difficulties in interpreting the scope of legal representation in relation to adults with incapacity. For an account of the history of *inter alia* tutors as guardians to adults, see Ward *The Power to Act*.

Subs. (4)
This subsection refers to changes of address. Section 76 refers to changes in the adult's place of habitual residence. The intended difference, and the reasons for it, are not clear.

The Public Guardian must not notify the adult if she considers that this would be likely to pose a serious risk to the adult's health (see s.11 (2)).

Subs. (5)
Power to purchase assets, services or accommodation is frequently conferred upon trustees administering discretionary trusts with disabled beneficiaries, and often found to be useful. For such powers to be readily available to guardians assists them in giving, with less difficulty than was the case under curatory, an appropriate service to adults with incapacities.

Under para. 1(1) of Sched. 2, a management plan is required in all cases where property and financial powers are granted, unless the sheriff specifically directs otherwise.

Paragraph 6 of Sched. 2 deals with the purchase or disposal of accommodation.

Subs. (6)
This provision is helpful in relation to personal welfare powers, as well as financial powers, and in a variety of situations, such as where the guardian is not the day to day carer, or where

Adults with Incapacity (Scotland) Act 2000 (Pt. 6)

the adult goes for respite care or for a group holiday. The guardian may delegate the actual carrying out of functions, but not responsibility for them. The demarcation may not always be obvious. It may be unobjectionable for a guardian to delegate routine decisions about matters such as diet and dress, but there would be a question as to the extent of delegation competent to deal with an emergency. There could be a similar question as to the extent to which delegation of management of funds would be competent (though guardians are not trustees in terms of the Trusts (Scotland) Act 1921 (11 & 12 Geo.5 c.58)).

Subs. (7)
A welfare guardian is not subject to a similar requirement to comply with orders and demands: see General Note to s.10. Welfare guardians are however under the supervision of local authorities (see s.10 (1)(a) and subject to the recall provisions of s.63).
As to applications to the sheriff, see ss.2 and 3.

Subs. (8)
For appointment of interim guardians, see s.57 (5) and (6).

Subs. (9)
Section 58 (7) specifies those to whom the guardianship order itself must be notified. See also ss.59 and 69 (2)–(4).
A significant criticism of the law prior to this Act is that while even a curator bonis (the approximate equivalent of a guardian with property and financial powers) had to be an individual, and not an impersonal entity or even a partnership (*McFarlane v Donaldson* (1835) 13S 725, *Brogan, Petr.*, 1986 SLT 420), the local authority could be a 1984 Act guardian (1984 Act s.37 (2)(a)). In relation to welfare powers even more than to property and financial powers, guardianship powers should only be exercised by an identified and known individual. This subsection is designed to ensure this, and was strengthened at stage 3 to require notification within seven days of initial appointment, and any change, of the identity of the officer responsible for carrying out guardianship functions conferred on the chief social work officer. It would appear that "his appointment" refers to the appointment of the officer responsible, so that there is not strictly speaking a time-limit for making the initial such appointment following the commencement of guardianship, but the importance attached to this matter in this section and in s.76 (3) indicates that the Parliament envisaged that the adult and others should not be left longer than seven days in ignorance of the identity of the individual actually responsible for guardianship functions.
See s.76 (3) where the adult moves to another local authority area.
The improvements compared to earlier law contained in this subsection do not apply to appointments under Criminal Procedure (Scotland) Act 1995 (c.46) as amended by s.84 and Sched. 5 para. 26 of this Act, under which the guardian is the local authority or a person approved by the local authority.

Subs. (10)
See s.11 (1) for circumstances in which the sheriff may order that intimation should not be given.

Subs. (11)
Regarding regulations, see s.86. There is no equivalent power to make regulations in relation to intervention orders, therefore it appears that the Parliament intended that the potential scope of intervention orders should not be similarly limited, so that it might be possible to obtain an intervention order to achieve something outwith the powers which might be conferred on a guardian. See General Note to s.53. No regulations have yet been made under this subsection.

Subs. (12)
Many provisions of importance appear in Sched. 2. It is not immediately obvious why matters such as gifts are dealt with in Pt. 6 (see s.66) while, for example, purchase and disposal of accommodation is dealt with in Sched. 2 (see para. 6).

Records: guardians
65. A guardian shall keep records of the exercise of his powers.

GENERAL NOTE
Guardians with property and financial powers are required to submit accounts as well as to keep records (Sched. 2, para. 7). Guardians with welfare powers only, like appointees under CPAs and WPAs (s.21) and intervention orders (s.54), are simply required to keep records of the exercise of their powers. Unlike record-keeping by withdrawers under s.30B, there is no provision for regulations. Guidance is given in codes of practice issued under s.13.

Gifts

66.—(1) A guardian having powers relating to the property or financial affairs of an adult may make a gift out of the adult's estate only if authorised to do so by the Public Guardian.

(2) Authorisation by the Public Guardian under subsection (1) may be given generally, or in respect of a particular gift.

(3) On receipt of an application in the prescribed form for an authorisation to make a gift, the Public Guardian shall, subject to subsection (4), intimate the application to the adult, his nearest relative, his primary carer[, his named person][132] and any other person who the Public Guardian considers has an interest in the application and advise them of the prescribed period within which they may object to the granting of the application; and he shall not grant the application without affording to any objector an opportunity of being heard.

(4) Where the Public Guardian is of the opinion that the value of the gift is such that intimation is not necessary, he may dispense with intimation.

(5) Having heard any objections as mentioned in subsection (3), the Public Guardian may grant the application.

(6) Where the Public Guardian proposes to refuse the application he shall intimate his decision to the guardian and advise him of the prescribed period within which he may object to the refusal; and he shall not refuse the application without affording to the guardian, if he objects, an opportunity of being heard.

(7) The Public Guardian may at his own instance or at the instance of the guardian or of any person who objects to the granting of the application remit the application for determination by the sheriff, whose decision shall be final.

(8) A decision of the Public Guardian—

(a) to grant an application under subsection (5) or to refuse an application; or

(b) to refuse to remit an application to the sheriff under subsection (7),

may be appealed to the sheriff, whose decision shall be final.

DEFINITIONS
"adult" : s.1 (6)
"nearest relative" : s.87 (1), subject to s.87 (2) and (3) (but see s.4)
"prescribed" : s.87 (1) (and see s.86)
"primary carer": s.87 (1)
"Public Guardian" : s.6 (1)

GENERAL NOTE
See comments on "benefit" in General Note to subs. (2) of s.1.

---

[132] Inserted by Mental Health (Care and Treatment) (Scotland) Act 2003 (Modification of Enactments) Order 2005 (SSI 2005/465), Sch.1, para.28(6).

Section 11 provides that the Public Guardian must not give intimation to the adult if that would be likely to pose a serious risk to the adult's health. Exercise by the Public Guardian of her discretion under subs. (4) would not relieve the guardian of his duty under s.1 (4)(a).

See ss.2 and 3 regarding remits and appeals to the sheriff.

Effect of appointment and transactions of guardian

67.—(1) The adult shall have no capacity to enter into any transaction in relation to any matter which is within the scope of the authority conferred on the guardian except in a case where he has been authorised by the guardian under section 64(1)(e); but nothing in this subsection shall be taken to affect the capacity of the adult in relation to any other matter.

(2) Where the guardian has powers relating to the property or financial affairs of the adult, the certificate of appointment issued to him by the Public Guardian shall, subject to the terms of the order appointing him, have the effect of—

(a) authorising the guardian to take possession of, manage and deal with any moveable or immoveable estate (wherever situated) of the adult;
(b) requiring any payment due to the adult to be made to the guardian,

in so far as the estate, payment or matter falls within the scope of the guardian's authority.

(3) A guardian having powers relating to the personal welfare of an adult may exercise these powers in relation to the adult whether or not the adult is in Scotland at the time of the exercise of the powers.

(4) The guardian shall be personally liable under any transaction entered into by him—

(a) without disclosing that he is acting as guardian of the adult; or
(b) which falls outwith the scope of his authority,

but where a guardian has acted as mentioned in paragraph (a) and is not otherwise in breach of any requirement of this Act relating to such guardians, he shall be entitled to be reimbursed from the estate of the adult in respect of any loss suffered by him in consequence of a claim made upon him personally by virtue of this subsection.

(5) Where a third party with whom the adult entered into a transaction was aware at the date of entering into the transaction that authority had been granted by the guardian under section 64(1)(e), the transaction shall not be void only on the ground that the adult lacked capacity.

(6) A transaction for value between the guardian purporting to act as such and a third party acting in good faith shall not be invalid on the ground only that—

(a) the guardian acted outwith the scope of his authority; or
(b) the guardian failed to observe any requirement, whether substantive or procedural, imposed by or under this Act, or by the sheriff or by the Public Guardian; or
(c) there was any irregularity whether substantive or procedural in the appointment of the guardian.

(7) In subsections (3) and (4) any reference to a guardian shall include a reference to a guardian (however called) appointed under the law of any

country to, or entitled under the law of any country to act for, an adult during his incapacity, if the guardianship is recognised by the law of Scotland.

DEFINITIONS
"adult" : s.1 (6)
"incapacity" : s.1 (6)
"Public Guardian" : s.6 (1)

GENERAL NOTE

Subs. (1)
See General Note on subs. (1) of s.64.
　Beyond the scope of the guardianship order, the presumption of capacity remains: see also General Note on subs. (5) below.

Subss. (3) and (4)
These provisions apply also to intervention orders, and by subs. (7) to equivalents of guardians under other jurisdictions—see General Note to s.1 (7).
　The entitlement to reimbursement in subs. (4) requires *inter alia* compliance with the general principles in s.1

Subs. (5)
It would appear that an adult acting within the authority of a guardian in terms of s.64 (1)(e), and parties transacting with such adults and aware of such authority, have unique guarantees that such transactions can never be challenged on grounds of lack of capacity.

Reimbursement and remuneration of guardian
68.—(1) A guardian shall be entitled to be reimbursed out of the estate of the adult for any outlays reasonably incurred by him in the exercise of his functions.
　(2) In subsection (1), "outlays", in relation to a guardian—

(a) who is someone other than the chief social work officer of a local authority, includes payment for items and services other than those items and services which the guardian is expected to provide as part of his functions;
(b) who is the chief social work officer of a local authority, includes payment for items and services only if they would not normally be provided free of charge by the local authority to a person who is in similar circumstances but who does not have a guardian.

　(3) The local authority shall, in relation to the cost of any application by them for appointment of their chief social work officer as guardian or of any subsequent application by that officer while acting as guardian—

(a) where the application relates to the personal welfare of the adult, meet such cost;
(b) where the application relates to the property or financial affairs of the adult, be entitled to recover such cost from the estate of the adult,

and where the application relates to the personal welfare and to the property or financial affairs of the adult the sheriff shall, in determining the application, apportion the cost as he thinks fit.
　(4) Remuneration shall be payable out of the adult's estate—

(a) in respect of the exercise of functions relating to the personal welfare of the adult, only in a case where special cause is shown;
(b) in respect of the exercise of functions relating to the property or financial affairs of the adult, unless the sheriff directs otherwise in the order appointing the guardian,

but shall not be payable to a local authority in respect of the exercise by their chief social work officer of functions relating to the personal welfare of the adult.

(5) In determining whether or not to make a direction under subsection (4)(b), the sheriff shall take into account the value of the estate and the likely difficulty of managing it.

(6) Any remuneration payable to the guardian and the amount of outlays to be allowed under subsection (1) shall be fixed by the Public Guardian—

(a) in a case where the guardian is required to submit accounts, when the guardian's accounts for that period are audited;
(b) in any other case, on an application by the guardian,

and in fixing the remuneration to be paid to the guardian the Public Guardian shall take into account the value of the estate.

(7) The Public Guardian may allow payments to account to be made by way of remuneration during the accounting period if it would be unreasonable to expect the guardian to wait for payment until the end of an accounting period.

(8) A decision by the Public Guardian—

(a) under subsection (6) as to the remuneration payable and the outlays allowable to the guardian;
(b) under subsection (7) as to payments to account to the guardian

may be appealed to the sheriff, whose decision shall be final.

DEFINITIONS
"adult" : s.1 (6)
"chief social work officer" : Social Work (Scotland) Act 1968 (c.49) s.3 (presumed)
"local authority" : s.87 (1) (referring to the Local Government etc. (Scotland) Act 1994 (c.39) s.2)
"outlays" : s.68 (2)
"Public Guardian" : s.6 (1)

GENERAL NOTE
Except for subs. (3), the provisions of this section are clearly expressed and require little comment. The general approach is that the guardian's outlays may be met from the adult's estate (subs. (1)); that there is a presumption against remuneration in the exercise of welfare powers (subs. (4)(b)); and that there is a presumption in favour of remuneration in the exercise of property and financial powers, though this will depend upon the size of the estate and the difficulty in managing it (subss. (4)(b) and (5)). Remuneration may be forfeited under s.69.

Subs. (3)
This subsection presents difficulties, firstly because it is clear from s.59 that only personal welfare powers, and not property or financial powers, may be conferred on the chief social work officer; and secondly because there is no provision as to how expenses should be dealt with in all other cases. Section 59 (2) provides that where the guardianship order confers both

welfare and financial powers and the chief social work officer is one of the guardians, he may have only welfare powers, and accordingly a joint guardian would be required to exercise the property and financial powers. That can be the only situation in which para. (b), and the apportionment provision which follows it, will apply.

Otherwise, the provisions regarding expenses in s.8 cover applications by local authorities (other than those to which this subsection applies), the Public Guardian and MWC only. It would appear that the expenses of all other applications are accordingly within the discretion of the sheriff under the general powers in s.3 or the inherent power of the sheriff to dispose of questions of expenses (see General Note to s.8).

Forfeiture of guardian's remuneration
69.—Where a guardian is in breach of any duty of care, fiduciary duty or obligation imposed by this Act the sheriff may, on an application being made to him by any person claiming an interest in the property, financial affairs or personal welfare of the adult, order the forfeiture (in whole or in part) of any remuneration due to the guardian.

DEFINITIONS
"adult" : s.1 (6)
"person claiming an interest" : s.87 (1)

GENERAL NOTE
See also s.81 (repayment of funds) and s.82 (limitation of liability), and the General Notes thereto. See also paras. 8(6) and (7) of Sched. 2.

Non-compliance with decisions of guardian with welfare powers
70.—(1) Where any decision of a guardian with powers relating to the personal welfare of the adult is not complied with by the adult [. . .][133], and the adult [. . .][134] might reasonably be expected to comply with the decision, the sheriff may, on an application by the guardian—

(a) make an order ordaining the adult [. . .][135] to implement the decision of the guardian;
(b) where the non-compliance relates to a decision of the guardian as to the place of residence of the adult, grant a warrant authorising a constable—
    (i) to enter any premises where the adult is, or is reasonably supposed to be;
    (ii) to apprehend the adult and to remove him to such place as the guardian may direct.

(2) Where any decision of a guardian with powers relating to the personal welfare of the adult is not complied with by any person other than the adult, and that person might reasonably be expected to comply with the decision, the sheriff may, on an application by the guardian make an order ordaining the person named in the order to implement the decision of the guardian.

---

[133] Repealed by Adult Support and Protection (Scotland) Act 2007 (asp 10), s.60(8)(a), subject to savings specified in SSI 2007/334, art.5.
[134] Repealed by Adult Support and Protection (Scotland) Act 2007 (asp 10), s.60(8)(a), subject to savings specified in SSI 2007/334, art.5.
[135] Repealed by Adult Support and Protection (Scotland) Act 2007 (asp 10), s.60(8)(a), subject to savings specified in SSI 2007/334, art.5.

(3) On receipt of an application in the prescribed form for an order or warrant under subsection (1) or for an order under subsection (2), the court shall intimate the application to the adult or, as the case may be, to the person named in the application as a person against whom the order or warrant is sought and shall advise them of the prescribed period within which they may object to the granting of the application; and the sheriff shall not grant the order or warrant without affording to any objector an opportunity of being heard.

(4) Having heard any objections as mentioned in subsection (3), the sheriff may grant the application.

[(4A) The sheriff may, on cause shown, disapply or modify the application of—

(a) subsection (3), and
(b) subsection (4) in so far as it requires the sheriff to hear objections.][136]

(5) A constable executing a warrant under subsection (1)(b) may use such force as is reasonable in the circumstances and shall be accompanied by the guardian or such person as the guardian may authorise in writing.

(6) In this section any reference to a guardian shall include a reference to a guardian (however called) appointed under the law of any country to, or entitled under the law of any country to act for, an adult during his incapacity, if the guardianship is recognised by the law of Scotland.

DEFINITIONS
"adult" : s.1 (6)
"incapacity" : s.1 (6)
"prescribed" : s.87 (1) (and see s.86)

GENERAL NOTE
In the Bill as introduced, subs. (1) dealt only with non-compliance by the adult, and subs. (2) only with non-compliance by others. At stage 2, subs. (1) was amended to refer also to "any other person". Assuming "any person other than the adult" in subs. (2) to be synonymous, subs. (2) then appeared—as regards persons other than the adult—to duplicate subs. (1), and to add nothing to it. The 2007 Act has rectified this anomaly by returning subs. (1) to the wording in the Bill as introduced, so that subs. (1) now refers only to the adult, and subs. (2) to third parties. The 2007 Act amendments have also removed the unintended effect of s.70 that a warrant could have been issued for the adult's removal from his or her place of residence where a third party had refused to comply with the guardian's decision.

Amendment at stage 2 also introduced the "might reasonably be expected to comply" qualification to both subsections, in response to expressions of concern by the Alliance and others that a guardian acting on behalf of an adult should not be empowered to make demands of third parties which the adult, if competent, would not be entitled to make, and that guardians should not in general terms be able to make unlimited demands. Without such qualification, these provisions risked challenge that they breached ECHR. These qualifications have been retained.

The granting and use of compulsive powers under this section should be seen as a last resort, and in relation to the adult must accord with the general principles in s.1

"Constable" is not defined in this Act, but is defined in Social Work (Scotland) Act 1968 (c.49) s.94 (1) as "a constable of a police force within the meaning of the Police (Scotland) Act 1967" (c.77).

The sheriff may under s.11 (1) direct that intimation should not be given to the adult where he considers that such intimation would be likely to pose a serious risk to the adult's health.

---

[136] Inserted by Adult Support and Protection (Scotland) Act 2007 (asp 10), s.60(8)(b), subject to savings specified in SSI 2007/334, art.5.

On subs. (6), see General Note to s.1 (7).

Subs. (4A)
Concerns about the procedure under s.70 were expressed at pp 11 *et seq* of the decision of Sheriff Baird in *Guardianship application in respect of A.D.*, February 8, 2005, Glasgow Sh. Ct., a lengthy decision otherwise mainly concerned with the facts of that application. The sheriff was particularly concerned about the cumbersomeness and duration of s.70 procedure in cases where the facts appeared to demand interim powers and a warrant for the immediate removal of the adult from where she was living. The 2007 Act introduced this subsection, under which the sheriff may now, on cause shown, disapply the intimation requirement and the corresponding right to object within a prescribed period. In some such situations the new adult protection powers under Pt. 1 of the 2007 Act may be the better option.

Regulations
See SSI 2002/98, reproduced in *Adult Incapacity*.

Termination and variation of guardianship and replacement, removal or resignation of guardian

Replacement or removal of guardian or recall of guardianship by sheriff

71.—(1) The sheriff, on an application made to him by an adult subject to guardianship or by any other person claiming an interest in the adult's property, financial affairs or personal welfare, may—

(a) replace a guardian by an individual or office holder nominated in the application if he is satisfied, in relation to an individual, that he is suitable for appointment having regard to the matters set out in section 59(3) to (5);

(b) remove a guardian from office if he is satisfied—

  (i) that there is a substitute guardian who is prepared to act as guardian; or

  (ii) in a case where there are joint guardians, that the remaining guardian is or remaining guardians are prepared to continue to act; or

(c) recall a guardianship order or otherwise terminate a guardianship if he is satisfied—

  (i) that the grounds for appointment of a guardian are no longer fulfilled; or

  (ii) that the interests of the adult in his property, financial affairs or personal welfare can be satisfactorily safeguarded or promoted otherwise than by guardianship,

and where an application under this subsection is granted, the sheriff clerk shall send a copy of the interlocutor to the Public Guardian.

(2) In making an order replacing a guardian by an individual with powers relating to the property or financial affairs of the adult or removing a guardian from office where there is a substitute guardian with such powers prepared to act as guardian, the sheriff [may][137] require an individual appointed as guardian or the substitute guardian to find caution [or to give such other security as the sheriff thinks fit][138].

(3) The Public Guardian on receiving a copy of the interlocutor under subsection (1) shall—

---

[137] Substituted by Adult Support and Protection (Scotland) Act 2007 (asp 10), s.60(9)(a)(i).
[138] Inserted by Adult Support and Protection (Scotland) Act 2007 (asp 10), s.60(9)(a)(ii).

Adults with Incapacity (Scotland) Act 2000 (Pt. 6)

(a) enter prescribed particulars in the register maintained by him under section 6(2)(b)(iv);
(b) where the sheriff—
   (i) replaces the guardian by the individual or office holder nominated in the application, when satisfied that, in the case of an individual, the individual has found caution [or given other security][139] if so required, issue him with a certificate of appointment;
   (ii) removes a guardian from office and a substitute guardian is prepared to act, when satisfied that the substitute guardian has found caution [or given other security][140] if so required, issue the substitute guardian with a certificate of appointment;
   (iii) removes a joint guardian from office and there is a joint guardian who is prepared to continue to act, issue a remaining joint guardian with a new certificate of appointment;
(a) notify the adult and the local authority and (in a case where the incapacity of the adult is by reason of, or reasons which include, mental disorder and the guardianship order relates to the adult's personal welfare or factors including it) the Mental Welfare Commission.

(4) Where the sheriff recalls the guardianship order he may at the same time make an intervention order.
(5) In this section any reference to a guardian shall include a reference to a guardian (however called) appointed under the law of any country to, or entitled under the law of any country to act for, an adult during his incapacity, if the guardianship is recognised by the law of Scotland; and "guardianship order" shall be construed accordingly.

DEFINITIONS
"adult" : s.1 (6)
"guardianship order" : s.58 (4)
"incapacity" : s.1 (6)
"intervention order" : s.53 (1)
"local authority" : s.87 (1) (referring to the Local Government etc. (Scotland) Act 1994 (c.39) s.2)
"mental disorder" : s.87 (1) (and see General Note to s.1 (6))
"Mental Welfare Commission" : s.87 (1) (referring to s.4 of the 2003 Act)
"office holder" : s.87 (1)
"person claiming an interest" : s.87 (1)
"prescribed" : s.87 (1) (and see s.86)
"Public Guardian" : s.6 (1)
"substitute guardian" : s.63 (2)

GENERAL NOTE
This section should be read in conjunction with the ensuing sections, especially the provisions of s.73 empowering the Public Guardian, MWC and local authorities to recall powers of the guardian. This section empowers the sheriff to replace the existing guardian with a new guardian (subs. (1)(a)), remove a guardian where a substitute or joint guardian will provide continuity (subs. (1)(b)), or simply end the guardianship if it is no longer required (subs.

---

[139] Inserted by Adult Support and Protection (Scotland) Act 2007 (asp 10), s.60(9)(b)(i).
[140] Inserted by Adult Support and Protection (Scotland) Act 2007 (asp 10), s.60(9)(b)(ii).

(1)(c)—as noted in the General Notes to ss.1 (3) and 58(1), subs. (1)(c)(ii) refers to any alternatives, not limited to those under this Act). For procedure in "subsequent applications" under subs. (1) see second paragraph of General Note to subs. (3) of s.58, SI 1999/929, and General Note to subs. (1) of s.60.

An application under subss. (1)(a) or (c) is required by a guardian wishing to resign, where there is no joint or substitute guardian who provides continuity, under s.75 (5).

In any case where a replacement guardian is appointed, it is important that powers conferred and duration of appointment be specified: see General Note to Sched. 4, which also considers the situation where these matters have not been specified.

Subsection (2) contains provisions regarding caution similar to those for new financial guardians under s.58 (6) (on which see note to that subsection), and subs. (3) provides for registration, certification and notification following upon an order under subs. (1). Under s.11 (2), the Public Guardian must not notify the adult where she considers that such intimation would be likely to pose a serious risk to the adult's health.

Subsection (4) empowers the sheriff to make an intervention order when recalling guardianship (see General Note to s.58 (3)), and subs. (5) contains the usual application to equivalents of guardians (see General Note to s.1 (7)).

Discharge of guardian with financial powers

72.—(1) At any time after—

(a) the recall of a guardianship order appointing a guardian with powers relating to the property or financial affairs of an adult;

[(aa) the expiry of such a guardianship order;][141]

(b) the resignation, removal or replacement of such a guardian; or

(c) the death of the adult,

the Public Guardian may, on an application by the former guardian or, if the former guardian has died, his representative, grant a discharge in respect of the former guardian's actings and intromissions with the estate of the adult.

(2) On receipt of an application in the prescribed form, the Public Guardian shall intimate the application to the adult, his nearest relative, his primary carer [his named person][142] and any other person who the Public Guardian considers has an interest in the application and advise them of the prescribed period within which they may object to the granting of the application; and he shall not grant the application without affording to any objector an opportunity of being heard.

(3) Having heard any objections as mentioned in subsection (2) the Public Guardian may grant the application.

(4) Where the Public Guardian proposes to refuse the application he shall intimate his decision to the applicant and advise him of the prescribed period within which he may object to the refusal; and he shall not refuse the application without affording to the applicant, if he objects, an opportunity of being heard.

(5) The Public Guardian may at his own instance or at the instance of the applicant or of any person who objects to the granting of the application remit the application for determination by the sheriff, whose decision shall be final.

(6) A decision of the Public Guardian—

(a) to grant a discharge under subsection (1) or to refuse a discharge;

(b) to grant an application under subsection (3) or to refuse an application;

---

[141] Inserted by Adult Support and Protection (Scotland) Act 2007 (asp 10), s.60(10).
[142] Inserted by Mental Health (Care and Treatment) (Scotland) Act 2003 (Modification of Enactments) Order 2005 (SSI 2005/465), Sch.1, para.28(7).

(c) to refuse to remit an application to the sheriff under subsection (5)

may be appealed to the sheriff, whose decision shall be final.

DEFINITIONS
"adult" : s.1 (6)
"guardianship order" : s.58 (4)
"nearest relative" : s.87 (1), subject to s.87 (2) and (3) (but see s.4)
"prescribed" : s.87 (1) (and see s.86)
"primary carer": s.87 (1)
"Public Guardian" : s.6 (1)

GENERAL NOTE
This section provides for the discharge of financial guardians. Subsection (1)(aa) makes good an omission in the 2000 text. Regarding the intimation provisions of subs. (2), note that under s.11 (2) the Public Guardian must not intimate to the adult where she considers that such intimation would be likely to pose a serious risk to the adult's health.

Recall of powers of guardian

73.—(1) The Public Guardian, at his own instance or on an application by any person (including the adult himself) claiming an interest in the property and financial affairs of an adult in respect of whom a guardian has been appointed, may recall the powers of a guardian relating to the property or financial affairs of the adult if it appears to him that—

(a) the grounds for appointment of a guardian with such powers are no longer fulfilled; or
(b) the interests of the adult in his property and financial affairs can be satisfactorily safeguarded or promoted otherwise than by guardianship.

(2) Where the Public Guardian recalls the powers of a guardian under subsection (1) he shall—

(a) enter prescribed particulars in the register maintained by him under section 6(2)(b)(iv);
(b) notify the adult, the guardian and the local authority.

(3) The Mental Welfare Commission or the local authority in whose area an adult in respect of whom a guardian has been appointed habitually resides [. . .][143], at their own instance or on an application by any person (including the adult himself) claiming an interest in the personal welfare of the adult, may recall the powers of a guardian relating to the personal welfare of the adult if it appears to them that—

(a) the grounds for appointment of a guardian with such powers are no longer fulfilled; or
(b) the interests of the adult in his personal welfare can be satisfactorily safeguarded or promoted otherwise than by guardianship.

[(3A) The Mental Welfare Commission may recall the powers of a guardian under subsection (3) only if those powers were granted in a case

---

[143] Repealed by Adult Support and Protection (Scotland) Act 2007 (asp 10), s.60(11)(a).

where the adult's incapacity is by reason of, or reasons which include, mental disorder.][144]
(4) Where the Mental Welfare Commission or the local authority recall the powers of a guardian under subsection (3) they shall notify the other and the Public Guardian who shall—

- (a) enter prescribed particulars in the register maintained by him under section 6(2)(b)(iv);
- (b) notify the adult and the guardian.

(5) The Public Guardian, Mental Welfare Commission or local authority, as the case may be, shall—

- (a) where acting on an application, on receipt of the application in the prescribed form intimate it;
- (b) where acting at his or their own instance, intimate the intention to recall the powers of a guardian,

to the adult, his nearest relative, his primary carer[, his named person][145] and any person who he or they consider has an interest in the recall of the powers and advise them of the prescribed period within which they may object to such recall; and he or they shall not recall the powers without affording to any objector an opportunity of being heard.

(6) Having heard any objections as mentioned in subsection (5) the Public Guardian, Mental Welfare Commission or local authority may recall the powers of a guardian.

(7) Where the Public Guardian, Mental Welfare Commission or local authority proposes or propose to refuse the application he or they shall intimate the decision to the applicant and the adult and advise them of the prescribed period within which they may object to the refusal; and he or they shall not refuse the application without affording to the applicant or the adult, if he objects, an opportunity of being heard.

(8) The Public Guardian, Mental Welfare Commission or local authority may at his or their own instance or at the instance of an applicant or of any person who objects to the recall of the powers of the guardian remit the matter for determination by the sheriff whose decision shall be final.

(9) A decision of—

- (a) the Public Guardian, Mental Welfare Commission or local authority to recall the powers of a guardian under subsection (6);
- (b) the Public Guardian, Mental Welfare Commission or local authority to remit or not to remit the matter to the sheriff under subsection (8),

may be appealed to the sheriff, whose decision shall be final, and the decision of the Public Guardian, Mental Welfare Commission or local authority as to the recall of the powers of a guardian shall remain in force pending the final determination of the appeal.

(10) The Scottish Ministers may prescribe the forms and procedure for the purposes of any recall of guardianship powers by the Mental Welfare Commission or the local authority.

---

[144] Inserted by Adult Support and Protection (Scotland) Act 2007 (asp 10), s.60(11)(b).
[145] Inserted by Mental Health (Care and Treatment) (Scotland) Act 2003 (Modification of Enactments) Order 2005 (SSI 2005/465), Sch.1, para.28(8).

[(11) Section 73A modifies the application of this section in relation to the recall by a local authority of guardianship powers held by their chief social work officer.][146]

DEFINITIONS
"adult" : s.1 (6)
"chief social work officer" : Social Work (Scotland) Act 1968 (c.49) s.3 (presumed)
"local authority" : s.87 (1) (referring to the Local Government etc. (Scotland) Act 1994 (c.39) s.2)
"Mental Welfare Commission" : s.87 (1) (referring to s.4 of the 2003 Act)
"nearest relative" : s.87 (1), subject to s.87 (2) and (3) (but see s.4)
"person claiming an interest" : s.87 (1)
"prescribe" : s.87 (1) (and see s.86)
"prescribed" : s.87 (1) (and see s.86)
"primary carer": s.87 (1)
"Public Guardian" : s.6 (1)

GENERAL NOTE
Regarding intimations to the adult, note that under s.11 (2) the Public Guardian must not intimate if she considers that such intimation would be likely to pose a serious risk to the adult's health.

Subs. (1)
The Public Guardian has substantial functions and powers in relation to financial guardians, including supervision under s.6 (2)(a), making orders and demands under s.64 (7), and recalling financial powers under this subsection, subject to remit (subs. (8)) or appeal (subs. (9)) to the sheriff. See ss.2 and 3 regarding proceedings before the sheriff.

Subss. (3) and (3A)
The function of supervising welfare guardians rests with the local authority (under s.10 (1)(a)) rather than MWC. Neither has a power to make orders or demands similar to those of the Public Guardian under s.64 (7), but either may recall welfare powers under this subsection, subject (in the case of MWC) to the limitation in subs. (3A), subject (in the case of local authorities whose chief social work officer is guardian) to the provisions of s.73A, and in all cases subject to remit (subs. (8)) or appeal (subs. (9)) to the sheriff.

Subs. (10)
See s.86.

Regulations
See SSI 2002/97 as amended by SSI 2008/53.

Recall of chief social work officer's guardianship powers
[73A.—(1) This section applies where—

(a) a local authority's chief social work officer is appointed as a guardian; and
(b) either—
   (i) the local authority wish to recall their chief social work officer's guardianship powers at their own instance; or
   (ii) another person (including the adult himself) applies to the local authority for such a recall.

(2) Where this section applies—

---
[146] Inserted by Adult Support and Protection (Scotland) Act 2007 (asp 10), s.60(11)(c).

(a) the local authority shall, for the purposes of section 73(5), treat the Public Guardian and the Mental Welfare Commission as persons whom they consider to have an interest in the recall of the guardian's powers; and
(b) if the Public Guardian, the Mental Welfare Commission or any other person to whom intimation is given under section 73(5) objects to the recall of the guardian's powers, the local authority—
  (i) shall not recall the guardian's powers; but
  (ii) shall instead remit the matter for determination by the sheriff under section 73(8).][147]

DEFINITIONS
"adult" : s.1 (6)
"chief social work officer" : Social Work (Scotland) Act 1968 (c.49) s.3 (presumed)
"local authority" : s.87 (1) (referring to the Local Government etc. (Scotland) Act 1994 (c.39) s.2)
"Mental Welfare Commission" : s.87 (1) (referring to s.4 of the 2003 Act)
"Public Guardian" : s.6 (1)

GENERAL NOTE
This section, added by the 2007 Act, regulates proposed recall by the local authority of welfare guardianship powers held by the authority's chief social work officer.

Variation of guardianship order

74.—(1) The sheriff, on an application by any person (including the adult himself) claiming an interest in the property, financial affairs or personal welfare of the adult, may vary the powers conferred by the guardianship order and may vary any existing ancillary order.

(2) In varying powers relating to the property or financial affairs of the adult conferred by the guardianship order or in varying any ancillary order in relation to such powers the sheriff [may][148] require the guardian to find caution [or to give such other security as the sheriff thinks fit][149].

(3) In considering an application under subsection (1), the sheriff shall have regard to any intervention order or guardianship order which may have been previously made in relation to the adult or any other order varying such an order, and to any order ancillary to such an order.

(4) Notwithstanding subsection (1), an application which seeks to vary the powers conferred by a guardianship order or to vary an ancillary order so that—

(a) a guardian, appointed only in relation to the personal welfare of an adult, shall be appointed also or instead in relation to the property or financial affairs of the adult; or
(b) a guardian, appointed only in relation to the property or financial affairs of an adult, shall be appointed also or instead in relation to the personal welfare of the adult;

shall be made under section 57.

(5) Where the sheriff varies the powers conferred by a guardianship order or varies an ancillary order under this section, the sheriff clerk shall

---

[147] Inserted by Adult Support and Protection (Scotland) Act 2007 (asp 10), s.60(12).
[148] Substituted by Adult Support and Protection (Scotland) Act 2007 (asp 10), s.60(13)(a)(i).
[149] Inserted by Adult Support and Protection (Scotland) Act 2007 (asp 10), s.60(13)(a)(ii).

Adults with Incapacity (Scotland) Act 2000 (Pt. 6)

send a copy of the interlocutor containing the order to the Public Guardian who shall—

    (a) enter prescribed particulars in the register maintained by him under section 6(2)(b)(iv);
    (b) notify the adult and the local authority and (in a case where the incapacity of the adult is by reason of, or reasons which include, mental disorder and the guardianship order relates to the adult's personal welfare or factors including it) the Mental Welfare Commission; and
    (c) if he is satisfied that the guardian has caution [or other security][150], if so required, which covers the varied order, issue a new certificate of appointment where necessary.

DEFINITIONS
"adult" : s.1 (6)
"guardianship order" : s.58 (4)
"incapacity" : s.1 (6)
"intervention order" : s.53 (1)
"local authority" : s.87 (1) (referring to the Local Government etc. (Scotland) Act 1994 (c.39) s.2)
"mental disorder" : s.87 (1) (and see General Note to s.1 (6))
"Mental Welfare Commission" : s.87 (1) (referring to s.4 of the 2003 Act)
"person claiming an interest" : s.87 (1)
"prescribed" : s.87 (1) (and see s.86)
"Public Guardian" : s.6 (1)

GENERAL NOTE
This section provides for variation of existing guardianship orders. For applications to the sheriff generally, see ss.2 and 3. For procedure in "subsequent applications", see second paragraph of General Note to subs. (3) of s.58, SI 1999/929, and General Note to subs. (1) of s.60. The provisions of subs. (2) regarding caution are similar to those of s.58 (6) (see note to s.58 (6)). Where it is proposed that property or financial powers should be conferred on a guardian hitherto having welfare powers only, or vice versa, the procedure under s.57 for a new order must be followed (subs. (4)). It would appear that, in consequence, the normal maximum initial duration for such new powers will be three years (see General Note to s.58 (4)).

Regarding subs. (5)(b), the Public Guardian must not notify the adult if she considers that such intimation would be likely to pose a serious risk to the adult's health (s.11 (2)).

Resignation of guardian
75.—(1) A joint guardian, or a guardian in respect of whom a substitute guardian has been appointed, may resign by giving notice in writing of his intention to do so to the Public Guardian and the local authority and (in a case where the incapacity of the adult is by reason of, or reasons which include, mental disorder and the guardianship order relates to the adult's personal welfare or factors including it) the Mental Welfare Commission.

    (2) The resignation of a guardian as mentioned in subsection (1)—

    (a) shall not take effect unless—

        (i) the remaining joint guardian is willing to continue to act; or
        (ii) the substitute guardian is willing to act;

    (b) shall take effect on the receipt by the Public Guardian of notice in writing under subsection (1) together with evidence as to the matters contained in paragraph (a)(i) or (ii).

---
[150] Inserted by Adult Support and Protection (Scotland) Act 2007 (asp 10), s.60(13)(b).

(3) On receiving notice in writing and evidence as mentioned in subsection (2)(b), the Public Guardian shall—

(a) enter prescribed particulars in the register maintained by him under section 6(2)(b)(iv);
(b) if satisfied that the substitute guardian has found caution [or given other security][151] if so required, issue him with a new certificate of appointment;
(c) issue a remaining joint guardian with a new certificate of appointment;
(d) notify the adult.

(4) A substitute guardian who has not subsequently become guardian by virtue of section 63 may resign by giving notice in writing to the Public Guardian and the local authority and (in the case mentioned in subsection (1)) the Mental Welfare Commission and the resignation shall take effect on the date of receipt of the notice by the Public Guardian; and on its becoming effective, the Public Guardian shall—

(a) notify the guardian and the adult; and
(a) enter prescribed particulars in the register maintained by him under section 6(2)(b)(iv).

(5) A guardian—

(a) who has no joint guardian; or
(b) in respect of whom no substitute guardian has been appointed; or
(c) being a joint guardian or guardian in respect of whom a substitute has been appointed who cannot effectively resign by reason of subsection (2)(a)(i) or (ii),

shall not resign until a replacement guardian has been appointed under section 71.

DEFINITIONS
"adult" : s.1 (6)
"guardianship order" : s.58 (4)
"incapacity" : s.1 (6)
"local authority" : s.87 (1) (referring to the Local Government etc. (Scotland) Act 1994 (c.39) s.2)
"mental disorder" : s.87 (1) (and see General Note to s.1 (6))
"Mental Welfare Commission" : s.87 (1) (referring to s.4 of the 2003 Act)
"prescribed" : s.87 (1) (and see s.86)
"Public Guardian" : s.6 (1)
"substitute guardian" : s.63 (2)

GENERAL NOTE
This section permits a guardian to resign provided that either there is continuity of guardianship or a judicial determination that a guardian is no longer required. Accordingly, a guardian may resign if a joint or substitute guardian provides continuity, but otherwise requires to apply to the sheriff under s.71 (1)(a) or (c) for his own removal and either replacement (s.71 (1)(a)) or a judicial determination that a guardian is no longer required (s.71 (1)(c)).

---

[151] Inserted by Adult Support and Protection (Scotland) Act 2007 (asp 10), s.60(14).

Under s.11 (2), notification to the adult must not be given under subss. (3)(d) or (4)(a) if the Public Guardian considers that such intimation would be likely to pose a serious risk to the adult's health.

Death of guardian
[**75A.** The personal representatives of a guardian who dies shall, if aware of the existence of the guardianship, notify the Public Guardian who shall—

(a) notify—
  (i) the adult;
  (ii) the local authority; and
  (iii) in a case where the adult's incapacity is by reason of, or reasons which include, mental disorder and the guardianship order relates to the adult's personal welfare or factors including it, the Mental Welfare Commission;
(b) enter prescribed particulars in the register maintained under section 6(2)(b)(iv); and
(c) issue a new certificate of appointment—
  (i) to any surviving joint guardian;
  (ii) where the Public Guardian is satisfied that any substitute guardian appointed in respect of the dead guardian is willing to act and has found caution or given other security if so required, to the substitute guardian.][152]

DEFINITIONS
"adult" : s.1 (6)
"local authority" : s.87 (1) (referring to the Local Government etc. (Scotland) Act 1994 (c.39) s.2)
"mental disorder" : s.87 (1) (and see General Note to s.1 (6))
"Mental Welfare Commission" : s.87 (1) (referring to s.4 of the 2003 Act)
"prescribed" : s.87 (1) (and see s.86)
"Public Guardian" : s.6 (1)
"substitute guardian" : s.63 (2)

GENERAL NOTE
The provisions of this section are self-explanatory, as is their purpose, but were not contained in the 2000 text and have now been added by the 2007 Act.

Under s.11 (2), notification to the adult must not be given under para. (a)(i) if the Public Guardian considers that such intimation would be likely to pose a serious risk to the adult's health.

See General Note to s.78 on the omission from that section of reference to this s.75A

Change of habitual residence
76.—(1) Where the guardian is the chief social work officer of the local authority and the adult changes his place of habitual residence to the area of another local authority, the chief social work officer of the first mentioned local authority shall notify the chief social work officer of the second mentioned local authority (the "receiving authority") who shall become guardian on receipt of the notification and shall within 7 days of that receipt notify the Public Guardian and (in a case where the incapacity of the adult is by reason of, or reasons which include, mental disorder and the guardianship order relates to the adult's personal welfare or factors which include it) the Mental Welfare Commission.

---

[152] Inserted by Adult Support and Protection (Scotland) Act 2007 (asp 10), s.60(15).

(2) The Public Guardian shall—

(a) enter prescribed particulars in the register maintained by him under section 6(2)(b)(iv) and issue a certificate of appointment to the new guardian; and
(b) subject to subsection (4), notify the adult within 7 days of receipt of the notification from the receiving authority.

(3) Subject to subsection (4), the chief social work officer of the receiving authority shall, within 7 working days of receipt of the notification, notify any person who received notification under section 58(7) of the appointment of the name of the officer responsible at any time for carrying out the functions and duties of guardian.

(4) If, in relation to the original application for a guardianship order, the sheriff has directed that intimation or notification of any application or other proceedings should not be given to the adult, the Public Guardian and the chief social work officer shall not notify the adult under subsection (2)(b) or (3) as the case may be.

DEFINITIONS
"adult" : s.1 (6)
"chief social work officer" : Social Work (Scotland) Act 1968 (c.49) s.3 (presumed)
"guardianship order" : s.58 (4)
"incapacity" : s.1 (6)
"local authority" : s.87 (1) (referring to the Local Government etc. (Scotland) Act 1994 (c.39) s.2)
"mental disorder" : s.87 (1) (and see General Note to s.1 (6))
"Mental Welfare Commission" : s.87 (1) (referring to s.4 of the 2003 Act)
"prescribed" : s.87 (1) (and see s.86)
"Public Guardian" : s.6 (1)

GENERAL NOTE
This section applies where the chief social work officer is guardian and the adult moves to another local authority area. Under 1984 Act guardianship there was experience in practice of unsatisfactory discontinuity when the adult under guardianship made such a move. In response to concerns about this, the requirement of subs. (3) to notify within seven days the identity of the responsible officer was added by amendment at stage 3. See General Note to s.64 (9).

See also s.64 (4) regarding change of address of the guardian or the adult.

Termination of authority to intervene and guardianship on death of adult

Termination of authority to intervene and guardianship on death of adult
77.—(1) An intervention order or a guardianship order in respect of an adult under this Part shall cease to have effect on his death.

(2) A person authorised under an intervention order or a guardian having powers relating to the property or financial affairs of the adult shall, until he becomes aware of the death of the adult or of any other event which has the effect of terminating his authority, be entitled to act under those powers if he acts in good faith.

(3) Where the authority of a person authorised under an intervention order or of a guardian (including a joint guardian) is terminated or otherwise comes to an end, a third party in good faith is entitled to rely on the authority of the person or guardian if he is unaware of the termination or ending of that authority.

(4) No title to any interest in heritable property acquired by a third party in good faith and for value from a person authorised under an intervention

order or from a guardian having powers relating to the property or financial affairs of the adult shall be challengeable on the grounds only of the termination or coming to an end of the authority of the person or of the guardian.

(5) In this section any reference to a guardian shall include a reference to a guardian (however called) appointed under the law of any country to, or entitled under the law of any country to act for, an adult during his incapacity, if the guardianship is recognised by the law of Scotland.

DEFINITIONS
"adult" : s.1 (6)
"guardianship order" : s.58 (4)
"incapacity" : s.1 (6)
"intervention order" : s.53 (1)

GENERAL NOTE
The heading to this section is misleading, in that subss. (3) and (4) apply where the authority of the appointee "is terminated or otherwise comes to an end", for any reason.

Subsections (1) and (2) provide that the order terminates upon death of the adult, but that the appointee may continue to act (provided that he does so in good faith) until he becomes aware of the death. See also s.78 (1)(b) in relation to guardianship but not intervention orders.

Subsections (3) and (4) provide protection for third parties who rely in good faith upon the authority of the appointee. See also s.79.

Subsection (5) contains the usual application to equivalent appointees—see General Note to s.1 (7).

Amendment of registration under section 61 on events affecting guardianship or death of adult

78.—(1) The Public Guardian shall—

(a) where under section 71(3)(a), 73(2)(a), 74(5)(a) or 75(3)(a) he enters in the register maintained by him under section 6(2)(b)(iv) prescribed particulars relating to a guardianship order in respect of which the appointment of the guardian was recorded or registered under section 61; or

(b) where an adult in respect of whom there was such a guardianship order has died,

apply forthwith to the Keeper of the Registers of Scotland for the recording of the interlocutor or other document vouching the event giving rise to the entry or, as the case may be, the certificate of the death or, as the case may be, the registering of the event or the death in the Land Register of Scotland.

(2) On an application under subsection (1), the Keeper shall, as appropriate—

(a) record the interlocutor or other document or certificate in the Register of Sasines and endorse it that it has been so recorded;
(b) update the title sheet of the heritable property accordingly.

DEFINITIONS
"adult" : s.1 (6)
"guardianship order" : s.58 (4)
"prescribed" : s.87 (1) (and see s.86)
"Public Guardian" : s.6 (1)

GENERAL NOTE
See General Note to s.61.

It is not clear why the provisions referred to in subs. (1)(a) do not include s.75A. There seems to be no reason why s.78 should apply to removal or resignation, but not the death, of a guardian.

Protection of third parties: guardianship

79. Where a third party has acquired, in good faith and for value, title to any interest in heritable property from a guardian that title shall not be challengeable on the ground only—

(a) of any irregularity of procedure in making the guardianship order; or

(b) that the guardian has acted outwith the scope of his authority.

DEFINITIONS
"guardianship order" : s.58 (4)

GENERAL NOTE
See also s.77 (4), and General Note to s.61.

[Guardianship orders: children

Guardianship orders: children

79A. Sections 57 to 79 apply in relation to a child who will become an adult within 3 months as they apply in relation to an adult; but no guardianship order made in relation to a child shall have effect until the child becomes an adult.][153]

DEFINITIONS
"adult" : s.1 (6)
"guardianship order" : s.58 (4)

GENERAL NOTE
This section is designed to permit continuity from child to adult guardianship for young people whose incapacities necessitate such continuity.

PART 7

MISCELLANEOUS

GENERAL NOTE
The content of Pt. 7 is summarised in the Introduction and General Note.

Future appointment of curator bonis etc. incompetent

80. In any proceedings begun after the commencement of this Act it shall not be competent to appoint a curator bonis, tutor-dative or tutor-at-law to a person who has attained the age of 16 years.

GENERAL NOTE
It remains competent to appoint a curator bonis to a person under 16, though it is curious that this should be so, and there is no self-evident advantage in not having replaced all forms of curatory with the new form of guardianship, though provisions such as the general principles in s.1 would have required modification (see, for example, comments on "best interests" in

---

[153] Inserted by Adult Support and Protection (Scotland) Act 2007 (asp 10), s.60(16).

General Note to subs. (4)(a) of s.1. While the long title and scope of this Act restrict its provisions to those aged 16 and over (subject to s.79A), the effect of the repeals in Sched. 6 of parts of the Judicial Factors Act 1849 (12 & 13 Vict. c.51) appears to be to remove curators to both adults and children from relevant provisions, including the definition of judicial factors.

Where curators are appointed to persons under 16, now or in the future, the appointee will become a guardian under this Act on the ward's 16th birthday (Sched. 4, para. 1(2)). Wilkinson and Norrie (*Parent and Child*, 2nd Ed. para. 15.64) recommend such curatory where financial guardianship is likely to continue to be required into adulthood. They also point out (ibid) that curatory, unlike appointment of a legal representative under The Children (Scotland) Act 1995 (c.36) s.11 (2)(b), is subject to the responsibilities of accounting and supervision contained in The Judicial Factors Act 1849 (12 & 13 Vict. c.51)—an advantage apparently removed by the repeals in Sched. 6.

Apart from the above curiosity, it has not been possible to appoint new curators or tutors since April 1, 2002. For transitional provisions see Sched. 4.

Many of the amendments in Sched. 5 and the repeals in Sched. 6 were consequential upon this section. Note in particular para. 1 of Sched. 5, which provides that, both in enactments and in documents, references to curators and tutors to adults are now to be construed as references to guardians with similar powers appointed under this Act.

Repayment of funds

81.—(1) Where—

(a) a continuing attorney;
(b) a welfare attorney;
(c) a withdrawer;
(d) a guardian;
(e) a person authorised under an intervention order; or
(f) the managers of an authorised establishment within the meaning of Part 4,

uses or use any funds of an adult in breach of their fiduciary duty or outwith their authority or power to intervene in the affairs of the adult or after having received intimation of the termination or suspension of their authority or power to intervene, they shall be liable to repay the funds so used, with interest thereon at the rate fixed by Act of Sederunt as applicable to a decree of the sheriff, to the account of the adult.

(2) Subsection (1) shall be without prejudice to sections 69 and 82.

DEFINITIONS
"adult" : s.1 (6)
"authorised establishments" : s.35 (2)
"continuing attorney" : s.15 (2)
"intervention order" : s.53 (1)
"managers" : s.35 (5) and Sched. 1, para. 1
"welfare attorney" : s.16 (2)
"withdrawer" : s.25 (6)

GENERAL NOTE
Common law fiduciary duties and duties of care apply to appointees under this Act, subject to specific provisions of this Act. Their obligation to repay in the various situations specified under subs. (1) is, in terms of subs. (2), without prejudice to the provisions of s.69 regarding forfeiture of a guardian's remuneration and those of s.82 regarding limitation of liability.

In relation to guardians, see also Sched. 2, para. 8 (6) and (7).

Public Guardian's power to obtain records

81A.—(1) The Public Guardian may, when carrying out an investigation under section 6(2)(c) or (d) or inquiries under section 30B(2)—

(a) require any person falling within subsection (2) to provide the Public Guardian with—

  (i) the person's records of the exercise of the person's powers in relation to the adult to whom the investigation relates; and
  (ii) such other information relating to the exercise of those powers as the Public Guardian may reasonably require,

(b) require any person who holds (or who has held) funds on behalf of the adult to whom the investigation relates to provide the Public Guardian with—

  (i) its records of the account; and
  (ii) such other information relating to those accounts as the Public Guardian may reasonably require.

(2) A person falls within this subsection if the person is or has been—

  (a) a continuing attorney appointed by the adult to whom the investigation relates;
  (b) a withdrawer with authority to intromit with that adult's funds;
  (c) a person authorised under an intervention order to act in relation to that adult; or
  (d) that adult's guardian.

(3) A fundholder may charge a reasonable fee for complying with a requirement under subsection (1)(b) and may recover that fee from the account concerned.][154]

DEFINITIONS
"adult" : s.1 (6)
"continuing attorney" : s.15 (2)
"fundholder" : s.33 (2)
"guardian" : s.33 (1)(a)
"Public Guardian" : s.6 (1)
"withdrawer" : s.25 (6)

GENERAL NOTE
This section ensures that the Public Guardian can obtain relevant records and information for the purpose of investigations under s.6 (2)(c) of complaints, under s.6 (2)(d) of circumstances where an adult's property or financial affairs appear to her to be at risk, and under s.30B (2) into the exercise of a withdrawer's functions under Pt. 3.

Limitation of liability
82.—(1) No liability shall be incurred by a guardian, a continuing attorney, a welfare attorney, a person authorised under an intervention order, a withdrawer or the managers of an establishment for any breach of any duty of care or fiduciary duty owed to the adult if he has or they have—

  (a) acted reasonably and in good faith and in accordance with the general principles set out in section 1; or
  (b) failed to act and the failure was reasonable and in good faith and in accordance with the said general principles.

---

[154] Inserted by Adult Support and Protection (Scotland) Act 2007 (asp 10), s.61, subject to transitional provisions specified in SSI 2007/334, art.3.

(2) In this section any reference to—

(a) a guardian shall include a reference to a guardian (however called) appointed under the law of any country to, or entitled under the law of any country to act for, an adult during his incapacity, if the guardianship is recognised by the law of Scotland;
(b) a continuing attorney shall include a reference to a person granted, under a contract, grant or appointment governed by the law of any country, powers (however expressed), relating to the granter's property or financial affairs and having continuing effect notwithstanding the granter's incapacity; and
(c) a welfare attorney shall include a reference to a person granted, under a contract, grant or appointment governed by the law of any country, powers (however expressed) relating to the granter's personal welfare and having effect during the granter's incapacity.

DEFINITIONS
"adult" : s.1 (6)
"continuing attorney" : s.15 (2)
"incapacity" : s.1 (6)
"intervention order" : s.53 (1)
"managers of an establishment" : s.35 (5) and Sched. 1
"welfare attorney" : s.16 (2)
"withdrawer" : s.25 (6)

GENERAL NOTE
As noted in relation to s.81, common law fiduciary duties and duties of care apply to appointees under this Act, subject to specific provisions of this Act. At common law, breach of such duties normally gives rise to personal liability. Subsection (1) exempts appointees from such liability for acts or omissions which are reasonable, in good faith and in accordance with the general principles in s.1. Subsection (2) contains the usual extension to equivalent appointees—see General Note to s.1 (7).

Offence of ill-treatment and wilful neglect
83.—(1) It shall be an offence for any person exercising powers under this Act relating to the personal welfare of an adult to ill-treat or wilfully neglect that adult.
(2) A person guilty of an offence under subsection (1) shall be liable—

(a) on summary conviction, to imprisonment for a term not exceeding 6 months or to a fine not exceeding the statutory maximum or both;
(b) on conviction on indictment, to imprisonment for a term not exceeding 2 years or to a fine, or both.

DEFINITIONS
"adult" : s.1 (6)

GENERAL NOTE
This is the only provision of this Act which created a new offence.

Application to guardians appointed under Criminal Procedure (Scotland) Act 1995
84.—(1) Parts 1, 5, 6 and 7 shall apply to a guardian appointed under section 57(2)(c) or section 58(1) of the Criminal Procedure (Scotland) Act

1995 (c.46) ("the 1995 Act") as they apply to a guardian with powers relating to the personal welfare of an adult appointed under Part 6; and accordingly the 1995 Act shall be amended as follows.

(2) After section 58 there shall be inserted—

Application of Adults with Incapacity (Scotland) Act 2000
58A. (1) Subject to the provisions of this section, the provisions of Parts 1, 5, 6 and 7 of the Adults with Incapacity (Scotland) Act 2000 (asp 4) ("the 2000 Act") apply—

  (a) to a guardian appointed by an order of the court under section 57(2)(c), 58(1) or 58(1A) of this Act (in this section referred to as a "guardianship order") whether appointed before or after the coming into force of these provisions, as they apply to a guardian with powers relating to the personal welfare of an adult appointed under section 58 of that Act;
  (b) to a person authorised under an intervention order under section [60B][155] of this Act as they apply to a person so authorised under section 53 of that Act.

(2) In making a guardianship order the court shall have regard to any regulations made by the Scottish Ministers under section 64(11) of the 2000 Act and—

  (a) shall confer powers, which it shall specify in the order, relating only to the personal welfare of the person;
  (b) may appoint a joint guardian;
  (c) may appoint a substitute guardian;
  (d) may make such consequential or ancillary order, provision or direction as it considers appropriate.

(3) Without prejudice to the generality of subsection (2), or to any other powers conferred by this Act, the court may—

  (a) make any order granted by it subject to such conditions and restrictions as appear to it to be appropriate;
  (b) order that any reports relating to the person who will be the subject of the order be lodged with the court or that the person be assessed or interviewed and that a report of such assessment or interview be lodged;
  (c) make such further inquiry or call for such further information as appears to it to be appropriate;
  (d) make such interim order as appears to it to be appropriate pending the disposal of the proceedings.

(4) Where the court makes a guardianship order it shall forthwith send a copy of the interlocutor containing the order to the Public Guardian who shall—

  (a) enter prescribed particulars of the appointment in the register maintained by him under section 6(2)(b)(iv) of the 2000 Act;

---

[155] Words substituted by Regulation of Care (Scotland) Act 2001 (asp 8), Sch.3, para.23(5).

(b) unless he considers that the notification would be likely to pose a serious risk to the person's health notify the person of the appointment of the guardian; and
(c) notify the local authority and the Mental Welfare Commission of the terms of the interlocutor.

(5) A guardianship order shall continue in force for a period of 3 years or such other period (including an indefinite period) as, on cause shown, the court may determine.

(6) Where any proceedings for the appointment of a guardian under section 57(2)(c) or 58(1) of this Act have been commenced and not determined before the date of coming into force of section 84 of, and paragraph 26 of schedule 5 to, the Adults with Incapacity (Scotland) Act 2000 (asp 4) they shall be determined in accordance with this Act as it was immediately in force before that date.".

DEFINITIONS
"adult" : s.1 (6)
"guardianship order" : s.58 (4)
"intervention order" : s.53 (1)
"local authority" : s.87 (1) (referring to the Local Government etc. (Scotland) Act 1994 (c.39) s.2)
"Mental Welfare Commission" : s.87 (1) (referring to s.4 of the 2003 Act)
"prescribed" : s.87 (1) (and see s.86)
"Public Guardian" : s.6 (1)
"substitute guardian" : s.63 (2)

GENERAL NOTE
The amendments to the Criminal Procedure (Scotland) Act 1995 (c46) in terms of this section should be read in conjunction with the further amendments to that Act in terms of para. 26 of Sched. 5.

Under that Act, the High Court and the sheriff court had powers to place under 1984 Act guardianship a person suffering from mental disorder convicted of offences punishable by imprisonment. 1984 Act guardianship was abolished by this Act (by the repeal of ss.36—52 of the 1984 Act in terms of Sched. 6). This section and para. 26 of Sched. 5 confer on the criminal courts a similar power to make intervention or welfare guardianship orders, and integrate such intervention and guardianship orders into the regime under this Act. It is accordingly necessary for the court to specify the powers conferred by such guardianship orders, and the court may on cause shown vary the normal duration, which is three years. Powers and duration were fixed under 1984 Act guardianship. The guardian is the local authority or someone approved by the local authority, rather than an appointee in terms of s.59 (see comments in General Note to s.64 (9)), but joint and substitute appointments are competent. Other provisions include requirements for registration with the Public Guardian.

Jurisdiction and private international law
85. Schedule 3 shall have effect for the purposes of defining the jurisdiction, in respect of adults who are incapable within the meaning of this Act, of the Scottish judicial and administrative authorities and for making provision as to the private international law of Scotland in that respect.

DEFINITIONS
"adult" : s.1 (6)
"incapable" : s.1 (6)

GENERAL NOTE
See Sched. 3 and General Note thereto.

Regulations
86.—(1) Any power of the Scottish Ministers to make regulations under this Act shall be exercisable by statutory instrument subject to annulment in pursuance of a resolution of the Scottish Parliament.

(2) Any such power may be exercised to make different provision for different cases or classes of case and includes power to make such incidental, supplemental, consequential or transitional provision or savings as appear to the Scottish Ministers to be appropriate.

GENERAL NOTE
Relevant regulations (or the most important parts thereof) are reproduced in *Adult Incapacity* and in Appendix 2 of this book.

Interpretation
87.—(1) In this Act, unless the context otherwise requires—
 "adult" shall be construed in accordance with section 1;
 "continuing attorney" shall be construed in accordance with section 15;
 "guardianship order" shall be construed in accordance with section 58;
 "incapable" and "incapacity" shall be construed in accordance with section 1;
 "intervention order" shall be construed in accordance with section 53;
 "local authority" means a council constituted under section 2 of the Local Government etc. (Scotland) Act 1994 (c.39), and references to a local authority shall be construed as references to the local authority for the area in which the adult resides;
 "managers of an establishment" shall be construed in accordance with schedule 1;
 "mental disorder" [has the meaning given by section 328 of the 2003 Act][156];
 ["mental health officer" has the meaning given by section 329 of the 2003 Act;][157]
 "Mental Welfare Commission" means the Mental Welfare Commission for Scotland continued in being by [section 4 of the 2003 Act][158];
 ["named person" has the meaning given by section 329 of the 2003 Act;][159]
 "nearest relative" [has the meaning given by section 254 of the 2003 Act][160];
 "office holder", in relation to a guardian, means the chief social work officer of the local authority;
 "person claiming an interest" includes the local authority, the Mental Welfare Commission and the Public Guardian;
 "power of attorney" includes a factory and commission;
 ["practising solicitor" means a solicitor holding a practising certificate issued in accordance with Part 2 of the Solicitors (Scotland) Act 1980 (c.46);][161]

---

[156] Words substituted by Mental Health (Care and Treatment) (Scotland) Act 2003 (asp 13), Sch.4, para.9(5)(a).
[157] Inserted by Mental Health (Care and Treatment) (Scotland) Act 2003 (asp 13), Sch.4, para.9(5)(b).
[158] Words substituted by Mental Health (Care and Treatment) (Scotland) Act 2003 (asp 13), Sch.4, para.9(5)(c).
[159] Inserted by Mental Health (Care and Treatment) (Scotland) Act 2003 (Modification of Enactments) Order 2005 (SSI 2005/465), Sch.1, para.28(9).
[160] Words substituted by Mental Health (Care and Treatment) (Scotland) Act 2003 (asp 13), Sch.4, para.9(5)(d).
[161] Inserted by Adult Support and Protection (Scotland) Act 2007 (asp 10), s.57(9)

"prescribe", except for the purposes of anything which may be or is to be prescribed by the Public Guardian, means prescribe by regulations; and "prescribed" shall be construed accordingly;
"primary carer" in relation to an adult, means the person or organisation primarily engaged in caring for him;
"Public Guardian" shall be construed in accordance with section 6;
"State hospital" shall be construed in accordance with section 102 of the National Health Service (Scotland) Act 1978 (c.29);
"substitute guardian" shall be construed in accordance with section 63;
"welfare attorney" shall be construed in accordance with section 16;
"withdrawer" shall be construed in accordance with section 26;
"the 1984 Act" means the Mental Health (Scotland) Act 1984 (c.36);
["the 2003 Act" means the Mental Health (Care and Treatment) (Scotland) Act 2003 (asp 13).][162]

[(1A) Any power under this Act to prescribe anything by regulations is exercisable by the Scottish Ministers.][163]
(2)–(3) [. . .][164]
(4) For the purposes of this Act, a person is bankrupt if his estate has been sequestrated for insolvency or he has granted a trust deed which has become a protected trust deed under Schedule 5 to the Bankruptcy (Scotland) Act 1985 (c.66), or he has been adjudged bankrupt in England and Wales, or he has become bankrupt (however expressed) under the law of any other country.

DEFINITIONS
"adult" : s.1 (6)
"nearest relative" : s.87 (1), subject to s.87 (2) and (3) (but see s.4)

GENERAL NOTE
Further definitions are limited to Parts and sections of this Act, and are given where appropriate in the General Notes to individual sections. This Act appears to apply some definitions from other legislation without specifically incorporating them, including the following:-
"chief social work officer"—see Social Work (Scotland) Act 1968 (c.49) ("the 1968 Act") s.3
"constable"—see the 1968 Act s.94 (1)

Subs. (1)
"mental disorder"—see General Note to s.1 (6)
"nearest relative"—see s.4. As early as an informal preliminary hearing prior to introduction of the Bill, the Justice and Home Affairs Committee was concerned about aspects of the 1984 Act "nearest relative" provisions. Section 4 was added by amendment at stage 2, and the former subss. (2) and (3) of this section at stage 3. Those subsections allowed a same-sex partner, in the circumstances defined, to be "nearest relative" for the purposes of this Act. Those improvements related to this Act only, and not to the 1984 Act "nearest relative" provisions. Mental health legislation "caught up" and was further improved by the 2003 Act, the definition in which is now incorporated in this Act without amendment.
"withdrawer"—the definition is now in s.25 (6)

Subs. (4)
See s.15 (5), and also s.16 (7).

---
[162] Inserted by Mental Health (Care and Treatment) (Scotland) Act 2003 (asp 13), Sch.4, para.9(5)(e).
[163] Inserted by Adult Support and Protection (Scotland) Act 2007 (asp 10), Sch.1, para.5(e).
[164] Repealed by Mental Health (Care and Treatment) (Scotland) Act 2003 (asp 13), Sch.5.

Continuation of existing powers, minor and consequential amendments and repeals
88.—(1) Schedule 4, which contains provisions relating to the continuation of existing powers, shall have effect.

(2) Schedule 5, which contains minor amendments and amendments consequential on the provisions of this Act, shall have effect.

(3) The enactments mentioned in schedule 6 are hereby repealed to the extent specified in the second column of that schedule.

NOTE
Section 88(3) as amended by correction slip

GENERAL NOTE
Note that para. 1 of Sched. 5 applies generally to documents as well as to enactments.

Citation and commencement
89.—(1) This Act may be cited as the Adults with Incapacity (Scotland) Act 2000.

(2) This Act shall come into force on such day as the Scottish Ministers may by order made by statutory instrument appoint and different days may be appointed for different purposes.

(3) Without prejudice to the provisions of schedule 4, an order under subsection (2) may make such transitional provisions and savings as appear to the Scottish Ministers necessary or expedient in connection with any provision brought into force by the order; and where it does so, the statutory instrument under which it is made shall be subject to annulment in pursuance of a resolution of the Scottish Parliament.

GENERAL NOTE

Subs. (1)
The Scottish Law Commission Discussion Paper No. 94, published September, 1991, referred to "mentally disabled adults", and the Commission's draft Bill, published with the SLC Report, to "incapable adults". The title adopted for this Act seems to have been accepted without adverse comment, and sits appropriately beside that of the Age of Legal Capacity (Scotland) Act 1991 (c.50).

Subss. (2) and (3)
See section on *Implementation, Review and Amendment* in the Introduction and General Note.

SCHEDULE 1

MANAGERS OF AN ESTABLISHMENT

1. For the purposes of Part 4"the managers" of an establishment means—

    (a) in relation to a hospital vested in the Scottish Ministers under the National Health Service (Scotland) Act 1978 (c.29), the Health Board responsible for the administration of that hospital;
    (b) in relation to a hospital managed by a National Health Service trust established under section 12A of the said Act of 1978, the directors of the trust;
    (c) in relation to a State hospital—
        (i) the Scottish Ministers;
        (ii) [. . .][165]; or

---

[165] Repealed by Mental Health (Care and Treatment) (Scotland) Act 2003 (asp 13), Sch.5.

Adults with Incapacity (Scotland) Act 2000 (Sched. 1)

      (iii) if the management of that hospital has been delegated to a Health Board, to a Special Health Board, to a National Health Service trust or to the Common Services Agency for the Scottish Health Service, that Board, trust or Agency, as the case may be, or any person appointed by the Board, trust or agency, as the case may be, to manage the hospital;

  [(d) in relation to a care service or limited registration service—

      (i) the person identified under section 7(2)(b) of the Regulation of Care (Scotland) Act 2001 (asp 8) in the application for registration of the service;
     (ii) if the application is made under section 33(1) of that Act, the local authority or any person appointed by the local authority to manage the service; or
    (iii) if another person has been identified in pursuance of regulations under section 29(7)(j) of that Act, the other person so identified,

and in paragraph (d) above "care service" and "limited registration service" have the same meanings as in the Regulation of Care (Scotland) Act 2001.][166]

2. The Scottish Ministers may by regulations amend the list of managers in paragraph 1.

DEFINITIONS
"establishments" : s.35 (1)
"local authority" : s.87 (1) (referring to the Local Government etc. (Scotland) Act 1994 (c.39) s.2)
"managers" : s.35 (5) and Sched. 1, para. 1
"nursing home" : The Nursing Homes Registration (Scotland) Act 1938 (c.73) s.10 (2) and (3)
"State hospital" : s.87 (1) (referring to the National Health Service (Scotland) Act 1978 (c.29) s.102)

GENERAL NOTE
This Schedule sets out in para. 1 who are "the managers", for the purposes of management by "authorised establishments" under Pt. 4, of the various categories of establishments which, in terms of s.35 (1), are included within the definition of "authorised establishments". Paragraph 2 provides for amendment by regulations—see s.86. With reference to para. 1(c), at time of passing of this Act the only state hospital was, and at time of preparation of these updated annotations still is, the State Hospital at Carstairs Junction, Lanarkshire, managed by a Special Health Board (the State Hospitals Board for Scotland).

SCHEDULE 2

MANAGEMENT OF ESTATE OF ADULT

Management plan
1.—(1) A guardian with powers relating to the property and financial affairs of the adult shall, unless the sheriff otherwise directs, prepare a plan (a "management plan"), taking account of any directions given by the sheriff in the order appointing him, for the management, investment and realisation of the adult's estate and for the application of the estate to the adult's needs, so far as the estate falls within the guardian's authority.

---

[166] Words substituted by Regulation of Care (Scotland) Act 2001 (asp 8), Sch.3, para.23(6).

(2) The management plan shall be submitted in draft by the guardian to the Public Guardian for his approval, along with the inventory of the adult's estate prepared under paragraph 3, not more than one month, or such other period as the Public Guardian may allow, after the submission of the inventory.

(3) The Public Guardian may approve the management plan submitted to him under sub-paragraph (2) or he may approve it with amendments and the plan as so approved or as so amended shall be taken account of by the guardian in the exercise of his functions in relation to the adult.

(4) Before the management plan is approved, the guardian shall, unless the sheriff on appointing him has conferred wider powers, have power only to—

(a) ingather and take control of the assets of the adult's estate so as to enable him, when the management plan has been approved, to intromit with them;
(b) make such payments as are necessary to provide for the adult's day to day needs.

(5) The Public Guardian may authorise the guardian to exercise any function within the scope of his authority before the management plan is approved, if it would be unreasonable to delay him exercising that function until the plan had been approved.

(6) The guardian shall keep the management plan under review and shall put forward to the Public Guardian proposals for variation of it whenever it appears to him to be appropriate.

(7) The Public Guardian—

(a) may at any time propose any variation to the management plan; and
(b) shall review the plan whenever the guardian submits his accounts for audit.

(8) The Public Guardian shall notify the guardian of any variation which he proposes to make to the management plan and shall not make any such variation without affording the guardian an opportunity to object.

(9) Having heard any objections by the guardian as mentioned in sub-paragraph (8) the Public Guardian may make the variation with or without amendment.

Directions from sheriff
2. Where the guardian disagrees with any decision made by the Public Guardian in relation to a management plan prepared under paragraph 1, he may apply to the sheriff for a determination in relation to the matter and the sheriff's decision shall be final.

Inventory of estate
3.—(1) A guardian with powers relating to the property or financial affairs of the adult shall, as soon after his appointment as possible and in any event within 3 months of the date of registration of his appointment or such other period as the Public Guardian may allow, submit to the Public Guardian for examination and approval a full inventory of the adult's estate in so far as it falls within the scope of the guardian's authority, along with such supporting documents and additional information as the Public Guardian may require.

Adults with Incapacity (Scotland) Act 2000 (Sched. 2)

(2) The inventory shall be in a form, and contain information, prescribed by the Public Guardian.

(3) Errors in and omissions from the inventory which are discovered by the guardian after the inventory has been approved by the Public Guardian shall be notified by him to the Public Guardian within 6 months of the date of discovery or when submitting his next accounts to the Public Guardian, whichever occurs sooner.

(4) The Public Guardian may dispense with the need for the guardian to submit an inventory under sub-paragraph (1) or may require the guardian to take such other action as he thinks appropriate in lieu of submitting an inventory.

Money
4. The guardian shall deposit all money received by him as guardian in a bank or a building society in an account in the name of the adult and shall ensure that all sums in excess of £500 (or such other sum as may be prescribed) so deposited shall earn interest.

Powers relating to investment and carrying on of business by guardian
5.—(1) Subject to the following provisions of this paragraph, a guardian with powers relating to the property or financial affairs of the adult shall be entitled—

> after obtaining and considering proper advice, to retain any existing investment of the adult;
> to use the adult's estate to make new investments in accordance with the management plan prepared under paragraph 1 or with the consent of the Public Guardian.

(2) For the purpose of sub-paragraph (1)—

> (a) proper advice is the advice of a person [who has permission for the purposes of the Financial Services and Markets Act 2000 to advise on investments][167] who is not the guardian or any person who is an employer, employee or business partner of the guardian; and
> (b) the advice must be given or subsequently confirmed in writing.

[(2A) Sub-paragraph (2) must be read with—

> (a) section 22 of the Financial Services and Markets Act 2000;
> (b) any relevant order under that section; and
> (c) Schedule 2 to that Act.][168]

(3) The guardian shall keep every investment under review and in doing so shall have regard to the following principles—

> (a) that the investment must be prudent;
> (b) that there must be diversification of investments; and

---

[167] Words substituted by Financial Services and Markets Act 2000 (Consequential Amendments and Repeals) Order 2001 (SI 2001/3649), s.235(2).
[168] Inserted by Financial Services and Markets Act 2000 (Consequential Amendments and Repeals) Order 2001 (SI 2001/3649), s.235(3).

(c) that the investment must be suitable for the adult's estate.

(4) The Public Guardian may at any time direct the guardian to realise any investment.

(5) The guardian may, subject to any direction given by the Public Guardian, carry on any business of the adult.

(6) Any decision by the Public Guardian—

(a) under sub-paragraph (4) as to directing the guardian to realise investments;
(b) under sub-paragraph (5) as to giving directions to the guardian in carrying on the business of the adult,

may be appealed to the sheriff, whose decision shall be final.

Purchase or disposal of accommodation
6.—(1) The guardian shall not, without the consent of the Public Guardian—

(a) in principle; and
(b) to the purchase or selling price,

purchase accommodation for, or dispose of any accommodation used for the time being as a dwelling house by, the adult.

(2) On receipt of an application for consent in principle under sub-paragraph (1)(a) in the prescribed form, the Public Guardian shall intimate the application to the adult, his nearest relative, his primary carer[, his named person][169] and any person who the Public Guardian considers has an interest in the application and advise them of the prescribed period within which they may object to the granting of the application.

(3) The Public Guardian shall remit any objection under sub-paragraph (2) for determination by the sheriff (whose decision shall be final) and—

(a) if the sheriff upholds the objection, shall refuse the application;
(b) if the sheriff dismisses the objection, shall grant the application.

(4) Where the Public Guardian proposes to refuse the application other than under sub-paragraph (3)(a) he shall intimate his decision to the applicant and advise him of the prescribed period within which he may object to the refusal; and he shall not refuse the application without affording the applicant, if he objects, an opportunity of being heard.

(5) Having heard any objections as mentioned in sub-paragraph (4) or where there is no objection as mentioned in sub-paragraph (2), the Public Guardian may grant the application.

(6) The Public Guardian may at his own instance or at the instance of any person who objects to the granting or refusal (other than a refusal under sub-paragraph (3)(a)) of the application remit the application to the sheriff for determination by the sheriff, whose decision shall be final.

(7) If consent in principle to the purchase or disposal of the accommodation is given, the guardian shall apply to the Public Guardian for consent under sub-paragraph (1)(b) to the purchase or selling price.

(8) A decision of the Public Guardian—

---

[169] Inserted by Adult Support and Protection (Scotland) Act 2007 (asp 10), Sch.1, para.5(f).

Adults with Incapacity (Scotland) Act 2000 (Sched. 2)

    (a) to grant or to refuse (other than under sub-paragraph (3)(a)) an application; or
    (b) to refuse to remit an application to the sheriff under sub-paragraph (6),

may be appealed to the sheriff, whose decision shall be final.

  (9) A decision of the Public Guardian to give or to refuse consent under sub-paragraph (1)(b) shall be final.

Accounting and auditing
7.—(1) A guardian with powers relating to the property or financial affairs of the adult shall submit accounts in respect of each accounting period to the Public Guardian within one month from the end of the accounting period or such longer period as the Public Guardian may allow.

  (2) There shall be submitted with the accounts under sub-paragraph (1) such supporting documents as the Public Guardian may require, and the Public Guardian may require the guardian to furnish him with such information in connection with the accounts as the Public Guardian may determine.

  (3) For the purposes of this paragraph, the first accounting period shall commence with the date of appointment of the guardian and end at such date not later than 18 months after the date of registration of the guardian's appointment as the Public Guardian may determine; and thereafter each accounting period shall be a year commencing with the date on which the immediately previous accounting period ended.

  (4) Notwithstanding the foregoing provisions of this paragraph, the Public Guardian may at any time—

    (a) give directions as to the frequency of accounting periods;
    (b) dispense with the need for the submission of accounts by the guardian; or
    (c) require the guardian to do anything which the Public Guardian thinks appropriate in lieu of submitting accounts.

  (5) The accounts shall be in such form as is prescribed by the Public Guardian and different forms may be prescribed for different cases or descriptions of case.

  (6) Where the estate of the adult includes a business or an interest in a business that part of the accounts which relates to the business or to the interest in the business shall be accompanied by a certificate from such person and in such form as may be prescribed by the Public Guardian, certifying the accuracy of that part of the accounts.

  (7) The accounts submitted to the Public Guardian under sub-paragraph (1) (other than any part to which a certificate as mentioned in sub-paragraph (6) relates) shall be audited by the Public Guardian or by an accountant appointed by, and responsible to, the Public Guardian for that purpose.

Approval of accounts
8.—(1) After the accounts of the guardian have been audited, the Public Guardian shall, if the accounts appear to him—

    (a) to be a true and fair view of the guardian's management of the adult's estate, approve them and fix the remuneration (if any) due to the guardian;

(b) not to be a true and fair view of the guardian's management of the adult's estate, prepare a report as to the extent to which they do not represent such a true and fair view and adjusting the accounts accordingly.

(2) The Public Guardian may approve the accounts, notwithstanding any minor inconsistencies or absence of full documentation in the accounts, if he is satisfied that the guardian acted reasonably and in good faith.

(3) The Public Guardian shall send any report prepared by him under sub-paragraph (1)(b) to the guardian, who may object to anything contained in the report within 28 days of it being sent to him.

(4) If no objection is taken to the report, the accounts as adjusted by the Public Guardian shall be regarded as approved by him.

(5) Where any objection taken to the report cannot be resolved between the guardian and the Public Guardian, the matter may be determined by the sheriff on an application by the guardian, and the sheriff's decision shall be final.

(6) Without prejudice to sub-paragraph (7), the guardian shall be liable to make good any deficiency revealed by the accounts as approved by the Public Guardian under sub-paragraph (1)(a).

(7) Where a deficiency is revealed as mentioned in sub-paragraph (6), the Public Guardian may require the guardian to pay interest to the adult's estate on the amount of the deficiency at the rate fixed by Act of Sederunt as applicable to a decree of the sheriff in respect of the period for which it appears that the deficiency has existed.

DEFINITIONS
"adult" : s.1 (6)
"named person" : s.87 (1) (referring to the definition in s.329 of the 2003 Act)
"nearest relative" : s.87 (1), subject to s.87 (2) and (3) (but see s.4)
"prescribed" : s.87 (1) (and see s.86)
"primary carer": s.87 (1)
"Public Guardian" : s.6 (1)

GENERAL NOTE
This Schedule sets out provisions, in addition to those in Pt. 6 and elsewhere in this Act (including in particular the general principles in s.1), regarding management by guardians upon whom property and financial powers have been conferred.

The overall approach is to replace the fixed provision, applicable to all appointments, which characterised "old law" (see *"Old law" and "new law"* in the Introduction and General Note) with an individualised package of provision tailored to the needs and circumstances of each case. Thus where curators operated within a generalised regime of usual powers, powers obtainable from the Accountant of Court, and special powers obtainable from the court, under this Act the emphasis shifted to the individual management plan (para. 1). Investment provisions (para. 5) are less rigid than under curatory, and include a specific requirement that investments must be suitable for the adult's estate. There is flexibility to adapt accounting requirements to particular cases (paras. 7(4) and (5)). Likewise in accordance with the principles of "new law", there are requirements to keep the management plan (paras. 1(1), (6) and (7)) and investments (para. 5(3)) under review.

Under Sched. 4, para. 6(6), the Public Guardian was empowered to determine the extent (if any) to which the provisions of this Schedule apply to curators and tutors who became guardians by virtue of Sched. 4.

The specific provisions of this Schedule are generally clearly expressed and laid out, and require little further comment.

Paras. 1(1) and (4)
The exceptions to both of these paragraphs require consideration at time of application—see General Note to s.57.

Para. 1(5)
For this provision to have meaning, "the scope of his authority" means the powers granted to the guardian without reference to the limitation in terms of para. 1(4).

Para. 6
Only principle and price require the consent of the Public Guardian. It is good practice to deal with matters of principle in good time: the Office of the Public Guardian usually responds swiftly when thereafter an offer is drafted or received. Where proposed terms (other than price) are unusual or cause difficulty, advice is available from the Public Guardian in terms of s.6 (2)(e).

Paras. 8(6) and (7)
It would appear that the guardian would be excused liability under this provision if s.82 were to apply.
See also the general liability to repay in terms of s.81.

SCHEDULE 3
JURISDICTION AND PRIVATE INTERNATIONAL LAW

General
1.—(1) The Scottish judicial and administrative authorities shall have jurisdiction to dispose of an application or other proceedings and otherwise carry out functions under this Act in relation to an adult if—

  (a) the adult is habitually resident in Scotland; or
  (b) property which is the subject of the application or proceedings or in respect of which functions are carried out under this Act is in Scotland; or
  (c) the adult, although not habitually resident in Scotland is there or property belonging to the adult is there and, in either case, it is a matter of urgency that the application is or the proceedings are dealt with; or
  (d) the adult is present in Scotland and the intervention sought in the application or proceedings is of a temporary nature and its effect limited to Scotland.

(2) As from the ratification date, the Scottish judicial and administrative authorities shall, in addition to the jurisdiction mentioned in sub-paragraph (1) in the circumstances set out therein, have the jurisdiction mentioned in that sub-paragraph in the following circumstances—

  (a) the adult—
    (i) is a British citizen; and
    (ii) has a closer connection with Scotland than with any other part of the United Kingdom; and
  (b) Article 7 of the Convention has been complied with,

or if the Scottish Central Authority, having received a request under Article 8 of the Convention from an authority of the State in which the adult is habitually resident and consulted such authorities in Scotland as would, under this Act, have functions in relation to the adult, have agreed to the request.

(3) As from the ratification date, the provisions of the Convention shall apply to the exercise of jurisdiction under this schedule where the adult—

  (a) is habitually resident in a Contracting State other than the United Kingdom; or

(b) not being habitually resident in Scotland, is or has been the subject of protective proceedings in such a Contracting State.

(4) As from the ratification date, any application made to a Scottish judicial or administrative authority under this Act which—

(a) relates to an adult who is not habitually resident in Scotland; and
(b) does not require to be determined as a matter of urgency,

shall be accompanied by information as to which State the adult habitually resides in and as to any other application relating to the adult which has been dealt with or is being made, or proceedings so relating which have been or are being brought, in any Contracting State other than the United Kingdom.

(5) For the purposes of this paragraph, an adult—

(a) whose habitual residence cannot be ascertained; or
(b) who is a refugee or has been internationally displaced by disturbance in the country of his habitual residence,

shall be taken to be habitually resident in the State which he is in.

Appropriate sheriff
2.—(1) The sheriff having jurisdiction under this schedule to take measures is the sheriff in whose sheriffdom—

(a) in relation to a case falling within paragraph 1(1)(a), the adult is habitually resident;
(b) in relation to a case falling within paragraph 1(1)(b), the property is located;
(c) in relation to a case falling within paragraph 1(1)(c), the adult or property belonging to the adult is present;
(d) in relation to a case falling within paragraph 1(1)(d), the adult is present.

(2) The sheriff shall also have jurisdiction to vary or recall any intervention order or guardianship order made by him under this Act if no Contracting State other than the United Kingdom has, by way of its judicial or administrative authorities, jurisdiction; and—

(a) no other court or authority has jurisdiction; or
(b) another court or authority has jurisdiction but—
   (i) it would be unreasonable to expect an applicant to invoke it; or
   (ii) that court or authority has declined to exercise it.

(3) Notwithstanding that any other judicial or administrative authority has jurisdiction under sub-paragraph (1)(a) to take measures, a sheriff shall have jurisdiction to take measures if—

(a) the adult is present in the sheriffdom; and
(b) the sheriff considers that it is necessary, in the interests of the adult, to take the measures immediately.

(4) Where, by operation of paragraph 1, jurisdiction falls to be exercised by a sheriff but the case is one appearing to fall outside sub-paragraphs (1)

and (2), the sheriff having jurisdiction is the Sheriff of the Lothians and Borders at Edinburgh.

Applicable law
3.—(1) The law applicable to anything done under this Act by a Scottish judicial or administrative authority in relation to an adult is the law of Scotland.

(2) Sub-paragraph (1) does not prevent a Scottish judicial or administrative authority from applying the law of a country other than Scotland if, in circumstances which demonstrate a substantial connection with that other country and having regard to the interests of the adult, it appears appropriate to do so.

(3) Such an authority shall, however, in the exercise of the powers conferred by section [20][170] of this Act, take into consideration to the extent possible the law which, as provided in paragraph 4, governs the power of attorney.

(4) Where a measure for the protection of an adult has been taken in one State and is implemented in another, the conditions of its implementation are governed by the law of that other State.

(5) Any question whether a person has authority by virtue of any enactment or rule of law to represent an adult shall be governed—

(a) where such representation is for the purposes of the immediate personal welfare of the adult and the adult is in Scotland, by the law of Scotland; and
(b) in any other case, by the law of the country in which the adult is habitually resident.

4.—(1) The law governing the existence, extent, modification and extinction of continuing or welfare powers of attorney (including like powers, however described) shall be that of the State in which the granter habitually resided at the time of the grant of these powers.

(2) Where, however, the granter of such a power of attorney so provides in writing, the law so applicable shall instead be the law of a State—

(a) of which the granter is a national;
(b) in which the granter was habitually resident before the grant; or
(c) in which the property of the granter is located.

(3) The manner of exercise of such a power shall be governed by the law of the State in which its exercise takes place.

(4) The law of a State may be applied under sub-paragraph (2)(c) above only in respect of the property referred to in that provision.

(5) Nothing in sub-paragraphs (1) and (2) prevents the sheriff from exercising powers under section 20 of this Act if a power of attorney is not being exercised so as to safeguard the welfare or property of the granter.

(6) It is not an objection to the validity of any contract or other transaction between a person acting or purporting to act as the representative of an adult and any other person that the person so acting or purporting to act was not entitled so to act under the law of a country other than the country where the contract or other transaction was concluded.

(7) Sub-paragraph (6) does not, however, apply where the other person knew or ought to have known that the entitlement so to act of the person

---

[170] Substituted by Adult Support and Protection (Scotland) Act 2007 (asp 10), Sch.1, para.5(g).

acting or purporting to act as representative was governed by the law of that other country.

(8) Sub-paragraph (6) applies only if the persons entering into the contract or other transaction were, when they did so, both (or all) in the same country.

5. Nothing in this schedule displaces any enactment or rule of law which has mandatory effect for the protection of an adult with incapacity in Scotland whatever law would otherwise be applicable.

6. Nothing in this schedule requires or enables the application in Scotland of any provision of the law of a country other than Scotland so as to produce a result which would be manifestly contrary to public policy.

Recognition and enforcement
7.—(1) Any measure taken under the law of a country other than Scotland for the personal welfare or the protection of property of an adult with incapacity shall, if one of the conditions specified in sub-paragraph (2) is met, be recognised by the law of Scotland.

(2) These conditions are—

- (a) that the jurisdiction of the authority of the other country was based on the adult's habitual residence there;
- (b) that the United Kingdom and the other country were, when the measure was taken, parties to the Convention and the jurisdiction of the authority of the other country was based on a ground of jurisdiction provided for in the Convention.

(3) Recognition of a measure may, however, be refused—

- (a) if, except in a case of urgency—
  - (i) the authority which took it did so without the adult to whom it related being given an opportunity to be heard; and
  - (ii) these circumstances constituted a breach of natural justice;
- (b) if it would be manifestly contrary to public policy to recognise the measure;
- (c) if the measure conflicts with any enactment or rule of law of Scotland which is mandatory whatever law would otherwise be applicable;
- (d) if the measure is incompatible with a later measure taken in Scotland or recognised by the law of Scotland;
- (e) if the measure would have the effect of placing the adult in an establishment in Scotland and—
  - (i) the Scottish Central Authority has not previously been provided with a report on the adult and a statement of the reasons for the proposed placement and has not been consulted on the proposed placement; or
  - (ii) where the Authority has been provided with such a report and statement and so consulted, it has, within a reasonable time thereafter, declared that it disapproves of the proposed placement.

8.—(1) A measure which is enforceable in the country of origin and which is recognised under paragraph 7 by the law of Scotland may, in accordance with rules of court, be registered.

(2) A measure so registered shall be as enforceable as a measure having the like effect granted by a court in Scotland.

9.—(1) For the purposes of recognition or enforcement of a measure taken outside Scotland in relation to an adult, findings of fact going to jurisdiction made by the authority taking the measure are conclusive of the facts found.

(2) The validity or merits of a measure falling to be recognised by the law of Scotland by virtue of this schedule shall not be questioned in any proceedings except for the purposes of ascertaining its compliance with any provision of this schedule.

10.—(1) The Scottish Ministers may, by order, provide for the recognition and enforcement of orders made and other measures taken by authorities in any part of the United Kingdom other than Scotland.

(2) The provision so made shall accord no less recognition and secure that these orders and measures are no less enforceable than if they were measures which are recognised by the law of Scotland under paragraph 7.

Co-operation, avoidance of conflict of jurisdiction and compliance with the Convention

11.—(1) Her Majesty may by Order in Council confer on the Scottish Central Authority, and the Scottish judicial and administrative authorities such powers, and impose on them such duties additional, in each case, to those which they have under this Act, as are necessary or expedient to enable them to give effect in Scotland to the Convention on and after the ratification date.

(2) An Order in Council under sub-paragraph (1) shall be subject to annulment in pursuance of a resolution of the Scottish Parliament.

(3) A certificate delivered in pursuance of Article 38 of the Convention by a designated authority of a Contracting State other than Scotland shall be proof of the matters stated in it unless the contrary is proved.

General

12. No provision of this schedule deriving from or giving effect to the Convention extends to any matter to which the Convention, by Article 4 thereof, does not apply.

13. Orders or regulations under this schedule shall be made by statutory instrument subject to annulment in pursuance of a resolution of the Scottish Parliament.

14. In this schedule—

> "the Convention" means the Hague Convention of 13 January 2000 on the International Protection of Adults;
> a "measure for the personal welfare or protection of the property" of an adult with incapacity includes any order, direction or decision effecting or relating to—
>> (a) the determination of the incapacity and the institution of appropriate measures of protection;
>> (b) the placing of the adult under the protection of a judicial or administrative authority;
>> (c) guardianship, curatorship or analogous institutions;
>> (d) the appointment and functions of any person or body having charge of the adult's person or property or otherwise representing the adult;
>> (e) the placement of the adult in an establishment or other place where the personal welfare of the adult is safeguarded;

(f) the administration, conservation or disposal of the adult's property; or
(g) the authorisation of a specific intervention for the personal welfare or protection of the property of the adult;

the "ratification date" means the date when the Convention is ratified as respects Scotland;
the "Scottish Central Authority" means—

(a) an authority designated under Article 28 of the Convention for the purposes of acting as such; or
(b) if no authority has been so designated any authority appointed by the Scottish Ministers for the purposes of carrying out the functions to be carried out under this schedule by the Scottish Central Authority;

the "Scottish judicial and administrative authorities" means the courts having functions under this Act and the Public Guardian, the Mental Welfare Commission, local authorities and supervisory bodies.

DEFINITIONS
"adult" : s.1 (6)
"continuing power of attorney" : s.15 (2)
"Convention, the" : Sched. 3, para. 14
"establishments" : s.35 (1)
"guardianship order" : s.58 (4)
"incapacity" : s.1 (6)
"intervention order" : s.53 (1)
"local authority" : s.87 (1) (referring to the Local Government etc. (Scotland) Act 1994 (c.39) s.2)
"measure for the personal welfare or protection of the property" : Sched. 3, para. 14
"Mental Welfare Commission" : s.87 (1) (referring to s.4 of the 2003 Act)
"power of attorney" : s.87 (1)
"Public Guardian" : s.6 (1)
"ratification date" : Sched. 3, para. 14
"Scottish Central Authority" : Sched. 3, para. 14
"Scottish judicial and administrative authorities" : Sched. 3, para. 14
"supervisory body" : s.40 (1)
"welfare power of attorney" : s.16 (2)

GENERAL NOTE
Paragraph 2 defines which sheriffdom has jurisdiction under this Act. The remainder of this Schedule contains private international law provisions in accordance with the Convention, dealing with jurisdiction, applicable law, recognition and related matters.

SCHEDULE 4

CONTINUATION OF EXISTING CURATORS, TUTORS, GUARDIANS AND ATTORNEYS UNDER THIS ACT

Curators and tutors
1.—(1) On the relevant date, any person holding office as curator bonis to an adult shall become guardian of that adult with power to manage the property or financial affairs of the adult.
(2) Where a person—

(a) before the relevant date, holds office as curator bonis to a person who has not attained the age of 16 years and does not hold such

office for the sole reason that the person has not attained the age of 16 years; or
  (b) after the relevant date, is appointed as curator bonis to such a person,

he shall become guardian of that person when that person attains the age of 16 years, with power to manage his property or financial affairs.

(3) Where any proceedings for the appointment of a curator bonis to an adult have been commenced and not determined before the relevant date, they shall be determined in accordance with the law as it was immediately before that date; and any person appointed curator bonis shall become guardian of that adult with power to manage the property or financial affairs of the adult.

(4) On the relevant date, any person holding office as tutor-dative to an adult shall become guardian of that adult and shall continue to have the powers conferred by the court on his appointment as tutor-dative.

(5) Where any proceedings for the appointment of a tutor-dative to an adult have been commenced and not determined before the relevant date, they shall be determined in accordance with the law as it was immediately before that date; and any person appointed tutor-dative shall become guardian of that adult with such power to manage the property, financial affairs or personal welfare of the adult as the court may determine.

(6) On the relevant date, any person holding office as tutor-at-law to an adult shall become guardian of that adult with power to manage the property, financial affairs or personal welfare of the adult.

(7) Where any proceedings for the appointment of a tutor-at-law to an adult have been commenced and not determined before the relevant date, they shall be determined in accordance with the law as it was immediately before that date; and any person appointed tutor-at-law shall become guardian of that adult with power to manage the property, financial affairs or personal welfare of the adult.

Guardians
2.—(1) On the relevant date, any person holding office as guardian of an adult under the 1984 Act shall become guardian of that adult under this Act and shall continue to have the powers set out in paragraphs (a) to (c) of section 41(2) of that Act notwithstanding the repeal of that section by this Act.

(2) Where any proceedings for the appointment of such a guardian of an adult have been commenced and not determined before the relevant date, they shall be determined in accordance with the 1984 Act as it was in force immediately before that date; and any person appointed guardian shall become guardian of that adult under this Act with the powers set out in the said paragraphs (a) to (c) of section 41(2) of the 1984 Act.

Proceedings relating to existing appointments
3. Where any proceedings in relation to the functions of an existing curator bonis, tutor-dative, tutor-at-law or guardian have been commenced and not determined before the relevant date, they shall be determined in accordance with the law as it was immediately before that date.

Attorneys
4.—(1) On the relevant date, any person holding office as—
  (a) an attorney under a contract of mandate or agency with powers relating solely to the property or financial affairs of an adult shall become a continuing attorney under this Act;

(b) an attorney under a contract of mandate or agency with powers relating solely to the personal welfare of an adult shall become a welfare attorney under this Act;
(c) an attorney under a contract of mandate or agency with powers relating both to the property and financial affairs and to the personal welfare of an adult shall become a continuing attorney and a welfare attorney under this Act.

(2) Where, under the provisions of a contract of mandate or agency executed before the relevant date, a person is appointed as an attorney after that date he shall be a continuing attorney, a welfare attorney or a continuing and welfare attorney, as provided for in sub-paragraph (1), under this Act.

[(3) Sections 6(2)(c)(i), 15, 19, 20(3)(a), 21, 22, and 23 shall not apply to persons who have become continuing attorneys by virtue of sub-paragraph (1)(a) or (c).

(4) Sections 16(1) to (4) and (7), 19, 20(3)(a), 21, 22, and 23 shall not apply to persons who have become welfare attorneys by virtue of sub-paragraph (1)(b) or (c).][171]

Note
Sch.4, para.4 as amended by correction slip

Managers
5.—(1) Any managers of a hospital who have received and hold money and valuables on behalf of any person under section 94 of the 1984 Act may continue to do so under this Act for a period not exceeding 3 years from the relevant date.

(2) This Act applies to managers as mentioned in sub-paragraph (1) notwithstanding that no certificate has been issued under section 37 in respect of the owner of the money or valuables.

(3) Sections 35 and 38 shall not apply in the case of managers who continue to hold money by virtue of sub-paragraph (1).

(4) Where the managers have authority from the Mental Welfare Commission to hold and manage money and other property in excess of the aggregate value mentioned in section 39 they may do so in relation to the money and valuables of any person which they continue to hold under sub-paragraph (1).

Note
Sch.4, para.5(4) as amended by correction slip.

Application of Act to persons who become guardians by virtue of this schedule
6.—(1) For the purposes of their application to persons who have become guardians by virtue of this schedule, the following provisions shall have effect as modified or disapplied by this paragraph.

(2) In section 67(2) the reference to the certificate of appointment issued under section 58 shall be construed as a reference to the order of the court appointing the person as curator bonis, tutor-dative, tutor-at-law or guardian under the 1984 Act, as the case may be.

(3) Section 60 shall apply to a person who has become a guardian to an adult by virtue of this schedule and who was a curator bonis, tutor dative or

---

[171] Substituted by Adult Support and Protection (Scotland) Act 2007 (asp 10), Sch.1, para.5(h).

Adults with Incapacity (Scotland) Act 2000 (Sched. 4)

tutor-at-law to that adult; and, for the purpose of that application, for the reference in section 60(1) to a period in respect of which a guardianship order has been made or renewed there shall be substituted a reference[—

(a) in the case of a curator bonis who, under paragraph 1(2), became guardian to a person on the person attaining the age of 16 years, to the period of 2 years from the later of the following dates—

    (i) the date on which section 60(17) (which amends this paragraph) of the Adult Support and Protection (Scotland) Act 2007 (asp 10) came into force;
    (ii) the date on which the person attained the age of 16 years,

(b) in any other case, to the period of 2 years from the date on which section 60(17) (which amends this paragraph) of the Adult Support and Protection (Scotland) Act 2007 (asp 10) came into force.][172]

[(3A) A person who has become a guardian to an adult by virtue of this schedule and who was a curator bonis, tutor dative or tutor-in-law to that adult shall cease to be authorised to act as that adult's guardian—

(a) where the person does not apply for renewal of guardianship within the 2 year period set by sub-paragraph (3), on the expiry of that period;
(b) where—

    (i) the person applies for such a renewal within that period; and
    (ii) the sheriff refuses the application,

on the date of refusal;
(c) where—

    (i) the person applies for such a renewal within that period; and
    (ii) the sheriff grants the application,

in accordance with the provisions of this Act.

(3B) Sub-paragraph (3A) does not prevent the authority of a guardian of the type mentioned in that sub-paragraph from being terminated (by virtue of the terms on which the guardian is authorised to act or sections 71, 73, 75 or 79A) earlier than the date on which it would otherwise terminate by operation of that subparagraph.

(3C) Where—

(a) a person ("G") who was a curator bonis, tutor dative or tutor-at-law to an adult becomes the adult's guardian by virtue of this schedule; and
(b) another person is appointed under section 62 as an additional guardian to the adult before G's appointment as guardian has been renewed in accordance with the provisions of this Act,

subsection (3A) applies in relation to the additional guardian as it applies in relation to G.

(3D) The Public Guardian must take reasonable steps to give notice of the effect of sub-paragraph (3A) to any person who—

---

[172] Substituted by Adult Support and Protection (Scotland) Act 2007 (asp 10), s.60(17)(a).

(a) is a guardian to an adult by virtue of this schedule;
(b) was a curator bonis to that adult; and
(c) has not applied for renewal of guardianship.

(3E) A local authority must take reasonable steps to give notice of the effect of subparagraph (3A) to any person who—

(a) is a guardian to an adult residing within the local authority's area by virtue of this schedule;
(b) was a tutor dative or tutor-in-law to that adult; and
(c) has not applied for renewal of guardianship.][173]

(4) Section 60 shall not apply to a person who has become a guardian to an adult by virtue of this schedule and who was a guardian of that adult under the 1984 Act, in which case the powers shall continue until such time as they would have continued had he not become a guardian by virtue of this schedule to this Act.

(5) In sections 68(2) and (3) and 76 the references to the chief social work officer of the local authority shall be construed as including references to the local authority.

(6) Schedule 2 shall apply only—

(a) in a case where; and
(b) to the extent that,

the Public Guardian has determined that it should apply.

(7) Any determination by the Public Guardian under sub-paragraph (6), or a decision by him not to make such a determination, may be appealed to the sheriff, whose decision shall be final.

(8) No reference in this Act to registration shall have effect in relation to any person who becomes a guardian by virtue of this schedule.

Transitional Provisions
7. Until Part 6 comes into force—

(a) the references in section 23(1)(c) to a guardian shall be omitted;
(b) in section 31(7), the reference in paragraph (a) to the appointment of a guardian shall be construed as a reference to the appointment of a curator bonis or tutor-dative or tutor-at-law with powers relating to the funds or accounts in question and paragraph (b) shall be omitted;
(c) in section 34(1), the reference in paragraph (a) to a guardian shall be construed as a reference to a curator bonis or tutor-dative or tutor-at-law with powers relating to the funds or account in question and paragraph (b) shall be omitted;
(d) in section 46(1), the reference in paragraph (a) to a guardian shall be construed as a reference to a curator bonis or tutor-dative or tutor-at-law with powers relating to the matter and paragraph (b) shall be omitted.

Interpretation
8. In this schedule the "relevant date" in relation to any paragraph in which it appears means the date of coming into force of that paragraph.

---

[173] Inserted by Adult Support and Protection (Scotland) Act 2007 (asp 10), s.60(17)(b).

Adults with Incapacity (Scotland) Act 2000 (Sched. 4)

DEFINITIONS
"1984 Act, the" : The Mental Health (Scotland) Act 1984 (c.36) (per s.87 (1))
"adult" : s.1 (6)
"chief social work officer" : Social Work (Scotland) Act 1968 (c.49) s.3 (presumed)
"continuing attorney" : s.15 (2)
"guardianship order" : s.58 (4)
"local authority" : s.87 (1) (referring to the Local Government etc. (Scotland) Act 1994 (c.39) s.2)
"managers" : s.35 (5) and Sched. 1, para. 1
"Mental Welfare Commission" : s.87 (1) (referring to s.4 of the 2003 Act)
"Public Guardian" : s.6 (1)
"relevant date" : Sched. 4, para. 8
"welfare attorney" : s.16 (2)

GENERAL NOTE
Section 80 provides that no curators or tutors to adults might be appointed after the relevant provisions of this Act came into force (on April 1, 2002). The repeal of ss.36—52 of the 1984 Act in Sched. 6 abolished guardianship under that Act. Paragraphs 1, 2, 3 and 6 of this Schedule contain the principal consequential provisions. On April 1, 2002 curators became guardians will full property and financial powers (para. 1(1)); tutors-at-law became guardians with full property, financial and personal welfare powers (para. 1(6)); and tutors-dative and 1984 Act guardians became guardians with the same powers as previously (paras. 1(4) and 2(1) respectively). Applications and other proceedings pending at that date continued to be dealt with under the previous law (paras. 1(3), (5) and (7), 2(2) and 3).

Appointment of curators to children remains competent (see General Note to s.80), but such curators, whenever appointed, become guardians with full property and financial powers on the ward's 16th birthday (para. 1(2)). Section 79A permits applications under this Act to be commenced up to three months prior to the 16th birthday of children who will require guardians under this Act on and from that birthday.

Paragraph 6 applies to guardians who became such by virtue of any of the foregoing provisions. Paragraph 6(3) in the 2000 text had a curious, and perhaps not the intended, effect. The official Explanatory Notes to this Act suggested that previous appointments of curators and tutors "will have to be re-considered by the court within 5 years". That seemed to be incorrect. The Bill as introduced provided (in para. 6(4) of what was then Sched. 3) that previous appointments would continue for their duration, if the order creating them specified a duration, and otherwise indefinitely. That provision did not appear in this Act as enacted, but in the absence of any contrary provision its terms still appeared to represent the then position under this Act. The effect of the original para. 6(3) in conjunction with s.60 (which contains renewal provisions) was to create a time-limit for renewal applications. The only practical effect was that if an appointment of limited duration was to continue beyond the relevant five-year period, it could not have been renewed unless the application for renewal had been made within the five-year period. After that, a fresh application would have been required. That was a peculiar and rather meaningless provision, given that up until April 1, 2008 the procedures for fresh applications and for renewals were the same.

It is believed that the original para. 6 (3) did not reflect the original policy intention. The 2007 Act substantially amended para. 6 (3) and inserted new paras. 6 (3A)—(3E). All transitional appointments will expire two years after these changes came into force on October 5, 2007, if not renewed within that period. The new simplified renewal procedure (see note to s.60) will be applicable. In response to concerns by the Law Society that some adults might lose their guardianships because their guardians were unaware of this change, a successful amendment requires the Public Guardian to notify financial guardians of the new provisions, and local authorities to notify welfare guardians; and in response to concerns by the Law Society about the status of joint guardians appointed under this Act to transitional guardians, it has been clarified that the relevant new provisions of para. 3 apply also to such joint guardians.

Subject to the point addressed in the next paragraph, these mandatory renewal provisions do not apply to replacement guardians appointed in place of transitional guardians. Such replacement guardians have become guardians by virtue of their interlocutors of appointment under this Act, not by virtue of the transitional provisions of this Schedule. They were not former curators bonis or tutors for the purposes of any of the provisions of this Schedule.

Paragraph 6 (3C) explicitly extends the renewal requirement to joint guardians appointed under s.62 as additional guardians to transitional guardians: a similar express provision would have been required to bring replacement guardians within the scope of para. 6. The duration of appointment of such replacement guardians is determined by the interlocutor of appointment, and para. 6 does not apply.

However, it is understood that some such interlocutors may have failed to specify duration and/or powers in relation to replacement guardians. It could reasonably be argued that the only possible interpretation of such interlocutors is that the sheriff has impliedly carried forward into the replacement appointment the terms of the appointment of the guardian who was replaced. It is difficult to identify any other possibility. This means that the powers of the replacement guardian will be the same as the powers of the previous guardian; and it means that the duration of the appointment will be the same as that of the predecessor. If that is correct, then mandatory renewal will apply in this situation, not as a direct consequence of the terms of this Act, but because if the predecessor was a curator bonis or tutor and if the only possible interpretation of the interlocutor is that the term of appointment is the same as that of the predecessor transitional guardian, then it would seem that the application of para. 6 of this Schedule will have been imported by the implied terms of the interlocutor.

Paragraph 6(2) refers to s.67 (2), under which the certificate of appointment authorises the guardian to take possession of, manage and deal with the adult's estate and to require payment to the guardian of sums due to the adult. See comments in General Note to s.61 on renewal of transitional guardianships where there is heritable property.

As regards powers of attorney, s.18 provides that powers granted after commencement of the relevant provisions of this Act will only be effective following incapacity if granted in accordance with s.15 (in the case of CPAs) or s.16 (in the case of WPAs). Section 71 of the Law Reform (Miscellaneous Provisions) (Scotland) Act 1990 (c.40), which previously provided for powers of attorney to remain in force following incapacity of the granter, was repealed by Sched. 6. Paragraph 4 of this Schedule was designed to contain consequential provisions, but unfortunately as originally enacted was seriously garbled. That has now been rectified. Attorneys in office on the relevant date (para. 4(1)) or coming into office thereafter under documents executed before the relevant date (para. 4(2)) on the relevant date became continuing attorneys, welfare attorneys or both, depending upon the nature of the powers held. Paragraphs 4 (3) and (4) disapply certain provisions of this Act in relation to CPAs and WPAs respectively.

Disapplied in relation to CPAs only are:- s.6 (2)(c)(i) (receipt and investigation of complaints by the Public Guardian) and s.15 (formalities for granting a CPA). Disapplied in relation to WPAs only are:- s.16 (1)—(4) (formalities for granting a WPA) and s.16 (7) (power not ended by bankruptcy of granter or attorney). Disapplied in relation to both CPAs and WPAs are ss.19 and 20 (3)(a) (registration provisions), s.21 (requirement to keep records), s.22 (notification to Public Guardian) and s.23 (provisions regarding resignation of attorneys). All other provisions of this Act (including the general principles in s.1, the other general provisions of Pt. 1 other than the single exception noted above, and the remainder of Pt. 2) apply to attorneys acting after April 2, 2001 for adults with incapacity under documents executed before that date.

Hospital management under s.94 of the 1984 Act was abolished by the repeal of that section in Sched. 6 of this Act, and was replaced by the scheme of management of residents' finances under Pt. 4 of this Act. Paragraph 5 of this Schedule allowed hospital managers holding funds and valuables under s.94 of the 1984 Act on the relevant date to continue to do so under this Act for up to three years thereafter (para. 5(1)). Certificates in respect of individual residents under s.37 were not required (para. 5(2)). Sections 35 (definition of what are authorised establishments and who are their managers) and 38 (financial procedures and controls) are both disapplied (para. 5(3)). Section 39 provides for limitation by regulation of the maximum value of the matter managed (subject to increases in individual cases approved by the relevant supervisory body). Paragraph 5(4) preserved any existing authorisation by MWC under s.94 of the 1984 Act to hold and administer in excess of the 2000 Act limits.

The transitional provisions of para. 7 were necessary because Pts. 2, 3 and 4 came into force before Pt. 6.

SCHEDULE 5
Minor and Consequential Amendments

General

1. With effect from the commencement of this paragraph any reference in any enactment or document to a curator bonis or a tutor or curator of a

person of or over the age of 16 years shall be construed as a reference to a guardian with similar powers appointed to that person under this Act.

Defence Act 1842 (c.94)
2.—(1) In section 15 of the Defence Act 1842—

    (a) after "nonage" in both places there shall be inserted "or mental incapacity";
    (b) "or not of whole mind" shall be repealed;
    (c) for "out of prison, within this land, or of whole mind" there shall be substituted "within this land".

(2) In section 27 of that Act for "lunacy" there shall be substituted "mental incapacity".

Judicial Factors Act 1849 (c.51)
3. In section 34A of the Judicial Factors Act 1849 for "recovery, death or coming of age of the ward" there shall be substituted "coming to an end of the situation giving rise to it".

Improvement of Land Act 1864 (c.114)
4. [. . .]¹⁷⁴

Titles to Land (Consolidation) (Scotland) Act 1868 (c.101)
5.—(1) In section 24 of the Titles to Land (Consolidation) (Scotland) Act 1868 for "mental disorder within the meaning of the Mental Health (Scotland) Act 1960" there shall be substituted "mental or other incapacity".

(2) In section 62 of that Act for "of insane mind" there shall be substituted "mental or other incapacity".

Judicial Factors (Scotland) Act 1889 (c.39)
6.—(1) In section 2 of the Judicial Factors (Scotland) Act 1889 at the beginning there shall be inserted "Without prejudice to section 6(1) of the Adults with Incapacity (Scotland) Act 2000 (asp 4) (Accountant of Court to be Public Guardian)".

(2) In section 6 of that Act, in the proviso, after "apply to" there shall be inserted "guardians appointed under the Adults with Incapacity (Scotland) Act 2000 (asp 4), to".

Heritable Securities (Scotland) Act 1894 (c.44)
7. In section 13 of the Heritable Securities (Scotland) Act 1894—

    (a) after "(b) trustees" there shall be inserted—

        "(c) the person entitled to act as the legal representative of any such person";

    (b) "tutors, curators," shall be repealed.

---

[174] Repealed by Adult Support and Protection (Scotland) Act 2007 (asp 10), Sch.2.

National Assistance Act 1948 (c.29)
8. In section 49 of the National Assistance Act 1948 as it applies to Scotland—

> (a) immediately before "the council" where last occurring there shall be inserted "or applies for an intervention order or for appointment as a guardian under the Adults with Incapacity (Scotland) Act 2000 (asp 4)";
> (b) immediately before "in so far as" there shall be inserted "or his functions under the intervention order or as guardian".

Offices, Shops and Railway Premises Act 1963 (c.41)
9. In section 90(1) of the Offices, Shops and Railway Premises Act 1963 in the definition of "owner" for ", tutor or curator" there shall be substituted "or person entitled to act as legal representative of a person under disability by reason of nonage or mental or other incapacity".

Social Work (Scotland) Act 1968 (c.49)
10.—11. [. . .][175]

Medicines Act 1968 (c.67)
12. In section 72 of the Medicines Act 1968—

> (a) in subsection (1) for "curator bonis" there shall be substituted "guardian";
> (b) in subsections (3)(d) and (4)(c) "curator bonis," shall be repealed.

Sheriff Courts (Scotland) Act 1971 (c.58)
13. In section 32(1) of the Sheriff Courts (Scotland) Act 1971 after paragraph (j) there shall be inserted—

> "(k) prescribing the procedure to be followed in appointing a person under section 3(4) of the Adults with Incapacity (Scotland) Act 2000 (asp 4) and the functions of such a person.".

Land Registration (Scotland) Act 1979 (c.33)
14. In section 12(3) of the Land Registration (Scotland) Act 1979 after paragraph (k) there shall be inserted—

> "(kk) the loss is suffered by an adult within the meaning of the Adults with Incapacity (Scotland) Act 2000 (asp 4) because of the operation of sections 24, 53, 67, 77 or 79 of that Act, or by any person who acquires any right, title or interest from that adult;".

NOTE
Sch.5, para.14 as amended by correction slip.

Solicitors (Scotland) Act 1980 (c.46)
15. In section 18(1) of the Solicitors (Scotland) Act 1980—

> (a) in paragraph (a) "or becomes subject to guardianship" shall be repealed;

---

[175] Repealed by Regulation of Care (Scotland) Act 2001 (asp 8), Sch.4.

Adults with Incapacity (Scotland) Act 2000 (Sched. 5)

(b) for paragraph (b) there shall be substituted—

"(b) a guardian is appointed to a solicitor under the Adults with Incapacity (Scotland) Act 2000 (asp 4);".

Law Reform (Miscellaneous Provisions) (Scotland) Act 1980 (c.55)
16. In group C of Part I of Schedule 1 to the Law Reform (Miscellaneous Provisions) (Scotland) Act 1980 for paragraphs (b) and (c) there shall be substituted—

"(b) persons for the time being subject to guardianship under the Adults with Incapacity (Scotland) Act 2000 (asp 4).".

Mental Health (Scotland) Act 1984 (c.36)
17.—(1) In section 3 of the Mental Health (Scotland) Act 1984—

(a) in subsection (1) "guardianship or" shall be repealed;
(b) in subsection (2) in paragraph (b) "or who are subject to guardianship" shall be repealed.

(2) In section 5(2) of that Act "and the guardian of any person subject to guardianship under this Act" shall be repealed.
(3)—(24) [. . .][176]

Insolvency Act 1986 (c.45)
18. In section 390(4)(c) of the Insolvency Act 1986 at the end there shall be added "or has had a guardian appointed to him under the Adults with Incapacity (Scotland) Act 2000 (asp 4).".

Legal Aid (Scotland) Act 1986 (c.47)
19. In section 36(3) of the Legal Aid (Scotland) Act 1986, after paragraph (b) there shall be inserted—

"(bb) is concerned as claiming or having an interest in the property, financial affairs or personal welfare of an adult under the Adults with Incapacity (Scotland) Act 2000 (asp 4);".

Financial Services Act 1986 (c.60)
20. In section 45(1)(d) of the Financial Services Act 1986 at the end there shall be added "or when acting in the exercise of his functions as Public Guardian under the Adults with Incapacity (Scotland) Act 2000 (asp 4);".

Access to Health Records Act 1990 (c.23)
21. In section 3 of the Access to Health Records Act 1990, in subsection (3) after paragraph (e) there shall be inserted—

"(ee) where the record is held in Scotland and the patient is incapable, within the meaning of the Adults with Incapacity (Scotland) Act 2000 (asp 4) in relation to making or authorising the application, any person entitled to act on behalf of the patient under that Act.".

Child Support Act 1991 (c.48)
22. In section 50 of the Child Support Act 1991 in subsection (8)(c) for paragraphs (i) and (ii) there shall be substituted "a guardian or other

---

[176] Repealed by Mental Health (Care and Treatment) (Scotland) Act 2003 (asp 13), Sch.5.

person entitled to act on behalf of the person under the Adults with Incapacity (Scotland) Act 2000 (asp 4).".

Social Security Administration Act 1992 (c.5)
23. In section 123 of the Social Security Administration Act 1992 in subsection (10)(c) for paragraphs (i) and (ii) there shall be substituted "a guardian or other person entitled to act on behalf of the person under the Adults with Incapacity (Scotland) Act 2000 (asp 4).".

Health Service Commissioners Act 1993 (c.46)
24. In section 7A of the Health Service Commissioners Act 1993 after "patients)" there shall be inserted "or", "or 50 (orders discharging patients from guardianship)" shall be repealed, and at the end there shall be inserted "or section 73 of the Adults with Incapacity (Scotland) Act 2000 (asp 4)".

Clean Air Act 1993 (c.11)
25. In section 64 of the Clean Air Act 1993 in subsection (1) in the definition of "owner" for "tutor or curator" there shall be substituted "or person entitled to act as the legal representative of a person under disability by reason of nonage or mental or other incapacity".

Criminal Procedure (Scotland) Act 1995 (c.46)
26.—(1) In section 57 of the Criminal Procedure (Scotland) Act 1995—

    (a) in subsection (2)(c) for first "person" there shall be substituted "person's personal welfare";
    (b) in subsection (4) after "58(1)," there shall be inserted "58(1A),";
    (c) at the end there shall be added—

        "(6) Section 58A of this Act shall have effect as regards guardianship orders made under subsection (2)(c) of this section.".

(2) In section 58 of that Act—

    (a) for subsection (1) there shall be substituted—

        "(1) Where a person is convicted in the High Court or the sheriff court of an offence, other than an offence the sentence for which is fixed by law, punishable by that court with imprisonment, and the court—

            (a) is satisfied on the written or oral evidence of two medical practitioners (complying with section 61 of this Act) that the grounds set out in section 17(1) of the Mental Health (Scotland) Act 1984 apply in relation to the offender;
            (b) is of the opinion, having regard to all the circumstances including the nature of the offence and the character and antecedents of the offender and to the other available methods of dealing with him, that the most suitable method of disposing of the case is by means of an order under this subsection,

        the court may, subject to subsection (2) below, by order authorise his admission to and detention in such hospital as may be specified in the order.
          (1A) Where a person is convicted as mentioned in subsection (1) above and the court is satisfied—

(a) on the evidence of two medical practitioners (complying with section 61 of this Act and with any requirements imposed under section 57(3) of the Adults with Incapacity (Scotland) Act 2000 (asp 4)) that the grounds set out in section 58(1)(a) of that Act apply in relation to the offender;

(b) that no other means provided by or under this Act would be sufficient to enable the offender's interests in his personal welfare to be safeguarded or promoted,

the court may, subject to subsection (2) below, by order place the offender's personal welfare under the guardianship of such local authority or of such other person approved by a local authority as may be specified in the order.";

(b) in subsections (2), (3) and (10) for "subsection (1)" there shall be substituted "subsection (1) or (1A)";

(c) in subsections (5) and (7) after "subsection (1)" there shall be inserted "or paragraph (a) of subsection (1A),";

(d) for subsection (6) there shall be substituted—

"(6) An order placing a person under the guardianship of a local authority or of any other person (in this Act referred to as "a guardianship order") shall not be made under this section unless the court is satisfied—

(a) on the report of a mental health officer (complying with any requirements imposed by section 57(3) of the Adults with Incapacity (Scotland) Act 2000 (asp 4)) giving his opinion as to the general appropriateness of the order sought, based on an interview and assessment of the person carried out not more than 30 days before it makes the order, that it is necessary in the interests of the personal welfare of the person that he should be placed under guardianship;

(b) that any person nominated to be appointed a guardian is suitable to be so appointed;

(c) that the authority or person is willing to receive that person into guardianship; and

(d) that there is no other guardianship order, under this Act or the Adults with Incapacity (Scotland) Act 2000 (asp 4), in force relating to the person.";

(e) at the end there shall be added—

"(11) Section 58A of this Act shall have effect as regards guardianship orders made under subsection (1) of this section.".

(3) After section [60A][177] of that Act there shall be inserted—

"Intervention orders
[60B][178]. The court may instead of making a hospital order under section 58(1) of this Act or a guardianship order under section 57(2)(c) or 58(1A) of this Act, make an intervention order [(as defined in section 53(1) of the Adults with Incapacity

---

[177] Substituted by Regulation of Care (Scotland) Act 2001 (asp 8), Sch.3, para.23(7)(a).
[178] Substituted by Regulation of Care (Scotland) Act 2001 (asp 8), Sch.3, para.23(7)(b).

Adults with Incapacity Legislation

(Scotland) Act 2000 (asp 4)][179] where it considers that it would be appropriate to do so.".

(4) [. . .][180]

---

[179] Inserted by Regulation of Care (Scotland) Act 2001 (asp 8), Sch.3, para.23(7)(c).
[180] Repealed by Adult Support and Protection (Scotland) Act 2007 (asp 10), Sch.2.

Adults with Incapacity (Scotland) Act 2000 (Sched. 6)

SCHEDULE 6

Repeals

Enactment	Extent of Repeal
Curators Act 1585 (c.25(S))	The whole Act.
Judicial Factors Act 1849 (12 & 13 Vict. c.51)	In section 1, "and curator bonis" and the words from "the word "tutor"" to "Act 1960" where second occurring. In section 7, the words from "and if any factor" to "not subject to appeal". In section 10, "tutors and curators". Section 25(1). Section 26. In section 27, "or Court of Exchequer, as the case may be," and "tutors and curators". Section 28. In section 31, "tutor or curator" and "or curator bonis". In section 32, "tutor or curator". In section 33, "tutor or curator". In section 34, "tutor, or curator". In section 34A, "tutors and curators" and "tutory or curatory". In section 36, "tutories, and curatories". In section 37, "tutor, or curator". In section 40, the words from "and the manner of applying" to "curators" where first occurring and "tutors, and curators,".
Improvement of Land Act 1864 (27 & 28 Vict. c.114)	In section 24, "tutors,", "curators,", "tutor," and "curator,".
Titles to Land (Consolidation) (Scotland) Act 1868 (31 & 32 Vict. c.101)	In section 3 in the definition of "judicial factor", "or curators bonis".
Judicial Factors (Scotland) Act 1880 (43 & 44 Vict. c.4)	In section 3, "a curator bonis".
Judicial Factors (Scotland) Act 1889 (52 & 53 Vict. c.39)	In section 13, "tutor, curator" in both places.
Heritable Securities (Scotland) Act 1894 (57 & 58 Vict. c.44)	In section 13, "tutors, curators".
Trusts (Scotland) Act 1921 (11 & 12 Geo.5 c.58)	In section 2 in each of the definitions of "trust" and "trust deed" the words "tutor, curator, guardian or" and in the definition of "trustee" the words "tutor, curator, guardian"; in the definition of "judicial factor" the words "or curator"; the definitions of "curator", "tutor" and "guardian".
U.S.A. Veterans' Pensions Act 1949 (12 & 13 Geo.6 c.45)	In section 1(4), "tutor, factor loco tutoris," and "curator bonis or".
Medicines Act 1968 (c.67)	In section 72(3)(d) and (4)(c), "curator bonis,".
Solicitors (Scotland) Act 1980 (c.46)	In section 18(1)(a), "or becomes subject to guardianship".
Mental Health Act 1983 (c.20)	In section 110, in subsection (1) "curator bonis, tutor or"; in subsection (2) "curator bonis, tutor, or".
Mental Health (Scotland) Act 1984 (c.36)	In section 3 in subsection (1) "guardianship or"; in subsection (2)(b), "or who are subject to guardianship". In section 5(2) "or subject to guardianship under the following provisions of this Act".

Adults with Incapacity Legislation

Enactment	Extent of Repeal
Mental Health (Scotland) Act 1984 (c.36)—*cont.*	In section 7(1)(b), "under the following provisions of this Act".
In section 10(1)(b) "the following provisions of this Act or under".
In section 29 in subsection (1), paragraphs (b) and (c) and "or" which precedes them; in subsection (2), "or, as the case may be, by the local authority concerned"; in subsection (3), paragraph (b).
Sections 36 to 52.
In section 53(3), "or his reception into guardianship".
Section 55(3).
In section 57(4), "or subject to guardianship" and "or so subject" wherever occurring.
In section 59, subsections (1)(b) and (2) and in subsection (3), "or 44".
Section 61.
In section 76(1) paragraph (b) and ", a guardianship order".
In section 77, in subsection (1) "or subject to guardianship" and "or, as the case may be, for receiving him into guardianship"; subsection (3).
In section 78, in subsection (1), "or reception into guardianship"; in subsection (2), "or his reception into guardianship".
In section 80(1), "or subject to guardianship" and "or, as the case may be, for receiving him into guardianship".
Section 84(4).
In section 87(1), "or subject to guardianship" and "or placed under guardianship."
In section 92, subsection (1) and in subsection (2)(a), "or subject to guardianship thereunder".
Sections 93 and 94.
In section 105(2), "subject to his guardianship under this Act or otherwise".
In section 107(1)(b), "subject to his guardianship under this Act or is otherwise".
In section 108(1)(a), "or being subject to guardianship".
In section 110 in subsection (1), ", or in the case of a patient subject to guardianship, the local authority concerned", "or subject to guardianship", "or guardianship" in both places, "or his reception into guardianship"; in subsection (4), "or, as the case may be, the local authority concerned in relation to a patient subject to guardianship as aforesaid".
In section 112, "or his reception into guardianship".
In section 113(1), "or for reception into guardianship".
In section 119, "guardianship under this Act".
In section 121 in subsection (1)(b), "or subject to guardianship", "or 44"; in subsection (2), "or subject to guardianship", "or 44", "and subsection (2) of the said section 44"; in subsection (6), the words from "(in the case of" where first occurring to "guardianship)", "or section 44", "respectively", "or the said section 44 (as the case may be)".

Adults with Incapacity (Scotland) Act 2000 (Sched. 6)

Enactment	Extent of Repeal
Mental Health (Scotland) Act 1984 (c.36)—*cont.*	In section 125 in subsection (4), "or subject to guardianship"; in subsection (5), "or received, or liable to be received, into guardianship", "(other than under Part V thereof)", "or received or liable to be received into guardianship".
Law Reform (Miscellaneous Provisions) (Scotland) Act 1990 (c.40)	Section 71.
Criminal Procedure (Scotland) Act 1995 (c.46)	In section 59(2), "or section 39".
	In section 61(1), "or section 39".
	In section 230(1), "or 39".
	In schedule 4, in paragraph 2(1)(b), "or 39".

APPENDIX 1

SOCIAL WORK (SCOTLAND) ACT 1968 (C.49)

Provision of services to incapable adults

[181]**13ZA.**—(1) Where—
- (a) a local authority have decided under section 12A of this Act that an adult's needs call for the provision of a community care service; and
- (b) it appears to the local authority that the adult is incapable in relation to decisions about the service,

the local authority may take any steps which they consider would help the adult to benefit from the service.

(2) Without prejudice to the generality of subsection (1) above, steps that may be taken by the local authority include moving the adult to residential accommodation provided in pursuance of this Part.

(3) The principles set out in subsection (2) to (4) of section 1 of the 2000 Act apply in relation to any steps taken under subsection (1) above as they apply to interventions in the affairs of an adult under or in pursuance of that Act.

(4) Subsection (1) does not authorise a local authority to take steps if they are aware that—
- (a) there is a guardian or welfare attorney with powers relating to the proposed steps;
- (b) an intervention order has been granted relating to the proposed steps; or
- (c) an application has been made (but not yet determined) for an intervention order or guardianship order under Part 6 of the 2000 Act relating to the proposed steps.

(5) In this section—
- (a) "the 2000 Act" means the Adults with Incapacity (Scotland) Act 2000 (asp 4);
- (b) "adult" has the meaning given in section 1(6) of the 2000 Act;
- (c) "community care service" has the meaning given in section 5A of this Act;
- (d) "incapable" has the meaning given in section 1(6) of the 2000 Act;
- (e) "intervention order" is to be construed in accordance with section 53 of the 2000 Act";
- (f) the reference to a guardian includes a reference to—
    - (i) a guardian appointed under the 2000 Act; and
    - (ii) a guardian (however called) appointed under the law of any country to, or entitled under the law of any country to act for, an adult during his incapacity, if the guardianship is recognised by the law of Scotland;
- (g) the reference to a welfare attorney includes a reference to—
    - (i) a welfare attorney within the meaning of section 16 of the 2000 Act; and

---

[181] Section 13ZA inserted by Adult Support and Protection (Scotland) Act 2007 (asp 10), s.64.

(ii) a person granted, under a contract, grant or appointment governed by the law of any country, powers (however expressed) relating to the granter's personal welfare and having effect during the granter's incapacity.".

GENERAL NOTE
By inserting the provisions of this section in the 1968 Act, the Parliament has placed them outwith the scope of s.58 (1)(b) of the Incapacity Act, which permits guardianship orders only where "no other means provided by or under this Act" (i.e. the Incapacity Act) will suffice to safeguard or promote the adult's interests in the adult's property, financial affairs or personal welfare. This s.13ZA nevertheless does introduce a new situation in which guardianship (or an intervention order) may no longer be required when such an order might well have been required previously. It follows much debate and discussion about "When to invoke the Act?" (i.e. the Incapacity Act).

Under the Incapacity Act, the only methods for dealing with non-medical welfare interventions are guardianship and intervention orders. There is a need for proportionality not only as to measures put in place, but as to the procedure to do so. The simplest intervention order still requires three reports and court procedure. We have the simpler procedures for authority to intromit under Pt. 3, management of residents' finances under Pt. 4, and authority to treat under Pt. 5. These all require a medical certificate of incapacity, and some other appropriate requirements, but no court procedure. However, at this level of simpler procedure there was a gap. There was no such simpler procedure to authorise non-medical welfare acts and decisions. To what extent, accordingly, was it necessary to go through guardianship or intervention order procedure to authorise simple welfare interventions, or more significant welfare interventions which could be shown to be entirely non-controversial? This issue became focused upon a matter of great practical importance for social work authorities. Did they require to obtain guardianship or an intervention order every time it was proposed to move an adult from one residential setting to another, for example from hospital to other accommodation, when no-one with an interest in the matter was in disagreement and the adult was compliant but not capable even of the simple act of assenting to the move? One local authority obtained Opinion of Counsel, which was widely circulated, advising that local authorities should use the procedure provided by the Incapacity Act to obtain guardianship or an intervention order, and should not proceed informally. Where there is no relevant capacity, compliance cannot equate to consent, and is irrelevant: "The presence or lack of resistance may of itself be symptomatic of the very vulnerability which the Act seeks to ensure is not exploited". MWC hosted a discussion which elicited a range of interesting and valuable views, but achieved no clear consensus.

The story thereafter can be followed through (a) circular dated July 30, 2004 from Scottish Executive, Social Work Services Inspectorate, (b) paper published by MWC and written by Hilary Patrick entitled *Authorising significant interventions for adults who lack capacity* (August 2004) and the updated version issued October 2005, (c) the decision in *Muldoon, Applicant* (Sh Ct) 2005 SCLR 611 and the cases therein considered, (d) Scottish Executive, Justice Department, Civil Law Division circular dated September 29, 2005 entitled *Interventions under the Adults with Incapacity (Scotland) Act 2000*, (e) the decisions of the European Court of Human Rights in *H.M. v Switzerland* (2002) ECHR 157 and *H.L. v U.K.* (the "Bournewood case") (2004) 40 EHRR 761, (f) *Making Sense of Bournewood*, R. Robinson and L. Scott-Moncrieff, Journal of Mental Health Law, May 2005, p17, (g) draft guidance for local authorities on when to invoke the Incapacity Act issued by the Scottish Executive, and (h) s.64 of the 2007 Act and relevant guidance mentioned below.

It remains relevant to query whether local authorities in fact had a problem. The financial memorandum which accompanied the Bill which became the Incapacity Act predicted 1,500 Pt. 6 applications by local authorities each year, so the prediction was that there would have been 4,500 such applications in the first three years. In fact, there were only 996. The precise figures are quoted in the commentary on *Muldoon* (above), which commentary challenged the assumption that the requirements of the Incapacity Act were proving unexpectedly burdensome for local authorities, and which suggested that there must be concern that substantial numbers of adults might still be subject to significant interventions to which they are not capable of consenting, without due process or proper authority.

Nevertheless, it can hardly be realistically argued that Pt. 6 orders are necessary to justify every simple and minor welfare intervention. It would be likely to be unacceptable in Scotland

Social Work (Scotland) Act 1968 (C.49)

to introduce any equivalent to England's general authority to intervene in matters of "care or treatment" without procedure or express authorisation simply on the basis that the intervener considers himself (or herself) to be acting in the "best interests" of the adult (Mental Capacity Act 2000 c9, s.5). That danger lurked for so long as these issues were not sensibly resolved.

The Scottish Executive guidance suggested that the Social Work (Scotland) Act 1968 contained hitherto unidentified authority for local authorities to make decisions on behalf of incapable adults. It would appear that very few lawyers who had considered the point agreed with the Scottish Executive position on this. If Scottish Executive had been right, then the 1968 Act provided an additional technique for making decisions on behalf of incapable adults which escaped the notice of the Scottish Law Commission and everyone else who addressed the topic in over a decade of careful consideration preceding the Incapacity Act. Prior to insertion of this section, the 1968 Act was concerned quite clearly with public law matters of "making available" (the words of that Act) facilities and services, not with private law matters of making decisions about accepting those services and their consequences, such as being removed from one's own home and placed elsewhere.

It is by this route that we now have this s.13ZA, which came into force on March 22, 2007, the day after Royal Assent to the 2007 Act, which inserted it in the 1968 Act. This provision applies where a local authority has decided that an adult's needs call for provision of a community care service and the adult is incapable in relation to decisions about the service. In that situation the local authority "may take any steps which they consider would help the adult to benefit from the service", including (without prejudice to that generality) moving the adult to residential accommodation provided under the 1968 Act. The first four principles in s.1 of the Incapacity Act apply. The authority under the 1968 Act is disapplied where a guardian or welfare attorney has relevant powers, an intervention order has been granted relating to the proposed steps, or an application has been made (but not yet determined) for an intervention or guardianship order relating to the proposed steps. Theoretically, such an application could be refused to allow s.13ZA of the 1968 Act to be applied. However, that section should be read along with s.5 of the 1968 Act which requires local authorities to act under the general guidance of Scottish Ministers and to comply with their directions. The relevant guidance is entitled *Guidance for Local Authorities (March 2007) Provision of community care services to adults with incapacity*. The guidance sets out procedures and criteria which in effect permit use of this new procedure under the 1968 Act only in situations which are genuinely non-controversial, and where the adult is entirely compliant. The guidance concludes by stating that intervention under said Act of 2000 may be appropriate where: "the carer/family members have expressed a different view to that of the person and/or the health and social work professionals involved with the needs assessment and care plan, or there is disagreement amongst professionals. In such cases, where no agreement can be reached, local authorities may conclude that the only way to protect the personal welfare of the individual would be through an application for an order and a hearing in front of a sheriff. Even where there is doubt about how convincing the evidence may be in court, where concerns remain over the capacity of the individual to protect their own welfare and there is such a disagreement, the matter should be placed before the court for a decision.". It is therefore difficult to visualise circumstances in which it would ever be appropriate for a sheriff to refuse an application under Pt. 6 of the Incapacity Act on the grounds that the new procedure under the 1968 Act is available, because under the guidance the 1968 Act procedure will be inapplicable where there is such disagreement as results in someone who claims an interest making application under Pt. 6.

Section 64 of the 2007 Act would appear to clarify a further point. The section creates a new procedure to authorise certain welfare decisions. It does not purport to regulate an existing authority previously to be found in the 1968 Act. It contains no declaratory provision such as is contained in the new s.15 (5) of the Incapacity Act as inserted by s.57 (1)(d) of the 2007 Act. No authority to make welfare decisions about accepting services, and consenting to their implementation, is to be inferred from the duties under the 1968 Act to make such services available. That point would appear to be of more general application. Hitherto undiscovered authority to make welfare decisions, or indeed any decisions, on behalf of incapable adults is not to be inferred in the absence of either express authority or a procedure which is expressly capable of conferring such authority. In the absence of any such express alternative source of authority, the procedures under Pt. 6 of the Incapacity Act are required in order to provide lawful authority to make decisions in matters of personal welfare, or concerning property and finances, in relation to an adult not capable of making the decision(s) in question.

Adults with Incapacity Legislation

In this broader context *Muldoon, Applicant* (Sh Ct) 2005 SCLR 611 remains important. In that case the proposed appointment of a welfare guardian was opposed by reference to the arguments in the MWC paper *Authorising significant interventions for adults who lack capacity* referred to above. Sheriff Baird reviewed the authorities available to him at the time of his decision on January 18, 2005 (though not the circular of July 30, 2004). He held that where an adult is compliant with a regime, but legally incapable of consenting to or disagreeing with it, then to impose the regime deprives the adult of his or her liberty in breach of Article 5 of ECHR; and that such a step should not be taken without express authority. In such a situation the appropriate statutory intervention was a guardianship order, because in every case where the court is dealing with an incapable but compliant adult, the least restrictive option would be the granting of a guardianship order under the Act (provided that all the other statutory requirements are satisfied): only in that way would the necessary safeguards and statutory and regulatory framework to protect the adult (and the guardian) come into play. One would only add that, though not mentioned by the sheriff, where there are no ongoing guardianship needs an intervention order would be equally appropriate.

One has to record some surprise that the *Muldoon* decision was not referred to in the Scottish Executive circular of September 29, 2005. The decision nevertheless appears to be vindicated by the introduction by the Executive, by amendment at an advanced stage of parliamentary procedure, of what is now s.64 of the 2007 Act, inserting this s.13ZA into the 1968 Act.

In the broader context of the Incapacity Act and adult incapacity law, some points which arose in the "When to invoke the Act?" debate remain relevant and important.

The incidence of resource-consuming issues about whether to invoke Pt. 6 of the Incapacity Act in relation to significant welfare interventions can be reduced in various ways. The whole circumstances and requirements should always be reviewed. As well as the issues in immediate contemplation, there may be other factors or potential factors putting it beyond doubt that Pt. 6 procedure is required. On the other hand adults at risk of progressive impairment of capacity should be encouraged to grant welfare powers of attorney while still competent to do so, or to make advance decisions. Most importantly, where an adult with impaired capacity nevertheless has the relatively limited capacity necessary to assent to a proposed significant welfare intervention in circumstances where there is no realistic alternative, that adult's ability to give such assent should always be respected and facilitated.

The debate sometimes seemed to assume that there is something optional about the extent of efforts which must be made to ascertain whether the adult can decide or assent, and if so to facilitate this. That is fundamentally incorrect. The requirement to determine whether the adult has relevant capacity, and if so to enable the adult to exercise that capacity, is absolute (see s.1 (6) of the Incapacity Act and Note thereto). In all cases it is necessary to analyse the decision or assent required and to determine whether the adult, even with all necessary assistance, is incapable of such decision or assent. There is a large difference in the degree of capacity required, on the one hand, to decide whether and where to move when there is realistic choice, and on the other hand to assent to the act of moving when that is all that is required. There are of course issues about definition of situations of "no realistic choice" and about ascertainment of them.

The debate also frequently assumed that Pt. 6 procedure is slow and costly. Properly and efficiently followed, it may not be significantly slower nor significantly more costly of resources than s.13ZA procedure. The timetable for Pt. 6 procedure is tight, both before and after the application is lodged, and in case of urgency an interim order can be sought. It is not self-evident that the time or resources necessary to follow s.13ZA procedure properly, in accordance with the Scottish Executive guidance, will always be significantly less than is required to obtain a Pt. 6 order.

The debate spanned the period during which the "Bournewood case" (above) was proceeding, ultimately to the European Court on Human Rights. This understandably resulted in much emphasis upon the question of what interventions would amount to "deprivation of liberty" in terms of Article 5 of ECHR. That issue was addressed in Ms Patrick's paper, and again in "Annexe D" to the Scottish Executive guidance of March 2007. There are also, particularly in the context of a move from one residential setting to another, issues as to the relevance of compliance, of potential abduction and assault, and of the fundamental concerns which gave rise to our modern incapacity legislation.

As stressed above, when there is no adequate capacity, there can be no valid consent, and compliance is irrelevant. The Incapacity Act addresses incapacity in relation both to deciding and to acting. It does so, for example, in the definition of "incapable" in s.1 (6), in the criteria for an intervention order in s.53(1), and in the criteria for a guardianship order in s.58 (1)(a). There is no definition of a precise boundary between deciding and acting, but in relation to a move from one residential setting to another it seems reasonable to suggest that "deciding" would encompass deciding whether and where to move, where there is choice, and "acting" would encompass actually assenting to the physical act of moving. It is significant that the Parliament has chosen to include in the options available under Pt. 6 an option, in the form of an intervention order where an adult is incapable of acting, only for the purpose of a situation where the adult is compliant. Section 70 contains provisions to deal with situations of non-compliance only in relation to the decisions of welfare guardians, and not in relation to the decisions of appointees under intervention orders, therefore welfare intervention orders are only appropriate where the adult is expected to be compliant. The Parliament cannot have intended that Pt. 6 should not be used in the situation of a significant welfare intervention where the adult is compliant but incapable of competent assent, when the range of measures provided under Pt. 6 includes one which addresses *inter alia* that situation.

On abduction, Gordon *Criminal Law*, 3rd edition, 2001 (para. 29.52), and the authorities there referred to, do not address the situation of adults lacking relevant capacity. The only distinction made is between (impliedly capable) adults and children. Force is necessary to demonstrate abduction in the case of the former, but not in the case of the latter. The principle to be drawn, it would appear, is that compliance is only relevant in the case of persons able to make a valid decision as to whether they consent to what is happening or not, and could reasonably be expected to resist if they did not consent. Gordon and the authorities which he quotes do not address the situation of an adult whose apparent compliance derives from incapacity rather than from competent though tacit assent to what is happening. It seems improbable that it would not be held to be criminal for anyone whatsoever to "capture" an adult with incapacity and spirit that adult away to some quite other location. If our law were not to provide such protection, that would be a breach of ECHR (cf *X and Y v The Netherlands*, decision 26 March 1985 on application No 16/1983/72/110). If there is doubt, the ECHR-compliant interpretation of our law should be favoured.

If any physical intervention, including the act of removing a compliant but incapable adult from one home setting to another, were to involve any physical contact, even touching, that would be likely to be at least technically an assault in criminal law if not lawfully authorised (see Scottish Law Commission Discussion Paper No 94 *Mentally Disabled Adults*, para 3.4 and authorities there cited, *Stair Memorial Encyclopaedia*, vol. 14, para 1130 and authorities there cited). The principle of necessity could justify such intervention, but not where there is no such urgency as would render it impossible or impractical to obtain lawful authorisation by one of the routes provided by the Parliament. Any abduction or assault would of course be actionable as a civil wrong.

Fundamentally, Pt. 6 procedure—when it is appropriate—is a right of the adult, not an imposition upon the adult: "The mentally retarded person has a right to a qualified guardian when this is required to protect his personal wellbeing and interests" (Article V, United Nations Declaration on the Rights of Mentally Retarded Persons). This author has sought many times to put over this fundamental point. "No-one has any automatic right to make decisions for another adult, however handicapped. In every legal system, specific procedure is required in order to appoint someone to such a supervisory role. The essential elements of such procedure will include an assessment of whether such an appointment is needed, and a decision as to who should be appointed. Such an appointment does represent a diminution of the rights of the adult, but if the powers conferred are limited to those which are necessary, the only rights lost will be those which the adult is unable to exercise for himself. There is greater risk of infringement of the rights of the adult where there is no judicial determination that such an appointment is necessary, yet someone simply assumes such a role without any legal authority to do so." (*The Power to Act*, 1990, pp 11—12). "It is often necessary to balance two different types of limitations on a person's rights and freedoms in personal matters. Firstly, it is a limitation of a person's rights and freedoms to impose any special legal provisions, such as appointing a guardian. But secondly, it is also an infringement of the person's rights and freedoms if someone else is in fact making decisions, or exercising the control of a guardian, without any legal authority to do so. There should be no intervention in the form of special legal provisions, except when shown to be necessary. Such intervention should be limited to the extent shown to be necessary, but to that extent it should be provided." (*A New View*, English-language edition, 1993, pp.33–34).

Adults with Incapacity Legislation

In matters fundamental to the rights and freedoms of adults not capable of protecting their rights and freedoms for themselves, the safeguard for all concerned of independent and authoritative consideration and determination by a court, and with it the proper separation of the roles of judiciary and executive, should not be lightly dispensed with.

APPENDIX 2

NOTE: The Statutory Instruments set out in this Appendix do not include those reproduced in Appendix 2 to *Adult Incapacity* which remain fully in force and unamended. They are as follows:

Adults with Incapacity (Supervision of Welfare Attorneys by Local Authorities) (Scotland) Regulations 2001 (SSI 2001/77)
Adults with Incapacity (Scotland) Act 2000 (Commencement No.1) Order 2001 (SSI 2001/81)
Adults with Incapacity (Non-compliance with Decisions of Welfare Guardians) (Scotland) Regulations 2002 (SSI 2002/98)
Adults with Incapacity (Scotland) Act 2000 (Commencement No.2) Order 2002 (SSI 2002/189)
Adults with Incapacity (Specified Medical Treatments) (Scotland) Regulations 2002 (SSI 2002/275)

ACT OF SEDERUNT (SUMMARY APPLICATIONS, STATUTORY APPLICATIONS AND APPEALS ETC. RULES)

(SI 1999/929)

PART XVI

ADULTS WITH INCAPACITY (SCOTLAND) ACT 2000

Interpretation

3.16.1 In this Part—
[. . .][182]
"the 2000 Act" means the Adults with Incapacity (Scotland) Act 2000;
["the 2003 Act" means the Mental Health (Care and Treatment)(Scotland) Act 2003][183]
["adult" means a person who is the subject of an application under the 2000 Act and—
(a) has attained the age of 16 years; or
(b) in relation to an application for a guardianship order, will attain the age of 16 years within 3 months of the date of the application;][184]
"authorised establishment" has the meaning ascribed to it in section 35(2) of the 2000 Act;
"continuing attorney" means a person on whom there has been conferred a power of attorney granted under section 15(1) of the 2000 Act;
"guardianship order" means an order made under section 58(4) of the 2000 Act;
"incapable" has the meaning ascribed to it at section 1(6) of the 2000 Act, and "incapacity" shall be construed accordingly;
"intervention order" means an order made under section 53(1) of the 2000 Act;
"local authority" has the meaning ascribed to it by section 87(1) of the 2000 Act;
"managers" has the meaning ascribed to it in paragraph 1 of Schedule 1 to the 2000 Act;
"Mental Welfare Commission" has the meaning ascribed to it by section 87(1) of the 2000 Act;
["named person" has the meaning ascribed to it by section 329 of the Mental Health (Care and Treatment) (Scotland) Act 2003;][185]
"nearest relative" means, subject to section 87(2) of the 2000 Act, the person who would be, or would be exercising the functions of, the adult's nearest relative under sections 53 to 57 of the 1984 Act if the

---

[182] Repealed by Mental Health (Care and Treatment) (Scotland) Act 2003 (Modification of Subordinate Legislation) Order 2005 (SSI 2005/445), Sch.1.
[183] Inserted by Mental Health (Care and Treatment) (Scotland) Act 2003 (Modification of Subordinate Legislation) Order 2005 (SSI 2005/445), Sch.1.
[184] Substituted by Act of Sederunt (Summary Applications, Statutory Applications and Appeals etc. Rules) Amendment (Adult Support and Protection (Scotland) Act 2007) 2008 (SSI 2008/111), r.3(1).
[185] Inserted by Act of Sederunt (Summary Applications, Statutory Applications and Appeals etc. Rules) Amendment (Adult Support and Protection (Scotland) Act 2007) 2008 (SSI 2008/111), r.2(1).

Act of Sederunt (Summary Applications etc. Rules) (SI 1999/929)

adult were a patient within the meaning of that Act and notwithstanding that the person neither is or was caring for the adult for the purposes of section 53(3) of that Act;
"power of attorney" includes a factory and commission;
"primary carer" means the person or organisation primarily engaged in caring for an adult;
"Public Guardian" shall be construed in accordance with section 6 of the 2000 Act; and
"welfare attorney" means a person on whom there has been conferred a power of attorney granted under section 16(1) of the 2000 Act.

Appointment of hearing
3.16.2 On an application or other proceedings being submitted under or in pursuance of the 2000 Act the sheriff shall—

(a) fix a hearing;
(b) order answers to be lodged (where he considers it appropriate to do so) within a period that he shall specify; and
(c) appoint service and intimation of the application or other proceedings.

[Place, and privacy, of any hearing
3.16.3 The sheriff may, where he considers it appropriate in all the circumstances, appoint that the hearing of an application or other proceedings shall take place—

(a) in a hospital, or any other place than the court building;
(b) in private][186]

Service of application
3.16.4—(1) Service of the application or other proceedings shall be made in Form 20 on—

(a) the adult;
(b) the nearest relative of the adult;
(c) the primary carer of the adult (if any);
[(ca) the named person of the adult (if any);][187]
(d) any guardian, continuing attorney or welfare attorney of the adult who has any power relating to the application or proceedings;
(e) the Public Guardian;
(ea) where appropriate, the Mental Welfare Commission;
(eb) where appropriate, the local authority; and
(f) any other person directed by the sheriff.

(2) Where the applicant is an individual person without legal representation service shall be effected by the sheriff clerk.
(3) Where the adult is in an authorised establishment the person effecting service shall not serve Form 20 on the adult under paragraph

---

[186] Substituted by Act of Sederunt (Ordinary Cause, Summary Application, Summary Cause and Small Claim Rules) Amendment (Miscellaneous) 2004 (SSI 2004/197), r.3(7).
[187] Inserted by Act of Sederunt (Summary Applications, Statutory Applications and Appeals etc. Rules) Amendment (Adult Support and Protection (Scotland) Act 2007) 2008 (SSI 2008/111), r.2(2).

(1)(a) but shall instead serve Forms 20 and 21, together with Form 22, on the managers of that authorised establishment by—

    (a) first class recorded delivery post; or
    (b) personal service by a sheriff officer.

(4) On receipt of Forms 20 and 21 in terms of paragraph (3) the managers of the authorised establishment shall, subject to rule 3.16.5—

    (a) deliver the notice in Form 20 to the adult; and
    (b) as soon as practicable thereafter complete and return to the sheriff clerk a certificate of such delivery in Form 22.

(5) Where the application or other proceeding follows on a remit under rule 3.16.9 the order for service of the application shall include an order for service on the Public Guardian or other party concerned.

(6) Where the application is for an intervention order or a guardianship order, copies of the reports lodged in accordance with section 57(3) of the 2000 Act (reports to be lodged in court along with application) shall be served along with Form 20, or Forms 20, 21 and 22 as the case may be.

Dispensing with service on adult
3.16.5—(1) Where, in relation to any application or proceeding under or in pursuance of the 2000 Act, two medical certificates are produced stating that intimation of the application or other proceeding, or notification of any interlocutor relating to such application or other proceeding, would be likely to pose a serious risk to the health of the adult the sheriff may dispense with such intimation or notification.

(2) Any medical certificates produced under paragraph (1) shall be prepared by medical practitioners independent of each other.

(3) In any case where the incapacity of the adult is by reason of mental disorder, one of the two medical practitioners must be a medical practitioner approved for the purposes of [section 22(4) of the 2003 Act][188] as having special experience in the diagnosis or treatment of mental disorder.

Hearing
3.16.6—(1) A hearing to determine any application or other proceeding shall take place within 28 days of the interlocutor fixing the hearing under rule 3.16.2 unless any person upon whom the application is to be served is outside Europe.

(2) At the hearing referred to in paragraph (1) the sheriff may determine the application or other proceeding or may order such further procedure as he thinks fit.

Prescribed forms of application
3.16.7—(1) An application submitted to the sheriff under or in pursuance of the 2000 Act, other than an appeal or remitted matter, shall be in Form 23.

(2) An appeal to the sheriff under or in pursuance of the 2000 Act shall be in Form 24.

---

[188] Substituted by Mental Health (Care and Treatment) (Scotland) Act 2003 (Modification of Subordinate Legislation) Order 2005 (SSI 2005/445), Sch.1.

Act of Sederunt (Summary Applications etc. Rules) (SI 1999/929)

Subsequent applications
3.16.8—(1) Unless otherwise prescribed in this Part or under the 2000 Act, any application or proceedings subsequent to an initial application or proceeding considered by the sheriff, including an application to renew an existing order, shall take the form of a minute lodged in the process.

(1A) Except where the sheriff otherwise directs, any such minute shall be lodged in accordance with, and regulated by, Chapter 14 of the Ordinary Cause Rules.

(2) Where any subsequent application or proceedings under paragraph (1) above are made to a court in another sheriffdom the sheriff clerk shall transmit the court process to the court dealing with the current application or proceeding.

(3) Transmission of the process in terms of paragraph (2) shall be made within 4 days of it being requested by the sheriff clerk of the court in which the current application or proceedings have been raised.

(4) Where the application is for renewal of a guardianship order, [a copy of any report lodged under section 60 of the 2000 Act][189] shall be served along with the minute.

[(5) Where the application is for renewal of a guardianship order, a copy shall be served on the local authority and, where it relates to the adult's personal welfare where incapacity is by reason of mental disorder, on the Mental Welfare Commission.][190]

Remit of applications by the Public Guardian etc.
3.16.9 Where an application is remitted to the sheriff by the Public Guardian or by any other party authorised to do so under the 2000 Act the party remitting the application shall, within 4 days of the decision to remit, transmit the papers relating to the application to the sheriff clerk of the court where the application is to be considered.

[Caution and Other Security][191]
3.16.10—(1) Where the sheriff requires a person authorised under an intervention order or any variation of an intervention order, or appointed as a guardian, to find caution he shall specify the amount and period within which caution is to be found in the interlocutor authorising or appointing the person or varying the order (as the case may be).

[(1A) The amount of caution specified by the sheriff in paragraph (1) may be calculated and expressed as a percentage of the value of the adult's estate.][192]

(2) The sheriff may, on application made by motion before the expiry of the period for finding caution and on cause shown, allow further time for finding caution in accordance with paragraph (1).

---

[189] Substituted by Act of Sederunt (Summary Applications, Statutory Applications and Appeals etc. Rules) Amendment (Adult Support and Protection (Scotland) Act 2007) 2008 (SSI 2008/111), r.3(2)(a).

[190] Inserted by Act of Sederunt (Summary Applications, Statutory Applications and Appeals etc. Rules) Amendment (Adult Support and Protection (Scotland) Act 2007) 2008 (SSI 2008/111), r.3(2)(b).

[191] Substituted by Act of Sederunt (Summary Applications, Statutory Applications and Appeals etc. Rules) Amendment (Adult Support and Protection (Scotland) Act 2007) 2008 (SSI 2008/111), r.4(2).

[192] Inserted by Act of Sederunt (Summary Applications, Statutory Applications and Appeals etc. Rules) Amendment (Adult Support and Protection (Scotland) Act 2007) 2008 (SSI 2008/111), r.4(1)(a).

(3) Caution shall be lodged with the Public Guardian.
(4) Where caution has been lodged to the satisfaction of the Public Guardian he shall notify the sheriff clerk.
(5) The sheriff may at any time while a requirement to find caution is in force—

- (a) increase the amount of, or require the person to find new, caution; or
- (b) authorise the amount of caution to be decreased.

[(6) Where the sheriff requires the person referred to in paragraph (1) to give security other than caution, the rules of Chapter 27 of the Ordinary Cause Rules shall apply with the necessary modifications.][193]

Appointment of interim guardian
3.16.11 An application under section 57(5) of the 2000 Act (appointment of interim guardian) may be made in the crave of the application for a guardianship order to which it relates or, if made after the submission of the application for a guardianship order, by motion in the process of that application.

Registration of intervention order or guardianship order relating to heritable property
3.16.12 Where an application for an intervention order or a guardianship order seeks to vest in the person authorised under the order, or the guardian, as the case may be, any right to deal with, convey or manage any interest in heritable property which is recorded or capable of being recorded in the General Register of Sasines or is registered or capable of being registered in the Land Register of Scotland, the applicant must specify the necessary details of the property in the application to enable it to be identified in the Register of Sasines or the Land Register of Scotland, as the case may be.

Non-compliance with decisions of guardians with welfare powers
3.16.13—(1) Where the court is required under section 70(3) of the 2000 Act to intimate an application for an order or warrant in relation to non-compliance with the decision of a guardian with welfare powers, the sheriff clerk shall effect intimation in Form 20 in accordance with paragraphs (2) and (3).
(2) Intimation shall be effected—

- (a) where the person is within Scotland, by first class recorded delivery post, or, in the event that intimation by first class recorded delivery post is unsuccessful, by personal service by a sheriff officer; or
- (b) where the person is furth of Scotland, in accordance with rule 2.12 (service on persons furth of Scotland).

(3) Such intimation shall include notice of the period within which any objection to the application shall be lodged.

---

[193] Inserted by Act of Sederunt (Summary Applications, Statutory Applications and Appeals etc. Rules) Amendment (Adult Support and Protection (Scotland) Act 2007) 2008 (SSI 2008/111), r.4(1)(b).

Act of Sederunt (Summary Applications etc. Rules) (SI 1999/929)

SCHEDULE

FORM 20

Rule 3.16.4(1)

FORM OF NOTICE OF AN APPLICATION UNDER THE ADULTS WITH INCAPACITY (SCOTLAND) ACT 2000

To *(insert name and address)*

Attached to this notice is a copy of an application for *(insert type of application)* under the Adults with Incapacity (Scotland) Act 2000.

The hearing will be held at (insert place) on (insert date) at (insert time)

You may appear personally at the hearing of this application.

In any event, if you are unable or do not wish to appear personally you may appoint a legal representative to appear on your behalf.

If you are uncertain as to what action to take you should consult a solicitor. You may be eligible for legal aid, and you can obtain information about legal aid from any solicitor. You may also obtain information from any Citizens Advice Bureau or other advice agency.

If you do not appear personally or by legal representative, the sheriff may consider the application in the absence of you or your legal representative.

(insert place and date)

(signed)

Sheriff Clerk

or

[P.Q.] Sheriff Officer

or

[X.Y.], Solicitor

Adults with Incapacity Legislation

FORM 21

Rule 3.16.4(3)

FORM OF NOTICE TO MANAGERS

To *(insert name and address of manager)*

A copy of an application made under the Adults with Incapacity (Scotland) Act 2000 and notice of hearing is sent with this notice.

1. You are requested to deliver it personally to (name of adult) and to explain the contents of it to him or her.

2. You are further requested to complete and return to the sheriff clerk in the enclosed envelope the certificate (Form 22) appended hereto before the date of the hearing.

(insert place and date) (signed)

Sheriff Clerk

or

[P.Q.], Sheriff Officer

or

[X.Y.], Solicitor

Act of Sederunt (Summary Applications etc. Rules) (SI 1999/929)

FORM 22

Rule 3.16.4(4)

FORM OF CERTIFICATE OF DELIVERY BY MANAGER

I, *(insert name and designation)*, certify that—

I have on *(insert date)* personally delivered to (name of adult) a copy of the application and the intimation of the hearing and have explained the contents to him/her.

Date *(insert date) (signed)*

Manager

(add designation and address)

Adults with Incapacity Legislation

FORM 23

Rule 3.16.7(1)

SUMMARY APPLICATION UNDER THE ADULTS WITH INCAPACITY (SCOTLAND) ACT 2000

SHERIFFDOM OF *(insert name of sheriffdom)*
AT *(insert place of Sheriff Court)*
[A.B.] *(design and state capacity in which the application is made)*, Pursuer

The applicant craves the court *(state here the specific order(s) sought by reference to the provisions in the Adults with Incapacity (Scotland) Act 2000.)*

STATEMENTS OF FACT
(State in numbered paragraphs the facts on which the application is made, including:
1. *The designation of the adult concerned (if other than the applicant).*
2. *The designation of:*

(a) *the adult's nearest relative;*
(b) *the adult's primary carer;*
[(ba) *the adult's named person;*][194]
(c) *any guardian, continuing attorney or welfare attorney of the adult; and*
(d) *any other person who may have an interest in the application.*

3. *The adult's place of habitual residence and/or the location of the property which is the subject of the application.)*

(insert place and date) (signed)

[A.B.], Pursuer or

[X.Y.], *(state designation and business address)*

Solicitor for the Pursuer
Note. This Form should not be used for appeals to the Sheriff. Appeals should be made in Form 24.

---

[194] Inserted by Act of Sederunt (Summary Applications, Statutory Applications and Appeals etc. Rules) Amendment (Adult Support and Protection (Scotland) Act 2007) 2008 (SSI 2008/111), r.2(3).

Act of Sederunt (Summary Applications etc. Rules) (SI 1999/929)

FORM 24

Rule 3.16.7(2)

APPEAL TO THE SHERIFF UNDER THE ADULTS WITH INCAPACITY (SCOTLAND) ACT 2000

SHERIFFDOM OF *(insert name of sheriffdom)*
AT *(insert place of Sheriff Court)*
[A.B.] *(design and state capacity in which the appeal is being made)*, Pursuer

This appeal is made in respect of *(state here the decision concerned, the date on which it was intimated to the pursuer, and refer to the relevant provisions in the Adults with Incapacity (Scotland) Act 2000).*

(State here, in numbered paragraphs:

1. The designation of the adult concerned (if other than the applicant).

2. The designation of:

    (a) the adult's nearest relative;
    (b) the adult's primary carer;
  [(ba) the adult's named person;][195]
    (c) any guardian, continuing attorney or welfare attorney of the adult; and
    (d) any other person who may have an interest in the application.

3. The adult's place of habitual residence and/or the location of the property which is the subject of the application.)

The pursuer appeals against the decision on the following grounds *(state here in separate paragraphs the grounds on which the appeal is made)*.

The pursuer craves the court *(state here orders sought in respect of appeal)*.

(insert place and date) *(signed)*

[A.B.], Pursuer

or

[X.Y.], *(state designation and business address)*

Solicitor for the Pursuer

---

[195] Inserted by Act of Sederunt (Summary Applications, Statutory Applications and Appeals etc. Rules) Amendment (Adult Support and Protection (Scotland) Act 2007) 2008 (SSI 2008/111), r.2(3).

ADULTS WITH INCAPACITY (EVIDENCE IN RELATION TO DISPENSING WITH INTIMATION OR NOTIFICATION) (SCOTLAND) REGULATIONS

(SSI 2001/79)

Made	7th March 2002
Laid before the Scottish Parliament	8th March 2002
Coming into force	2nd April 2002

The Scottish Ministers, in exercise of the powers conferred by sections 7(1)(d) and 86(2) of the Adults with Incapacity (Scotland) Act 2000 and of all other powers enabling them in that behalf, hereby make the following Regulations:

Citation and commencement
1. These Regulations may be cited as the Adults with Incapacity (Evidence in Relation to Dispensing with Intimation or Notification) (Scotland) Regulations 2001 and shall come into force on 2nd April 2001.

Evidence to be taken into account
2.—(1) For the purposes of section 11(2) of the Adults with Incapacity (Scotland) Act 2000, the evidence which the Public Guardian shall take into account when deciding whether to dispense with intimation or notification to the adult shall be two medical certificates stating that intimation or notification could be likely to pose a serious risk to the health of the adult.

(2) Those medical certificates shall be prepared by medical practitioners independent of each other.

(3) In any case where the incapacity of the adult is by reason of mental disorder, one of the two medical practitioners must be a medical practitioner approved for the purposes of [section 22(4) of the Mental Health (Care and Treatment) (Scotland) Act 2003][196] as having special experience in the diagnosis or treatment of mental disorder.

---

[196] Words substituted by Mental Health (Care and Treatment) (Scotland) Act 2003 (Modification of Subordinate Legislation) Order 2005, SSI 2005/445, Sch.1, para.32.

ADULTS WITH INCAPACITY (SUPERVISION OF WELFARE GUARDIANS ETC. BY LOCAL AUTHORITIES) (SCOTLAND) REGULATIONS

(SSI 2002/95)

Made   5th March 2002
Laid before the Scottish Parliament   7th March 2002
Coming into force   1st April 2002

The Scottish Ministers, in exercise of the powers conferred by sections 10(3)(a) and (b)(i) and 86(2) of the Adults with Incapacity (Scotland) Act 2000 and of all other powers enabling them in that behalf, hereby make the following Regulations:

Citation and commencement
1. These Regulations may be cited as the Adults with Incapacity (Supervision of Welfare Guardians etc. by Local Authorities) (Scotland) Regulations 2002 and shall come into force on 1st April 2002.

Duties of local authority
2.—(1) Where a guardian with functions in relation to the personal welfare of an adult has been appointed for a period of one year or more the local authority shall arrange for—

(a) that adult to be visited on behalf of the local authority from time to time but in any case within three months of the guardianship order being granted and thereafter at intervals of not more than [six][197] months; and
(b) that guardian (except where the guardian is the chief social work officer) to be visited on behalf of the local authority from time to time but in any case [within three months of the guardianship order being granted and thereafter at intervals of not more than six months][198].

(2) Where that guardian has been appointed for a period of less than one year the local authority shall arrange for the adult and guardian to be visited on behalf of the local authority—

(a) within fourteen days before or after the midpoint of that period of appointment; and
(b) within fourteen days before the end of that period of appointment.

(3) Where the local authority is supervising a person authorised under an intervention order, it shall arrange for the adult who is the subject of the intervention order, and where appropriate the person authorised under the intervention order, to be visited on behalf of the local authority as often as required by the sheriff and, where no such requirement has been specified,

---

[197] Substituted by Adults with Incapacity (Supervision of Welfare Guardians etc. by Local Authorities) (Scotland) Amendment Regulations 2005 (SSI 2005/630), reg.2(2)(a).
[198] Substituted by Adults with Incapacity (Supervision of Welfare Guardians etc. by Local Authorities) (Scotland) Amendment Regulations 2005 (SSI 2005/630), reg.2(2)(b).

at intervals of not more than one month for the period of time fixed by the sheriff for supervision by the local authority.

(4) Where the local authority considers it appropriate, any visit to the adult in accordance with this regulation may take place at the same time as a visit to the guardian or person authorised under an intervention order as the case may be.

(5) Where the circumstances of an adult are such that it is not possible for a local authority to visit that adult within the time periods specified in this regulation, that local authority shall visit the adult at a time as close to the time when the visit should have taken place, as the adult's circumstances will allow.

Information to be provided
3. For the purpose of enabling the local authority to carry out its supervisory functions—

(a) a guardian shall from time to time provide the local authority with any reports or other information about the personal welfare of the adult, or the exercise by that guardian of that guardian's powers in relation to the personal welfare of the adult, as the local authority may reasonably require; and
(b) a person authorised under an intervention order shall from time to time provide the local authority with any reports or other information about the personal welfare of the adult, or the exercise by that person of that person's functions, as the local authority may reasonably require.

Revocation
4. Regulations 4, 5, 6 and 7 of the Mental Health (Specified Treatments, Guardianship Duties etc.) (Scotland) Regulations 1984 are hereby revoked.

ADULTS WITH INCAPACITY (REPORTS IN RELATION TO GUARDIANSHIP AND INTERVENTION ORDERS) (SCOTLAND) REGULATIONS

(SSI 2002/96)

Made	5th March 2002
Laid before the Scottish Parliament	7th March 2002
Coming into force	1st April 2002

The Scottish Ministers, in exercise of the powers conferred by sections 57(3) and 86(2) of the Adults with Incapacity (Scotland) Act 2000 and of all other powers enabling them in that behalf, hereby make the following Regulations:

Citation and commencement
1. These Regulations may be cited as the Adults with Incapacity (Reports in Relation to Guardianship and Intervention Orders) (Scotland) Regulations 2002 and shall come into force on 1st April 2002.

Interpretation
2. Any reference in these Regulations—

(a) to a numbered section is a reference to the section bearing that number in the Adults with Incapacity (Scotland) Act 2000; and
(b) to a numbered Schedule is a reference to the Schedule bearing that number in these Regulations.

Report from medical practitioner
3. The reports by medical practitioners under section 57(3)(a)[, or, as the case may be, section 60(3)(a),][199] in relation to an application for—

(a) a guardianship order;
(b) renewal of a guardianship order; or
(c) an intervention order,

shall be in the form set out in Schedule 1.

Report from mental health officer
4. A report by the mental health officer under section 57(3)(b) [in respect of applications for a category (a) or (c) order below, or by a mental health officer under section 60(3)(b) in respect of an application for a category (b) order below][200]—

(a) a guardianship order shall be in the form set out in Schedule 2;
(b) renewal of a guardianship order shall be in the form set out in Schedule 3; and
(c) an intervention order shall be in the form set out in Schedule 4.

---

[199] Words inserted by Adults with Incapacity (Reports in Relation to Guardianship and Intervention Orders) (Scotland) Amendment Regulations 2008 (SSI 2008/55), reg 2(2).
[200] Words substituted by Adults with Incapacity (Reports in Relation to Guardianship and Intervention Orders) (Scotland) Amendment Regulations 2008 (SSI 2008/55), reg 2(3).

Report from chief social work officer
5. A report by the chief social work officer under section 57(3)(b) [in respect of applications for a category (a) or (c) order below, or under section 60(3)(b) in respect of an application for a category (b) order below][201]—

    (a) a guardianship order shall be in the form set out in Schedule 5;
    (b) renewal of a guardianship order shall be in the form set out in Schedule 6; and
    (c) an intervention order shall be in the form set out in Schedule 7.

Report from person with sufficient knowledge
6. A report, by a person with sufficient knowledge as to the matters referred to in section 57(3)(b)(i) and (ii), under section 57(3)(c) [in respect of applications for a category (a) or (c) order below, or by the Public Guardian under section 60(3)(c) in respect of an application for a category (b) order below][202]—

    (a) a guardianship order shall be in the form set out in Schedule 8;
    (b) renewal of a guardianship order shall be in the form set out in Schedule 9; and
    (c) an intervention order shall be in the form set out in Schedule 10.

---

[201] Words substituted by Adults with Incapacity (Reports in Relation to Guardianship and Intervention Orders) (Scotland) Amendment Regulations 2008 (SSI 2008/55), reg 2(4).
[202] Words substituted by Adults with Incapacity (Reports in Relation to Guardianship and Intervention Orders) (Scotland) Amendment Regulations 2008 (SSI 2008/55), reg 2(5).

A with I (Guardianship and Intervention Orders) (S) Regs (SSI 2002/96)

SCHEDULE 1

Regulation 3

Report of incapacity to accompany
application for guardianship*
application for renewal of guardianship*
application for intervention order*

AWI[1]
ADULTS WITH INCAPACITY
(SCOTLAND) ACT 2000
[sections 57(3)(a) and 60(3)(a)][189]

Note: fill in Part A1 where the adult is examined in Scotland and Part A2 where the adult is examined outwith Scotland.[204]

PART A1   DETAILS OF REPORT WRITER AND ADULT FOR EXAMINATIONS IN SCOTLAND

I [   ] (name)

being a medical practitioner with the following professional address:

[   ] (state full postal address for contact)

Telephone [   ]   E-mail [   ]

[*complete the following box if applicable*[(a)] *otherwise, delete*]

and being approved by the [   ] Health Board/by the State Hospital's Board (*please delete one*)

for the purposes of section 22 of the Mental Health (Care and Treatment) (Scotland) Act 2003 as having special experience in the diagnosis and treatment of mental disorder,

hereby confirm that I examined and assessed the following adult ("the adult")

Name [   ]

Residing at [   ] (state full postal address)

Date of birth [   ]

On [   ] (give date of examination and assessment)
OR

* delete the two which do not apply
(a) Where the incapacity is by reason of mental disorder, one of the medical practitioners must be approved for the purposes of section 22 of the 2003 Act as having special experience in the diagnosis and treatment of mental disorder (section 57(6B) of the Act).

---

[203] Words substituted by Adults with Incapacity (Reports in Relation to Guardianship and Intervention Orders) (Scotland) Amendment Regulations 2008 (SSI 2008/55), reg 2(6)(a).
[204] Parts A1 and A2 substituted in place of Part A by Adults with Incapacity (Reports in Relation to Guardianship and Intervention Orders) (Scotland) Amendment Regulations 2008 (SSI 2008/55), reg 2(6)(b).

Adults with Incapacity Legislation

Regulation 3

SCHEDULE 1

PART A2 DETAILS OF REPORT WRITER AND ADULT FOR EXAMINATIONS OUTWITH SCOTLAND

I [_____] (name)

being a medical practitioner with the following professional address:

[_____] (state full postal address for contact)

Telephone [_____] E-mail [_____]

having the following qualification and special experience in relation to the treatment of mental disorder

[_____]

and having consulted the Mental Welfare Commission[a] about this report [ ] (*please tick box*)

hereby confirm that I examined and assessed the following adult ("the adult")

Name [_____]

Residing at [_____] (state full postal address)

Date of birth [_____]

On [_____] (give date of examination and assessment)

At [_____] (insert place and address of assessment)

---

[a] Postal address: The Mental Health Welfare Commission, Floor K, Argyle House, 3 Lady Lawson Street, Edinburgh, EH3 9SH. Telephone: 0131 222 6111. Website: www.mwcscot.org.uk

A with I (Guardianship and Intervention Orders) (S) Regs (SSI 2002/96)

Regulation 3
SCHEDULE 1

PART B   PURPOSE OF EXAMINATION AND ASSESSMENT

The examination and assessment was in connection with a proposed application for (tick whichever applies)

A guardianship order /renewal of guardianship order /an intervention order
a)   with power over personal welfare

b)   with power over property and/or financial affairs

c)   with power over personal welfare, property and/or financial affairs.

Name of applicant or person requesting report

Name(s) of person or persons nominated in application (if known)

PART C   FINDINGS OF EXAMINATION AND ASSESSMENT

On the basis of my examination and assessment I am of the opinion that the adult named in Part A has

(tick box for whichever of the following applies and add comments on nature)

a) Mental disorder[1]

Nature

And/or

b) Inability to communicate because of physical disability

Nature

---

* delete the two which do not apply

[[1]mental disorder has the meaning given to it in section 328 of the Mental Health (Care and Treatment) (Scotland) Act 2003, namely that it means any mental illness; personality disorder or learning disability however caused or manifested; but an adult is not mentally disordered by reason only of sexual orientation; sexual deviancy; transsexualism; transvestism; dependence on, or use of, alcohol or drugs, behaviour that causes, or is likely to cause, harassment, alarm or distress to any other person; or acting as no prudent person would act.][205]

---

[205] Footnote text in form substituted by Adults with Incapacity (Reports in Relation to Guardianship and Intervention Orders) (Scotland) Amendment Regulations 2008 (SSI 2008/55), reg 2(6)(c).

Adults with Incapacity Legislation

SCHEDULE 1
Regulation 3

I am of the opinion that the condition mentioned in Part C has impaired the capacity of the adult named in Part A to make decisions about or to act to safeguard or promote his/her interests in his/her property, financial affairs or personal welfare in relation to the matters covered in the proposed application. The reason for my opinion is given below.

Please indicate the findings of your examination and assessment, so far as they relate to the adult's capacity in relation to the matters which are the subject of the application.

Please indicate the likely duration of the incapacity

Please indicate the extent to which you have been able to communicate with the adult,

Please indicate the extent to which you have been able to consult the nearest relative, primary carer, [named person][206] and anyone else having an interest in, or knowledge of, the adult.

---

[206] Words inserted by Adults with Incapacity (Reports in Relation to Guardianship and Intervention Orders) (Scotland) Amendment Regulations 2008 (SSI 2008/55), reg 2(6)(d).

A with I (Guardianship and Intervention Orders) (S) Regs (SSI 2002/96)

[*Note: Schedules 2–7 have not been reproduced here.*]

Regulation 6(a)

SCHEDULE 8

Report to accompany application for guardianship relating to property and financial affairs

AW1 [8]
ADULTS WITH INCAPACITY (SCOTLAND) ACT 2000
Section 57(3)(c)

PART A   **AUTHOR OF THE REPORT**

I []

am a person with sufficient knowledge to make this report, because of my position as:

[]

(Give contact address)   Address []

Tel No []   E-mail []

PART B   **THE ADULT**

On [] (Give date of interview and assessment of the adult

I interviewed and assessed the adult who is the subject of this application

[] (name)

(Give full name, address and date of birth of the adult, as on the application) of [] (address)

[] (DOB)

PART C   **THE APPLICANT**

This report is written in relation to the application by

(Name of applicant) []

Adults with Incapacity Legislation

SCHEDULE 8

Regulation 6(a)

PART D

Please state your opinion in terms of the general principles as set out in section (1) of the Act where possible

APPROPRIATENESS OF THE ORDER APPLIED FOR

I have read the application, have taken note of the powers sought and the period of guardianship being applied for. My opinion as to the appropriateness of the order sought is as follows:-

1. Will the proposed order (a) benefit the adult and (b) will the benefit be unable to be reasonably achieved without the order?

(a) Describe how the proposed order will benefit the adult

(b) Describe how the benefit will be unable to be reasonably achieved without the order.

2. Whether the proposed order is the least restrictive opinion in relation to the freedom of the adult, consistent with the propose of the order.

(Describe any alternatives considered. These may include a measure outwith the 2000 Act, a different measure under the 2000 Act or an order containing less restrictive powers. State whether you support the terms of the order sought or support it subject to amendment.)

A with I (Guardianship and Intervention Orders) (S) Regs (SSI 2002/96)

SCHEDULE 8

Regulation 6(a)

3 | What are the past and present wishes and feelings of the adult?

State
(a) the past and present wishes and feelings of the adult about the order sought and the powers requested, so far as you have been able to ascertain them.

(b) If you have not been able to ascertain the adult's wishes and feelings, please explain the barriers to this.

(c) describe the efforts you made to overcome these barriers.

Adults with Incapacity Legislation

SCHEDULE 8

Regulation 6(a)

| 4 | What are the views of the nearest relative of the adult? |

Name:

Relationship:

State

(a) the views of the nearest relative about the order sought if you have obtained these. Note this section relates to the relative's own views. Information which the relative wishes to provide about the adult's wishes and feelings should be included (and attributed) in section 3(a).

(b) Do you agree with these views?

(c) If you have not obtained these views, why was it not reasonable or practicable to do so?
Note: the nearest relative should not be consulted where an order to that effect has been made under section 4 of the Act.

A with I (Guardianship and Intervention Orders) (S) Regs (SSI 2002/96)

SCHEDULE 8
Regulation 6(a)

5 | What are the views of the primary carer of the adult?

Name:

Relationship:

State
(a) the views of the primary carer about the order sought if you have obtained these.

(b) do you agree with these views?

(c) If you have not obtained these views, why was it not reasonable or practicable to do so?

Adults with Incapacity Legislation

Regulation 6(a)
SCHEDULE 8

| 5A[207] | What are the views of the adult's named person? |

Name:

Relationship:

State
(a) the views of the adult's named person about the order sought if you have obtained these.

(b) do you agree with these views?

(c) If you have not obtained these views, why was it not reasonable or practicable to do so?

---

[207] Paragraph 5A inserted by Adults with Incapacity (Reports in Relation to Guardianship and Intervention Orders) (Scotland) Amendment Regulations SSI 2008/55, reg 2(7).

A with I (Guardianship and Intervention Orders) (S) Regs (SSI 2002/96)

Regulation 6(a)

SCHEDULE 8

Complete if applicable

6 | What are the views of any guardian, continuing attorney or welfare attorney?

Name:

Appointment (e.g. financial guardian:)

State
(a) the views of the such a person about the order sought if you have obtained these.

(b) Do you agree with these views?

(c) If you have not obtained these views, why was it not reasonable or practicable to do so? (Continue on a separate sheet if there is more than one such person).

Adults with Incapacity Legislation

SCHEDULE 8

Regulation 6(a)

Complete if applicable

7 | What are the views of any other relevant person which have been made known to you?

Name:

Connection to adult:

State

(a) the views of any other relevant person which have been made known to you and which are relevant to the order sought.

(b) Do you agree with these views? (Continue on a separate sheet if there is more than one such person).

8 | Are there any other matters which seem to you to be relevant?

A with I (Guardianship and Intervention Orders) (S) Regs (SSI 2002/96)

Regulation 6(a)

SCHEDULE 8

PART E   PROPOSED GUARDIAN'S SUITABILITY

(If there is more than one proposed guardian with powers over property and/or financial affairs please duplicate Part E and complete for each proposed guardian.)

Name of proposed guardian:

Relationship to adult:

Sections 59(3) & (4) of the Act require the sheriff to consider certain factors before appointing an individual as a guardian; comment on the suitability of the person nominated under the headings in Part E where possible. Refer as appropriate to discussion with him or her.

My opinion as to the suitability of the person nominated is as follows:-

1. Awareness of the adult's circumstances and conditions and of the needs arising from such circumstances and conditions.

2. Awareness of the functions of a guardian.

3. | Accessibility to adult and primary carer. |

| |

4. | Ability to carry out the functions of a guardian with personal welfare powers. |

| |

5. | Any likely conflict of interest between the guardian and the adult. (NB: Being a close relative or living in the same household as the adult does *not* on its own count as conflict of interest.) |

| |

6. | Any undue concentration of power which is likely to arise in the proposed guardian over the adult. (NB: Being a close relative or living in the same household as the adult does *not* on its own count as undue concentration of power.) |

| |

A with I (Guardianship and Intervention Orders) (S) Regs (SSI 2002/96)

SCHEDULE 8
Regulation 6(a)

7. Any adverse effects which the appointment of the proposed guardian would have on the interests of the adult.

8. Any other matters which seem to you to be relevant.

Adults with Incapacity Legislation

SCHEDULE 8

Regulation 6(a)

PART F   CONCLUSION

My general conclusions on the appropriateness of the order sought and the suitability of the proposed guardian(s) are as follows:

[   ]

PART G: DECLARATION OF INTEREST

Delete (a) or (b)   (a) I am not related to the adult

(b) I am related to the adult being his /her (state relationship)

[   ]

AND

Delete (c) or (d)   (c) I have no pecuniary interest in the appointment of a guardian or guardians

(d) I have a pecuniary interest in the appointment of a guardian or guardians

The nature and extent of that interest is

[   ]

Signed[208]   [   ]

Dated   [   ]

---

[208] Please note that the application and accompanying reports will be served on interested parties.

A with I (Guardianship and Intervention Orders) (S) Regs (SSI 2002/96)

SCHEDULE 9[209]

Regulation 6(b)

Public Guardian's report to accompany
application for renewal of guardianship relating to property or financial affairs

AW1 [9]
ADULTS WITH INCAPACITY
(SCOTLAND) ACT 2000
Section 60(3)(c)

I _____ (name)

of the Office of the Public Guardian, Hadrian House, Callendar Business Park, Callendar Road, Falkirk, FK1 1XR,

Tel No _____ E-mail _____

having considered the guardianship by _____ (insert name of guardian)

in relation to _____ (insert name of adult)

(state opinion as to (1) the applicant's conduct as the guardian and (2) the suitability of the applicant continuing as guardian)

Signed _____

Dated _____

---

[209] Schedule 9 substituted by Adults with Incapacity (Reports in Relation to Guardianship and Intervention Orders) (Scotland) Amendment Regulations 2008 (SSI 2008/55), reg 2(10).

Adults with Incapacity Legislation

SCHEDULE 10
Regulation 6(c)

Report to accompany application for intervention order relating to property and financial affairs

AW1 [10]
ADULTS WITH INCAPACITY (SCOTLAND) ACT 2000
Section 57(3)(c)

PART A   **AUTHOR OF THE REPORT**

I [ ]

am a person with sufficient knowledge to make this report because of my position as:

[ ]

(Give contact address)   Address [ ]

Tel No [ ]   E-mail [ ]

PART B   **THE ADULT**

On [ ] (Give date of interview and assessment of the adult

I interviewed and assessed the adult who is the subject of this application

[ ] (name)

(Give full name, address and date of birth of the adult, as on the application) of [ ] (address)

[ ] (DOB)

PART C   **THE APPLICANT**

This report is written in relation to the application by

(Name of applicant) [ ]

A with I (Guardianship and Intervention Orders) (S) Regs (SSI 2002/96)

SCHEDULE 10

Regulation 6(c)

PART D

Please state your opinion in terms of the general principles as set out in section (1) of the Act where possible

APPROPRIATENESS OF THE ORDER APPLIED FOR

I have read the application, have taken note of the powers sought and the period being applied for (if applicable). My opinion as to the appropriateness of the order sought is as follows:-

1 | Will the proposed order (a) benefit the adult and (b) will the benefit be unable to be reasonably achieved without the order?

(a) Describe how the proposed order will benefit the adult.

(b) Describe how the benefit will be unable to be reasonably achieved without the order.

2 | Whether the proposed order is the least restrictive opinion in relation to the freedom of the adult, consistent with the propose of the order.

(Describe any alternatives considered. These may include a measure outwith the 2000 Act, a different measure under the 2000 Act or an order containing less restrictive powers. State whether you support the terms of the order sought or support it subject to amendment.)

Adults with Incapacity Legislation

SCHEDULE 10

Regulation 6(c)

3 | What are the past and present wishes and feelings of the adult?

State
(a) the past and present wishes and feelings of the adult about the order sought and the powers requested, so far as you have been able to ascertain them.

(b) If you have not been able to ascertain the adult's wishes and feelings, please explain the barriers to this.

(c) describe the efforts you made to overcome these barriers.

A with I (Guardianship and Intervention Orders) (S) Regs (SSI 2002/96)

Regulation 6(c)

SCHEDULE 10

| 4 | What are the views of the nearest relative of the adult? |

Name:

Relationship:

State

(a) the views of the nearest relative about the order sought if you have obtained these. Note this section relates to the relative's own views. Information which the relative wishes to provide about the adult's wishes and feelings should be included (and attributed) in section 3(a).

(b) Do you agree with these views?

(c) If you have not obtained these views, why was it not reasonable or practicable to do so?
Note: the nearest relative should not be consulted where an order to that effect has been made under section 4 of the Act.

Adults with Incapacity Legislation

Regulation 6(c)

SCHEDULE 10

| 5 | What are the views of the primary carer of the adult? |

Name:

Relationship:

State
(a) the views of the primary carer about the order sought if you have obtained these.

(b) do you agree with these views?

(c) If you have not obtained these views, why was it not reasonable or practicable to do so?

A with I (Guardianship and Intervention Orders) (S) Regs (SSI 2002/96)

SCHEDULE 10
Regulation 6(c)

5A[210] | What are the views of the adult's named person?

Name:

Relationship:

State

(a) the views of the adult's named person about the order sought if you have obtained these.

(b) do you agree with these views?

(c) If you have not obtained these views, why was it not reasonable or practicable to do so?

---

[210] Para 5A inserted by Adults with Incapacity (Reports in Relation to Guardianship and Intervention Orders) (Scotland) Amendment Regulations SSI 2008/55, reg 2(7).

Adults with Incapacity Legislation

Regulation 6(c)

SCHEDULE 10

Complete if applicable

6 | What are the views of any guardian, continuing attorney or welfare attorney?

Name:

Appointment (e.g. financial guardian:)

State
(a) the views of the such a person about the order sought if you have obtained these.

(b) Do you agree with these views?

(c) If you have not obtained these views, why was it not reasonable or practicable to do so? (Continue on a separate sheet if there is more than one such person).

A with I (Guardianship and Intervention Orders) (S) Regs (SSI 2002/96)

SCHEDULE 10

Regulation 6(c)

Complete if applicable

7 | What are the views of any other relevant person which have been made known to you?

Name:

Connection to adult:

State

(a) the views of any other relevant person which have been made known to you and which are relevant to the order sought.

(b) Do you agree with these views? (Continue on a separate sheet if there is more than one such person).

8 | Are there any other matters which seem to you to be relevant?

Adults with Incapacity Legislation

Regulation 6(c)

SCHEDULE 10

PART E   **SUITABILITY OF PERSON NOMINATED TO BE AUTHORISED UNDER AN INTERVENTION ORDER**

(Complete in all cases where under section 53(5)(b) a person is nominated in the application to take action or make a decision, including those where the person nominated is an officer of the local authority.)

Name of nominee:

Relationship to adult:

Sections 59(3) & (4) of the Act require the sheriff to consider certain factors before appointing an individual as a guardian; These provide useful guidance as to what information should be contained in the report on the suitability of a person named in an application for an intervention order. Please therefore comment on the suitability of the person nominated under the headings in Part E where possible. Refer as appropriate to discussion with him or her.

My opinion as to the suitability of the person nominated is as follows:-

1. Awareness of the adult's circumstances and conditions and of the needs arising from such circumstances and conditions.

2. Awareness of the functions of a person authorised under an intervention order.

A with I (Guardianship and Intervention Orders) (S) Regs (SSI 2002/96)

3. | Accessibility to adult and primary carer. |

4. | Ability to carry out the functions of a person authorised under an intervention order with power over property and/or financial powers. |

5. | Any likely conflict of interest between the person nominated and the adult. (NB: Being a close relative or living in the same household as the adult does *not* on its own count as conflict of interest.) |

6. | Any undue concentration of power which is likely to arise in the person nominated over the adult. (NB: Being a close relative or living in the same household as the adult does *not* on its own count as undue concentration of power.) |

Adults with Incapacity Legislation

Regulation 6(c)

SCHEDULE 10

7. Any adverse effects which the appointment of the person nominated would have on the interests of the adult.

8. Any other matters which seem to you to be relevant.

A with I (Guardianship and Intervention Orders) (S) Regs (SSI 2002/96)

SCHEDULE 10

Regulation 6(c)

PART F   CONCLUSION

My general conclusions on the appropriateness of the order sought and the suitability of the person nominated (if any) are as follows:

[ ]

PART G: DECLARATION OF INTEREST

Delete (a) or (b)   (a) I am not related to the adult

(b) I am related to the adult being his /her (state relationship)

[ ]

AND

Delete (c) or (d)   (c) I have no pecuniary interest in the order sought

(d) I have a pecuniary interest in the order sought

The nature and extent of that interest is

[ ]

Signed[211]   [ ]

Dated   [ ]

---

[211] Please note that the application and accompanying reports will be served on interested parties.

THE ADULTS WITH INCAPACITY (RECALL OF GUARDIANS' POWERS) (SCOTLAND) REGULATIONS 2002

(SSI 2002/97)

Made	*5th March 2002*
Laid before the Scottish Parliament	*7th March 2002*
Coming into force	*1st April 2002*

The Scottish Ministers, in exercise of the powers conferred by sections 73(5), (7) and (10) and 86(2) of the Adults with Incapacity (Scotland) Act 2000 and of all other powers enabling them in that behalf, hereby make the following Regulations:

Citation and commencement
1. These Regulations may be cited as the Adults with Incapacity (Recall of Guardians' Powers) (Scotland) Regulations 2002 and shall come into force on 1st April 2002.

Interpretation
2 Any reference in these Regulations—

(a) to a numbered section is a reference to the section bearing that number in the Adults with Incapacity (Scotland) Act 2000; and
(b) to a numbered Schedule is a reference to the Schedule bearing that number in these Regulations.

Applications for recall
3. An application under section 73(3) for recall of a guardian's powers—

(a) by the Mental Welfare Commission shall be in the form set out in Schedule 1; or
(b) by the local authority shall be in the form set out in Schedule 2,

and, where the person making the application considers that the adult is no longer incapable, shall be accompanied by a medical report in the form set out in Schedule 3.

Intimation of application to recall or intention to recall by the Mental Welfare Commission
4. An intimation by the Mental Welfare Commission under section 73(5) of—

(a) an application for recall of a guardian's powers; or
(b) their intention at their own instance to recall the powers of a guardian,

shall be in the form set out in Schedule 4.

A with I (Recall of Guardians' Powers) (S) Regs (SSI 2002/97)

Intimation of application to recall or intention to recall by the local authority
5. An intimation by the local authority under section 73(5) of—

(a) an application for recall of a guardian's powers; or
(b) its intention at its own instance to recall the powers of a guardian,

shall be in the form set out in Schedule 5.

Period for objection to recall
6. A person may object under section 73(5) to the recall of a guardian's powers within 21 days of receipt of intimation of the application for recall, or intention to recall, by the Mental Welfare Commission or local authority, as the case may be.

Intimation of a decision by the Mental Welfare Commission to refuse recall
7. Where the Mental Welfare Commission proposes to refuse an application for recall under section 73(7), the intimation of that decision shall be in the form set out in Schedule 6.

Intimation of a decision by the local authority to refuse recall
8. Where the local authority proposes to refuse an application for recall under section 73(7), the intimation of that decision shall be in the form set out in Schedule 7.

Period for objection to decision as to recall
9. A person may object under section 73(7) to the decision by the Mental Welfare Commission or local authority, as the case may be, to refuse an application for recall of a guardian's powers within 21 days of receipt of intimation of that decision.

Form for recording decision by the Mental Welfare Commission
10. A decision by the Mental Welfare Commission to—

(a) recall the powers of a guardian under section 73(6);
(b) refuse an application to recall such powers; or
(c) remit, or not remit, the decision on recall to the sheriff under section 73(8), shall be in the form set out in Schedule 8.

Form for recording decision by the local authority
11. A decision by the local authority to—

(a) recall the powers of a guardian under section 73(6);
(b) refuse an application to recall such powers; or
(c) remit, or not remit, the decision on recall to the sheriff under section 73(8),

shall be in the form set out in Schedule 9.

Notification of decisions
12.—(1) Where the Mental Welfare Commission decides to recall the powers of a guardian they shall send a copy of the form provided for at regulation 10 above to the applicant, the local authority and the Public Guardian.

(2) Where the local authority decides to recall the powers of a guardian it shall send a copy of the form provided for at regulation 11 above to the applicant, the Mental Welfare Commission and the Public Guardian.

A with I (Recall of Guardians' Powers) (S) Regs (SSI 2002/97)

SCHEDULE 1

Regulation 3(a)

Application to Mental Welfare Commission for recall of powers of a guardian relating to personal welfare

AWI[11]
ADULTS WITH INCAPACITY (SCOTLAND) ACT 2000
Section 73(3)

PART A   PERSON MAKING THE APPLICATION

(Give your full name and name of local authority for whom you are acting in this case if applicable or provide details of your interest in the personal welfare of the adult.)

Name
Local authority /statement of interest

Address

Post Code

Tel No

E-mail

PART B   THE ADULT

This application is for recall of the powers of a guardian/guardians relating to the personal welfare of:

☐ (name)

of

(Give full name, address and date of birth of the adult or insert "as above" if adult is person making the application)

☐ (address including postcode)

☐ (DOB)

[*Note: The Mental Welfare Commission may not be asked to recall welfare powers other than those granted in cases where the adult's incapacity is by reason of, or reasons which include, mental disorder.*][212]

---

[212] Words inserted by Adults with Incapacity (Recall of Guardians' Powers) (Scotland) Amendment Regulations SSI 2008/53, reg 2(2)(a).

Adults with Incapacity Legislation

SCHEDULE 1

Regulation 3(a)

PART C DETAILS OF GUARDIANSHIP

(Insert date, court and court case number if known)	The guardianship order currently in force to which this application relates was made on: Court: Court case number:
(Insert name and address)	The guardianship order appointed the following person(s) as guardian(s) with powers relating to personal welfare: Name: Address: Post Code: Tel no: Fax No: e-mail address: **Note: If available please provide a copy of the guardianship order**

Where the chief social work officer was appointed guardian, the officer responsible under section 64(9) of the Act to carry out the functions and duties of guardian is:

(Insert name and contact details or delete as applicable)	Name: Address: Post Code: Tel no: Fax No: e-mail address:

The guardianship order also appointed the following person(s) as guardian(s) with powers relating to property or financial affairs:

(Insert details or delete as applicable)	Name(s): Address(es): Post Code Tel no: Fax No: e-mail address:

A with I (Recall of Guardians' Powers) (S) Regs (SSI 2002/97)

Regulation 3(a)

SCHEDULE 1

PART D GROUNDS ON WHICH RECALL IS SOUGHT

(Delete (a) or (b), unless both apply.)	I apply for the powers relating to personal welfare in the order described in Part C above to be recalled because:
	(a) the grounds for appointment of a guardian with such powers are no longer fulfilled (this could relate to either the adult's capacity or the adult's needs).
NB: the applicant must ensure that the doctor providing such a report is informed of the powers in the order.	(Explain why this is the case and, if applicable, attach a report by a medical practitioner stating that the adult is no longer incapable in relation to decisions about, or of acting to safeguard or promote his interests in his/her personal welfare, in relation to the matters covered in the guardianship order.)
(Describe alternatives proposed)	(b) the interests of the adult in his/her personal welfare can be satisfactorily safeguarded or promoted otherwise than by guardianship. (Describe the alternative means by which the adult's interests are to be safeguarded or promoted.)

Adults with Incapacity Legislation

Regulation 3(a)

SCHEDULE 1

PART E CONSULTATION

In making the application, I have consulted the following persons:

1. | the adult |

(State the past and present wishes and feelings of the adult about the proposed recall of guardianship, so far as you have been able to ascertain them. If you have not been able to ascertain the adult's wishes and feelings, please explain the barriers to this and explain the efforts you made to help the adult overcome these barriers.)

2. | The nearest relative of the adult |

Name:
Address

Relationship to adult:

(State the views of the nearest relative on the proposed recall if you have obtained these. Do you agree with these views? If you have not obtained these views, why was it not reasonable or practicable to do so?) Note: the nearest relative of the adult should not be consulted where an order to that effect has been made under section 4 of the Act.

A with I (Recall of Guardians' Powers) (S) Regs (SSI 2002/97)

Regulation 3(a)
SCHEDULE 1

3. | The views of the primary carer of the adult |

    Name:
    Address

    Relationship to adult:

(State the views of the primary carer on the proposed recall if you have obtained these. Do you agree with these views? If you have not obtained these views, why was it not reasonable or practicable to do so?)

3A.[213] | The views of the adult's named person |

    Name:
    Address

    Relationship to adult:

(State the views of the adult's named person on the proposed recall if you have obtained these. Do you agree with these views? If you have not obtained these views, why was it not reasonable or practicable to do so?)

---

[213] Paragraph 3A inserted by Adults with Incapacity (Recall of Guardians' Powers) (Scotland) Amendment Regulations SSI 2008/53, reg 2(2)(b).

Adults with Incapacity Legislation

SCHEDULE 1

Regulation 3(a)

4. | The views of the guardian(s) at Part C |

Name(s): [   ]

Appointment e.g. financial guardian [   ]

(State the views of any guardian named at Part (C) on the proposed recall if you have obtained these. Do you agree with these views? If you have not obtained these views, why was it not reasonable or practicable to do so?).

5. | The views of any other relevant person including any other guardian, continuing or welfare attorney which have been made known to you and any person whom the sheriff has directed to be consulted |

Name:
Address [   ]

Connection to adult: [   ]

(State the views of any other relevant person which have been made known to you and which are relevant to the proposed recall. Do you agree with these views?) (Continue on a separate sheet if there is more than one such person.)

A with I (Recall of Guardians' Powers) (S) Regs (SSI 2002/97)

Regulation 3(a)
SCHEDULE 1

PART F CONCLUSION

List any other matters which seem to you to be relevant.

Sign and date the form

Signed:
Date:

Adults with Incapacity Legislation

SCHEDULE 2

Regulation 3(b)

Application to local authority for recall of powers of a guardian relating to personal welfare

AWI[12]
ADULTS WITH INCAPACITY (SCOTLAND) ACT 2000
Section 73(3)

PART A   PERSON MAKING THE APPLICATION

(Give your full name and name of local authority for whom you are acting in this case if applicable or provide details of your interest in the personal welfare of the adult. [. . .][214])

Name
Local authority /statement of interest

Address

Post Code

Tel No

E-mail

PART B   THE ADULT

This application is for recall of the powers of a guardian/guardians relating to the personal welfare of:

☐ (name)

of

(Give full name, address and date of birth of the adult or insert "as above" if adult is person making the application)

☐ (address including postcode)

☐ (DOB)

---

[214] Footnote repealed by Adults with Incapacity (Recall of Guardians' Powers) (Scotland) Amendment Regulations SSI 2008/53, reg 2(3)(a).

A with I (Recall of Guardians' Powers) (S) Regs (SSI 2002/97)

Regulation 3(b)

SCHEDULE 2

PART C DETAILS OF GUARDIANSHIP

(Insert date, court and court case number if known)	The guardianship order currently in force to which this application relates was made on: Court: Court case number:
(Insert name and address)	The guardianship order appointed the following person(s) as guardian(s) with powers relating to personal welfare: Name: Address: Post Code: Tel no: Fax No: e-mail address: **Note: If available please provide a copy of the guardianship order**

The guardianship order also appointed the following person(s) as guardian(s) with powers relating to property or financial affairs:

(Insert details or delete as applicable)	Name(s): Address(es): Post Code Tel no: Fax No: e-mail address:

Adults with Incapacity Legislation

Regulation 3(b)

SCHEDULE 2

PART D GROUNDS ON WHICH RECALL IS SOUGHT

(Delete (a) or (b), unless both apply.)	I apply for the powers relating to personal welfare in the order described in Part C above to be recalled because: (a) the grounds for appointment of a guardian with such powers are no longer fulfilled (this could relate to either the adult's capacity or the adult's needs).
NB: the applicant must ensure that the doctor providing such a report is informed of the powers in the order.	(Explain why this is the case and, if applicable, attach a report by a medical practitioner stating that the adult is no longer incapable in relation to decisions about, or of acting to safeguard or promote his interests in his/her personal welfare, in relation to the matters covered in the guardianship order.)
(Describe alternatives proposed)	(b) the interests of the adult in his/her personal welfare can be satisfactorily safeguarded or promoted otherwise than by guardianship. (Describe the alternative means by which the adult's interests are to be safeguarded or promoted.)

A with I (Recall of Guardians' Powers) (S) Regs (SSI 2002/97)

Regulation 3(b)
SCHEDULE 2

PART E **CONSULTATION**

In making the application, I have consulted as follows:

1. the adult

(State the past and present wishes and feelings of the adult about the proposed recall of guardianship, so far as you have been able to ascertain them. If you have not been able to ascertain the adult's wishes and feelings, please explain the barriers to this and explain the efforts you made to help the adult overcome these barriers.)

2. The nearest relative of the adult

Name:
Address

Relationship to adult:

(State the views of the nearest relative on the proposed recall if you have obtained these. Do you agree with these views? If you have not obtained these views, why was it not reasonable or practicable to do so?) Note: the nearest relative of the adult should not be consulted where an order to that effect has been made under section 4 of the Act.

Adults with Incapacity Legislation

Regulation 3(b)
SCHEDULE 2

3. | The views of the primary carer of the adult

Name:
Address

Relationship to adult:

(State the views of the primary carer on the proposed recall if you have obtained these. Do you agree with these views? If you have not obtained these views, why was it not reasonable or practicable to do so?)

3A.[215] | The views of the adult's named person

Name:
Address:

Relationship to adult:

(State the views of the adult's named person on the proposed recall if you have obtained these. Do you agree with these views? If you have not obtained these views, why was it not reasonable or practicable to do so?)

---

[215] Paragraph 3A inserted by Adults with Incapacity (Recall of Guardians' Powers) (Scotland) Amendment Regulations SSI 2008/53, reg 2(3)(b).

A with I (Recall of Guardians' Powers) (S) Regs (SSI 2002/97)

SCHEDULE 2

Regulation 3(b)

4. The views of the guardian(s) at Part C

Name(s):

Appointment e.g. financial guardian

(Only complete if applicable.)
(State the views of any guardian(s) named at Part (C) on the proposed recall if you have obtained these. Do you agree with these views? If you have not obtained these views,
why was it not reasonable or practicable to do so?)

5. The views of any other relevant person including any other guardian, continuing attorney or welfare attorney which have been made known to you and any person whom the sheriff has directed to be consulted

Name:
Address

Connection to adult:

(State the views of any other relevant person which have been made known to you and which are relevant to the proposed recall. Do you agree with these views?) (Continue on a separate sheet if there is more than one such person.)

Adults with Incapacity Legislation

SCHEDULE 2   Regulation 3(b)

PART F   CONCLUSION

List any other matters which seem to you to be relevant.

Sign and date the form

Signed:

Date:

A with I (Recall of Guardians' Powers) (S) Regs (SSI 2002/97)

SCHEDULE 3

Regulation 3

Report of capacity to accompany applications to the Mental Welfare Commission or local authority under section 73(3) of the Act for recall of powers of a guardian relating to personal welfare

Adults with Incapacity (Scotland) Act 2000

AWI[13]

Section 73(3)

PART A DETAILS OF REPORT WRITER AND ADULT

I [   ] (name)

being a medical practitioner with the following professional address:

[   ] (state full postal address for contact)

Telephone [   ] E-mail [   ]

hereby confirm that I examined and assessed the following adult ("the adult")

Name [   ]

Residing at [   ] (state full postal address)

Date of birth [   ]

On [   ] (give date of examination and assessment)

251

Adults with Incapacity Legislation

SCHEDULE 3

Regulation 3

PART B DETAILS OF APPLICATION

Name of applicant or person requesting report

Date of application (if known)

PART C FINDINGS OF EXAMINATION AND ASSESSMENT

On the basis of my examination and assessment I am of the opinion that the adult named in Part A is no longer incapable in relation to decisions about, or of acting to safeguard or promote his/her interests in his/her personal welfare in relation to the matters covered in the guardianship order. The reason for my opinion is given below.

Please indicate the findings of your examination and assessment, so far as they relate to the adult's capacity in relation to the matters which are the subject of the guardianship order.

Please indicate the extent to which you have been able to communicate with the adult,

Please indicate the extent to which you have been able to consult the nearest relative, primary carer, and anyone else having an interest in, or knowledge of, the adult.

Signed

Date

A with I (Recall of Guardians' Powers) (S) Regs (SSI 2002/97)

SCHEDULE 4   Regulation 4

Intimation by Mental Welfare Commission of
 (i) **application or**
(ii) **intention to recall powers of a guardian relating to personal welfare**

AWI[14]
ADULTS WITH INCAPACITY
(SCOTLAND) ACT 2000
Section 73(5)

PART A   PERSONS TO WHOM THIS INTIMATION IS ADDRESSED

(Insert details of those listed in section 73(5) of the Act—see notes on Part A, at end of form.)

Name	
Status under section 73(5)	
Address	
Name	
Status under section 73(5)	
Address	
Name	
Status under section 73(5)	
Address	

Adults with Incapacity Legislation

SCHEDULE 4   Regulation 4

PART B   **PERSON WHO IS THE SUBJECT OF THE APPLICATION OR INTENTION TO RECALL ("THE ADULT")**

This intimation is in respect of the powers relating to personal welfare conferred on the guardian(s) of:

[ ] (name)

(Give full name, address and date of birth of the adult, as on the application)

[ ] (address)

[ ] DOB

PART C   **DETAILS OF GUARDIANSHIP**

The guardian(s) with powers relating to the personal welfare of the adult is/are:

Name(s):

Address(es):

Note: If available please provide a copy of the guardianship order

A with I (Recall of Guardians' Powers) (S) Regs (SSI 2002/97)

Regulation 4

SCHEDULE 4

PART D   **APPLICATION RECEIVED OR INTENTION TO RECALL**

(Delete (a) or (b))	(a) The Mental Welfare Commission has received an application for recall of the powers relating to personal welfare conferred on the guardian(s) of the adult named in Part B. The application was made by:
(Insert details of applicant)	Name: Address: The application was made on: Date: The reason(s) why the application was made is (are): OR (b) The Mental Welfare Commission, acting at its own instance intends to recall the powers relating to personal welfare conferred on the guardian(s) of the adult named in Part B. The reason(s) why it is intended to recall the powers are:

Adults with Incapacity Legislation

SCHEDULE 4

Regulation 4

PART E   OBJECTIONS TO RECALL

> You may object to recall of the powers relating to personal welfare conferred on the guardian(s) of the adult named in Part B.
>
> Objections must be made within 21 days of the date of receipt of this form.
> Objections must be made in writing, and should be sent to:
>
> Name:
>
> Address:
>
> Tel No:
>
> e-mail address:
>
> Fax:

NOTES ON PART A

Under section 73(5) of the Adults with Incapacity (Scotland) Act 2000, the following should receive intimation of applications for recall or the intention of the Mental Welfare Commission to recall the powers of a guardian relating to personal welfare:

(a)   the adult, unless the sheriff has determined under section 11(1) of the Act that he/she should not be so notified;

(b)   the adult's nearest relative as defined in the Act. The nearest relative should not receive intimation of this form, however, where a court has made an order to that effect under section 4 of the Act;

(c)   the adult's primary carer;

(ca)[216]   the adult's named person;

(d)   any guardian(s) with powers relating to personal welfare (unless an application for recall has been received from that person);

(e)   any person who the Mental Welfare Commission considers has an interest in the recall of the powers.

---

[216] Inserted by Adults with Incapacity (Recall of Guardians' Powers) (Scotland) Amendment Regulations SSI 2008/53, reg 2(4).

A with I (Recall of Guardians' Powers) (S) Regs (SSI 2002/97)

SCHEDULE 5

Regulation 5

Intimation by local authority of
 (i) application or
 (ii) intention to recall powers of a guardian relating to personal welfare

AWI[15]
ADULTS WITH INCAPACITY
(SCOTLAND) ACT 2000
Section 73(5)

PART A   PERSONS TO WHOM THIS INTIMATION IS ADDRESSED

(Insert details of those listed in section 73(5) of the Act—see notes on Part A, at end of form.)

Name

Status under section 73(5)

Address

Name

Status under section 73(5)

Address

Name

Status under section 73(5)

Address

Adults with Incapacity Legislation

Regulation 5

SCHEDULE 5

PART B   **PERSON WHO IS THE SUBJECT OF THE APPLICATION OR INTENTION TO RECALL ("THE ADULT")**

This intimation is in respect of the powers relating to personal welfare conferred on the guardian(s) of:

[ ] (name)

(Give full name, address and date of birth of the adult, as on the application)

[ ] (address)

DOB

PART C   **DETAILS OF GUARDIANSHIP**

The guardian(s) with powers relating to the personal welfare of the adult is/are:

Name(s):

Address(es):

Note: If available please provide a copy of the guardianship order

A with I (Recall of Guardians' Powers) (S) Regs (SSI 2002/97)

SCHEDULE 5

Regulation 5

PART D   APPLICATION RECEIVED OR INTENTION TO RECALL

(Delete (a) or (b)) (Insert name of local authority)

(a) _____ has received an application for recall of the powers relating to personal welfare conferred on the guardian(s) of the adult named in Part B. The application was made by:

(Insert details of applicant)

Name:

Address:

The application was made on:

Date:

The reason(s) why the application was made is (are):

OR

(Insert name of local authority

(b) _____ acting at its own instance intends to recall the powers relating to personal welfare conferred on the guardian(s) of the adult named in Part B.

The reason(s) why it is intended to recall the powers are:

Regulation 5

SCHEDULE 5

PART E   OBJECTIONS TO RECALL

> You may object to recall of the powers relating to personal welfare conferred
> on the guardian(s) of the adult named in Part B.
>
> Objections must be made within 21 days of the date of receipt of this form.
> Objections must be made in writing, and should be sent to:
>
> Name:
>
> Address:
>
> Tel No:
>
> e-mail address:
>
> Fax:

NOTES ON PART A

Under section 73(5) of the Adults with Incapacity (Scotland) Act 2000, the following should receive intimation of applications for recall or the intention of the Mental Welfare Commission to recall the powers of a guardian relating to personal welfare:

(a)   the adult, unless the sheriff has determined under section 11(1) of the Act that he/she should not be so notified;

(b)   the adult's nearest relative as defined in the Act. The nearest relative should not receive intimation of this form, however, where a court has made an order to that effect under section 4 of the Act;

(c)   the adult's primary carer;

(ca)[217] the adult's named person;

(d)   any guardian(s) with powers relating to personal welfare (unless an application for recall has been received from that person);

(e)   any person who the Mental Welfare Commission considers has an interest in the recall of the powers.

---

[217] Inserted by Adults with Incapacity (Recall of Guardians' Powers) (Scotland) Amendment Regulations SSI 2008/53, reg 2(5).

A with I (Recall of Guardians' Powers) (S) Regs (SSI 2002/97)

SCHEDULE 6   Regulation 7

Intimation by Mental Welfare Commission of proposal to refuse application for recall of powers of a guardian relating to personal welfare

AWI[16]
ADULTS WITH INCAPACITY (SCOTLAND) ACT 2000
Section 73(7)

PART A   **PERSON WHO IS THE SUBJECT OF THE APPLICATION TO RECALL ("THE ADULT")**

This intimation is in respect of the powers relating to personal welfare conferred on the guardian(s) of:

(Give full name, address and date of birth of the adult, as on the application)

                 (name)

                 (address)

DOB

PART B   **PERSONS TO WHOM THIS INTIMATION IS ADDRESSED**

(a) Adult (see details above) unless the sheriff has determined under section 11(1) of the Act that he/she should not be so notified;

(b) the person who submitted the application for recall.

Name:
Address:

PART C   **DETAILS OF GUARDIANSHIP**

The guardian(s) with powers relating to the personal welfare of the adult is/are:

Name(s):

Address(es):

Adults with Incapacity Legislation

SCHEDULE 6

Regulation 7

PART D   **REASONS FOR PROPOSAL TO REFUSE APPLICATION FOR RECALL**

> The Mental Welfare Commission has received an application for recall of the powers relating to personal welfare conferred on the guardian(s) of the adult named in Part B. The application was made by:
>
> (Insert details of applicant)
>
> Name:
>
> Address:
>
>
> The application was made on:
>
> Date:
>
> The reason(s) why it is proposed to refuse the application for recall is (are):

PART E   **OBJECTIONS TO REFUSAL TO RECALL**

> You may object to the proposed refusal to recall the powers relating to personal welfare conferred on the guardian(s) of the adult named in Part B.
>
> Objections must be made within 21 days of the date of receipt of this form. Objections must be made in writing, and should be sent to:
>
> Name:
>
> Address:
>
>
> Tel No:
> e-mail address:
> Fax:

A with I (Recall of Guardians' Powers) (S) Regs (SSI 2002/97)

SCHEDULE 7

Regulation 8

Intimation by local authority of proposal to refuse application for recall of powers of a guardian relating to personal welfare

AWI[17]
ADULTS WITH INCAPACITY (SCOTLAND) ACT 2000
Section 73(7)

PART A   PERSON WHO IS THE SUBJECT OF THE APPLICATION TO RECALL ("THE ADULT")

This intimation is in respect of the powers relating to personal welfare conferred on the guardian(s) of:

(Give full name, address and date of birth of the adult, as on the application)

(name)

(address)

DOB

PART B   PERSONS TO WHOM THIS INTIMATION IS ADDRESSED

(a) Adult (see details above) unless the sheriff has determined under section 11(1) of the Act that he/she should not be so notified;

(b) the person who submitted the application for recall.

Name:
Address:

PART C   DETAILS OF GUARDIANSHIP

The guardian(s) with powers relating to the personal welfare of the adult is/are:

Name(s):

Address(es):

263

Adults with Incapacity Legislation

Regulation 8

SCHEDULE 7

PART D **REASONS FOR PROPOSAL TO REFUSE APPLICATION FOR RECALL**

(Insert name of local authority)

_____ has received an application for recall of the powers relating to personal welfare conferred on the guardian(s) of the adult named in Part B. The application was made by:

(Insert details of applicant)

Name:

Address:

The application was made on:

Date:

The reason(s) why it is proposed to refuse the application for recall is (are):

PART E **OBJECTIONS TO REFUSAL TO RECALL**

You may object to the proposed refusal to recall the powers relating to personal welfare conferred on the guardian(s) of the adult named in Part B.

Objections must be made within 21 days of the date of receipt of this form. Objections must be made in writing, and should be sent to:

Name:

Address:

Tel No:
e-mail address:
Fax:

A with I (Recall of Guardians' Powers) (S) Regs (SSI 2002/97)

SCHEDULE 8   Regulation 10

Decision by Mental Welfare Commission on recall of powers of a guardian relating to personal welfare

AWI[18]
ADULTS WITH INCAPACITY (SCOTLAND) ACT 2000
Section 73(6)

PART A   **THE ADULT UNDER GUARDIANSHIP**

This decision concerns the powers of a guardian/guardians relating to the personal welfare of:

[_____] (name)

of

(Give full name, address and date of birth of the adult under guardianship)

[_____] (address)

[_____] DOB

PART B   **DETAILS OF GUARDIANSHIP**

(Insert date, court and court case number if known)

The guardianship order currently in force to which this application relates was made on:
Court:
Court case number:

(Insert name and address)

The guardianship order appointed the following person(s) as guardian(s) with powers relating to personal welfare:

Name:
Address

Adults with Incapacity Legislation

Regulation 10

SCHEDULE 8

PART C   APPLICATION FOR RECALL

Delete part C if not applicable

(Insert details of applicant)

The Mental Welfare Commission has received an application for recall of the powers relating to personal welfare conferred on the guardian(s) named in Part B.

The application was made by:

Name

Address:

(Insert details from application)

The capacity in which the applicant claimed an interest in the adult's personal welfare was:

The application was made on: (date)

PART D   CONFIRMATION OF INTIMATIONS TO POTENTIAL OBJECTORS

I confirm that the application OR the mental welfare commission's intention to recall the personal welfare powers at Part B was intimated to:

(Insert names and details of those who received intimations under sections 73(5) and (7) of the Act)

A with I (Recall of Guardians' Powers) (S) Regs (SSI 2002/97)

Regulation 10

SCHEDULE 8

PART E   **OBJECTIONS RECEIVED**

(Insert details of objections including name of objector(s) and capacity in which he/she/they objected)

The following objections to recall were received:

Adults with Incapacity Legislation

SCHEDULE 8   Regulation 10

PART F   DECISION

Please delete those sections (a)–(d) which are not applicable.

The decision of the Mental Welfare Commission is as follows:-

(a) to recall the personal welfare powers of the guardian(s) named at Part B in relation to the adult named at Part A.

The decision was made because either (i) or (ii) or both are applicable (delete as necessary)

(i) the grounds for appointment of the guardian with personal welfare powers named at Part B are no longer fulfilled

(ii) the interests of the adult named at Part A in his/her personal welfare can be satisfactorily safeguarded or promoted otherwise than by guardianship

(b) to refuse to recall the personal welfare powers at Part B of the guardian(s) of the adult at Part A.

The decision was made because either (i) or (ii) or both are applicable (delete as necessary)

(i) the grounds for appointment of a guardian with the personal welfare powers at Part B are still fulfilled

(ii) the interests of the adult at Part A in his/her personal welfare cannot be satisfactorily safeguarded or promoted otherwise than by guardianship

(c) to remit to the sheriff the decision on recall of the personal welfare powers of the guardian(s) named at Part B in relation to the adult named at Part A

Insert the reasons why the decision at (c) was made

(d) not to remit to the sheriff the decision on recall of the personal welfare powers of the guardian(s) named at Part B in relation to the adult named at Part A where the issue of remit has been considered.

Insert the reasons why the decision at (d) was made

Local Authority and Public Guardian hereby notified in terms of section 73(4) of the Act.

Signed   Date

On behalf of the Mental Welfare Commission.

A with I (Recall of Guardians' Powers) (S) Regs (SSI 2002/97)

SCHEDULE 9

Regulation 11

Decision by local authority on recall of powers of a guardian relating to personal welfare

AWI[19]
ADULTS WITH INCAPACITY (SCOTLAND) ACT 2000
Section 73(6)

PART A   ADULT UNDER GUARDIANSHIP

This decision concerns the powers of a guardian/guardians relating to the personal welfare of:

[_____] (name)

of

(Give full name, address and date of birth of the adult under guardianship)

[_____] (address)

[_____] DOB

PART B   DETAILS OF GUARDIANSHIP

(Insert date, court and court case number if known)

The guardianship order currently in force to which this application relates was made on:
Court:
Court case number:

(Insert name and address)

The guardianship order appointed the following person(s) as guardian(s) with powers relating to personal welfare:

Name:
Address:

269

Adults with Incapacity Legislation

SCHEDULE 9   Regulation 11

PART C   APPLICATION FOR RECALL

Delete part C if not applicable

(Insert name of local authority)

_____ has received an application for recall of the powers relating to personal welfare conferred on the guardian(s) named in Part B.

(Insert details of applicant)

The application was made by:

Name

Address:

(Insert details from application)

The capacity in which the applicant claimed an interest in the adult's personal welfare was:

The application was made on: (date)

PART D   CONFIRMATION OF INTIMATIONS TO POTENTIAL OBJECTORS

I confirm that the application OR the authority's intention to recall the personal welfare powers at Part B was intimated to:

(Insert names and details of those who received intimations under sections 73(5) and (7) of the Act)

A with I (Recall of Guardians' Powers) (S) Regs (SSI 2002/97)

SCHEDULE 9

Regulation 11

PART E **OBJECTIONS RECEIVED**

(Insert details of objections including name of objector(s) and capacity in which he/she/they objected)

The following objections to recall were received:

Adults with Incapacity Legislation

SCHEDULE 9

Regulation 11

PART F   DECISION

Please delete those sections (a)–(d) which are not applicable.

The decision of the local authority is as follows:-

(a) to recall the personal welfare powers of the guardian(s) named at Part B in relation to the adult named at Part A.

The decision was made because either (i) or (ii) or both are applicable (delete as necessary)

(i) the grounds for appointment of the guardian with personal welfare powers named at Part B are no longer fulfilled

(ii) the interests of the adult named at Part A in his/her personal welfare can be satisfactorily safeguarded or promoted otherwise than by guardianship

(b) to refuse to recall the personal welfare powers at Part B of the guardian(s) of the adult at Part A.

The decision was made because either (i) or (ii) or both are applicable (delete as necessary)

(i) the grounds for appointment of a guardian with the personal welfare powers at Part B are still fulfilled

(ii) the interests of the adult at Part A in his/her personal welfare cannot be satisfactorily safeguarded or promoted otherwise than by guardianship

(c) to remit to the sheriff the decision on recall of the personal welfare powers of the guardian(s) named at Part B in relation to the adult named at Part A

Insert the reasons why the decision at (c) was made

(d) not to remit to the sheriff the decision on recall of the personal welfare powers of the guardian(s) named at Part B in relation to the adult named at Part A where the issue of remit has been considered.

Insert the reasons why the decision at (d) was made

Mental Welfare Commission and Public Guardian hereby notified in terms of section 73(4) of the Act.

Signed   Date
On behalf of the local authority.

ADULTS WITH INCAPACITY (ETHICS COMMITTEE) (SCOTLAND) REGULATIONS

(SSI 2002/190)

Made				15th April 2002
Laid before the Scottish Parliament	17th April 2002
Coming into force			1st July 2002

The Scottish Ministers, in exercise of the powers conferred by sections 51(6) and (7) and 86(2) of the Adults with Incapacity (Scotland) Act 2000 and of all other powers enabling them in that behalf, hereby make the following Regulations:

Citation and commencement
1. These Regulations may be cited as the Adults with Incapacity (Ethics Committee) (Scotland) Regulations 2002 and come into force on 1st July 2002.

Ethics Committee
2. There is hereby constituted an Ethics Committee ("the Committee") for the purposes specified in section 51 of the Adults with Incapacity (Scotland) Act 2000.

Membership of the Committee
3.—(1) The members of the Committee may be appointed by the Scottish Ministers on such terms and conditions as the Scottish Ministers consider appropriate.
   (2) No more than [30][218] members shall be appointed to the Committee at any time.
   (3) The membership of the Committee shall, so far as practical, include at least—

   (a) one person who has experience in relation to the treatment of adults who are incapable;
   (b) one medical practitioner who provides personal, or general, medical services under sections 17C or 19 of the National Health Service (Scotland) Act 1978;
   (c) one registered nurse or registered midwife;
   (d) one registered medical practitioner having experience in clinical pharmacology;
   (e) one [pharmacist registered in Part 1 of one of the register maintained under article 10(1) of the Pharmacists and Pharmacy Technicians Order 2007][219] or a registered person as defined by Article 2(2) of the Pharmacy (Northern Ireland) Order 1976;
   (f) one registered medical practitioner who holds the position of hospital consultant;
   (g) one registered medical practitioner having experience in the field of public health medicine;

---

[218] Substituted by Adults with Incapacity (Ethics Committee) (Scotland) Amendment Regulations 2007 (SSI 2007/22), reg.2(2).
[219] Substituted by Pharmacists and Pharmacy Technicians Order 2007 (SI 2007/289), Sch.1, para.30.

(h) one member who is registered as a member of a profession to which the [Health Professions Order 2001][220] applies; and
(i) three lay members.

(4) Each member may be appointed for a period not exceeding 5 years but no member may be appointed for consecutive periods exceeding 10 years.

(5) Where a person has been appointed as a member for a total of 10 years consecutively that person may only be appointed again as a member under paragraph (4) above after the expiration of a period of 2 years from the end of the person's previous membership.

Chair and Vice-Chair
4. Subject to regulation 3(4) and (5) above, the Scottish Ministers may appoint, from among the members of the Committee, a Chair and a Vice-Chair of the Committee for such period or periods as the Scottish Ministers consider appropriate.

Remuneration
5. The Scottish Ministers may pay, to members of the Committee, such expenses related to their membership of the Committee as the Scottish Ministers consider appropriate.

Approval of Research
6. Before approving any research under section 51 of the Adults with Incapacity (Scotland) Act 2000 the Committee must take into account—

(a) the objectives, design, methodology, statistical considerations and organisation of the research;
(b) the relevance of the research and the study design;
(c) the justification of predictable risks and inconveniences weighed against the anticipated benefits for the research participants and future participants;
(d) the suitability of the lead researcher;
(e) the adequacy of the written information to be given and the procedure for obtaining consent; and
(f) the arrangements for the recruitment of research participants.

Procedures
7.—(1) Subject to the provision of this regulation, the Committee shall consider applications in such manner as it considers appropriate in the circumstances.

(2) No approval of research shall be granted by the Committee unless at least [7 members are present][221] and those members include—

(a) the Chair, or in the Chair's absence, the Vice-Chair;
(b) two members from among those appointed under sub-paragraphs (a) to (h) of regulation 3(3) above; and
(c) two members from among those appointed under sub-paragraph (i) of regulation 3(3) above.

---

[220] Substituted by Health Professions Order 2001 (Consequential Amendments) Order 2003 (SI 2003/1590), Sch.1, para.10.
[221] Substituted by Adults with Incapacity (Ethics Committee) (Scotland) Amendment Regulations 2007 (SSI 2007/22), reg.2(3).

(3) The proceedings of the Committee shall not be invalidated by death or other vacancy in its membership.

(4) Application to the Committee for approval of research shall be in such form as the Committee may determine.

(5) The Committee may call for such information from an applicant as it may reasonably require in order to determine the application and may seek such assistance from other persons as it considers necessary for that determination.

(6) The Committee may refer to one or more of its members for report or recommendation on such matters as it considers appropriate in relation to its consideration of an application.

ADULTS WITH INCAPACITY (MANAGEMENT OF RESIDENTS' FINANCES) (NO. 2) (SCOTLAND) REGULATIONS

(SSI 2003/266)

Made	29th May 2003
Laid before the Scottish Parliament	3rd June 2003
Coming into force	1st October 2003

The Scottish Ministers, in exercise of the powers conferred by sections 37(2) and (9), 39(3), 41(d) and 86 of the Adults with Incapacity (Scotland) Act 2000, and of all other powers enabling them in that behalf, hereby make the following Regulations:

Citation, commencement and interpretation
1.—(1) These Regulations may be cited as the Adults with Incapacity (Management of Residents' Finances) (No. 2) (Scotland) Regulations 2003 and shall come into force on 1st October 2003.

(2) In these Regulations "the Act" means the Adults with Incapacity (Scotland) Act 2000.

Certificate of incapacity of managing affairs
2. The certificate issued by a medical practitioner under section 37(2) of the Act (certificate of incapacity of managing affairs) shall be in the form set out in Schedule 1 to these Regulations.

Evidence to be taken into account under section 37(8) of the Act
3.—(1) The evidence which the supervisory body shall take into account in reaching a decision under section 37(8) of the Act (as to whether a direction should be given authorising the managers of an authorised establishment to dispense with certain matters) shall be the evidence provided in two certificates, each signed by a medical practitioner certifying as to whether or not, in the opinion of that medical practitioner, it would pose a serious risk to the health of the resident for the resident to be—

(a) notified that the resident is to be examined under section 37(2) of the Act;
(b) sent a copy of the certificate issued by a medical practitioner under that section (certificate of incapacity of managing affairs); or
(c) notified that the managers of the authorised establishment intend to manage the resident's affairs.

(2) A certificate granted under paragraph (1) shall be in the form set out in Schedule 2 to these Regulations.

(3) Each certificate under paragraph (1) shall be prepared and signed by a medical practitioner who has examined the resident outwith the presence of the other medical practitioner.

(4) Section 37(6) applies to a medical practitioner who certifies under paragraph (1) as it applies to a medical practitioner who certifies under section 37.

(5) In any case in which the resident's incapacity is wholly or partly by reason of mental disorder, at least one of the certificates under paragraph (1) shall be signed by a medical practitioner who is a practitioner approved

Adults with Incapacity (Residents' Finances) (No. 2) (S) Regs (SSI 2003/266)

for the purposes of [section 22(4) of the Mental Health (Care and Treatment) (Scotland) Act 2003][222] as having special experience in the diagnosis or treatment of mental disorder.

Value of matter for the purposes of section 39(3) of the Act
4. The value which is prescribed for the purposes of section 39(3) (which prevents the managers of an authorised establishment from managing, without the consent of the supervisory body, any matter if its value is greater than that which is prescribed) is—

(a) £100 in the case of any matter which consists of a disposal under section 39(1)(d) (disposal of moveable property other than money) irrespective of the number of items of moveable property comprised in the disposal; and
(b) £10,000 in the case of any other matter.

Placing funds to earn interest
5. For the purpose of section 41(d) of the Act (investment for interest of funds held), the sum which is prescribed is £500.

---

[222] Substituted by Mental Health (Care and Treatment) (Scotland) Act 2003 (Modification of Subordinate Legislation) Order 2005 (SSI 2005/445), Sch.1.

Regulation 2

SCHEDULE 1

Adults with Incapacity (Scotland) Act 2000 ("the Act")

Certificate of incapacity in relation to decisions as to, or safeguarding interest in, resident's affairs.

I .... (full name of medical practitioner) of ....
.... (professional address) have examined .... (resident's name), .../.../... (resident's date of birth), of ....
....
...... (authorised establishment where resident lives) on ../../.. (date) in my capacity as .... *.
I am of the opinion that he/she is incapable in relation to:

- decisions as to**
- safeguarding his/her interests in **

any of the affairs referred to in section 39 of the Act.
This is because of:
- mental disorder**
- inability to communicate because of physical disability**

....
....
....
....
(brief description of nature of mental disorder/inability to communicate).

I am not related to the resident or to any of the managers of the authorised establishment in which he/she resides, nor do I have any direct or indirect financial interest in the authorized establishment.

In assessing the capacity of the resident, I have given effect to the principles set out in section 1 of the Act.

.... (signature of medical practitioner)
.... (printed name)
.../.../... (date)

Note: In accordance with section 37(7) of the Act, this certificate shall expire on .... (three years after date of signature), but it shall be reviewed before that date where it appears that there has been any change in the condition or circumstances of the resident named in this certificate bearing on that resident's incapacity.

* the person signing the certificate must be a medical practitioner; insert as appropriate eg GP, specialist in mental disorder.
** one of these must be deleted unless both apply.

Adults with Incapacity (Residents' Finances) (No. 2) (S) Regs (SSI 2003/266)

Regulation 3(2)
SCHEDULE 2

Adults with Incapacity (Scotland) Act 2000 ("the Act")

Certificate to inform decision whether to dispense with intimation under section 37(3) or action under section 37(4).
I .... (full name of medical practitioner) of ....
.... (professional address) have examined .... (resident's name), .../.../... (resident's date of birth),
of ....
....
......(authorised establishment where resident lives) on ../ ../ .. (date) in my capacity as .... *.
I am of the opinion that it would pose a serious risk to the health of the resident named above for him/her to be notified:
- that his/her capacity is to be medically examined under section 37(2) of the Act;
- of the result of that medical examination;
- that his/her affairs are to be managed under section 37 of the Act.**

The reason for this opinion is ....
....
....
....
(brief description of reason(s)).

I am not related to the resident or to any of the managers of the authorised establishment in which he/she resides, nor do I have any direct or indirect financial interest in the authorised establishment.

***I am a medical practitioner approved by .... (approving body) for the purposes of [section 22(4) of the Mental Health (Care and Treatment) (Scotland) Act 2003][223] as having special experience in the diagnosis or treatment of mental disorder.
.... (signature of medical practitioner)
.... (printed name)
.../ .../ ... (date)

  * the person signing the certificate must be a medical practitioner; insert as appropriate eg GP, specialist in mental disorder,
 ** If any alternative is inappropriate, please delete it.
*** Delete if this is not the case.

---

[223] Substituted by Mental Health (Care and Treatment) (Scotland) Act 2003 (Modification of Subordinate Legislation) Order 2005 (SSI 2005/445), Sch.1.

ADULTS WITH INCAPACITY (CONDITIONS AND CIRCUMSTANCES APPLICABLE TO THREE YEAR MEDICAL TREATMENT CERTIFICATES) (SCOTLAND) REGULATIONS

(SSI 2007/100)

Made   *21st February 2007*
Laid before the Scottish Parliament   *22nd February 2007*
Coming into force   *23rd March 2007*

The Scottish Ministers, in exercise of the powers conferred by section 47(5)(b)(ii) and (6)(b)(ii) of the Adults with Incapacity (Scotland) Act 2000, and of all other powers enabling them in that behalf, hereby make the following Regulations:

Citation, commencement and interpretation
1.—(1) These Regulations may be cited as the Adults with Incapacity (Conditions and Circumstances Applicable to Three Year Medical Treatment Certificates) (Scotland) Regulations 2007 and shall come into force on 23rd March 2007.
(2) In these Regulations—

"the Act" means the Adults with Incapacity (Scotland) Act 2000; and "severe or profound learning disability" means a condition which results from the arrested or incomplete physical development of the brain, or severe damage to the brain, and which involves severe impairment of intelligence and social functioning.

Issue of medical treatment certificates for a period of up to three years
2. For the purpose of section 47(5)(b)(ii) of the Act the conditions and circumstances prescribed are that—

    (a) the adult is suffering from—

        (i) a severe or profound learning disability;
        (ii) dementia; or
        (iii) a severe neurological disorder,

    such that the adult is incapable in respect of decisions about medical treatment of the adult; and
    (b) what the adult is suffering from under paragraph (a) is unlikely to improve.

Issue of new medical treatment certificates for a period of up to three years
3. For the purpose of section 47(6)(b)(ii) of the Act the conditions and circumstances prescribed are that—

    (a) the adult is suffering from—

        (i) a severe or profound learning disability;
        (ii) dementia; or
        (iii) a severe neurological disorder,

A with I (Conditions and Circumstances) (S) Regs (SSI 2007/100)

    such that the adult is incapable in respect of decisions about medical treatment of the adult; and
(b) what the adult is suffering from under paragraph (a) is unlikely to improve.

ADULTS WITH INCAPACITY (MEDICAL TREATMENT CERTIFICATES) (SCOTLAND) REGULATIONS

(SSI 2007/104)

Made   *21st February 2007*
Laid before the Scottish Parliament   *22nd February 2007*
Coming into force   *23rd March 2007*

The Scottish Ministers, in exercise of the powers conferred by section 47(5) of the Adults with Incapacity (Scotland) Act 2000 and of all other powers enabling them in that behalf, hereby make the following Regulations:

Citation and commencement
1. These Regulations may be cited as the Adults with Incapacity (Medical Treatment Certificates) (Scotland) Regulations 2007 and shall come into force on 23rd March 2007.

Medical treatment certificates
2. A certificate for the purposes of section 47(1) of the Adults with Incapacity (Scotland) Act 2000 (authority of persons responsible for medical treatment) shall be in the form set out in the Schedule to these Regulations.

Revocation
3. The Adults with Incapacity (Medical Treatment Certificates) (Scotland) Regulations 2002 are revoked.

A with I (Medical Treatment Certificates) (S) Regs (SSI 2007/104)

SCHEDULE

Regulation 2

Certificate of Incapacity for the purposes of Section 47(1) of the Adults with Incapacity (Scotland) Act 2000

I .... (name)
of .... (address)
* am the medical practitioner primarily responsible for the medical treatment of; or

* am a person who is * a dental practitioner / an ophthalmic optician / a registered nurse and who satisfies such requirements as are prescribed by the Adults with Incapacity (Requirements for Signing Medical Treatment Certificates) (Scotland) Regulations 2007 and who is primarily responsible for medical treatment of the kind in question of
.... (name)
of .... (address) .../.../... (date of birth)

for whom the *guardian/welfare attorney/person appointed by intervention order/nearest relative/carer is ....

I have examined the patient named above on ..../..../.... (Date). I am of the opinion that *he/she is incapable within the meaning of the Adults with Incapacity (Scotland) Act 2000 ("the 2000 Act") in relation to a decision about the following medical treatment:—
....
....
because of (nature of incapacity) ....
....
This incapacity is likely to continue for .... months.

*I therefore consider it appropriate for the authority conferred by section 47(2) of the 2000 Act to subsist from ... / ... / ... (date of examination) until ... / ... / ..., being a period which does not exceed one year from the *date of the examination on which this certificate is based/ date of revocation of the certificate issued previously by me; or

*I am of the opinion that (a) *he/she is suffering from *a severe or profound learning disability/ dementia/a severe neurological disorder; and (b) *what he/she is suffering from is unlikely to improve within the meaning of the Adults with Incapacity (Conditions and Circumstances Applicable to Three Year Medical Certificates) (Scotland) Regulations 2007/ and therefore consider it appropriate for the authority conferred by section 47(2) of the 2000 Act to subsist until / / being a period which does not exceed three years from the *date of the examination on which this certificate is based / date of revocation of the certificate issued previously by me.

The authority conferred by section 47(2) of the 2000 Act shall subsist for the period specified above or until such earlier date as this certificate is revoked.

In assessing the capacity of the patient, I have observed the principles set out in section 1 of the 2000 Act.

Signed ....

Date ....

*delete as appropriate

ADULTS WITH INCAPACITY (REQUIREMENTS FOR SIGNING MEDICAL TREATMENT CERTIFICATES) (SCOTLAND) REGULATIONS

(SSI 2007/105)

Made 21st February 2007
Laid before the Scottish Parliament 22nd February 2007
Coming into force 23rd March 2007

The Scottish Ministers, in exercise of the powers conferred by section 47(1A)(b) of the Adults with Incapacity (Scotland) Act 2000 and of all other powers enabling them in that behalf, hereby make the following Regulations:

Citation and commencement
1. These Regulations may be cited as the Adults with Incapacity (Requirements for Signing Medical Treatment Certificates) (Scotland) Regulations 2007 and shall come into force on 23rd March 2007.

Requirements to be satisfied by relevant health professional signing medical treatment certificate
2. The requirements prescribed for the purposes of section 47(1A)(b) of the Adults with Incapacity (Scotland) Act 2000 are that the person concerned must have completed and passed the course entitled "Adults with Incapacity: Part 5 Amendment—Assessment of Incapacity for Health Professionals" administered by Napier University, Craiglockhart Campus, Edinburgh.

ADULTS WITH INCAPACITY (ACCOUNTS AND FUNDS) (SCOTLAND) REGULATIONS

(SSI 2008/51)

Made   *20th February 2008*
Laid before the Scottish Parliament   *21st February 2008*
Coming into force   *1st April 2008*

The Scottish Ministers make the following Regulations in exercise of the powers conferred by sections 24D(7), 27B and 27E(2) of the Adults with Incapacity (Scotland) Act 2000 and all other powers enabling them to do so.

Citation, commencement and interpretation
1.—(1) These Regulations may be cited as the Adults with Incapacity (Accounts and Funds) (Scotland) Regulations 2008 and come into force on 1st April 2008.

(2) In these Regulations, "the Act" means the Adults with Incapacity (Scotland) Act 2000.

Particulars of account to be notified to the Public Guardian
2. For the purposes of section 24D(7) of the Act, the following particulars are prescribed:—

- (a) title on the account;
- (b) name of bank;
- (c) address of bank;
- (d) type of account; and
- (e) (i) sort code and account number; or
       (ii) roll number.

Certificate from a medical practitioner
3. For the purposes of section 27B of the Act the certificate from a medical practitioner shall be in the form set out in the Schedule.

Period for objections
4. For the purposes of section 27E(2) of the Act the period of 21 days is prescribed.

Revocation
5. The Adults with Incapacity (Certificates from Medical Practitioners) (Accounts and Funds) (Scotland) Regulations 2001 are revoked.

Adults with Incapacity Legislation

Regulation 3
SCHEDULE

Adults with Incapacity (Scotland) Act 2000 ("the Act")

Certificate of incapacity to accompany an application to the Public Guardian under section 24C, 24D or 25

I. .... (full name)
of ....
(professional address) in my capacity as .... [1]
have examined the following patient on .... (date),
.... patient's name)
of ....
.... (address) .... / .... / .... (date of birth)

I am of the opinion that he/she is incapable in relation to decisions about, or incapable of acting to safeguard or promote his/her interests in, his/her funds.

I am of the opinion that the patient named above is incapable in terms of section 27B of the Act because of:

mental disorder[2] and/or

inability to communicate because of physical disability[3]

Brief description of mental disorder/inability to communicate ....
....
....
.... (signed) .... (date)

[1] the person signing the certificate must be a medical practitioner; insert as appropriate, eg GP, specialist in mental disorder
[2] mental disorder has the meaning given to it in section 328 of the Mental Health (Care and Treatment) (Scotland) Act 2003, namely that it means any mental illness; personality disorder or leaning disability however caused or manifested, but an adult is not mentally disordered by reason only of sexual orientation; sexual deviancy; transsexualism; transvestism; dependence on, or use of, alcohol or drugs; behaviour that causes, or is likely to cause, harassment, alarm or distress to any other person; or acting as no prudent person would act.
[3] one of these **must** be deleted unless both apply

ADULTS WITH INCAPACITY (PUBLIC GUARDIAN'S FEES) (SCOTLAND) REGULATIONS

(SSI 2008/52)

Made   *20th February 2008*
Laid before the Scottish Parliament   *21st February 2008*
Coming into force   *1st April 2008*

The Scottish Ministers make the following Regulations in exercise of the powers conferred by sections 7(2) and 86(2) of the Adults with Incapacity (Scotland) Act 2000 and all other powers enabling them to do so.

Citation, commencement and interpretation
1.—(1) These Regulations may be cited as the Adults with Incapacity (Public Guardian's Fees) (Scotland) Regulations 2008 and come into force on 1st April 2008.
(2) In these Regulations, "the Act" means the Adults with Incapacity (Scotland) Act 2000 and references to sections are references to sections in that Act.

Fees payable to Public Guardian
[**2.** The fees payable to the Public Guardian in respect of matters specified in column 1 of the Table of Fees in the Schedule shall be the fees specified in relation to those matters in column 2 of that Table (the previous fees payable being shown in column 3 of that Table).][224]

Exemption from fees
3. A fee regulated by these Regulations shall not be payable by a person if—

(a) the person is in receipt of legal aid within the meaning of section 13(2) of the Legal Aid (Scotland) Act 1986 in respect of the matter in the Table of Fees in connection with which the fee is payable; or
(b) the person's solicitor is undertaking work in relation to the matter in the Table of Fees in connection with which the fee is payable on the basis of any regulations made under section 36 of the Legal Aid (Scotland) Act 1986 providing for legal aid in a matter of special urgency.

Revocation of the Adults with Incapacity (Public Guardian's Fees) (Scotland) Regulations 2001
4. The Adults with Incapacity (Public Guardian's Fees) (Scotland) Regulations 2001 are revoked.

---

[224] Substituted by Adults with Incapacity (Public Guardian's Fees) (Scotland) Amendment Regulations 2008 (SSI 2008/238), reg.2(2).

Adults with Incapacity Legislation

SCHEDULE 1[225]

Regulation 2(3)(a), as read with regulation 1

TABLE OF FEES PAYABLE TO PUBLIC GUARDIAN

Fees payable from 1st August 2008

Column 1 (Matters)	Column 2 (Fee payable) £	Column 3 (Fee formerly payable)(a) £
1. Search of registers under section 6(2)(b) of the Act (per half hour or any part thereof)	15	8
2. Submission of a document conferring a continuing or welfare power of attorney under section 19 of the Act	65	60
3. Provision of a duplicate or replacement of a certificate issued under section 19(2) of the Act	10	11
4. Audit of accounts submitted by a continuing attorney under section 20(2)(b) of the Act	95	87
5. Processing of an application for authorisation to obtain information about the adult's funds under section 24C of the Act, and where such an application is granted, the issue of a certificate authorising any fundholder to provide the applicant with such information	65	60
6. Where there is no application under section 24C or where the certificate granted under section 24C is more than 4 months old, processing of an application for authorisation to intromit with funds under section 25 of the Act, and where such an application is granted, the issue of a certificate of authority to the withdrawer	65	60
7. Processing of an application for appointment as a joint withdrawer under section 26B of the Act, and where such an application is granted, the issue of a certificate of authority to the joint withdrawer	10	11
8. Processing of an application for appointment as a reserve withdrawer under section 26D	10	11

(a) Column 3 shows the fees which were payable under S.S.I. 2008/52 immediately before the coming into force of this Schedule. Where there is no entry in column 3 but an entry in column 2 the matter is new or has been amended such that no direct comparison can be made with the fee formerly payable.

---

[225] Schedule 1 substituted by Adults with Incapacity (Public Guardian's Fees) (Scotland) Amendment Regulations 2008 (SSI 2008/238), reg.2(3)(a). The fees specified in this table shall cease to have effect on 1st April 2009. For the fees payable from 1st April 2009 and from 1st April 2010, please see Schedules 2 and 3 to SSI 2008/238.

Adults with Incapacity (Public Guardian's Fees) (S) Regs (SSI 2008/52)

Column 1 (Matters)	Column 2 (Fee payable) £	Column 3 (Fee formerly payable)(a) £
9. Provision of a certificate of authority to the reserve withdrawer under section 26E(3)(b) where the certificate is not applied for at the same time as the application under section 26D is made	10	11
10. Processing of an application for variation of a withdrawal certificate under section 26F of the Act, and where such an application is granted, the issue of a varied withdrawal certificate to the withdrawer	10	11
11. Where an application for authority to transfer a specified sum under section 26G of the Act is not made at the same time as an application under section 25, processing of an application under section 26G, and where such an application is granted, the issue of a certificate to the applicant	10	11
12. Provision of a duplicate or replacement of a certificate of authority issued under sections 24C(3), 24D(3), 25(4)(b), 26B(4)(b), 26E(3)(b), 26F(3)(b) or 26G(4)(b)	10	11
13. Processing of an application for renewal of authority to intromit with funds under section 31B of the Act, and where such an application is granted, the issue of a certificate of authority to the joint withdrawer	40	35
14. Provision of a copy of any document— (a) up to 10 pages (b) each page thereafter (c) on a computer disc or in other electronic form per document	5 0.50 5	– 0.20 3
15. Registration under section 6(2) of the Act of— (a) a guardianship order; (b) an intervention order; (c) a variation of a guardianship order; (d) a variation of an intervention order; or (e) a renewal of a guardianship order, made under Part 6 of the Act (including, where appropriate, checking caution or other security and issuing certificates)	65	60
16. Authorisation of a gift out of the adult's estate under section 66(1) of the Act, where the gift has a value in excess of £2,500	45	41

Adults with Incapacity Legislation

Column 1 (Matters)	Column 2 (Fee payable) £	Column 3 (Fee formerly payable)(a) £
17. Recall of the powers of a guardian under section 73 of the Act—		
(a) for an estate with no heritable property	45	41
(b) for an estate with heritable property	95	87
18. Approval of guardian's management plan and inventory, in accordance with paragraphs 1 and 3 of schedule 2 to the Act—		
Estate value (excluding heritable property)		
£0 to £30,000	45	41
£30,001 to £50,000	190	174
£50,001 to £100,000	375	348
£100,001 to £500,000	630	580
£500,001 and over	945	870
19. Granting an application for consent made in accordance with paragraph 6 of schedule 2 to the Act	125	116
20. Audit (except final audit) of accounts submitted in accordance with paragraph 7 of schedule 2 to the Act—		
Estate value (excluding heritable property)		
£0 to £30,000	65	58
£30,001 to £50,000	160	145
£50,001 to £100,000	440	406
£100,001 to £250,000	565	522
£250,001 to £750,000	755	696
£750,001 to £2,000,000	1,510	1,392
£2,000,001 and over	2,200	2,030
21. Final audit of accounts submitted in accordance with paragraph 7 of schedule 2 to the Act—		
Estate value (excluding heritable property)		
£0 to £30,000	115	108
£30,001 to £50,000	210	195
£50,001 to £100,000	495	456
£100,001 to £250,000	620	572
£250,001 to £750,000	810	746
£750,001 to £2,000,000	1,565	1,442
£2,000,001 and over	2,255	2,080

ADULTS WITH INCAPACITY (CERTIFICATES IN RELATION TO POWERS OF ATTORNEY) (SCOTLAND) REGULATIONS

(SSI 2008/56)

Made *20th February 2008*
Laid before the Scottish Parliament *21st February 2008*
Coming into force *1st April 2008*

The Scottish Ministers make the following Regulations in exercise of the powers conferred by sections 7(1)(c), 15(3)(c), 16(3)(c) and 22A(2)(b) of the Adults with Incapacity (Scotland) Act 2000 and all other powers enabling them to do so.

Citation, commencement and interpretation
1.—(1) These Regulations may be cited as the Adults with Incapacity (Certificates in Relation to Powers of Attorney) (Scotland) Regulations 2008 and come into force on 1st April 2008.
(2) In these Regulations—

"the Act" means the Adults with Incapacity (Scotland) Act 2000;
"the 2001 Regulations" means the Adults with Incapacity (Certificates in Relation to Powers of Attorney) (Scotland) Regulations 2001.

Certificates for use in connection with continuing and welfare powers of attorney and revocation notices
2. For the purposes of sections 15(3)(c) and 16(3)(c) of the Act, the certificate to be incorporated in a written document granting a continuing power of attorney, or a welfare power of attorney, or both, shall be in the form set out in Schedule 1.
3. For the purposes of section 22A(2)(b) of the Act, the certificate to be incorporated in a notice revoking part or all of a continuing power of attorney, or a welfare power of attorney, or both, shall be in the form set out in Schedule 2.

Classes of persons for the purposes of sections 15(3)(c), 16(3)(c) or 22A(2)(b) of the Act
4. For the purposes of sections 15(3)(c), 16(3)(c) and 22A(2)(b) of the Act, the following classes are prescribed:—

(a) practising members of the Faculty of Advocates; and
(b) registered medical practitioners.

Revocation and savings
5.—(1) Subject to paragraph (2) the 2001 Regulations are revoked.
(2) The 2001 Regulations continue to have effect on or after 1st April 2008 in relation to certificates signed before that date.

Adults with Incapacity Legislation

SCHEDULE 1

Regulation 2

CERTIFICATE UNDER SECTIONS 15(3)(c) AND/OR 16(3)(c) OF THE ADULTS WITH INCAPACITY (SCOTLAND) ACT 2000 TO BE INCORPORATED IN A DOCUMENT GRANTING A POWER OF ATTORNEY

1. This certificate is incorporated in the document subscribed by

Insert name of granter

2. On

Insert date subscribed

3. That confers a

Tick appropriate box—tick one box only

- ☐ • Continuing power of attorney (i.e. confers property or financial powers only)
- ☐ • Welfare power of attorney (i.e. confers welfare powers only)
- ☐ • Combined power of attorney (i.e. confers both property or financial and welfare powers)

4. Appointing as Attorney(s)

Insert name(s) of Attorney(s)

Adults with Incapacity (Certificates) (S) Regs (SSI 2008/56)

5. Declaration of Certifier

Note: any person signing this certificate should not be the person to whom this power of attorney has been granted.

I certify that

1. I interviewed the granter *immediately* before he/she subscribed this power of attorney;
2. I am satisfied that, at the time this power of attorney was granted, the granter understood its nature and extent; and

    I have satisfied myself of this:
    Please tick appropriate box. (Both may apply but one must apply)

    ☐ (a) because of my own knowledge of the granter;

    and/or

    ☐ (b) because I have consulted the following person who has knowledge of the granter on the matter

Insert name, address and relationship with granter, of person consulted

```
┌─────────────────────────────────────────────┐
│                                             │
│                                             │
│                                             │
│                                             │
└─────────────────────────────────────────────┘
```

3. I have no reason to believe the granter was acting under undue influence or that any other factor vitiates the granting of this power of attorney.

Signed: ....

Print name: ....

Profession: ....

Address: ....

....

....

Date: ....

Adults with Incapacity Legislation

SCHEDULE 2

Regulation 3

CERTIFICATE UNDER SECTIONS 22A(2)(b) OF THE ADULTS WITH INCAPACITY (SCOTLAND) ACT 2000 TO BE INCORPORATED IN NOTICE REVOKING A POWER OF ATTORNEY

1. This certificate is incorporated in the revocation notice subscribed by

Insert name of granter

2. On

Insert date subscribed

3. That revokes

(tick the appropriate box to indicate what is being revoked)

- ☐ • All powers granted in the power of attorney
  or
- ☐ • Specific powers granted in the power of attorney (which power or powers have been specified in the revocation notice of which this forms part)

4. In relation to

Insert name(s) of Attorney(s) whose powers are being revoked

5. Declaration of Certifier

Note: any person signing this certificate should not be the person to whom the power of attorney was granted.

I certify that

Adults with Incapacity (Certificates) (S) Regs (SSI 2008/56)

1. I interviewed the granter *immediately* before he/she subscribed this revocation notice;
2. I am satisfied that, at the time this revocation notice was subscribed, the granter understood its effect; and

    I have satisfied myself of this:
    Please tick appropriate box. (Both may apply but one must apply)

    ☐ (a) because of my own knowledge of the granter;

    and/or

    ☐ (b) because I have consulted the following person who has knowledge of the granter on the matter

    Insert name, address and relationship with granter, of person consulted

3. I have no reason to believe the granter was acting under undue influence or that any other factor vitiates this revocation.

Signed: ....

Print name: ....

Profession: ....

Address: ....

....

....

Date: ....

ADULTS WITH INCAPACITY (PUBLIC GUARDIAN'S FEES)(SCOTLAND) AMENDMENT REGULATIONS 2008

(SSI 2008/238)

Made   *6th June 2008*
Laid before the Scottish Parliament   *6th June 2008*
Coming into force in accordance with regulation 1

The Scottish Ministers make the following Regulations in exercise of the powers conferred by section 7(2) of the Adults with Incapacity (Scotland) Act 2000 and of other powers enabling them to do so.

Citation and commencement
1.—(1) These Regulations may be cited as the Adults with Incapacity (Public Guardian's Fees) (Scotland) Amendment Regulations 2008 and, subject to paragraphs (2) and (3), shall come into force on 1st August 2008.

(2) Regulation 2(3)(b) and Schedule 2 shall come into force, and regulation 2(3)(a) and Schedule 1 shall cease to have effect, on 1st April 2009.

(3) Regulation 2(3)(c) and Schedule 3 shall come into force, and regulation 2(3)(b) and Schedule 2 shall cease to have effect, on 1st April 2010.

Amendment of the Adults with Incapacity (Public Guardian's Fees) (Scotland) Regulations 2008
2.—(1) The Adults with Incapacity (Public Guardian's Fees) (Scotland) Regulations 2008 shall be amended in accordance with the following paragraphs.

(2) For regulation 2 (fees payable to Public Guardian), substitute—

"**2.** The fees payable to the Public Guardian in respect of matters specified in column 1 of the Table of Fees in the Schedule shall be the fees specified in relation to those matters in column 2 of that Table (the previous fees payable being shown in column 3 of that Table)."

(3) The Table of Fees in the Schedule shall be substituted by—

(a) the Table of Fees in Schedule 1 to these Regulations on 1st August 2008;
(b) the Table of Fees in Schedule 2 to these Regulations on 1st April 2009; and
(c) the Table of Fees in Schedule 3 to these Regulations on 1st April 2010.

A with I (Public Guardian's Fees) (S) Amendment Regs 2008 (SSI 2008/238)

SCHEDULE 1

Regulation 2(3)(a), as read with regulation 1

TABLE OF FEES PAYABLE TO PUBLIC GUARDIAN

Fees payable from 1st August 2008

Column 1 (Matters)	Column 2 (Fee payable) £	Column 3 (Fee formerly payable)(a) £
1. Search of registers under section 6(2)(b) of the Act (per half hour or any part thereof)	15	8
2. Submission of a document conferring a continuing or welfare power of attorney under section 19 of the Act	65	60
3. Provision of a duplicate or replacement of a certificate issued under section 19(2) of the Act	10	11
4. Audit of accounts submitted by a continuing attorney under section 20(2)(b) of the Act	95	87
5. Processing of an application for authorisation to obtain information about the adult's funds under section 24C of the Act, and where such an application is granted, the issue of a certificate authorising any fundholder to provide the applicant with such information	65	60
6. Where there is no application under section 24C or where the certificate granted under section 24C is more than 4 months old, processing of an application for authorisation to intromit with funds under section 25 of the Act, and where such an application is granted, the issue of a certificate of authority to the withdrawer	65	60
7. Processing of an application for appointment as a joint withdrawer under section 26B of the Act, and where such an application is granted, the issue of a certificate of authority to the joint withdrawer	10	11
8. Processing of an application for appointment as a reserve withdrawer under section 26D	10	11

(a) Column 3 shows the fees which were payable under S.S.I. 2008/52 immediately before the coming into force of this Schedule. Where there is no entry in column 3 but an entry in column 2 the matter is new or has been amended such that no direct comparison can be made with the fee formerly payable.

Adults with Incapacity Legislation

Column 1 (Matters)	Column 2 (Fee payable) £	Column 3 (Fee formerly payable)(a) £
9. Provision of a certificate of authority to the reserve withdrawer under section 26E(3)(b) where the certificate is not applied for at the same time as the application under section 26D is made	10	11
10. Processing of an application for variation of a withdrawal certificate under section 26F of the Act, and where such an application is granted, the issue of a varied withdrawal certificate to the withdrawer	10	11
11. Where an application for authority to transfer a specified sum under section 26G of the Act is not made at the same time as an application under section 25, processing of an application under section 26G, and where such an application is granted, the issue of a certificate to the applicant	10	11
12. Provision of a duplicate or replacement of a certificate of authority issued under sections 24C(3), 24D(3), 25(4)(b), 26B(4)(b), 26E(3)(b), 26F(3)(b) or 26G(4)(b)	10	11
13. Processing of an application for renewal of authority to intromit with funds under section 31B of the Act, and where such an application is granted, the issue of a certificate of authority to the joint withdrawer	40	35
14. Provision of a copy of any document— (a) up to 10 pages (b) each page thereafter (c) on a computer disc or in other electronic form per document	5 0.50 5	– 0.20 3
15. Registration under section 6(2) of the Act of— (a) a guardianship order; (b) an intervention order; (c) a variation of a guardianship order; (d) a variation of an intervention order; or (e) a renewal of a guardianship order, made under Part 6 of the Act (including, where appropriate, checking caution or other security and issuing certificates)	65	60
16. Authorisation of a gift out of the adult's estate under section 66(1) of the Act, where the gift has a value in excess of £2,500	45	41

A with I (Public Guardian's Fees) (S) Amendment Regs 2008 (SSI 2008/238)

Column 1 (Matters)	Column 2 (Fee payable) £	Column 3 (Fee formerly payable)(a) £
17. Recall of the powers of a guardian under section 73 of the Act—		
(a) for an estate with no heritable property (b) for an estate with heritable property	45 95	41 87
18. Approval of guardian's management plan and inventory, in accordance with paragraphs 1 and 3 of schedule 2 to the Act—		
Estate value (excluding heritable property) £0 to £30,000 £30,001 to £50,000 £50,001 to £100,000 £100,001 to £500,000 £500,001 and over	45 190 375 630 945	41 174 348 580 870
19. Granting an application for consent made in accordance with paragraph 6 of schedule 2 to the Act	125	116
20. Audit (except final audit) of accounts submitted in accordance with paragraph 7 of schedule 2 to the Act—		
Estate value (excluding heritable property) £0 to £30,000 £30,001 to £50,000 £50,001 to £100,000 £100,001 to £250,000 £250,001 to £750,000 £750,001 to £2,000,000 £2,000,001 and over	65 160 440 565 755 1,510 2,200	58 145 406 522 696 1,392 2,030
21. Final audit of accounts submitted in accordance with paragraph 7 of schedule 2 to the Act—		
Estate value (excluding heritable property) £0 to £30,000 £30,001 to £50,000 £50,001 to £100,000 £100,001 to £250,000 £250,001 to £750,000 £750,001 to £2,000,000 £2,000,001 and over	115 210 495 620 810 1,565 2,255	108 195 456 572 746 1,442 2,080

Adults with Incapacity Legislation

SCHEDULE 2

Regulation 2(3)(b), as read with regulation 1

TABLE OF FEES PAYABLE TO PUBLIC GUARDIAN

Fees payable from 1st August 2009

Column 1 (Matters)	Column 2 (Fee payable) £	Column 3 (Fee formerly payable)(a) £
1. Search of registers under section 6(2)(b) of the Act (per half hour or any part thereof)	15	15
2. Submission of a document conferring a continuing or welfare power of attorney under section 19 of the Act	65	65
3. Provision of a duplicate or replacement of a certificate issued under section 19(2) of the Act	10	10
4. Audit of accounts submitted by a continuing attorney under section 20(2)(b) of the Act	95	95
5. Processing of an application for authorisation to obtain information about the adult's funds under section 24C of the Act, and where such an application is granted, the issue of a certificate authorising any fundholder to provide the applicant with such information	65	65
6. Where there is no application under section 24C or where the certificate granted under section 24C is more than 4 months old, processing of an application for authorisation to intromit with funds under section 25 of the Act, and where such an application is granted, the issue of a certificate of authority to the withdrawer	65	65
7. Processing of an application for appointment as a joint withdrawer under section 26B of the Act, and where such an application is granted, the issue of a certificate of authority to the joint withdrawer	10	10
8. Processing of an application for appointment as a reserve withdrawer under section 26D	10	10

(a) Column 3 shows the fees which were payable by virtue of Schedule 1 to these Regulations immediately before the coming into force of this Schedule.

A with I (Public Guardian's Fees) (S) Amendment Regs 2008 (SSI 2008/238)

Column 1 (Matters)	Column 2 (Fee payable) £	Column 3 (Fee formerly payable)(a) £
9. Provision of a certificate of authority to the reserve withdrawer under section 26E(3)(b) where the certificate is not applied for at the same time as the application under section 26D is made	10	10
10. Processing of an application for variation of a withdrawal certificate under section 26F of the Act, and where such an application is granted, the issue of a varied withdrawal certificate to the withdrawer	10	10
11. Where an application for authority to transfer a specified sum under section 26G of the Act is not made at the same time as an application under section 25, processing of an application under section 26G, and where such an application is granted, the issue of a certificate to the applicant	10	10
12. Provision of a duplicate or replacement of a certificate of authority issued under sections 24C(3), 24D(3), 25(4)(b), 26B(4)(b), 26E(3)(b), 26F(3)(b) or 26G(4)(b)	10	10
13. Processing of an application for renewal of authority to intromit with funds under section 31B of the Act, and where such an application is granted, the issue of a certificate of authority to the joint withdrawer	40	40
14. Provision of a copy of any document— (a) up to 10 pages (b) each page thereafter (c) on a computer disc or in other electronic form per document	5 0.50 5	5 0.50 5
15. Registration under section 6(2) of the Act of— (a) a guardianship order; (b) an intervention order; (c) a variation of a guardianship order; (d) a variation of an intervention order; or (e) a renewal of a guardianship order, made under Part 6 of the Act (including, where appropriate, checking caution or other security and issuing certificates)	65	65
16. Authorisation of a gift out of the adult's estate under section 66(1) of the Act, where the gift has a value in excess of £2,500	45	45

Column 1 (Matters)	Column 2 (Fee payable) £	Column 3 (Fee formerly payable)(a) £
17. Recall of the powers of a guardian under section 73 of the Act—		
(a) for an estate with no heritable property (b) for an estate with heritable property	45 95	45 95
18. Approval of guardian's management plan and inventory, in accordance with paragraphs 1 and 3 of schedule 2 to the Act— Estate value (excluding heritable property) £0 to £30,000 £30,001 to £50,000 £50,001 to £100,000 £100,001 to £500,000 £500,001 and over	 45 195 390 650 970	 45 190 375 630 945
19. Granting an application for consent made in accordance with paragraph 6 of schedule 2 to the Act	130	125
20. Audit (except final audit) of accounts submitted in accordance with paragraph 7 of schedule 2 to the Act— Estate value (excluding heritable property) £0 to £30,000 £30,001 to £50,000 £50,001 to £100,000 £100,001 to £250,000 £250,001 to £750,000 £750,001 to £2,000,000 £2,000,001 and over	 65 160 455 580 775 1,555 2,265	 65 160 440 565 755 1,510 2,200
21. Final audit of accounts submitted in accordance with paragraph 7 of schedule 2 to the Act— Estate value (excluding heritable property) £0 to £30,000 £30,001 to £50,000 £50,001 to £100,000 £100,001 to £250,000 £250,001 to £750,000 £750,001 to £2,000,000 £2,000,001 and over	 120 220 510 640 835 1,610 2,320	 115 210 495 620 810 1,565 2,255

A with I (Public Guardian's Fees) (S) Amendment Regs 2008 (SSI 2008/238)

SCHEDULE 3

Regulation 2(3)(c), as read with regulation 1

TABLE OF FEES PAYABLE TO PUBLIC GUARDIAN

Fees payable from 1st April 2010

Column 1 (Matters)	Column 2 (Fee payable) £	Column 3 (Fee formerly payable)(a) £
1. Search of registers under section 6(2)(b) of the Act (per half hour or any part thereof)	15	15
2. Submission of a document conferring a continuing or welfare power of attorney under section 19 of the Act	70	65
3. Provision of a duplicate or replacement of a certificate issued under section 19(2) of the Act	15	10
4. Audit of accounts submitted by a continuing attorney under section 20(2)(b) of the Act	100	95
5. Processing of an application for authorisation to obtain information about the adult's funds under section 24C of the Act, and where such an application is granted, the issue of a certificate authorising any fundholder to provide the applicant with such information	70	65
6. Where there is no application under section 24C or where the certificate granted under section 24C is more than 4 months old, processing of an application for authorisation to intromit with funds under section 25 of the Act, and where such an application is granted, the issue of a certificate of authority to the withdrawer	70	65
7. Processing of an application for appointment as a joint withdrawer under section 26B of the Act, and where such an application is granted, the issue of a certificate of authority to the joint withdrawer	15	10
8. Processing of an application for appointment as a reserve withdrawer under section 26D	15	10

(**a**) Column 3 shows the fees which were payable by virtue of Schedule 2 to these Regulations immediately before the coming into force of this Schedule.

Adults with Incapacity Legislation

Column 1 (Matters)	Column 2 (Fee payable) £	Column 3 (Fee formerly payable)(a) £
9. Provision of a certificate of authority to the reserve withdrawer under section 26E(3)(b) where the certificate is not applied for at the same time as the application under section 26D is made	15	10
10. Processing of an application for variation of a withdrawal certificate under section 26F of the Act, and where such an application is granted, the issue of a varied withdrawal certificate to the withdrawer	15	10
11. Where an application for authority to transfer a specified sum under section 26G of the Act is not made at the same time as an application under section 25, processing of an application under section 26G, and where such an application is granted, the issue of a certificate to the applicant	15	10
12. Provision of a duplicate or replacement of a certificate of authority issued under sections 24C(3), 24D(3), 25(4)(b), 26B(4)(b), 26E(3)(b), 26F(3)(b) or 26G(4)(b)	15	10
13. Processing of an application for renewal of authority to intromit with funds under section 31B of the Act, and where such an application is granted, the issue of a certificate of authority to the joint withdrawer	40	40
14. Provision of a copy of any document— (a) up to 10 pages (b) each page thereafter (c) on a computer disc or in other electronic form per document	5 0.50 5	5 0.50 5
15. Registration under section 6(2) of the Act of— (a) a guardianship order; (b) an intervention order; (c) a variation of a guardianship order; (d) a variation of an intervention order; or (e) a renewal of a guardianship order, made under Part 6 of the Act (including, where appropriate, checking caution or other security and issuing certificates)	70	65
16. Authorisation of a gift out of the adult's estate under section 66(1) of the Act, where the gift has a value in excess of £2,500	45	45

A with I (Public Guardian's Fees) (S) Amendment Regs 2008 (SSI 2008/238)

	Column 1 (Matters)	Column 2 (Fee payable) £	Column 3 (Fee formerly payable)(a) £
	17. Recall of the powers of a guardian under section 73 of the Act—		
	(a) for an estate with no heritable property	45	45
	(b) for an estate with heritable property	100	95
	18. Approval of guardian's management plan and inventory, in accordance with paragraphs 1 and 3 of schedule 2 to the Act—		
	Estate value (excluding heritable property)		
	£0 to £30,000	45	45
	£30,001 to £50,000	200	195
	£50,001 to £100,000	400	390
	£100,001 to £500,000	665	650
	£500,001 and over	1000	970
	19. Granting an application for consent made in accordance with paragraph 6 of schedule 2 to the Act	135	130
	20. Audit (except final audit) of accounts submitted in accordance with paragraph 7 of schedule 2 to the Act—		
	Estate value (excluding heritable property)		
	£0 to £30,000	65	65
	£30,001 to £50,000	165	160
	£50,001 to £100,000	465	455
	£100,001 to £250,000	600	580
	£250,001 to £750,000	800	775
	£750,001 to £2,000,000	1,600	1,555
	£2,000,001 and over	2,335	2,265
	21. Final audit of accounts submitted in accordance with paragraph 7 of schedule 2 to the Act— Estate value (excluding heritable property)		
	£0 to £30,000	125	120
	£30,001 to £50,000	225	220
	£50,001 to £100,000	525	510
	£100,001 to £250,000	660	640
	£250,001 to £750,000	860	835
	£750,001 to £2,000,000	1,660	1,610
	£2,000,001 and over	2,395	2,320

Index

Accountant of Court
supervisory function, 22, 24
Accommodation
acquisition of accommodation, 97, 98, 158
disposal, of, 158, 159
management of adult's estate, 155, 159
Accounts and funds
Access to Funds Revised Code of Practice, 48
accounts
approval, of, 159
auditing, 159
financial guardianship, 48
see also **Financial guardianship**
fundholders
see **Fundholders**
information provisions
authority to provide information, 50
confidential information, 50
release of information, 50
intervention orders, 47
see also **Intervention orders**
intromit
see **Authority to intromit**
joint accounts
see **Joint accounts**
management arrangements, 47
medical certificates, 285, 286
see also **Medical treatment certificates**
opening of account, 51
Public Guardian, applications to, 47, 49, 50, 51
repayment of funds, 48, 147
see also **Repayment of funds**
sheriff's directions, 47
state benefits, 47
transfer of funds, 53, 54, 58, 59
withdrawal certificates 53, 54, 65, 66, 68, 69
see also **Withdrawal certificates**
withdrawal of money, 47
withdrawers, 47, 48, 65, 66
see also **Withdrawers**
Additional guardians
joint guardians, 119
see also **Joint guardians**
Adult
definition, 10, 16, 152
Ancillary orders
variation of guardianship, 140
Appeals
decision as to incapacity, 31
financial guardians, 136

medical treatment, 93
Sheriff Court, 17, 18
withdrawers
refusal of application, 69
transition from guardianship, 69, 70
Applications
countersigning, 60, 61
determination of applications, 62, 63
fit and proper applicants, 62, 63
general requirements, 59, 60
intimation of applications, 61, 62
medical certificates, 61
multiple applications, 63, 64
referral to sheriff, 63
refusal, 69
representations, opportunity for, 63
Attorneys
see also **Powers of attorney**
continuation of powers, 166, 171, 172
continuing attorneys
see also **Continuing attorneys**
interventions, 10
powers, 10
welfare attorneys
see also **Welfare attorneys**
interventions, 10
powers, 10
Authority to intromit
application, 51
application procedure, 52, 53, 54
determination of applications, 63, 64
fit and proper applicants, 62, 63
generally, 48
intimation of applications, 61, 62
renewal, 67–68
Bankruptcy
definition, 153
welfare powers of attorney (WPAs), 34, 35
see also **Welfare powers of attorney (WPAs)**
Best interests
best interests test, 11
Body parts
removal, of, 36
Books of Council and Session
powers of attorney, 39
see also **Powers of attorney**
Breach of duty
continuing attorneys, 147
duty of care, 148, 149
fiduciary duties, 148, 149
guardians, 132, 147

Index

managers of establishments, 147
personal liability, 149
repayment of funds, 147
welfare attorneys, 147
withdrawers, 147
Caution
alternative security, 97, 100
finding caution
  guardianship orders, 94, 109, 111, 112, 118, 140, 141
  intervention orders, 94, 97, 100
  removal of guardians, 134, 135
  replacement of guardians, 134, 135
  variation of guardianship, 140, 141
no longer mandatory, 94
presumption, as to, 100
Certificates of incapacity
management of resident's finances, 276, 278, 279
medical treatment certificates, 283
Changes of address
intervention orders, 100
notification, 123, 126, 143
withdrawers, 65, 66
Chief social worker
appointment as guardian, 113, 114, 123, 129
change of address, 143
costs, 130
definition, 106
guardianship reports, 184
notification requirement, 143
powers
  recall powers, 139
  welfare powers, 131
Children
guardianship orders, 146, 147
Civil partners
continuing powers of attorney (CPAs), 46
  see also **Continuing powers of attorney (CPAs)**
welfare powers of attorney (CPAs), 46
  see also **Welfare powers of attorney (CPAs)**
Codes of Practice
Access to Funds Revised Code of Practice, 47, 48
consultation requirement, 31
guidance, 31
responsibility, for, 31
topics, covered by, 31
Consultation provisions
Codes of Practice, 31
interventions, 10, 15, 16
Mental Welfare Commission (MWC), 26, 27
Public Guardian, 23, 24
recall of powers, 234–236, 198–200
Continuation of existing powers
continuing attorneys, 166, 171, 172
curator bonis, 166, 170

guardians, 167–170
managers, 168
mandatory renewal provisions, 171
proceedings, 167
replacement guardians, 171
statutory provisions, 151
transitional appointments, 170
transitional guardians, 170
tutor-at-law, 166, 169
tutor-dative, 166, 169
welfare attorneys, 167, 171, 172
Continuing attorneys
see also **Continuing powers of attorney (CPAs)**
appointment, 39, 40
breach of duty, 147
certification provisions, 34, 280
continuation of powers, 166, 171, 172
definition, 23, 152
interpretation, 71
interventions, 10
limitation of liability, 148
management of resident's finances, 81
  see also **Management of resident's finances**
powers, 10
resignation, 44, 45
Continuing powers of attorney (CPAs)
accompanying certificate, 36
appointment, 39, 40
certification provisions, 34, 280
civil partners, involving, 46
creation, 33, 34
generally, 32
guidance, 32
ill-treatment offence, 32
investigation of complaints, 32
joint accounts, 71
jurisdiction, 32
legislative compliance, 37
limitation of liability, 32
married persons, involving, 46
not obliged to act, 37
Public Guardian, notification to, 41, 42
registration, 37, 38, 39, 41
repayment of funds, 32
revocation, 42–44
sheriff's powers, 39
"springing power", 34, 39
termination, 45, 46
transitional provisions, 32
wilful neglect offence, 32
willingness to act, 39
Court of Session
ascertainment of views, 22
jurisdiction, 18
powers, 20, 21
safeguarders, appointment of, 22
safeguarding of interests, 22
Court proceedings
see **Judicial proceedings**

Index

Criminal Procedure (Scotland) Act 1995
  amendments, to, 149–151, 176
  guardians, appointed under, 149, 151
  guardianship orders, 149–151
  intervention orders, 149, 151
  judicial powers, 150
  mentally ill offenders, 151
  registration requirement, 151
  sheriff's powers, 151
Curator bonis
  appointment, 105, 166, 170, 171
  continuation of powers, 166, 170
  determination of proceedings, 167
  future appointment, 146
  guardianship, 166, 168, 171
  individual, as, 127
Death of adult
  guardianship, 143, 144
Decision-making incapability
  authority for research, 91
  certification process, 82–85
  prescribed form, 83
Directions
  see also **Sheriff's powers**
  sheriff's directions
    accounts and funds, 48
    generally, 17–20
    joint guardians, 117
    management of adult's estate, 155
    management of resident's finances, 72
Disposal of accommodation
  management of adult's estate, 158, 159
Duty of care
  breach of duty, 147, 148
  guardians, 132
Ethics Committee
  authority for research, 90–92, 274
  establishment, 273
  membership, 273, 274
  procedures, 274, 275
  remuneration, 274
European Convention on Human Rights (ECHR)
  fair hearing, 9
Expenses
  award, of, 25, 26
  guardianship orders, 96
  intervention orders, 8, 89
  Public Guardian, 25
  sheriff's discretion, 23, 132
Fair hearing
  requirement, for, 9
Fees
  Public Guardian
    exemptions, 287
    fees payable, 287, 288, 296–305
Financial guardians
  annual accounting, 47
  applications, 47
  discharge
    appeals, 136
    application, for, 136
    determination by sheriff, 137
    intimation provisions, 137
    Public Guardian's role, 136, 139
  legislative compliance, 47–48
  powers
    discharge powers, 95
    financial powers, 124
    sheriff's powers, 47
  renewal procedure, 94
  simplified form, 47
Fundholders
  current account, 64
  interpretation, 71
  joint accounts, 70
  liability, 65
  meaning, 71
  original account, 64, 65
  second account, 64
General principles
  choice of forum, 9
  compliance provisions, 12
  financial affairs, 10
  first principle, 13
  fundamental rights, 9
  interventions, 10–13
    see also **Interventions**
  limitation of liability, 11
    see also **Limitation of liability**
  personal welfare, 10
  second principle 14
  skills development, 10, 11, 16
  substantive procedures, 9
General Register of Sasines
  heritable property interests, 118
Gifts
  application process, 128
  authorisation, 128, 129
  dispensing with intimation, 128
  Public Guardian's authority, 129
  value of gift, 128
Guardians
  application of statutory provisions, 168–170
  appointment
    certificate of appointment, 129, 172
    chief social worker, 113, 114, 124
    conditions of appointment, 113, 114
    effect, of, 129, 130
    generally, 11, 12
    joint guardians, 119
    medical treatment purposes, 86
    sheriff, by, 113, 114
    suitability, 105, 106
  authority
    authority for research, 90, 91
    conferred authority, 129
    presumption of capacity, 130
    termination, 144
  breach of duty, 132, 148
  change of address, 123, 126, 144

309

Index

continuation of powers, 167–170
death, of, 87, 143, 144
decisions
  implementation orders, 132, 133
  non-compliance, 132, 133
delegation, by, 114, 126
determination of proceedings, 167
duty of care, 132
financial guardians
  see **Financial guardians**
functions and duties
  compliance, 123
  defence of actions, 122
  legal representation, 123, 126
  management of estate, 123, 124
  notification requirements, 124, 127
  purchase of assets, 123, 126
  record-keeping, 127
  use of capital/income, 123
gifts
  application process, 128
  authorisation, 118, 128
  dispensing with intimation, 128
  Public Guardian's authority, 128
  value of gift, 128
interim guardianship, 95, 103, 105, 107, 124, 127
see also **Interim guardians**
interpretation, 71
joint guardians
  see **Joint guardians**
limitation of liability, 148
management of resident's finances, 81
  see also **Management of resident's finances**
mandatory renewal, 171
personal representatives, 95
powers
  additional powers, 125
  excessive powers, 125
  financial powers, 124
  generally, 5, 7
  intervention orders, 118
  joint accounts, 71
  limitation, of, 125
  personal welfare, 122, 124–126, 129
  powers conferred, 124
  property/financial powers, 122–124, 126, 127
  removal, of, 126
  review, of, 125
  welfare powers, 126, 127, 132
recall, 95, 99, 135–139
  see also **Recall of guardians**
reimbursement, 130
removal, 134, 135
  see also **Removal of guardians**
remuneration
  entitlement, 130, 131
  forfeiture, 131, 132
replacement guardians, 171

replacement of guardians, 134, 135
  see also **Replacement of guardians**
resignation
  continuity of guardianship, 142
  notice requirement, 141, 142
  removal/replacement, 142
substitute guardians
  see **Substitute guardians**
transactions
  conferred authority, 129
  personal liability, 129
  third parties, 129
  transaction for value, 129
transitional guardians, 96, 116–117, 171
welfare guardians
  see **Welfare guardians**
Guardianship
see also **Guardianship orders**
alternatives, 109
amendment of registration, 145
application of statutory provisions, 168–170
caution
  finding caution, 109, 111, 112
  no longer mandatory, 94
change of habitual address, 143
conferral of powers, 150
continuity, of, 142
curator bonis, 166, 167, 172
  see also **Curator bonis**
death of adult, 144, 145
determination of proceedings, 167
financial guardians
  see **Financial guardianship**
intervention orders, 99, 100
mandatory renewal, 171
reports
  see **Guardianship reports**
restrictive nature, 109
termination of authority, 144
third party protection, 145
transition from guardianship, 70
tutor-at-law, 167
  see also **Tutor-at-law**
tutor-dative, 167
  see also **Tutor-dative**
Guardianship orders
see also **Guardians; Guardianship**
applications
  accompanying reports, 103, 104, 106, 107
  commencement, 94
  disposal, of, 108, 109
  finding caution, 109, 112
  interim guardians, 105, 107
  joint guardians, 111, 113
  local authority, 29
  medical examinations, 103, 104
  medical treatment, 87
  personal welfare, 103, 106–108, 113
  previous orders, 108

Index

process, 102–108
property/financial affairs, 102–108, 112
recommencement, 109, 110
renewal applications, 106, 114
children, 146, 147
conferral of powers, 150
curator *ad litem*, 96
curatory petitions, 105, 110
definition, 23, 151
duration, 105, 108–111, 151
expenses, 96
expiry, 95
finding caution, 118
flexibility, 105, 107
jurisdiction, 10, 95
medical reports, 94
previous orders, 96, 100, 108, 109
procedure, 150
property/financial powers, 95
recall
  intervention orders, 99
  local authority, 95
registration
  heritable property, 118
  third party protection, 118
renewals
  accompanying reports, 115, 117
  applications, 106, 114–116
  conveyancing description, 118
  local authority renewals, 114, 116
  medical examinations, 117
  mental disorders, 115
  personal welfare, 115
  procedure, 117
  property/financial affairs, 115, 118
  refusal, 116, 118
  sheriff's powers, 116
  time limits, 115–117
scope, 105
termination, 144
variation
  ancillary orders, 140
  applications, for, 140, 141
  finding caution, 140, 141
  intimation provisions, 140, 141
  previous orders, 140
  procedure, 140
  property/financial affairs, 140, 141
  Public Guardian's role, 140, 141
  sheriff's powers, 140, 141
Guardianship reports
chief social worker, 204
incapacity reports
  examination outwith Scotland, 206
  examination within Scotland, 205
  findings of examination, 207
  Public Guardian's report, 209
  purpose of examination, 207
medical practitioners, 203
mental health officers, 203
persons with sufficient knowledge, 204

Hague Convention (International Protection of Adults)
application, 161, 164, 165
compliance, 161, 165
ratification date, 161, 166
recognition/enforcement of judgments, 164
Heritable property
guardianship orders, 115, 116
heritable property interests, 118, 144
intervention orders, 98, 99, 102, 144
Hospital management
abolition, of, 172
Ill-treatment
continuing powers of attorney (CPAs), 32
  see also **Continuing powers of attorney (CPAs)**
offence, 32, 149
Implementation orders
use, of, 132, 133
Incapable
decision-making incapability
  authority for research, 91, 93
  certification process, 83–85
  prescribed form, 83
definition 10, 17, 151
Incapacity
certificates
  see **Certificates of incapacity**
decisions
  appeals, 31
  communicating, 11
  decision-making, 12, 82–86, 89, 90, 93
  retained memory, 16
  understanding, 11
definition, 16, 152
inability to communicate, 16
mental disorder, 16
particular purposes, for, 17
Incapacity reports
see also **Certificates of incapacity**
medical examination
  findings, 207
  outwith Scotland, 206
  purpose, 207
  within Scotland, 205
Public Guardian's report, 209
Independent advocacy services
meaning, 20
Interest in property
heritable property
  see **Heritable property**
persons claiming an interest, 19, 20
Interim guardians
appointment, of, 103, 104, 107, 127
duration of guardianship, 105
powers, 124
Interpretation
interpretative provisions, 152–154, 170
Intervention orders
see also **Interventions**

Index

acquisition of accommodation, 97
applications
  local authority, 28, 97
caution
  alternative security, 100
  no longer mandatory, 94
  presumption, as to, 100
change of address, 100
curatory petitions, 100
death of authorised person, 102, 103
definition, 23, 152
effects, 97
emergency situations, 99
expenses, 96
heritable property, 98, 99, 101
interim orders, 99
joint accounts, 71
jurisdiction, 18, 19, 95, 99
management of resident's finances, 81
  see also **Management of resident's finances**
medical treatment, 88
  see also **Medical treatment**
personal welfare, 101
previous orders, 96, 100
procedure, 98
property/financial powers, 95, 96, 98
recall of guardians, 135
record-keeping, 100
registration, 101
scope, of 95, 98
sheriff's powers, 96–98
specified action, 98
specified decisions, 98
termination, 144
title to property, 98, 99
transactions for value, 97
variation, 96
Interventions
ascertainment of wishes, 10, 15
authorisation, 10, 13
  see also **Intervention orders**
benefit principle, 10, 13, 14
best interests test, 12
certification, 13
choice of procedure, 14
conditions, 10
consultation provisions, 10, 15, 16
continuing attorneys, 10
curatory procedure, 10, 16
effecting the intervention, 10, 13
formal measures, 14
general principles, 9–11
least restrictive intervention, 14
least restrictive option, 10
meaning, 12, 13
medical treatment, 87
  see also **Medical treatment**
minimum necessary intervention, 14
powers conferred, 13, 14
provision of facilities/services, 13

provision of treatment 13
Public Guardian, 13
  see also **Public Guardian**
welfare attorneys, 10
Intimation
discharge of guardian, 136
dispensing with, 30, 128
failure to intimate, 117
gifts, relating to, 128
intimation of applications, 62, 63
recall of powers
  local authorities, 257–260, 263, 264
  Mental Welfare Commission (MWC), 253–256, 261–262
variation of guardianship, 140, 141
Intromit
authority to intromit
  application procedure, 52, 53, 54
  applications, 51
  determination of applications, 62, 63
  fit and proper applicants, 62, 63
  generally, 47–49
  intimation of applications, 61, 62
  renewal, 67–68
continuing to intromit, 71
joint accounts, 71
Investigations
information requirements, 30
local authority, 30
Mental Welfare Commission (MWC), 30
Public Guardian, 30
safeguarding
  personal welfare, 30
  property/financial affairs, 30
Joint accounts
continuing powers of attorney, 71
continuing to intromit, 71
guardian's powers, 71
intervention orders, 71
  see also **Intervention orders**
Joint guardians
additional guardians, 119
applications, 119, 120
appointment, of, 105, 113, 119–120
consultation, between, 120
death of guardian, 143
disagreement, between, 120
exercise of individual function, 120
guardianship orders, 109, 111
joint and several liability, 120
liability, 119
property/financial powers, 130
removal, 134
resignation, 141, 142
sheriff's powers
  applications, 119, 120
  appointments, 119, 120
  directions, 120
third party reliance, 120
Judicial proceedings
Court of Session

Index

see **Court of Session**
expenses
  award, of, 25, 26
  sheriff's discretion, 26
Sheriff Court
  see **Sheriff Court**
Jurisdiction
  applicable law, 163, 164
  conflict of jurisdiction, 165
  continuing powers of attorney (CPAs), 32
    see also **Continuing powers of attorney (CPAs)**
  extent of jurisdiction, 151, 161
  generally, 161, 162, 166
  guardianship orders, 95
  habitual residence, 161, 162
  intervention orders, 18, 96,98
  judicial comity, 164
  private international law, 151
  recognition/enforcement of judgments, 164, 165
  Sheriff Courts, 162, 163
Limitation of liability
  continuing attorneys, 148
  continuing powers of attorney (CPAs), 32
  guardians, 148
  managers of establishments, 148
  welfare attorneys, 148
  withdrawers, 48, 148
Local authority
  applications
    guardianship orders, 28
    intervention orders, 28
  definition, 23, 151
  functions
    advice, 28, 29
    consultation, 28, 29
    information, 28, 29
    investigative, 28, 29, 30
    personal welfare, 27, 29
    provision of services, 183
    supervision, 27–29, 127, 184, 185
  intervention orders, 97
  recall of powers
    applications, 244, 257
    decision, 235
    details of guardianship, 245
    guardianship details, 245
    intention to recall, 235
    intimation provisions, 235, 257–260, 263–264
    objections to recall, 235, 256
    personal welfare guardians, 244–245
    provisions, for, 95
    subject of application, 244
  renewals
    guardianship orders, 115
Management of adult's estate
  see also **Management of resident's finances**
  accommodation

    disposal, of, 158
    purchase, of, 158
  accounts
    approval, of, 159
    auditing, 159
  carrying on business, 157
  inventory of estate, 156
  investment powers, 157
  management plans, 155, 157
  money, 157
  sheriff's directions, 156
Management of resident's finances
  see also **Management of adult's estate**
  certification, 76, 276, 278, 279
  continuing attorneys, 81
  entitlement, 74, 75
  evidence provisions, 276
  financial procedure/controls, 75
  general principles, 72
  good faith, 82
  guardians, 82
  intervention orders, 82
    see also **Intervention orders**
  investigative powers, 72
  investment for interest, 277
  management scheme, 72
  managers
    see **Managers of establishments**
  matters under management, 72, 76, 81
  medical examinations, 75
  notification requirement, 74, 75, 81
  records of transactions, 78
  registration, 74
  residents' establishments
    authorised establishments, 72–75, 155
    registered establishments, 72–75
    relevant establishments, 72
    unregistered establishments, 63–74
  responsibility, 76
  sheriff's directions, 72
  statement of resident's affairs, 79
  supervisory bodies, 72, 73–78, 276, 277
  value of property, 277
Managers of establishments
  authorised establishments, 78, 155, 172
  authority
    authorisation, 78
    certificate of authority, 78, 79
    cessation, of, 80
    revocation, 81
  breach of duty, 148
  care services, 155
  categories, 72, 73, 74
  compliance, 72, 75, 76, 81
  continuation of powers, 167, 168
  definition, 152, 153
  duties/functions, 77, 78
  financial management, 77, 78
  good faith, 78, 82
  limitation of liability, 148
  limited registration services, 155

Index

list of managers, 154
meaning, 72
records of transactions, 79
responsibility, 76
state hospitals, 155, 172
withdrawals, 78, 79
Married persons
continuing powers of attorney (CPAs), 46
see also **Continuing powers of attorney (CPAs)**
welfare powers of attorney (CPAs), 46
see also **Welfare powers of attorney (CPAs)**
Medical treatment
appeals, 93
authority
authorisation, 87
authority conferred, 82, 85
certification, 85
exceptions, 76
certificates
see **Medical treatment certificates**
dental practitioners, 83, 85
detention, use of, 84, 85
experienced medical practitioners, 200
force, use of, 84, 85
generally, 13
guardians
appointment, of, 87
guardianship orders, 86
incapable of decision-making
authority for research, 90
certification process, 83–86
prescribed form, 83
interdict, 85, 86
intervention
applications, 86
intervention orders, 87–88
meaning, 83
Mental Welfare Commission (MWC)
dispute resolution, 89, 90
nominated medical practitioners, 88
ophthalmic opticians, 83, 85
registered nurses, 83
responsible persons, 83, 85
second opinions, 86, 89
welfare attorney, appointment of, 87
Medical treatment certificates
certificate of incapacity, 283
issue, of, 280
renewal, 280
signature, 283
statutory form, 283
Memory
memory of decisions, 10, 16
retained memory, 16
Mental disorder
incapacity, caused by, 16
definition, 16, 152
experienced medical practitioners, 200
treatment, of, 36

Mental health officers
guardianship reports, 203
Mental Welfare Commission (MWC)
definition, 23, 152
function
advice, 26, 27
consultation, 26, 27
generally, 9, 16
information, 26, 27
investigative, 26, 27, 30
personal welfare, 26, 27
support, 27
medical treatment
see also **Medical treatment**
dispute resolution, 89, 90
nominated medical practitioners, 89, 90
recall of powers
applications, 234, 235, 237, 244, 251, 253, 257
decision, 268
guardianship details, 258, 265
intention to recall, 259
intimation provisions, 257–258, 261, 263–264, 266
objections to recall, 260, 267
personal welfare guardianship, 269–271
provisions, for, 101, 134, 137–139, 140, 234, 235, 239
refusal of application, 261–262
subject of applications, 237
Nearest relative
authority for research, 91
definition, 21, 152
judicial prohibitions
information, 20–21
intimation, 20–21
powers, 20–21
Notification
accounts and funds, 285
dispensing with, 24, 29–30, 192
guardians
death, 143
recall, 137
removal, 134–135
resignation, 141, 142
management of resident's finances, 74–76
see also **Management of resident's finances**
Public Guardian, 41, 42, 94
recall of powers, 234, 235
Office holders
definition, 152
Powers of attorney
Books of Council and Session, 39
certificates
continuing powers, 292
welfare powers, 292
continuing powers of attorney (CPAs)
see **Continuing powers of attorney (CPAs)**
definition, 23, 152

314

Index

duration, 172
effective, 172
incorporation, 292–295
revocation, 294
welfare powers of attorney (WPAs)
  see **Welfare powers of attorney (WPAs)**
Practising solicitor
  definition, 152
Primary carer
  definition, 153
Private international law
  applicable law, 163, 164
  habitual residence, 161, 162
  Hague Convention
    see **Hague Convention (International Protection of Adults)**
  judicial comity, 165
  jurisdiction, 151, 162, 165
  recognition/enforcement of judgments, 164, 165
Public Guardian
  Accountant of Court, 22, 24
  applications
    accounts and funds, 47, 49–51
    intimations of applications, 61, 62
    refusal, 69
  approval of accounts, 159, 160
  certificates, issued by, 25
  definition, 23, 153
  discharge powers, 95
  evidence, submitted to, 200
  expenses, 25
  fees
    exemptions, 287
    fees payable, 287 297–305
  functions
    consultation, 23, 24
    general advice, 23, 24
    information, 23, 24
    investigative function, 23, 24, 30, 72
    maintenance of registers, 22, 24, 41, 59
    party to proceedings, 23
    property/financial affairs, 23, 27
    supervision, 22, 23, 24
  gifts, authority regarding, 128
  guardians
    discharge, 136, 139
    recall, 135, 137, 138, 139
    removal, 134
    replacement, 134
  guardianship orders
    amendment of registration, 145
    variation, 140, 141
  incapacity reports, 205
  interventions, 12
    see also **Interventions**
  intimation, dispensing with, 279
  notification, 41, 42, 94, 95, 175
  power to obtain records, 147, 148
  prescribed fees, 25
  registration, with, 151

revocation notices, 43
transfer of funds, 58, 59
withdrawers
  refusal of application, 69
  suspension of authority, 67
  termination of authority, 67
  transition from guardianship, 69, 70
Recall of guardians
  see also **Recall of powers**
  chief social worker's powers, 139, 140
  intervention orders, 135
  intimation provisions, 136, 137
  Mental Welfare Committee (MWC), 135, 137,–139, 234, 235, 237, 251, 253, 261, 265
    see also **Mental Welfare Commission (MWC)**
  notification requirement, 137
  Public Guardian's role, 1135, 137–139
  sheriff, by, 134, 135
Recall of powers
  consultation, 240–242, 247–249
  grounds for recall, 239, 246
  intention to recall, 234, 235
  intimation provisions
    local authorities, 257–260
    Mental Welfare Commission (MWC), 253–255, 258
    objections to recall, 256
    period for objection, 235
    refusal to recall, 235
  local authorities, 235, 244–250, 257
    see also **Local authorities**
  Mental Welfare Commission (MWC), 135, 137–139, 234, 235, 237, 251, 253, 261, 265
    see also **Mental Welfare Commission (MWC)**
  notification of decisions, 234, 235
  period for objection, 235
  personal welfare powers, 244, 245, 251, 252
  Public Guardian, 134–138
  refusal to recall
    details of guardianship, 261, 263
    intimation provisions, 235, 261, 262
    local authority intimation, 263, 264
    Mental Welfare Commission (MWC) intimation, 261, 262
    objections to refusal, 262, 264
    reasons for refusal, 262, 264
  report of capacity
    findings of examination, 252
    local authorities, 251
    Mental Welfare Commission (MWC), 251
    welfare guardians, 251
Registration
  amendments, to, 145
  continuing powers of attorney (CPAs), 37–41

Index

guardianship orders, 116–118, 145
intervention orders, 101
management of resident's finances, 74
Public Guardian, with, 151
welfare powers of attorney (CPAs), 37–41
Regulations
consequential provisions, 152
power to make, 152
statutory instruments, 152
supplemental provisions, 152
transitional provisions/savings, 152
Removal of guardians
finding caution, 134, 135
joint guardians, 135
notification requirement, 135
Public Guardian's role, 134
sheriff, by, 134
substitute guardians, 134, 135
Renewal of powers
guardianship, 171
mandatory renewal provisions, 171
Repayment of funds
breach of duty, 147
excess of authority, 147
interest payments, 147
Repeals
statutory repeals, 179–181
Replacement guardians
continuation of powers, 172
duration of appointment, 172
powers, 172
Replacement of guardians
finding caution, 134, 135
Public Guardian's role, 134
sheriff, by, 134
substitute guardians, 134
Report of capacity
findings of examination, 252
local authorities, 251
Mental Welfare Commission (MWC), 251
welfare guardians, 251
Research
approved research, 91
beneficial research, 92, 93, 95
clinical trials, 91, 92
consent
guardians, 91, 92
nearest relative, 91
welfare attorneys, 91, 92
Ethics Committee, 91, 92, 93
legislative authority, need for, 93
minimal discomfort, 91
minimal foreseeable risk, 91
persons incapable of decision-making, 91, 93
Residents
ceasing to be resident, 80, 81
residents' establishments
authorised establishments, 73–77, 154, 155
registered establishments, 72–75
relevant establishments, 72
unregistered establishments, 72–74
resident's finances
see also **Management of resident's finances**
certificate of authority, 78, 79
financial management, 77, 78
records of transactions, 78
revocation of authority to manage, 81
statement of affairs, 79, 80
Resignation
continuing attorneys, 44, 45
guardians
continuity of guardianship, 1342
joint guardians, 142, 143
notice requirement, 142, 143
removal/replacement, 142
substitute guardians, 142, 143
welfare attorneys, 44, 45
Revocation
continuing powers of attorney (CPAs), 42–44, 294
see also **Continuing powers of attorney (CPAs)**
revocation notices, 43
welfare powers of attorney (WPAs), 42–44, 294
see also **Welfare powers of attorney (WPAs)**
Safeguarders
appointment, 19, 20, 224
function, 19, 20
powers, 19, 20
Scottish Law Commission
choice of forum, 9
procedural issues, 9
Sheriff Court
see also **Sheriff's powers**
appeals, 17, 18
directions, 17, 18
evidence, 17, 18
intimation, 18
jurisdiction
appropriate sheriff, 162, 163
guardianship orders, 17
intervention orders, 17, 18
notification, 18
summary applications, 17, 18
Sheriffs' powers
applications, referred to, 63
ascertainment of wishes/feelings, 14, 15
conditions/restrictions, 19, 20
consequential/ancillary orders, 18–20
continuing powers of attorney (CPAs), 40, 41
see also **Continuing powers of attorney (CPAs)**
directions
accounts and funds, 47, 48
generally, 9–12
joint guardians, 119, 120

316

Index

management of adult's estate, 156
management of resident's finances, 72
expenses, award of, 25, 26, 132
further inquiries, 19, 20
guardianship
  appointment of guardians, 113, 114, 119–122
  financial guardianship, 47
  guardianship orders, 118, 119
  joint guardianship, 119, 120
  substitute guardians, 121, 122
  variation, of, 140, 141
interests in property, 19, 20
interim orders, 19, 20
intervention orders, 94–96
lodging of reports/assessments/interviews, 19, 20
nearest relatives, involving, 20, 21
procedural powers, 18–20
recall powers, 134–136
removal powers, 134, 135
replacement powers, 134, 135
safeguarders, appointment of, 19, 20
safeguarding of interests, 19
variation of terms, 19
welfare powers of attorney (CPAs), 40, 41
  see also **Welfare powers of attorney (CPAs)**

Social Work (Scotland) Act 1968
guardians, 193
guardianship orders, 183, 184
intervention orders, 183, 184
interventions, 183, 184
local authority services, 183, 184
welfare attorneys, 183

State hospital
definition, 153
managers, 154, 155

Substitute guardians
applications, 121
appointments
  period of appointment, 121
  procedure, 121
  sheriff's powers, 121
death of guardian, 122, 136, 143
functions/powers, 122
notification requirement, 127
original guardian
  death/incapacity, 121, 122
  removal/resignation, 122
  unable to act, 121, 122
removal of guardians, 134–136
replacement of guardians, 134, 136
resignation, 134, 136, 141, 142

Transfer of funds
authority to transfer, 58, 59
Public Guardian, 58, 59
specified sums, 58, 59
withdrawal certificates, 53, 54

Transitional guardians
continuation of powers, 172
generally, 116–117

Transitional provisions
continuing powers of attorney (CPAs), 32
  see also **Continuing powers of attorney (CPAs)**
generally, 172

Tutor-at-law
appointment, 146, 168, 170
continuation of powers, 166–168
determination of proceedings, 167
guardianship, 167
powers, 167

Tutor-dative
additional tutors, 119, 120
appointment, 105, 114, 120, 146, 167, 168, 170
continuation of powers, 166–168
determination of proceedings, 167
guardianship, 167
joint tutors, 120
powers, 167
revival, of, 105, 117, 120

Welfare attorneys
see also **Welfare powers of attorney (WPAs)**
appointment
  generally, 40, 41
  medical treatment, 87
authority for research, 90–93
breach of duty, 148, 149
certification, 291
continuation of powers, 166, 171, 172
definition, 153
interpretation, 72
interventions, 11
limitation of liability, 147
not obliged to act, 37
powers, 5
resignation, 44, 45
willingness to act, 39

Welfare guardians
intervention orders, 94, 99
recall of powers, 244, 245, 251, 252, 261, 262
  see also **Recall of powers**
renewals, 94, 110
report of capacity, 251
supervision, of, 127, 201, 202
welfare powers, 125

Welfare powers of attorney (WPAs)
accompanying certificate, 36, 37
appointment, 40, 41
bankruptcy provisions, 33, 34
body parts, removal of, 36
certification, 291
civil partners, involving, 46
creation, 34–36
exercise, 34–36
generally, 32
married persons, involving, 46

317

Index

mental disorder, treatment of, 35, 36
not obliged to act, 37
Public Guardian, notification to, 41, 42
record-keeping, 41
registration, 37–39, 42, 43
revocation, 42–44
sheriff's powers, 39, 40
termination, 45, 46
willingness to act, 39

Wilful neglect
continuing powers of attorney (CPAs), 32
  see also **Continuing powers of attorney (CPAs)**
offence, 32, 149

Withdrawal certificates
designated accounts, 54
duration, 66–68
interpretation, 71
limits on withdrawals, 54
meaning, 71
overdrawing, 54
payment of funds, 53
renewal, 68
transfer of funds, 53, 54
validity, 64
variation, 58

Withdrawers
appeals
  refusal of application, 69
  transition from guardianship, 69, 70
authority
  duration, 66–68
  renewal, 67, 68
  suspension, 67
  termination, 67
breach of duty, 147
changes of address, 65, 66
corporate withdrawers, 52
definition, 23, 153
inquiries, 66
joint withdrawers, 54–56
limitation of liability, 48, 147
main withdrawers, 52, 56–58
record-keeping, 66
repayment of funds, 48
reserve withdrawers
  applications, 56, 60–63
  authority to act, 56–58
  generally, 52
use of funds, 65
variation of authority, 58